TREATING DISSOCIATIVE IDENTITY DISORDER

THE JOSSEY-BASS LIBRARY OF CURRENT CLINICAL TECHNIQUE

IRVIN D. YALOM, GENERAL EDITOR

NOW AVAILABLE

Treating Alcoholism
Stephanie Brown, Editor

Treating Schizophrenia
Sophia Vinogradov, Editor

Treating Women Molested in Childhood
Catherine Classen, Editor

Treating Depression
Ira D. Glick, Editor

Treating Eating Disorders
Joellen Werne, Editor

Treating Dissociative Identity Disorder
James L. Spira, Editor

FORTHCOMING

Treating Adolescents
Hans Steiner, Editor

Treating the Elderly
Javaid I. Sheikh, Editor

Treating Posttraumatic Stress Disorder
Charles R. Marmar, Editor

Treating Anxiety Disorders
Walton T. Roth, Editor

Treating Couples
Hilda Kessler, Editor

Treating Difficult Personality Disorders
Michael Rosenbluth, Editor

TREATING DISSOCIATIVE IDENTITY DISORDER

A VOLUME IN THE JOSSEY-BASS
LIBRARY OF CURRENT CLINICAL TECHNIQUE

James L. Spira, EDITOR

Irvin D. Yalom, GENERAL EDITOR

Jossey-Bass Publishers • San Francisco

Substantial discounts on bulk quantities of Jossey-Bass books are available to corporations, professional associations, and other organizations. For details and discount information, contact the special sales department at Jossey-Bass Inc., Publishers.
(415) 433–1740; Fax (800) 605–2665.

For sales outside the United States, please contact your local Simon & Schuster International Office.

TCF Manufactured in the United States of America on Lyons Falls Pathfinder Tradebook. This paper is acid-free and 100 percent totally chlorine-free.

Library of Congress Cataloging-in-Publication Data

Treating dissociative identity disorder/James L. Spira.
    p.   cm.—(A volume in the Jossey-Bass library of current clinical technique)
    Includes index.
    ISBN 0-7879-0157-1 (alk. paper)
    1. Multiple personality—Treatment. I. Spira, James L. II. Series: Jossey-Bass library of current clinical technique.
RC569.5.M8T74 1996
616.85'2360651—dc20   95-23765
                                                                      CIP

FIRST EDITION
HB Printing 10 9 8 7 6 5 4 3 2 1

CONTENTS

FOREWORD ix
Irvin D. Yalom, General Editor

PREFACE xiii
James L. Spira

INTRODUCTION: UNDERSTANDING AND TREATING
DISSOCIATIVE IDENTITY DISORDER xvii
James L. Spira

PART ONE

MODELS OF TREATMENT

CHAPTER 1
PSYCHOLOGICAL ASSESSMENT 3
Judith Armstrong

CHAPTER 2
DISSOCIATION, PSYCHOTHERAPY,
AND THE COGNITIVE SCIENCES 39
Daniel J. Siegel

CHAPTER 3
MODELS OF HELPING
The Role of Responsibility 81
Catherine G. Fine

CHAPTER 4
MEDICATIONS IN THE TREATMENT OF
DISSOCIATIVE IDENTITY DISORDER 99
Moshe S. Torem

❧

PART TWO

OUTPATIENT INTERVENTIONS

CHAPTER 5
TREATMENT OF EARLY ONSET 135
Gary Peterson

CHAPTER 6
AN OUTLINE FOR PSYCHOANALYTICAL TREATMENT 183
Stephen S. Marmer

CHAPTER 7
THE USE OF HYPNOSIS IN DIAGNOSIS AND TREATMENT 219
William Smith

CHAPTER 8
EXPRESSIVE THERAPY 239
Peggy L. Dawson and John F. Higdon

❧

PART THREE

INPATIENT INTERVENTIONS

CHAPTER 9
HOSPITAL TREATMENT 275
Richard P. Kluft

CHAPTER 10
SHORT-TERM, PROBLEM-ORIENTED INPATIENT TREATMENT 337
Colin A. Ross

ABOUT THE AUTHORS 367

INDEX 371

FOREWORD

At a recent meeting of clinical practitioners, a senior practitioner declared that more change had occurred in his practice of psychotherapy in the past year than in the twenty preceding years. Nodding assent, the others all agreed.

And was that a good thing for their practice? A resounding "No!" Again, unanimous concurrence—too much interference from managed care; too much bureaucracy; too much paper work; too many limits set on fees, length, and format of therapy; too much competition from new psychotherapy professions.

Were these changes a good or a bad thing for the general public? Less unanimity on this question. Some pointed to recent positive developments. Psychotherapy was becoming more mainstream, more available, and more acceptable to larger segments of the American public. It was being subjected to closer scrutiny and accountability—uncomfortable for the practitioner but, if done properly, of potential benefit to the quality and efficiency of behavioral health care delivery.

But without dissent this discussion group agreed—and every aggregate of therapists would concur—that astounding changes are looming for our profession: changes in the reasons that clients request therapy; changes in the perception and practice of mental health care; changes in therapeutic theory and technique; and changes in the training, certification, and supervision of professional therapists.

From the perspective of the clientele, several important currents are apparent. A major development is the de-stigmatization of psychotherapy. No longer is psychotherapy invariably a hush-hush affair, laced with shame and conducted in offices with separate entrance and exit doors to prevent the uncomfortable possibility of patients meeting one another.

Today such shame and secrecy have been exploded. Television talk shows—Oprah, Geraldo, Donahue—have normalized psychopathology and psychotherapy by presenting a continuous public parade of dysfunctional human situations: hardly a day passes without television fare of confessions and audience interactions with deadbeat fathers, sex addicts, adult children of alcoholics, battering husbands and abused wives, drug dealers and substance abusers, food bingers and purgers, thieving children, abusing parents, victimized children suing parents.

The implications of such de-stigmatization have not been lost on professionals who no longer concentrate their efforts on the increasingly elusive analytically suitable neurotic patient. Clinics everywhere are dealing with a far broader spectrum of problem areas and must be prepared to offer help to substance abusers and their families, to patients with a wide variety of eating disorders, adult survivors of incest, victims and perpetrators of domestic abuse. No longer do trauma victims or substance abusers furtively seek counseling. Public awareness of the noxious long-term effects of trauma has been so sensitized that there is an increasing call for public counseling facilities and a growing demand, as well, for adequate treatment provisions in health care plans.

The mental health profession is changing as well. No longer is there such automatic adoration of lengthy "depth" psychotherapy where "deep" or "profound" is equated with a focus on the earliest years of the patient's life. The contemporary field is more pluralistic: many diverse approaches have proven therapeutically effective, and the therapist of today is more apt to tailor the therapy to fit the particular clinical needs of each patient.

In past years there was an unproductive emphasis on territoriality and on the maintaining of hierarchy and status—with the more prestigious professions like psychiatry and doctoral-level psychology expending considerable energy toward excluding master's level therapists. But those battles belong more to the psychotherapists of yesterday; today there is a significant shift toward a more collaborative interdisciplinary climate.

Managed care and cost containment is driving some of these changes. The role of the psychiatrist has been particularly affected as cost efficiency has decreed that psychiatrists will less frequently deliver psychotherapy personally but, instead, limit their activities to supervision and to psychopharmacological treatment.

In its efforts to contain costs, managed care has asked therapists to deliver a briefer, focused therapy. But gradually managed care is realizing that the bulk of mental health treatment cost is consumed by inpatient care and that outpatient treatment, even long-term therapy, is not only salubrious for the patient but far less costly. Another looming change is that the field is turning more frequently toward the group and family therapies. How much longer can we ignore the many comparative research studies demonstrating that the group therapy format is equally or more effective than higher cost individual therapies?

Some of these cost-driven edicts may prove to be good for the patients; but many of the changes that issue from medical model mimicry—for example, efforts at extreme brevity and overly precise treatment plans and goals that are inappropriate to the therapy endeavor and provide only the illusion of efficiency—can hamper the therapeutic work. Consequently, it is of paramount importance that therapists gain control of their field and that managed care administrators not be permitted to dictate how psychotherapy or, for that matter, any other form of health care be conducted. That is one of the goals of this series of texts: to provide mental health professionals with such a deep grounding in theory and such a clear vision of effective therapeutic technique that they will be empowered to fight confidently for the highest standards of patient care.

ॐ

The Jossey-Bass Library of Current Clinical Technique is directed and dedicated to the frontline therapist—to master's and doctoral-level clinicians who personally provide the great bulk of mental health care. The purpose of this entire series is to offer state-of-the-art instruction in treatment techniques for the most commonly encountered clinical conditions. Each volume offers a focused theoretical background as a foundation for practice and then dedicates itself to the practical task of what to do for the patient—how to assess, diagnose, and treat.

I have selected volume editors who are either nationally recognized experts or are rising young stars. In either case, they possess a comprehensive view of their specialty field and have selected leading therapists of a variety of persuasions to describe their therapeutic approaches.

Although all the contributors have incorporated the most recent and relevant clinical research in their chapters, the emphasis in these volumes is the practical technique of therapy. We shall offer specific therapeutic guidelines, and augment concrete suggestions with the liberal use of clinical vignettes and detailed case histories. Our intention is not to impress or to awe the reader, and not to add footnotes to arcane academic debates. Instead, each chapter is designed to communicate guidelines of immediate pragmatic value to the practicing clinician. In fact, the general editor, the volume editors, and the chapter contributors have all accepted our assignments for that very reason: a rare opportunity to make a significant, immediate, and concrete contribution to the lives of our patients.

Irvin D. Yalom, M.D.
Professor Emeritus of Psychiatry
Stanford University School of Medicine

PREFACE

Perhaps no other psychological or medical disorder has raised as much controversy as that of Dissociative Identity Disorder (DID). Patients with the disorder and therapists who regularly treat such persons have no doubt whatsoever as to its existence or to the value of treatment. It is understandable, however, that those who have never witnessed this disorder firsthand would remain skeptical. After all, it appears to be so far removed from normal experience as to be a highly improbable, if not impossible, phenomenon. Yet, as this book shows, it is not so foreign after all. Rather, DID is an exaggeration of normal and natural psychological functioning that arises as a consequence of severe circumstances.

Even the name itself reflects the controversy surrounding the disorder. Although the existence of the disorder has been recorded for centuries, the name *Dissociative Identity Disorder* has evolved through many changes. Formerly known as *Multiple Personality Disorder* (*DSM-III-R*), the recent revision to Dissociative Identity Disorder (*DSM-IV*) serves several functions:

- It avoids confusion with being classified as a *personality disorder* (even though most persons with this disorder share many characteristics found in the personality disorders).

- It maintains consistency with the naming of other dissociative disorders, which currently all begin with the term *dissociative*, followed by their specific descriptor (for example, *Dissociative Amnesia, Dissociative Fugue*).

- It reduces the bias that results from the familiar term *Multiple Personality Disorder* being overascribed by patients and professionals, in order to accept fewer false positives—although this renaming may simultaneously increase the possibility of true cases being rejected.

The psychiatric literature has contained scattered discussions of the disorder during the past century; yet, relatively few articles have been published in the area. Only in the last decade have any books dedicated exclusively to the subject become available, including the following:

Kluft, R. P. (Ed.). (1985). *Childhood antecedents of multiple personality.* Washington, DC: American Psychiatric Press.

Braun, B. G. (Ed.). (1986). *Treatment of multiple personality disorder.* Washington, DC: American Psychiatric Press.

Putnum, F. W. (1989). *Diagnosis and treatment of multiple personality disorder.* New York: Guilford Press.

Ross, C. A. (1989). *Multiple personality disorder: Diagnosis, clinical features, and treatment.* New York: Wiley.

Kluft, R. P., & Fine, C. G. (Eds.). (1993). *Clinical perspectives on multiple personality disorder.* Washington, DC: American Psychiatric Press.

Although these books have gone far in advancing the field, they are not specifically targeted to the practicing psychotherapist, but rather are more academic in their intent. In contrast, this volume offers a broad range of perspectives and methods exclusively written for the practicing therapist. Principles and methods are presented in such a way that the experienced psychotherapist can understand and immediately put them into practice. Moreover, the field is developing so rapidly that an update including the latest methods in assessment and treatment is needed.

Each chapter provides an overview of a particular theoretical orientation, followed by specific methods of incorporating this theory into clinical practice. Authors offer case examples to facilitate application of principles, along with specific cautions or concerns required for appropriate usage.

This book is useful for a variety of readers. It is certainly of benefit for those already working with persons having DID—it can both help them refine their skills and further the range of their skills. For those familiar with treating other dissociative disorders, this book can provide, along with additional workshops and supervision, a strong foundation for effective diagnosis and treatment of DID. Therapists who have not treated dissociative disorders will discover a solid introduction to the field; however, additional training through more reading, workshops, and supervision is required before competent treatment can ensue for this disorder. Finally, researchers, academic psychologists, and students of psychology will find a fascinating study of dissociative processes in their extreme that will help them appreciate dissociative coping reactions over a plethora of psychological disorders while revealing much about the workings of the normal mind.

The authors represented in this volume are uniquely qualified to present a wide array of the most current approaches to the treatment of DID. The book has been organized so as to allow readers either to select those aspects of greatest interest to them or to read from cover to cover to get a complete treatment perspective. After a general introduction offering an overview of the disorder, its diagnosis, and treatment, Judith Armstrong, Daniel Siegel, Catherine Fine, and Moshe Torem offer guidelines for assessing and treating DID from several viewpoints. Then Gary Peterson, Stephen Marmer, William Smith, Peggy Dawson, and John Higdon discuss specific psychotherapeutic methods from various theoretical perspectives. Finally, Richard Kluft and Colin Ross offer insights into the hospital treatment of DID.

ACKNOWLEDGMENTS

I wish to acknowledge those without whom this book would not have been written, including Alan Rinzler for careful reading, editorial support, and constant encouragement; Irv Yalom, Bruce Arnow, and David Stewart for supervision and insight regarding the importance of present-focused interpersonal relationship in therapy, especially important when treating DID; Francis Dreher and Patrick Woods for sharing their respect for the value of controlled dissociation, the importance of always searching for the underlying benefits of uncontrolled dissociative coping reactions, and the value of communicating with all "parts" of the unconscious responsible for an unwanted behavior; Joshu Sasaki Roshi for teaching the value of suspending one's fixed self-image in order to appreciate the hermeneutic stance of others; Janet and Julia Spira for their patience and support during the many hours of writing and editing that allowed these fine chapters to come to press; the contributors, who took time from their busy schedules to share their insight, experience, and talent with those who will be in a position to help patients with this difficult disorder; and finally, the patients I have seen with dissociative disorders who taught me respect for the power of the mind and the will to survive.

September 1995   James L. Spira
                                              Durham, North Carolina

INTRODUCTION: UNDERSTANDING AND TREATING DISSOCIATIVE IDENTITY DISORDER

James L. Spira

Clearly, Dissociative Identity Disorder (DID) (formally Multiple Personality Disorder [MPD]) is poorly understood (at best) and even rejected as mere fantasy by much of the general population and many psychotherapists. Although its prevalence in the general and psychiatric populations is debated, most psychotherapists will never see a case of DID. And in this environment of brief therapy, writing about a topic that requires long-term care would seem to be, at the very least, unpopular. So why a text entirely devoted to treating DID? Certainly, those who treat DID need to be kept informed on the latest treatment modalities. Yet, studying treatments for DID can benefit even those who may never see such a case because the study of DID provides psychotherapists with insight into other dissociative disorders and other psychopathology (especially Axis II disorders, depressive and anxiety disorders, and repressive coping styles). Moreover, it provides insight into the nature of normal psychological functioning, revealing the interaction of unconscious and conscious processes.

With the growing restrictions on long-term intensive psychotherapy due to increased managed care, there is an urgent need to appreciate the nature of DID. Too often, the diagnosis has been considered either a factitious disease (in the minds of both patient and therapist) or simply a bizarre anomaly. While there may have been many instances of misdiagnosis (both errors of inclusion, as well as errors of omission) and while such persons appear strange indeed to those who do not understand the disorder, to practitioners who have treated persons with DID it is no more factitious or bizarre than any other psychological disorder.

When properly understood, DID can be appreciated as a style of coping that helped a tortured mind (and often body) deal with an otherwise overwhelming situation. Often initiated during the years when cognitive, emotional, and social development should be progressing normally, this illness was often the best way the child found to cope with continual and intense abuse. This coping style was thus learned at an early age and maintained for many years. For this reason, therapy for this disorder is not likely to be successful in teaching alternative coping styles in ten or twenty sessions. It is more likely that these persons will need therapy for most of their lives, to various extents, depending on their level of functioning and therapeutic stage.

Fortunately, long-term psychotherapy, on the one hand, is effective in helping persons with DID reduce disruption in daily function, reduce overall distress and suffering, and when the therapist is an expert with treating DID, even eliminate the dissociative disorder. Brief therapy, on the other hand, at best may serve to slightly reduce acute distress during a crisis but will do nothing to stop such occurrences from arising frequently throughout the patient's life. In fact, given the extreme sensitivity to interpersonal issues of trust and rejection, establishing a therapeutic alliance required for improvement is unlikely or may result in even greater distress at termination of therapy.

Thus, long-term psychotherapy is actually less expensive than ineffective brief therapy for persons with DID. Insurance companies, therefore, should be willing to support this effort, lest they end up paying far greater amounts for medical treatment of somatic disorders, suicide attempts, and frequent inpatient visits that will no doubt occur in the absence of ongoing long-term psychotherapy. The only exception is when a patient already in long-term therapy may require additional short-term support (see Ross, Chapter Ten).

For psychotherapy to be effective, the treating therapist must be able to (1) make a correct diagnosis, (2) appreciate the nature of the disorder, and (3) adequately treat the disorder throughout the various therapeutic stages. Without such expertise, the therapist can do harm both to the patient and to the professional discipline of those treating patients with dissociative disorders. Because of the skepticism that abounds not only in the general community but also in the psychotherapeutic community, only those who are well trained in diagnosing and treating dissociative disorders should enter into a therapeutic relationship with these clients.

With these concerns in mind, this text is intended for

Therapists who want a good introduction to the field of treating DID, should they wish to pursue active training and supervision under someone with relevant expertise

Therapists who wish to understand more about DID in order to detect it among their clientele and thus refer to an appropriate practitioner

Therapists with expertise in treating dissociative disorders, in order to broaden their range of skills

Professionals in affiliated fields who wish to gain an increased appreciation for persons with DID and to better understand appropriate methods of treatment

With these goals in mind, what follows is a basic foundation for understanding more advanced perspectives on treating DID.

DIAGNOSIS

Dissociative identity disorder is listed in the fourth edition of the *Diagnostic and Statistical Manual of Mental Disorders* (*DSM-IV*) under Axis I; Dissociative Disorders Section; 300.14; formerly

Multiple Personality Disorder. The diagnosis is based on the following criteria:

A. The presence of two or more distinct personality states (each with its own relatively enduring pattern of perceiving, relating to, and thinking about the environment and self).

B. At least two of these identities or personality states recurrently take control of the person's behavior.

C. The inability to recall important personal information that is too extensive to be explained by ordinary forgetfulness.

D. The disturbance is not due to the direct physiological effects of a substance (for example, blackouts or chaotic behavior during alcohol intoxication) or a general medical condition (for example, complex partial seizures). (Note: In children the symptoms are not attributable to imaginary playmates or other fantasy play.)

The *DSM-III-R* refers to *personality* as enduring traits across many situations, whereas *personality states* is referred to as characteristics that emerge in a specific setting. The number of personalities or personality states (referred to as *alters*) ranges from two to more than one hundred, with about ten being the mode. Switching between personalities is sudden and often dramatic, as if an entirely different person is suddenly present, with new and different name, age, body posture and movements, voice, vocabulary, accent, social skills, and possibly different physiological processes (such as visual acuity, health) or even different gender. The patient's environmental context may also be quite different. Alter personalities often become "fixed in time." They may believe the date to be the same as the age when their personality developed. If a forty-year-old patient has a six-year-old alter, this "six-year-old" may still think that Eisenhower is president and that the computer monitor on your desk is a "funny TV." If the patient moved here from a different state after age six, then he or she may be confused if you talk about the local state environment. And if you tell the patient that you will be a few minutes late next week because you will be giving a lecture at the university, he or she will ask who the bad person was that you have to lecture (scold).

Switching between personalities often takes seconds (or less) and can be facilitated by hypnosis in therapy. Such switching usually occurs when the patient becomes distressed because of some perceived psychosocial threat in his or her environment. In the best situations, switching allows a distressed alter to retreat while an alter more competent to handle the situation can emerge. In less adaptive circumstances, a hostile alter may emerge to disrupt and punish a functionally successful alter.

Certain alters are often unaware of the experiences or even the existence of other alters. Occasionally, an alter has access to the information of all the other alters but does not feel the emotion of the others. Although one or two predominant personalities is the norm, one of these is usually identified by the patient as the "original personality." If one is gentle and submissive, the other dominant personality is often strong and aggressive. It is not uncommon that one alter will attempt to harm or even kill other alters, with the belief that this "aggressive" alter will not be hurt. Usually at least one alter is depressed and may occasionally attempt suicide. It is not uncommon for an aggressive alter attempting to harm the "others" to take them out into the countryside and leave them there. When other alters emerge, they have no idea where they are.

Important questions to ask when interviewing persons suspected of having DID is whether they have periods of time they cannot account for, whether they frequently meet people who know them but whom they do not recognize, whether they find clothes or other new items in their possession they cannot recall purchasing, and so forth. Younger patients do not necessarily recognize that these occurrences are "all that unusual." Because most have been like this since young childhood, they may tend to think the world simply operates this way.

Patients with DID can function surprisingly well. Many have full-time jobs, where one personality will predominate (with occasional support from other alters who keep their identity secret to others). Different alters may emerge when going to or leaving work or in other contexts. Most persons with DID will have periods when they decompensate and require intensive urgent care (either on an inpatient or intensive outpatient basis; see Kluft, Chapter Nine, and Ross, Chapter Ten).

Differential Diagnosis

It is important to be able to discriminate DID from other dissociative disorders, including Fugue (dissociative travel) and Psychogenic Amnesia (inability to recall important episodes). Although persons with DID will have periods of fugue and amnesia, the DID diagnosis takes precedence.

DID is also frequently confused with Schizophrenia/Schizophreniform Psychosis, or Schizotypal Personality Disorder, because of what clinicians may interpret as bizarre and unreal mentation. As mentioned above, persons with DID frequently switch in stressful situations (such as an initial psychiatric interview) and may have a high degree of distrust and caution regarding others because of their traumatic past. The cognitive processes evident in DID, however, are substantially different from the attentional difficulties seen in disorganized (hebephrenic type) psychosis or the obsessive and distorted picture of paranoid type schizophrenia. Moreover, the "voices" that persons with DID hear are their voices within themselves, not other "outside" forces directing them. And although such patients are likely to have personality disorders as well, it is usually not of the schizotypal variety (acting bizarrely, claiming to hear strange voices or see unusual things, but otherwise functioning normally). Posttraumatic Stress Disorder (PTSD) is frequently ascribed to these patients as well because the cause of the disturbance can be seen as following a traumatic episode. For this diagnosis to apply, however, the patient must have current symptoms of hypervigilance (including startle, sleeplessness, intrusive thoughts), in which case a dual diagnosis may be considered.

Concomitant Diagnoses

Although patients with DID, like any other patients, may have any number of concomitant psychiatric diagnoses, several are most common. The difficulty with ascribing any secondary diagnosis to a patient with DID is that different alters will consistently display certain pathology. At times, however, the "overall picture" seems to dictate a dual diagnosis—especially if an urgent concern needs to be dealt with.

Depression (Major or Dysthymic) is frequently seen in at least one of the alter personalities. Despair of living is frequently discussed, and suicide is often threatened or attempted. Antidepressant medication is often prescribed with positive results. In fact, I have never seen a person with DID who did not benefit from psychopharmacology at some point during his or her treatment (see Torem, Chapter Four).

Personality disorders are a common secondary diagnosis. It often appears that treating a person with DID is like doing family therapy in which each family member has a diagnosis of borderline personality disorder. Indeed, the emotional and social lability of persons with DID often appears to fit this diagnosis. Although the borderline diagnosis may appear most often to "fit," other alters will display narcissistic, histrionic, or schizoid tendencies.

Careful diagnosis will help differentiate from Malingering or Factitious Disorders. Often, it is the referring therapist who put the idea of DID into the patient's mind, either rightly or wrongly. A thorough interview and testing must be made in an attempt to rule out DID.

Of course, PTSD may need to be considered on occasion as well (as discussed earlier). Although this diagnosis is less accurate and complete, some therapists assign it to avoid the stigma associated with DID.

The diagnosis of DID faces two threats to accuracy. The first threat is misdiagnosis due to disbelief of the existence of the disorder. The second and equally culpable threat is the overdiagnosis of the disorder. Because many therapists tend to overascribe this disorder to persons with other dissociative or psychotic disorders, in referrals I have received for their treatment, I have ruled out DID in more patients than I have confirmed the diagnosis. Because of the hype surrounding multiple personalities, therapists should be conservative with this diagnosis. My rule of thumb is to attempt to rule out DID until such time as the evidence is so strong that it leaves no doubt about the appropriateness of this diagnosis. Until such time, I may offer a temporary diagnosis of Dissociative Disorder-Not Otherwise Specified (DD-NOS). Such an attitude toward accurate diagnosis will not only help the patient and therapist but also go far in assisting the field to take the diagnosis of DID seriously.

Psychological Tests

Therapists may find several tests helpful in confirming a diagnosis of DID. These include scales directly assessing dissociation, such as the Dissociative Experience Scale (DES), the Structured Clinical Interview Device-Dissociative version (SCID-D), and the Tellegen Absorption Scale (TAS). Other psychological testing can be helpful as well in filling out the picture, including projective tests (Thematic Aptitude Test, Tree-House-Person, Rorschach), personality assessments (for example, MMPI, MCMI), and cognitive assessment (such as the WAIS-R). Additional considerations are important in testing persons suspected of having DID. For example, one alter may give different responses than another alter, or switching may occur during periods of stress or fatigue (see Armstrong, Chapter One).

Whichever method one uses for confirmation of the diagnosis, however, it is useful to begin with the following questions in first suspecting the diagnosis.

The following four features should be confirmed:

1. Time: Do you frequently have periods of time that you cannot account for? (Rule out single episodes of Dissociative Amnesia.)

2. Space: Do you frequently find yourself somewhere and then cannot remember how you got there? (Rule out single episode of Dissociative Fugue.)

3. Recognition: Have you ever found strange things among your possessions (for example, clothes, jewelry) that you had no recall of buying? Or do you ever meet people who seem to know you well but whom you don't recognize? (Rule out a single episode of Dissociative Amnesia; organic or functional memory loss due to illness or fatigue.)

4. Switching: [The therapist should personally witness evidence of switching to alternate personalities that is so clear, rapid, and extreme that it would be extremely difficult for the person to be acting. The therapist can "ask" an alter to appear or use hypnosis to facilitate the emergence of an alter personality (see Smith, Chapter Seven). Occasionally, Amytal (a therapeutic "truth serum") is used by psychiatrists to facilitate the initial emergence of alters if no other method is successful.]

The following three features are useful for supportive confirmation:

1. Alters: Do you feel as if several "persons" are inside this one body? Do these persons ever "take over" the body? (Rule out schizophrenia or schizotypal personality disorder.)

2. Safety: Are you unable to feel safe and comfortable, now or even in the past, either when alone or with another person? (Rule out solely personality disorders.)

3. Abuse: Were you ever abused as a child? How severe was this abuse, and how long did it last? Was there anyone to turn to for support? (Rule out solely posttraumatic stress disorder.)

Positive answers to these questions give a very strong indication that DID is a likely diagnosis.

ETIOLOGY

The development of DID is a multifaceted interaction among several factors. Appreciating the complexity and interaction of these factors will help the DID therapist better understand the current status of his or her patients and their difficulty and reluctance to abandon their personality style, and this understanding will help guide the treatment. Understanding the cause and maintenance of this disorder requires examining past abuse, the lack of a safe and comfortable resource to turn to for support in times of difficulty, the formation of a coping style that was found to be helpful in these developmental years, the ability to readily dissociate, and the discovery of splitting as a useful tool.

Abuse

DID is thought to be most frequently due to continuous severe abuse, often perpetrated by a loved one (parent, sibling) or in a trusted organization (such as a school or day care setting). Because the severity of trauma required to cause a dissociative reaction of this magnitude usually must occur over an extended period of time and in such a way that there are few supportive resources to turn to for help, abuse by family members is always a primary consideration. Recurrent abuse by a family member or close family associate can take many forms, including direct sexual or physical contact or the witnessing of abuse to one family member by another. Although a history of ongoing sexual or physical violence by a family member is frequently present, therapists must not assume a priori that family members were involved in the abuse or that direct sexual or physical violence is always the cause. Some patients with clear DID do not report or exhibit any evidence for ongoing abuse of any kind.

Also frequently reported is ritualistic abuse, such as in a cult. And there is just enough collaboration in the press of cult murders or organized child abuse to confirm its presence. However infrequently this type of activity occurs, the magnitude of every occurrence of this type of abuse is such that the "cult mania" in America these days probably extends it far beyond its actual prevalence. Thus, it is important to offer a cautionary note. Externalization of causality of one's problems is a universal coping strategy. It can be easier for patients to believe there is an organized threat against them that justifies their hesitancy at trust and intimacy than to place the responsibility for this continued isolation on themselves.

Further, it is too often the case that therapists jump to conclusions about the presence of cults. So, although there is no doubt that cults exist and although patients may truly believe they were or still are the target of cult abuse, it is important to search for confirmation whenever possible. This caution notwithstanding, it is therapeutically advantageous to *believe that the client believes* in the presence of previous or current cult influences while reserving belief regarding the objective reality of the matter.

Supportive Resources

If a child is being hurt outside the home, he or she can turn toward parents for comfort and safety. Even if the child is not able to voice concern (because of age or out of fear of reprisal, confusion, or guilt), the comfort of the family can be a place of retreat from the pain. In addition, the child can count on parents to be vigilant of and protective from harmful events. When the family is not a place of comfort, however, either because of family difficulties or because the family is the source of the abuse, then the child may have no external resources to rely on. When a child's faith and trust in parental safety and protection and comfort are lacking, all that remains is to make sense of the world through what internal devices the child has developed from observing the world around him or her.

Fairbairn stated that we incorporate the negative objects of the world into our own psyche in order to control them. If the developing child lacks models of comforting cooperation and instead only observes aggressiveness and helplessness, then this behavior becomes the internal model for handling the abuse as well. As discussed below, the therapist needs to provide a sense of comfort and protection and to model another way of interacting with the world (see Peterson, Chapter Five, and Marmer, Chapter Six).

Dissociative Ability

Another contributing factor to the development of DID may be that those persons who have a skill of or tendency toward high absorption and abstract imagery tend to develop a dissociative coping style, rather than a hypervigilant or depressive style. *Imagery* refers to any internal representation of a currently or previously perceived sensation and thus can be visual, auditory, or tactile. The ability to be aware of or manipulate imagery varies tremendously among people. Roughly one-fifth of the general population reports no conscious awareness of internal visual images, instead claiming to "think" in terms of words. Another one-fifth or so report only very concrete imagery, being able to consciously attend to internal representations of static objects. Yet, many persons can extend this imagery into creative fantasy of the object or event under consideration, imagining various permutations and possibilities that could occur. Finally, some persons have the ability to become so fully absorbed in abstract imagery that they are at times hard-pressed to distinguish between their fantasy and the reality of the current or past situation.

Those children who possess the ability to become highly absorbed in abstract fantasy may find DID a useful escape from their ongoing trauma, whereas other children with less of this ability may tend toward some other coping response. Add to this what every parent knows—a young girl's tendency toward emotional response, gentler play, and reflection, compared with a young boy's tendency to act out—and the overwhelming majority of female DID and borderline patients compared with antisocial behavior of male patients can be better understood.

However, one's strengths can also be one's weakness when the strength is an uncontrolled habit versus a developed skill to be used as needed (see Figure I.1). When the current situation is unbearable, it is helpful to escape. Escaping the current situation involves a dissociative suspension of awareness of current time, space, logic, and self-other distinction. This can be a useful skill to have when attempting to recall an important memory, in reducing pain in the dentist's chair, or when focusing completely on a chess game. Dissociation occurring whenever one is distressed, however, becomes extremely problematic. In the case of a person with DID, given the *ability* to dissociate, coupled with the *need* to continually dissociate because of years of continual abuse, such a tendency was not consciously developed as a useful skill, but instead arose as a deeply ingrained style

ALERT VIGILANCE
Problem Solving

Sensation	Focus on and interact with objects and persons in the present moment (without thought as to their past meaning)	Ability to focus on information from the past, present, or future, as needed to deal with a specific problem at hand	*Abstraction*
	Meditation: Ability to feel safe and comfortable in this moment, without the need for vigilance	Self-hypnosis for creative problem solving, or therapist-led hypnosis for assisting in switching mental states	

Recuperation
SUSPENDED VIGILANCE

Figure I.1
Controlled Dissociation

Note: Controlling dissociation can be a valuable therapeutic tool in working with patients with DID for helping avoid uncontrollable reactions when facing distress.

of coping. Developing this tendency as a consciously useful tool, in combination with the ability to be vigilant and to actively problem-solve in new ways, is an essential aspect of any treatment for DID.

Splitting as an Adaptive Coping Style

Not everyone who faces continuous abuse develops DID. An additional factor that contributes to the development of this disorder is the discovery by the person that "splitting" the distress works better than other ways of coping (see Siegel, Chapter Two, and Peterson, Chapter Five). Splitting into alternative personalities is the unconscious way of protecting the child and helping him or her survive as best as possible. The alternative could be even worse (such as suicide, severe recurrent major depression, paralyzing anxiety, violence to self, violence to others as occurs in antisocial personality). Because of the early age at which this occurs, however, such splitting is not so much a skill as it is an uncontrollable dissociative reaction (see Figure I.2).

When the abuse is so extreme that even simple dissociation (such as going to a safe fantasy place) cannot blunt the pain, it can be useful to divide the pain among various people and places within one's dissociative realm. Just as when a task is overwhelming, one often seeks the support of others so that each support person can take a manageable amount of effort, the person with DID also finds a way to divide up the pain and suffering. If no support persons are available, such support must be sought in dissociative fantasy.

To appreciate that the person with DID is overusing a normal dissociative strategy, it is useful to consider normal and natural dissociative experiences that most people use on a regular basis. Have you ever driven someplace, reached your destination, and couldn't remember which route you took because your mind had been daydreaming or thinking of some problem; had a problem you couldn't solve, gone to sleep, and awoke with a great solution; had trouble remembering something, switched to some

HYPERVIGILANT
PTSD

Anxious reactions to various limited stimuli, usually related to initial trauma	Intrusive thoughts and subsequent resistance to recall
Tendency to dissociate into the moment, without vigilant perspective	Tendency to dissociate into fantasy, without reality testing

Sensation (left side)   *Abstraction* (right side)

Dissociative Disorders
HYPOVIGILANT

Figure I.2
Uncontrolled Dissociation

Note: Patients with DID tend to cope through hypovigilant attention to abstraction, although various alters may have PTSD reactions or a tendency to suspend vigilance and to focus on sensation.

other task, and later found that the memory suddenly surfaced; or become so fully absorbed in a movie or a book that you forgot for a while where you were, so that when the movie ended or someone walked into the room where you were reading, it took you a moment to reorient to time and place and to regain self-awareness?

These types of phenomena are examples of normal and natural functioning of a mind that can divide to handle normal daily events and that can focus so intently that normal vigilance is suspended. Part of the mind can focus on environmental tasks while another part can take on a different task to help out. DID uses this normal and natural dissociative ability to help the person cope with severe and ongoing problems. Thus, one might imagine that the severity of the dissociative splitting is in direct relation to the severity of the ongoing trauma in which no other coping strategy appears to be available to the person.

Finally, it should be noted that some persons clearly meet the criteria for a DID diagnosis yet exhibit no clear evidence of severe ongoing abuse from a trusted adult and come from loving families. Thus, although the "rule" leads us to look for evidence of abuse, the exceptions caution us not to jump to conclusions.

Common factors in the development of DID include:

- Severe ongoing abuse
- Natural dissociative tendencies (the ability to easily absorb into abstract imagery)
- Having no other persons to count on for support, comfort, and protection
- Being a female child

TREATMENT

Because of frequent misdiagnosis, patients with DID are often initially treated for Borderline Personality Disorder, major depression, Conversion Disorder, Dissociative Disorder NOS, Schizotypal Personality Disorder, or even Schizophreniform Psychosis—all of which share many of the criteria for diagnosis of DID. When accurately diagnosed, appropriate treatment for DID can finally begin. Treatment occurs in various forms, depending on the stage of treatment and the severity of symptoms. Essential principles and practices of psychotherapy for patients with DID will be determined, in part, by the stage of treatment and the structure within which treatment occurs.

Modalities of Therapy

Treatment for DID occurs in various formats. These include hospital-based therapy, outpatient-based therapy, and medication-supported therapy. Treatment will no doubt occur within each of these modalities at some point during treatment for the patient with DID. Each can be optimally effective at some stage and can support treatment in other modalities.

Hospital-Based Therapy. Many patients with DID will have the need for hospitalization at some point during their lives. The frequency and duration of stay will depend in large part on the type of outpatient care they receive. Hospital-based treatment can be *brief* (several days or weeks) to assist with temporary acute reactions that are too great for the patients to handle on their own or in outpatient therapy (see Ross, Chapter Ten). Before a correct diagnosis is made, *longer-term* care may be needed in order to recommend appropriate outpatient therapy for DID or in case a major decompensation occurs because of a new trauma, such as rape or death of a family member (see Kluft, Chapter Nine).

Several hospitals have special Dissociative Disorders Units that are optimal for inpatient treatment of persons with DID. Most hospitals, however, place such patients on a locked ward along with others who have severe psychosis or mood disturbance. In this case, the staff must be educated, often by the outpatient therapist, as to the nature of DID and its treatment. This training is especially important because most persons with DID are especially sensitive to social interactions and staff intentions (not unlike a person with Borderline Personality Disorder). In addition, of course, the outpatient therapist should get a release to stay in close touch with the inpatient staff so that bidirectional communication remains possible throughout the hospital stay.

Outpatient-Based Therapy. Outpatient therapy typically is on a regular and often frequent basis (see Peterson, Chapter Five, and Marmer, Chapter Six). Initially, seeing a patient two or three times per week is not uncommon, especially if there is a need to help stabilize. Therapy can be *brief* to help cope with a specific problem (usually interpersonal or dealing with a cult recall). Whereas brief therapy may be initiated because of an undiagnosed patient presenting for assistance with a specific symptom, this approach has limited value and is better reserved for the final stages of therapeutic progress. *Long-term* therapy usually requires weekly or biweekly ongoing psychotherapy for years before integration (fusion) is achieved and then continues in some form as follow-up therapy for many years thereafter. The style of therapy used in long-term therapy usually combines an interpersonal approach, such as that described by Adler or Sullivan, in combination with brief techniques such as hypnosis (see Smith, Chapter Seven) or cognitive therapy models (see Siegel, Chapter Two).

Support with Medication. Most patients with DID find medication useful during their therapeutic development (see Torem, Chapter Four). Medication may include antidepressants (for example, SSRIs such as Prozac; tricyclics such as Elavil), anxiolytics (for example, benzodiazepines, especially Xanax), and even anti-inhibition/central acting drugs (specifically Amytal) for use in uncovering repressed information during therapy or the initial emergence of alter personalities. The use of Amytal in reducing ego strength to increase honest and uninhibited reporting is controversial because Amytal also increases dreamlike fantasy, albeit dreams openly reported by the patient.

Special problems in DID patients taking medication occur when, for example, one alter does not feel depressed and so stops taking the antidepressant. Unfortunately, this withdrawal results in the "depressed" alters becoming more pathological, not infrequently to the point of being suicidal. Or, an angry alter may attempt to sabotage another alter by hiding medication. Thus, contracts need to be maintained with all of the alters that the "body" will continue to take prescribed medication, no matter which alter is "out." Further contracts may need to be established to reduce the likelihood of attempting suicide through an overdose of medication.

Essentials of Psychotherapy

For each structural modality within which treatment occurs, and especially in ongoing outpatient psychotherapy, certain principles, though useful in most applications of psychotherapy, are especially important when applied to the treatment of DID. These principles include (1) developing immediate rapport, (2) gathering critical information about the origin of the disorder, along with subsequent successes and failures in psychosocial functioning, (3) communicating effectively with all of the alters, (4) establishing an interpersonal therapeutic relationship, (5) respecting the patient's existential motivation, (6) using cognitive-behavior therapy (CBT) to assist in coping with current stressful situations, and (7) using hypnosis, which can greatly facilitate the treatment of the patient with DID.

Developing Rapport. Persons with DID are extremely interpersonally sensitive and need lots of reassurance that they are understood and cared about. It is essential to develop a foundation of compassion, empathy, trust, and stability. This is not unlike the interpersonal relationship commonly used with patients seen for Borderline Personality Disorder. Irv Yalom once told me that 75 percent of the benefit derived from therapy for such persons stems simply from the therapist showing up and being there for the patient. The other 25 percent of the benefit comes from what the therapist and the patient say and do in the sessions.

Gathering Information. Gathering information in a slow and gentle fashion will go far in developing rapport in the early stages of therapy. Patients want very much to be understood, up to a point—that point at which an alter may not want to

1. Reveal information or feelings to him- or herself (Remember that the "splitting" occurred because the trauma was initially too overwhelming)
2. Reveal information or feelings to the therapist because of either
   a. Not yet trusting you or
   b. Wanting to protect you (for example, from a cult or perpetrator of his or her suffering, whether real or imagined)

For these reasons, it is essential to go slowly in the elicitation of information or affect. Moreover, although therapists tend to assume the role of detective in uncovering alters and relevant information, it is critical to approach the patient at all times first and foremost with compassion and caring. The therapist is at all times modeling healthy psychosocial style and behavior for the patient.

Communicating with the Alters.   It is valuable to communicate with all of the alters. If the therapist is not able to communicate directly with one or more alters, it is possible to have another personality "relay" a message to a specific alter with whom he or she has access or even to have an alter "broadcast" a message to all of the other alters.

Spending time with all of the alters is an important (albeit difficult) feature of therapy. Each alter may desire, and certainly deserves, to be "seen" by the therapist. Psychotherapists are used to taking up to an hour with only one person (and consequently only one personality) per session. Because persons with DID have many personalities, each with his or her own sense of being a whole and unique individual, one can see how giving even a fraction of this amount of time and attention quickly becomes difficult, if not impossible. Moreover, sometimes there is a crisis with one alter, so that most of the session is spent with that "person."

I find it useful to conceive of therapy as being like family therapy to some extent. If I conceptualize many members of the family as having many characteristics similar to borderline personality disorder, I become very sensitive to relevant interpersonal issues. Primary among these are extremes in interpersonal sensitivity such as jealously, fear of abandonment, and being easily angered by others' actions or lack of action. Therefore, I usually announce why I am speaking with one "person" rather than another. After settling down with whoever presents in the session, I try to talk first with the alter who most requires assistance for anything major going on. I then ask that alter whether I should know about any concerns that "others" may have. I frequently have the patient go into a hypnotic "trance," during which I can announce to the "group" that "anyone" who wants to speak to me should come out now or let the "person" who first comes out tell me of his or her desire to speak with me at some point today. In the initial sessions, I try to meet every alter personality and to chart out his or her unique features. In ongoing therapy, as in group therapy, I try to take stock of whom I have been spending more and less time with and attempt to check in with all of the alters at regular intervals. If an alter is especially young, shy, or distrustful, I may ask for an "introduction" from an alter with whom I have a good relationship.

Withholding information is a difficult topic. Many therapists believe that sharing secrets with one member of a couple or family is bound to lead to disaster. With DID, one alter may only be willing to reveal important information to you if you promise not to tell one or more other alters. Patients may tell you they can "block" the access of other alters during this conversation, and so what they tell you will be known only between the two of you. Setting a policy of sharing secrets (refusing to withhold information from others in the "group") allows you to model openness and honesty and keeps you out of trouble if you slip and mention some confidentially shared information. Of course, with any absolute policy, one runs the risk of being considered untrustworthy if the need for an exception arises. Exceptions to such a policy may well arise when an alter wants to give you information that is in the best interest of the entire patient or therapeutic progress, yet will only give it "confidentially." In such a case, it may be better to hear what the patient has to say. When this situation arises, I find that it is best to ask the patient to share the information with the others or to let the patient know that "we" are discussing something in private that the alter believes is in the best interest of the group. Although sharing secrets in therapy may tend to exaggerate the split between members of the group, stating that you are willing to receive such information only if it is truly in the best interest of the group can minimize the potential harm and often save the patient's life in the case of a planned suicide or an attack on other alters.

Establishing an Interpersonal Relationship. It is useful to pursue an Adlerian/Sullivarian approach to "reparenting" through establishing a trusting relationship—possibly the very first one the patient has ever had the opportunity to develop. In this type of therapeutic relationship, the therapist focuses on both the relationship between patient and therapist and the relationship between patient and others. Although the emphasis is on current relationships, it can be helpful to explore past relationships and how those experiences affect current relationships.

One must be careful, however, not to become overly interpretive with the patient by continually reflecting on how the patient's behavior is due to past experiences or beliefs. This approach sets up the therapist as a judgmental authority figure and builds further distance between therapist and patient. Instead, the majority of therapeutic interaction should be spent directly engaging in experiential dialogue, with the therapist attempting to compassionately understand what the patient has experienced, is currently experiencing, and anticipates experiencing with others. This approach establishes a more intimate, trusting, and authentic relationship in therapy and serves to model the type of relationship the patient can attempt to have with others.

An interpersonal approach to therapy is useful in helping with repair of personality as described by Object Relations theorists. Three stages of development, and corresponding repair of development, are usually pursued in this approach.

Bonding is an initial stage of development of personality that involves experiencing trust and comfort with another "object" (initially, the mother) and then incorporating this object into one's self, as part of one's self, to take this trust and comfort along with oneself and have it present wherever one goes or with whom one is interacting. Clearly, the patient with DID has difficulty with this process. Therefore, the therapist can assist in redeveloping this bonding by becoming the object of trust and by allowing the patient to feel comfortable in his or her presence. Initially attributed to the therapist, the patient eventually will be able to incorporate this comfort and trust as his or her own and take it to novel situations.

Individuation occurs once a child has learned to incorporate a sense of comfort and trust into one's self and it becomes one's own. The individual can then continue to develop a sense of him- or herself as distinct from the mother and pursue a set of attitudes that form the basis of a separate self. This process allows the child to begin leaving the mother and acting on his or her own and in his or her own way. Although clients with DID no doubt believe they have found a way to keep themselves safe from harm, they need to learn how to reidentify as a person who also can establish new appropriate boundaries with persons they can trust. Therapy can act as a place of stability where the patient can explore new types of boundaries and a more confident sense of self. This exploration will include periods of distancing from the therapist, as well as the patient's finding new limits of intimacy allowable in the therapeutic relationship, and indeed in all relationships.

Exploration of the child's environment, and especially the social environment, can proceed more successfully if the child has a sense of comfort and identity within him- or herself and if the child knows that a "mother" is always around who can be returned to in times of need. With this sense of trust in the self and the mother figure, the child can take the risks necessary to explore new ways of interacting with other things and people and openly face novel situations. The therapist can thus serve as that place of security to allow the patient to go out from and explore his or her social environment in new ways and return to in order to feel safe and discuss the results of his or her efforts. Although it is valuable to find the limits of one's trust, this is rarely a problem for the DID patient. Rather, the patient can learn when and to what degree to trust others and oneself within a variety of social interactions.

These stages can serve as landmarks along the path to recovery during therapy. Even though it is valuable to spend time on earlier stages before moving on, it will be necessary to continually reestablish successes in earlier stages as work proceeds into these later stages.

Respecting the Patient's Existential Motivation. Therapists will benefit by establishing long-term goals that will bring a greater sense of meaning, purpose, and value into the patient's life. At first, this existential focus appears difficult because different alters may have different goals. And the goals of some alters may be to the detriment of other alters (especially among angry alters). Yet, attempting to find common goals and value in life will help motivate the patient and will be an early step on the way to integration. It is also valuable to distinguish between a behavior that may appear to be maladaptive and the positive intention for using the behavior. For example, wanting to be angry may be a defence against forming an attachment that will end up being broken and lead to more pain and suffering. The underlying intention is to be protected from further emotional harm, and the angry behavior guarantees that no harm will be forthcoming since no attachments will be formed. Therefore, it is important to discuss the underlying purpose and value of actions and desires and to find new behaviors that will help the patient achieve goals in even better ways than the old behavior allowed him or her to achieve. Taken together, the values, purpose for living, and meaning derived from actions taken can offer a picture of a survivor bent on being safe and secure. It is important to respect this fundamental desire for safety, to help elucidate it, and to continually build on it.

Another existential feature that is valuable in working with the DID patient is that of being fully present in the reality of the moment. The temptation exists for many therapists to pursue certain lines of investigation with DID patients that lead to boundless realms of fantasy. However, pursuing such fantasies with a patient can serve to legitimize and extend such routes of escape. It is better to remain in the here and now, in open and honest communication with the patient. Certainly, one must acknowledge the tendency of the patient to go off into this realm of fantasy in a way that shows understanding and does not offend or threaten; after all, it allowed the patient to avoid overwhelming pain and suffering in the past. Yet, staying in the room and in direct communication with the patient will allow the patient to experience that solutions can be found in the here and now in relationship with another.

For example, during one session a neutral alter told me that "Jane" (a good alter) could not come out because "Janet" (a hostile alter) had locked her away, along with some others, in a prison located in a deep dark dungeon. I asked the neutral alter whether she could take me there so that I could talk with Jane. After some coaxing, she agreed, and we proceeded down a path fraught with obstacles that needed to be overcome through continually acknowledging comfort and confidence and trust in our relationship. Eventually, we reached a room with dozens of cells. We found a way to open the cells, one of which held Jane, and brought her and the other imprisoned alters back to the surface. I believed this process would be useful in demonstrating that wherever one finds oneself, basic interpersonal skills of comfort and risk taking still could be used. However, this began a period of emotional lability and cognitive instability. Not only acknowledging but also pursuing this fantasy served to justify and subsequently stimulate the patient's use of this coping strategy. It took weeks of repair by staying in the here and now and in authentic relationship with the patient before she was able to stabilize.

Using Cognitive-Behavior Therapy. Within the context of an interpersonal-existential therapeutic relationship, CBT tools can assist the patient to improve his or her functioning in daily life. This assistance can occur through discussion of distortions and training in daily skills of coping. Coping skills may include such exercises as discussing and practicing communication skills with others in a variety of contexts, finding alternatives to "switching" when distressed through a quick relaxation exercise, and taking a break from the setting for a few minutes.

Recognizing and gaining control over one's cognitive distortions of self and world, past and future, can occur through simple discussion of how the patient is "supersensitized" to certain interpersonal relationships because of his or her difficult past. I often use the analogy of an injured hand: if your hand is very tender, you will be hesitant to shake hands and will be very aware of others' intentions to reach out to take your hand. In the same way, a patient with DID will be supersensitive to interactions with others. I will often ask the patient, "What would others do in this situation if they were able to feel safe and comfortable?" For example, if a co-worker is obviously interested in a patient and begins flirting, or if a boss is demanding more at work, or if a therapist reschedules an appointment, the patient may have an extreme reaction. It is useful to demonstrate compassion and understanding of the reaction, to ask whether another person would have a similar reaction, and then to ask whether the patient had such a strong reaction because of his or her past. Such an approach helps detach a patient from his or her automatic reactions and build ego strength that comes from putting one's historically influenced habitual inclinations into perspective and allows awareness of and therefore control over this response.

It is critical, however, not to appear to be too challenging. First and foremost be compassionate and understanding about the patient's reaction. Only in this context will gentle reflection be tolerated. Thus, if you do challenge patients' beliefs about their interactions—and therefore their world model—be gently and compassionately persistent but never insistent.

Using Hypnosis. The use of hypnotic techniques within the therapeutic framework discussed above can be useful in gently and rapidly working through acute crises, as well as for progressing through the various therapeutic stages (see Smith, Chapter Seven). Both self-hypnosis and therapist-led hypnosis are of benefit.

The use of self-hypnosis for accessing a comfort state can teach a form of controlled dissociation to help reduce uncontrolled dissociative reactions during times of distress. The ability to access this comfort state can also be useful for alters who are distrustful, upset, or void of emotion. I make it a point to teach a simple meditation-based self-hypnosis exercise for accessing a feeling of comfort, safety, and calmness before progressing into any difficult cognitive or affective material. Then, if the patient becomes overly distressed during the session, we can quickly access this healthy comfort state, rather than require a dissociative switching. I also encourage patients to access this state whenever they feel distressed. Teaching patients with dissociative disorders a form of self-hypnosis based on Buddhist meditation appears to be more beneficial than an "abstract and dissociative" form of self-hypnosis (see Figure I.1). This approach teaches patients to attend to a comforting sensation that is effortless and occurring in the moment. In fact, because most patients with DID say they do not currently experience comfort, never have felt comfort, and do not know what others mean when they talk of comfort, I find that I must use this technique to help them understand what it means to feel comfortable, safe, and secure. I let them know that this is a natural condition, one that is always with them, and that they can access whenever they need to. The instructions for developing this state are quite simple and occur in four steps:

1. Place your hands over your abdomen and feel the breath gently moving your hands in and out, like a massage from the inside.

2. Move one hand to your chest and feel your heart beating, regular and strong, keeping you healthy.

3. Feel the warmth of your body, like a safe and secure blanket protecting you.

4. Just sit with this feeling. Whenever thoughts or feelings arise, just let them go and return to sitting simply with this feeling of comfort and safety.

The use of therapist-led hypnosis can often serve to facilitate switching for therapeutic purposes, especially for alters who are reluctant to emerge or are otherwise difficult to access. This approach is also useful in gathering information about the initial trauma or other difficult material that is easier to examine dispassionately in trance. Hypnosis can soften the abreaction frequently associated with uncovering traumatic cognitive and affective memories that were repressed during or following the trauma. Therapist-led hypnosis should have three components:

1. *The induction phase:* The therapist leads patients to a safe and comfortable state. In DID, it is better to access such a state through attention to a concrete here-and-now sensation than by taking the patients to some dissociated fantasy (as described above).

2. *The utilization phase:* Once patients are dissociated from their typical cognitive concerns and focus, the therapist can ask patients to access memories or creative solutions to problems.

3. *The integration phase:* After material has surfaced (whether from memory or creative consideration), the therapist can ask patients to integrate this information into their lives in order to live more fully.

Finally, hypnosis can be of substantial use in assisting with the fusion of personalities (see Table I.1). Various hypnotic devices can be used for this, including asking patients to go into trance so that all the alters can communicate important information to the main (original) personality. This approach also helps build a sense of self as unconscious potentials (various alters contributing their various skills) and leads to a sense of a focused, conscious self (main personality) that selects among alternative potential actions and manifests one activity that is appropriate for the situation at hand.

I have also found that often an alter exists that identifies itself as the "unconscious." This "unconscious" alter is only accessed during trance when the therapist defines the unconscious as "containing all past and present thoughts, feelings, skills, and knowledge" and then asks the patient to "go to sleep, rest, feeling as safe and comfortable as possible. . . . When you are able to let all conscious awareness rest, I would like to speak directly to the unconscious so that no conscious alter is aware of what is being discussed. This will prevent any alter from becoming upset. When the unconscious is ready, it can let me know by saying 'hello.'" Once this alter is accessed, agreement is usually made not to share with the other alters any information accessed here, unless this alter agrees it would be useful. This alter is different from the other alters because it has access to all past and present information and because the others are unaware of its presence. Although holding secrets is usually not a good idea in typical couples, family, or group therapy settings, holding off sharing all information derived from hypnosis is often lifesaving in working with patients with DID. Access to this "unconscious" alter can provide the therapist with invaluable information that otherwise would not be accessible. For example, I have frequently been told of upcoming suicide attempts or other problems during dialogue with the unconscious alter, whereas prior to this access, I only found out about the problem after the event occurred. Because this unconscious alter has access to all prior experiences, I have also been given information about early abuse, perpetrators, or "secret" cult information I could not previously access—all with no deleterious effects. I let the other alters know, quite honestly, that hypnosis allows me to gather information helpful for therapy but that some alters may not be ready to deal with what surfaces and so I'd like to keep it to myself until I think the others are ready to receive this information. This approach avoids sharing information with some alters but not others.

Table I.1
The Usual Developmental Course of DID

Listed below are some of the major events in the progression of DID. Many other scenarios are possible, but this is one of the most "classical."

Normal childhood personality development.

Severe ongoing trauma, usually in early or later childhood; child is overwhelmed with distress.

Splitting into experientially separate "personalities" (each with its own affect, set of skills, and memories) occurs when the child has little support and can find no better way to cope. This splitting is effective in reducing the distress experienced by any single personality.

Successful coping style is learned and continues to apply in times of stress, even beyond the initial causal trauma. Initially, aberrant behavior can be noticed, but splitting is rarely apparent.

Therapy is sought for concomitant problems or disorders (such as depression, personality disorders, medical problems). DID diagnosis is often missed.

Dissociative Identity Disorder diagnosis is eventually made, yet often not until college years or later.

Initial psychotherapy focuses on understanding of alters, the initiating trauma, and ongoing dilemmas.

Ongoing therapy involves developing understanding and cooperation among alters and eventually being able to discuss the original trauma. This process usually takes many years, with many crises.

Integration is attempted following an agreement to share all information, feelings, and resources. This agreement may take much time and bargaining. Old symptoms may temporarily return.

Fusion of alters into one predominant self is achieved. All experiences and strengths of the previous alters are maintained, although they now work together to assist in coping with the situation at hand. This collaboration is often achieved tenuously at first, with splitting still occurring in very difficult psychosocial settings. With time and the trust of the therapist and other alters, a more permanent ego personality takes charge.

Ongoing follow-up therapy focuses on further developing ego strength through reinforcing skills of coping in the present, planning for the future, improving self-esteem, and developing more intimate psychosocial bonds. This process may entail weekly therapy for many years following fusion, or it could occur on an "as needed" basis.

Stages of Treatment

Long-term psychotherapy for persons with DID in many ways parallels approaches taken for many other conditions. Of course, unique considerations must be appreciated at various stages of treatment for patients with DID.

Initial Stages. Initial sessions are usually concerned with confirming the diagnosis, establishing trust and rapport through understanding the patient's present concerns and past experiences, "charting" the alters, and understanding the special strengths and concerns of each alter.

Intermediate Stages. The long process of psychotherapy may occur once or twice a week over several years. During this time, it is important to continue the development of trust and understanding, individuation, and exploration, as described earlier. Modeling appropriate psychosocial relationships, as well as calm and considered reactions to crises, will help the patient gain the skills needed to cope more appropriately in a variety of circumstances. The therapist should also attempt to improve communication and cooperation among alters. Specific coping skills can also be directly taught, including finding ways to feel safe and comfortable by oneself and then around others, developing and then practicing social skills in a variety of social settings, and managing depression or anger. It is also important at some point to allow past memories held by one alter to be shared with other alters. Once this can be accomplished, the original need to split will no longer be required.

Integration and Fusion. After the therapist has helped the patient achieve these intermediate goals of therapy, integration of alters into a fused sense of self can be attempted. When first working toward integration, it is important to maintain the entire range of coping skills and experiences contained in the entire alter group. The therapist may work toward integration in several ways. One approach is to help each alter have access to all other alters' experiences and abilities. It is also possible to allow one alter to have access to all other alters' experiences and to identify the experiences as "one's own." The alter selected by the group to represent the group is usually the original personality or one that emerges from a "ceremony" or in hypnosis as a gestalt of the others—a being greater than the mere sum of the parts. Yet, this personality must be strengthened by borrowing the positive resources from the others so that it can manifest the range of personality styles necessary for successful interaction in a complex environment. To avoid a "fight" among the alters at this point, it is useful to frame this phase of therapy as a building of a strong and confident new self that contains all the resources of the group, rather than as the "death" or elimination of any of the alters. Let each alter know that he or she is a valuable contribution to the whole and that all he or she has contributed will continue to be a valuable asset in the future. Even the "negative" aspects of the alters are useful experiences—if nothing else than to better understand the experience in others and to know what to avoid in the future. Yet, instead of having different names and exclusive ownership of experiences and skills, the integrated whole person will possess a continuum of abilities and skills. Thus, only benefits will accrue from this cooperative arrangement—the same sort of arrangement used automatically by people without DID.

Follow-Up Maintenance. Scheduling sessions on a less regular or "as needed" basis is useful to help the patient cope with new stresses as well as old tendencies to dissociate or split in the face of stress. CBT and Interpersonal Therapy approaches work well during this phase. Table I.1 presents an overview of the lifetime progression for persons with DID.

OTHER CONSIDERATIONS

Undoubtedly, many other considerations can be addressed regarding DID, including forensic issues and changes in neurophysiology during various alter states. Within the confines of *treating*

DID, however, two additional issues common to all psychotherapists need to be addressed in terms of their relevance to DID.

Repressed Memories, False Memory Syndrome, and Dissociative Identity Disorder

Generally, the issue of repressed or false memories refers to abuse (usually sexual or extremely violent) that occurs in childhood, is repressed from conscious recall, and surfaces later in adulthood (or is created later in adulthood to rationalize/justify some adult psychosocial disturbance), often during psychotherapy. DID, by contrast, develops in childhood and persists into adulthood. Rarely are memories of abuse repressed entirely (although they may be segmented into certain alters to the exclusion of others' awareness).

These reactions represent two very different ways of dissociative coping: *repression* (out of associative consciousness) and *division* (among dissociative consciousness). If one accepts the presence of DID at all (rather than the disorder being factitious on the part of the patient or misdiagnosis on the part of the therapist), then what must be taken as tenuous is not that abuse occurred, but rather the specifics of the memories. Early abuse is, no doubt, mixed with fantasy prevalent in all childhood recall. Because children have less referential context with which to "understand" what is happening to them (see Siegel, Chapter Two, for a discussion of episodic memory), they are always in more of a dissociative state than adults. Thus, either at the time of encoding the events or of currently reconstructing the events, patients may have mixed the environmental situation with their dissociative representation of it (see Figure I.2). Therefore, although abuse may well have occurred, the patients represented it in a fantastic way (for example, dungeons, ritualistic ceremony, screams, blood). Although such occurrences may have actually occurred (corroborated by witnesses), children represent it in their own unique way—the way that made sense to them at that time. These memories persist into adulthood.

Repressed early memories and false current memories are of minimal interest in the treatment of DID. Nevertheless, the study of False Memory Syndrome may help therapists appreciate the way actual trauma has been encoded and recalled by patients with DID and how this can influence their therapeutic development.

Managed Care

Although managed care promises to help eliminate excessive treatments and bring health care costs down in general, any limitation on psychotherapy for patients with DID threatens the improvement of these patients. By restricting therapy, patient improvement becomes restricted, and such a policy will drain both the insurer and society as a whole. These drains will be in the form of increased expenditure for expensive hospital and medical treatment (directly related to the psychiatric disturbance), as well as decreased functioning and productivity within society. Thus, whereas consistent and intensive treatment holds promise of improvement, transient and sporadic treatment over the years does little to reverse the illness.

Certainly, there is a place for brief, time-limited therapy for patients with DID. Brief hospital stays on a dissociative disorders unit can be of great support to both patient and outpatient therapist in times of acute crisis (see Ross, Chapter Ten). The best time for brief outpatient care, however, occurs only after years of ongoing intensive psychosocial treatment for purposes of maintenance and termination of successful psychotherapy.

Although the picture of DID and its treatment appears to be exceptionally complicated, the effort is well worthwhile. With patience and perseverance, psychotherapy holds out the possibility of helping patients improve their quality of life. The study of DID also can assist therapists to extend their understanding of normal and abnormal human consciousness and functioning— an understanding that will extend to assisting many other types of patients. The study and treatment of individuals with DID, however, is a serious effort. This book is simply the next step in one's training.

GLOSSARY OF MAJOR TERMS

ABREACTION. The reliving of an experience in such a way that previously repressed emotions associated with it are released. This release can be valuable in the treatment of Posttraumatic Stress Disorder. If abreactions occur before a patient has sufficient resources to adequately handle the surfacing of such previously repressed emotions, however, the patient may have a serious setback in therapeutic development.

ABUSE. The misuse of something. Abuse leading to the coping style that becomes DID can be sexual, physical, or emotional (from absence of love on the part of a parent to inconsistent emotions, such as alternating love and anger) and result in a wide range of conflicting emotions within the patient. (Fairbairn stated that patients incorporate the negative into themselves in order to control it. This principle helps to explain the continued self-abuse seen by many patients with DID.)

ALTER. One of the various personalities that the patient "splits" into to cope with overwhelming distress. Each has its own set of personality traits, including affect, cognitive and motor skills, language ability, memories, style of speech, age, value systems, and even physiological factors.

AMYTAL. An anti-inhibition, central-acting medication for use in uncovering repressed information during therapy or the initial emergence of alter personalities. A video recording is frequently made during such interviews for later presentation to the patient or concerned parties.

CHARTING (MAPPING). Charting or mapping the array of alter personalities, each having its own name, age, skills, concerns, memories, and relationship to the therapist. Developing this sort of personality chart becomes quite difficult, and important, when the number of alters is large.

DEPERSONALIZATION DISORDER. A dissociative disorder characterized by a persistent or recurrent feeling of being detached from one's mental process or body that is accompanied by intact reality testing (*DSM-IV*).

DEREALIZATION. A descriptor that applies to the experience that the world is somehow odd, separate from one's normal sense of participation with it, that one is looking from the outside-in. Derealization often occurs briefly following a single traumatic event or for longer periods of time following ongoing trauma.

DISSOCIATION. The suspension of attention to current environmental context (time, space, logic, self-other distinction) or from aspects of one's self (thoughts, emotions, sensations, behaviors, and even consciousness). Dissociation can be either uncontrolled (as in dissociative coping strategy) in response to severe distress (see Figure I.2) or controlled (self-initiated) as in meditation or hypnosis (see Figure I.1).

DISSOCIATIVE AMNESIA (PREVIOUSLY, PSYCHOGENIC AMNESIA [*DSM-III-R*]). A disorder characterized by an inability to recall important personal information, usually of a traumatic or stressful nature, that is too extensive to be explained by ordinary forgetfulness (*DSM-IV*).

DISSOCIATIVE DISORDER–NOT OTHERWISE SPECIFIED (DD–NOS). A category included in the *DSM-IV* for dissociative disorders that do not meet the exact criteria for another dissociative disorder. Note that dissociative symptoms also are present in acute stress disorder, posttraumatic stress disorder, and somatization disorder.

DISSOCIATIVE FUGUE (PREVIOUSLY, PSYCHOGENIC FUGUE [*DSM-III-R*]). A state characterized by sudden, unexpected travel away from home or one's customary place of work, accompanied by an inability to recall one's past and confusion about personal identity or the assumption of a new identity (*DSM-IV*).

FUSION (INTEGRATION). The integration of various alter personalities (each with specific affect, skills, and memories) into one personality with access to a variety of affect potentials and skills and to all memories). A major goal of therapy.

GROUP ("FAMILY" OR "OTHERS"). The "collection" of alters that comprise the assemblage of personalities.

HYPNOSIS. A natural and normal recuperative state in which one can suspend vigilance to current contextual time, place, logic, and self-awareness, instead attending to memories or creative imagery (see Figure I.1). Hypnosis can be self-induced (self-hypnosis) or therapist-led.

INTEGRATION. See Fusion.

OBJECT RELATIONS. In contrast to Freud's drive theory, this theory of personality development was developed by Eric Erickson, Otto Kernberg, Margaret Mahler, W.R.D. Fairbairn, Karl Winnocot, H. Kohut, and others who focused on "functional" development of ego in relationship to others (the "object") and their environment. Three stages of development, and therefore repair of development, are usually pursued in this approach: *bonding, individuation,* and *exploration.* An interpersonal approach to therapy, of the sort advocated by Adler or Sullivan, has been found to be useful in "reparenting" and repairing damaged "object relations."

REFRAME. From the work of hypnotherapist Milton Erickson, the therapeutic device of (1) separating a positive desired intention (for example, feeling comfortable or safe) from an unwanted behavior (for example, drug use, yelling) used to achieve this positive goal and then (2) attempting to find a more beneficial behavior that can achieve the positive intention even better than the unwanted behavior could achieve (for example, meditation).

RITUAL ABUSE. Satanic or non-organized rituals (for example, abuse committed by one or more perpetrators in a regular fashion—as in getting drunk nightly, hitting the child, and then locking the child in a closet when she or he cries).

SPLITTING. The dividing into disparate personalities, each with its own affect, set of skills, and memories. These personalities may or may not have awareness or even knowledge of the other personalities. (Note: The use of the term *splitting* here is distinct from the effort by some patients, such as those with borderline personality disorder, to *split* the affinities between others in some social situation.)

SWITCHING. The emergence of an alter personality that has been in the background; this occurs when the previously foregrounded alter personality becomes overwhelmed with some distress, or when the patient enters a setting where a different alter usually takes charge, or when the therapist asks the patient to "switch" and allow another alter to emerge. Switching can occur many times an hour or only when a distress occurs.

NOTES

P. xvii, *its prevalence in the general and psychiatric populations is debated:* Ross, C. A. (1991). Epidemiology of multiple personality disorder and dissociation. *Psychiatric Clinics of North America, 14,* 503–518.

P. xx, *Multiple Personality Disorder:* American Psychiatric Association. (1994). *Diagnostic and statistical manual of mental disorders* (4th ed.). Washington, DC: Author.

P. xxii, *a dual diagnosis may be considered:* Spiegel, D., Fritzholtz, E., & Spira, J. (1993). Functional disorders of memory. In J. Oldham, M. Riba, & A. Tasman (Eds.), *Annual review of psychiatry* (Vol. 12, pp. 747–782). Washington, DC: American Psychiatric Association Press.

P. xxiv, *Tellegen Absorption Scale (TAS):* Bernstein (Carlson), E. B., & Putnum, F. (1989). Development, reliability, and validity of a dissociation scale. *Journal of Nervous and Mental Diseases, 174,* 727–735 [referring to the Dissociative Experience Scale-DES]; Steinberg, M. (1993). *Structured clinical interview for DSM-IV dissociative disorders* (SCID-D). Washington, DC: American Psychiatric Press; Tellegen, A., & Atkinson, G. (1974). Openness to absorbing and self-altering experiences ("absorption"), a trait related to hypnotic susceptibility. *Journal of Abnormal Psychology, 83,* 268–277.

P. xxvii, *we incorporate the negative objects:* Fairbairn, W.R.D. (1986). The repression and the return of bad objects (with special reference to the "war on neurosis"). In P. Buckley (Ed.), *Essential papers on object relations* (pp. 102–126). New York: New York University Press.

P. xxviii, *visual, auditory, or tactile:* Pavio, A. (1975). Perceptual comparison through the mind's eye. *Memory and Cognition, 3,* 638–652. See also works by Stephen Kossyln.

P. xxxviii, *described by Object Relations theorists:* Bowlby, J. (1986). The nature of the child's tie to his mother. In P. Buckley (Ed.), *Essential papers on object relations* (pp. 153–199). New York: New York University Press; Fairbairn, W.R.D. (1986). The repression and the return of bad objects (with special reference to the "war on neurosis"). In P. Buckley (Ed.), *Essential papers on object relations* (pp. 102–126). New York: New York University Press; Kohut, H. (1977). *The restoration of the self.* New York: International University Press; Mahler, M. H. (1986). On the first three sub-phases of the separation-individuation process. In P. Buckley (Ed.), *Essential papers on object relations* (pp. 222–232). New York: New York University Press; and Winnocot, K. (1986). The theory of the parent-infant relationship. In P. Buckley (Ed.), *Essential papers on object relations* (pp. 233–353). New York: New York University Press.

P. xl, *allowed him or her to achieve:* This follows the principles of a therapeutic reframe developed by Milton Erickson and his students.

P. xliii, *self-hypnosis based on Buddhist meditation:* Spira, J. (1995). *Tai Chi Chuan and sitting meditation.* Durham, NC: Duke University Medical Center.

P. xliii, *more beneficial than an "abstract and dissociative" form of self-hypnosis:* Spiegel, H., & Spiegel, H. (1987). *Trance and treatment: Clinical uses of hypnosis.* New York: Basic Books.

P. xliv, *repressed during or following the trauma:* Spiegel, D., & Spira, J. (1993). Hypnosis for psychiatric disorders. In D. Dunner (Ed.), *Current psychiatric therapy* (pp. 517–523). Philadelphia: Saunders.

P. l, *the study of False Memory Syndrome:* Loftus, E. (1993). The reality of repressed memories. *American Psychologist, 48,* 518–537; Terr, L. (1987). What happens to early memories of trauma? A study of twenty children under age five at the time of documented traumatic events. *Journal of the American Academy of Child and Adolescent Psychiatry, 27,* 96–104.

P. li, *patients incorporate the negative:* Fairbairn, W.R.D. (1986). The repression and the return of bad objects (with special reference to the "war on neurosis"). In P. Buckley (Ed.), *Essential papers on object relations* (pp. 102–126). New York: New York University Press.

P. liii, *An interpersonal approach to therapy:* Adler, A. (1959). *Understanding human nature.* New York: Premier Books; Sullivan, H. S. (1953). *The interpersonal theory of psychiatry.* New York: Norton.

For all those with Dissociative Identity Disorder:
past, present, and future

TREATING
DISSOCIATIVE IDENTITY
DISORDER

PART ONE

MODELS OF TREATMENT

I

PSYCHOLOGICAL ASSESSMENT

Judith Armstrong

In this chapter, I will discuss the ways psychological assessment can be used to aid in the diagnosis and treatment of patients with Dissociative Identity Disorder (DID). I will also describe the special challenges that DID patients bring to the testing situation. These challenges must be addressed regardless of the tests that are used in order for the evaluation to give an accurate and representative picture of the dissociating patient.

I will begin this chapter with a discussion of the goals of DID assessment. I will then examine the unique features of the DID testing process. To test for DID, we must have a framework for seeing dissociative phenomena on testing. I will therefore introduce some general principles that enable the assessor to recognize DID behaviors on testing. Next, I will move to a discussion of special issues in the testing of DID patients. In this section, I will introduce some interpersonal techniques designed to increase the accuracy of the assessment by maximizing the cooperative working relationship of the DID testee and the tester.

Then, I will look at a testing battery I have found useful for diagnosis and treatment planning for DID patients. This battery is appropriate for patients suspected of having DID. It is also helpful when the DID diagnosis is established but the patient and the therapist want to better understand specific treatment problems or to monitor treatment outcome. I will conclude the chapter with an outline of some important points in giving feedback to patients and their clinicians on the test results.

GOALS OF THE DID ASSESSMENT

Generally speaking, psychological assessment has proven to be a useful tool for making diagnostic decisions. A test battery can provide the clinician with information on a wide array of the patient's characteristics, from the cognitive, to the emotional, to the interpersonal. Information is gathered and scored under controlled conditions that minimize the chances the tester will bias the results. Abundant data have been collected on the typical test results of different diagnostic groups. This plethora enables the assessor to identify whether the patient's test pattern resembles those of patients diagnosed with various psychiatric syndromes. Moreover, because the aim of many tests is not at all obvious and because several measures also contain validity checks, concerns about suggestion and malingering can be addressed.

These qualities make testing especially useful when dealing with a complex and controversial diagnosis such as DID. Psychological assessment can be supportive to both the patient and the therapist in these trying circumstances because it provides objective data about the patient's disorder that help clarify and justify the diagnostic decision.

It has also been my experience, however, that the very ability of testing to place people in diagnostic categories is viewed by many clinicians as a limitation. Therapists are often more interested in providing better treatment for their patients than in categorizing them. They want testing to provide information about their patients' uniqueness, the central life issues that drive patients' conflicts, the coping strengths patients can mobilize to overcome treatment hurdles and life crises, and the weaknesses that put patients at risk for regression and acting out. Consequently, useful assessment should not simply pigeonhole a patient, but rather provide information to guide the treatment of a human being, who is always more complex than his or her diagnosis.

Thus, the DID assessment not only should be employed to help confirm or rule out a dissociative disorder diagnosis but also should provide a bridge between the diagnostic label and practical therapeutic action. I hope to show that the treatment of people with dissociative disorders can be more effective if their therapists have information from an assessment that clarifies these patients' individual needs and characteristics. The vignettes that appear throughout this chapter both illustrate typical DID test responses and describe the therapeutic implications of these responses.

General Considerations

The assessment process refers to roles and interactions of the tester and testee in assessment. In the sections that follow, I argue that an understanding of the test process is essential to a valid and objective assessment of DID. In this section, I lay the groundwork for why this is so.

The reader who is not familiar with the process of testing may well assume that assessment is like an X ray in that the measures are powerful and subtle enough to give a clear picture of the patient's internal workings. The truth is not that simple because testing, like therapy, is also an interpersonal experience. The test responses that patients give are not solely due to internal personality variables. They are also influenced by social variables such as patient and therapist expectations and rapport, qualities that determine whether and how much patients are encouraged and willing to be open and honest with themselves, and with us as therapists, in their assessment.

In some ways, perhaps the X-ray analogy is an apt one because just as a moving patient will provide a blurred X ray, so a frightened or uncooperative testee will give a misleading, fragmentary, or confused test pattern. Moreover, the clarity of the picture is not the whole story. An accurate interpretation of an X ray depends on the ability of the physician to know where and how to look. Similarly, an accurate psychological assessment depends on the effectiveness of the interpretations of the assessor.

The human element is always a factor in science. Our goal in scientific assessment, then, is to monitor the assessment process and to use our understanding of this process to inform our testing and the conclusions we reach.

THE DID TESTING PROCESS: SEEING DISSOCIATIVE PHENOMENA

In this section, I turn to some general strategies that will help testers and psychotherapists recognize and understand dissociative phenomena on testing. These principles can be applied to a gamut of tests so that you may well be able to include your favorite instrument in your own DID test battery.

Readers looking for a cookbook of ingredients for making the extremely complex diagnosis of DID will be disappointed. The strategies that follow all make it clear that we as therapists don't have a test formula to ensure a quick and easy diagnosis of DID. This is true, in part, because we don't have a significant test database on dissociative disordered patients and, in part, because the diagnosis of any complex disorder requires expertise and individualization, not simple formulas. Thus, if you are considering developing your DID testing experience, be aware that this activity will also test your ability to enjoy change and challenge in your professional life.

Consider New Ways of Looking at the Test Data

This point may seem too obvious to mention, but most assessment studies have been designed to diagnose DID, rather than to describe and understand what dissociation and alter switching look like on testing. Commonly, a group of DID patients is given test X and then the results are interpreted in a standard fashion, as they would be if these testees were not DID patients. Rather than see what dissociation can add to test theory, the approach has tended to be the other way around, with efforts being made to fit DID into a traditional testing framework. If you have ever used this method, you probably have found that working with the familiar does not lessen your confusion. For example, Colin Ross and associates, using several personality measures, found that their DID patients simultaneously met criteria for a large variety of Axis I and II disorders.

I am not suggesting that you discard your favorite theories or tests, but I think it is important to recognize that phenomena like childhood abuse, adult trauma, and dissociation have been documented for several centuries. Nevertheless, the usual approaches to testing have not helped therapists to take notice of this. Although traditional test strategies bring much to the field of dissociative disorders, they also bring something that has blinded us to these forms of human suffering. The following principles can aid in moving us beyond standard test attitudes to a framework that is more congenial to noticing dissociative phenomena when they do occur in testing.

Focus on the Testee's Behavior

One of the best ways to take a new look at things is to fall back on the most conservative assessment strategy of all: careful observation and documentation of the patient's behavior.

A dramatic example of the usefulness of this approach is a test report I came across that was written twenty years ago, during the first hospitalization of a patient who was diagnosed with DID fifteen years later. Although the assessment was done long before we testers had any inkling of dissociative disorders and their traumatic etiology, it is a model of an accurate and useful description of a DID patient.

The assessor began by noting distinctive test behaviors, which included lack of anxiety accompanied by excessive eye blinking.

He commented that although the patient's intellectual testing and achievement were above average, she inexplicably drew her pictures as though she were a five-year-old child. He felt free to document other inconsistencies in test findings, including the fact that although the patient demonstrated a strong need for interpersonal closeness, she tended to withdraw from people because she associated intimacy with sadism. Finally, the tester remarked on the perplexing fact that despite her history of suicidal behavior, she showed absolutely no sign of depression on any of the tests. I most admire this long-ago tester for his courageous conclusion at the end of his report that the patient did not present a clear-cut diagnostic picture!

With all of its contradictions and uncertainties—in fact, because of them—this test report has significant things to say about the patient's present diagnosis and her treatment issues. Recording behavioral observations remains the most powerful way I know of convincing people, including ourselves, of the reality of dissociative disorders.

Familiarize Yourself with the DID Theory and Treatment Literature

DID theory and treatment literatures will help you recognize the behavioral signs of dissociation. You will develop a cognitive framework that enables you to see such things as the moments of uncommunicative staring into space that may mark a brief dissociative episode, the abrupt changes in voice and relational style occurring alongside a sudden change in level of functioning that may signal an alter switch, the sudden forgetting of test directions or the inability to explain a previous response that can alert you to the testee's ongoing amnesia.

Your readings will also help you form new hypotheses about familiar observations. Consider a young woman being interviewed prior to testing by a male examiner. She suddenly veers from a businesslike and cool attitude to a blatantly sexual, little-girl presentation. Although we may have formerly understood this as manipulative seductiveness, we can now also entertain the idea that what we are seeing is a switch to a sexualized child state. Perhaps something happened in the tester-testee interaction that aroused this patient's fear of the tester, a fear that she is attempting to diminish by becoming a seductive child. We can look for evidence of this hypothesis in the personality testing by seeing, for example, whether her primary reaction to interpersonal interactions is fear, distrust, and safety seeking, rather than the sexual and social dominance that her overt behavior might appear to imply.

When you begin to recognize dissociative phenomena during testing, you can also begin to use your testees' help in identifying their dissociative processes. I have found that the best method of doing this is the least suggestive and least intrusive: I simply ask patients to tell me what is going on.

Familiarize Yourself with the PTSD Test Literature

Because dissociative disorders are now understood as developmental posttraumatic disorders and because severe trauma is often accompanied by dissociative symptomatology, it stands to reason that test findings on patients with Posttraumatic Stress Disorder (PTSD) should have much to tell us about our dissociative disordered testees. Fortunately, the PTSD test literature has become quite extensive. Knowing what acute PTSD looks like on tests can help us clarify important questions such as how well the dissociative barriers of DID protect these patients from full-blown PTSD. This can be extremely useful input for us to have in making decisions about the pacing of treatment. After we determine the extent of PTSD that our DID patient is presently experiencing, we can offer practical advice on how much supportive work will be needed before he or she can tolerate the uncovering of new traumatic material.

The PTSD literature also alerts us to the importance of considering test stimuli as traumatic triggers for DID testees. Keep in mind that elements of the test material can evoke flashbacks and traumatic associations in dissociative disordered patients. The resultant fear, pain, and disorientation may then cause patients to give responses that appear to be primitive and disorganized. We need to consider that what might appear on testing as a developmental vulnerability to regression might instead be a traumatic vulnerability to being overpowered by memories of a truly aggressive and disorganized reality.

Don't Overincorporate

If everything is dissociation, then dissociation no longer has any meaning. We need to consider a range of diagnostic possibilities during our assessment before we rule in or rule out the presence of a dissociative disorder. We also need to consider whether the dissociation that we do see is a major or minor part of the test picture.

For example, a recent trauma that brings up an unresolved earlier trauma might result in severe PTSD and depression, with relatively minor signs of dissociation and self-dividedness. Taking a good history is essential to clarifying the role of dissociation in the larger diagnostic picture.

Consider the Context of the Testing

Considering the context of the testing is an important point in any diagnostic situation, but it is of special importance now, given the current controversy over the validity of DID. Much has been made of the possibility that patients may mimic DID symptoms to receive social or personal rewards. We assessors would be naive if we didn't recognize that some patients may create, exaggerate, or sustain dissociative symptoms to gain such reinforcements as increased attention or approval, decreased anxiety and uncertainty, social control, or monetary reward.

An equally important element of symptom reinforcement, however, is the concealment of psychopathology to receive rewards or to avoid punishment. In DID, this manifests as the conscious hiding of true dissociative symptoms because the patient has much to gain by denying DID and/or much to lose by revealing the disorder. In the present social climate, increased attention, approval by one's family and friends, decreased anxiety and confusion, and monetary reward may also attend the negation and disbelief of one's DID.

Both facets of symptom reinforcement are of particular concern in forensic situations, in which the rewards for producing or camouflaging dissociative behaviors may be substantial. One of the first questions we ought to clarify, then, is whether the client stands to benefit greatly from a DID diagnosis for reasons external to the disorder or to lose substantially from getting a DID diagnosis for similarly external considerations. In both instances, for opposite reasons, we ought to be skeptical and careful in our questioning and conservative and balanced in our interpretive strategies. The general unfamiliarity of the public with the details of test findings in trauma and dissociation makes psychological assessment particularly valuable when issues of symptom reward arise.

THE TESTING ALLIANCE

The special test considerations that follow have as their goal the development of a testing alliance between the tester and the DID patient. Similar to the treatment alliance, the testing alliance describes the sense that both patient and tester have of working together, with equal effort, to better understand and improve the problems of the patient.

The unusual self-dividedness of DID patients, and their traumatic expectation that they will be abused, invaded, shamed, controlled, and betrayed by people, is a formidable challenge to the testing alliance. In our favor, however, is the ability of DID patients to organize themselves around a task (they feel better when they are working), as well as their intellectual interest in understanding themselves better.

Whom Do I Test?

Perhaps the most distinctive aspect of DID is that it raises the question of which of the patient's alters to test. This question has very practical implications not only for the test results but also for the time and energy of the tester who is contemplating the unappetizing notion of assessing numerous separate personalities. In this section, I suggest a solution that is helpful in both clarifying diagnosis and making appropriate treatment recommendations.

As I began my DID assessment career, it became clear to me that the issue of "whom" to test would be a true challenge. Expecting enthusiastic support from these patients' therapists, I was instead treated to a series of sardonic anecdotes about their past experiences with misleading test reports. These evaluations contained diagnostic formulations that ranged from seriously damaging to so far off the mark that they were funny. Two examples are the story of the consistently productive DID professor who was diagnosed as a profoundly regressed schizophrenic and the case of the successful DID artist who was determined to have a severe visuospatial learning disability!

Clearly, these patients' assessors should have been disturbed by the discrepancy between their findings and the objectively adaptive behavior of these patients. Somehow, they had evaluated a limited and nonrepresentative element of these patients' personalities.

In fact, the misdiagnoses described above should be of no surprise to DID clinicians. We quickly learn that our patients can be totally and honestly dysfunctional in some circumstances (for example, the therapy hour, a disability assessment) and a short time later act with extreme capability in another setting (for example, at work, during a crisis with a family member).

Situation-dependent changeability in style and level of functioning is a hallmark of DID. This is why test information gathered on a single alter (for example, the "host" personality) or even a series of testings on different alters can be misleading. Such information tells us little about the natural patterning of the DID patient's personality system, such as basic coping style, range of abilities and vulnerabilities, and the roles and interactions of the alters.

If we want a testing that is representative of the DID patient's full personality, we need to create a setting that encourages the participation of the patient's full alter system. As in treatment, we can better appreciate and work with the "parts" if we have an understanding of the "whole."

In most referrals for testing, the DID diagnosis is still open or the patient's acceptance of alters is inconsistent. Therefore, I have found it best to encourage the involvement of all of the patient's self-aspects in testing by framing my invitation of the divided personality system in everyday, normative terms. I indicate to the patient that sometimes people feel as though they have different sides to themselves, different aspects, or perhaps different moods. I ask the patient whether this is true for him or her and, if so, to describe these sides. Then, I ask whether the patient would be willing to express all of these aspects in the testing. To minimize suggestion, I use only the patient's terms for his or her self-aspects throughout the assessment.

With overtly DID patients, this "invitation" enables me to discuss the fears and concerns that various alters might have about being assessed. It also provides more "hidden" or questionable DID patients and myself with a means to recognize and talk about their self-dividedness or their unacceptable feelings in a safe fashion. In either case, the invitation allows me to discuss directly with the patient the roles of his or her various self-aspects in the testing.

ELAINE

For example, Elaine's testing occurred early in treatment, well before her DID diagnosis. Her dense amnesia for her childhood and adolescence made it difficult to get a clear etiology for her sudden suicidality. Elaine's MMPI showed a severe degree of general psychopathology

that was surprising, given her life accomplishments. During our discussion of her answers to the MMPI "critical items" (test items that
may pick up life crises), Elaine's demeanor suddenly changed. In an
energetic, emotionally charged voice, she told me about a highly
unusual, trauma-filled childhood. She insisted that it was essential I
get this information to her therapist and demanded that I include a
xerographic copy of the critical items with my test report because,
"I won't remember what I'm telling you as soon as I finish talking."

Making the Testing Safe

I have found that the major objection most testers have to inviting all of the self-aspects of the DID patient into testing is the
potential consequences of such an invitation being accepted.
After all, they might be encouraging the participation of violent
adult alters, as well as overwhelmed child alters, who can turn
the evaluation into chaos. This issue is foremost in the DID
patient's mind as well. The DID tester's first order of business,
then, is to set up a test structure that will ensure the safety of the
assessment process for everyone involved.

One essential element of trauma is that the basic routine of
life has been destroyed, resulting in the development of the perception that the world is an unsafe and uncontrollable place.
Thus, it is important to promote the traumatized testees' sense
of security in a simple but essential manner: we can familiarize
them with the test procedure so that they know what to expect.

Before we begin the actual testing, we can describe the tests
and the order in which they will be given. We can then ask
patients to voice any questions and concerns they might have
about the present assessment and to share with us any negative
past testing experiences so that we can avoid or correct misunderstandings. We can alert patients to the possibility that some
tests might make them anxious. Then, we can rehearse ways to
anticipate and handle potential safety problems. I find that if I
discuss safety techniques at the outset of testing, DID patients

will invariably offer helpful advice that is appropriate to their stage of self-awareness.

Safety issues can be handled in a direct fashion with overtly DID patients by calling on the coping capacities of their self-system. We can ask "everyone" to listen or ask the patient to "listen inside" to find out whether alters have questions or concerns about the testing. Usually, DID patients will either voice their fears about certain alters entering the testing or switch to an alter who has these concerns. The problem-solving process can then proceed in a fashion that promotes the working relationship between the patient's alter system and the tester.

We can model our safety techniques on basic DID treatment techniques. For example, violence-prone alters can make a contract to behave safely or, if they cannot, to speak through another alter. Frightened or nonverbal child alters can find some internal support system, such as an older alter, to explain testing to them or to help them explain themselves in testing. We can also encourage the natural coping of the self-system by asking the patient ("everyone") for advice on how potentially dangerous or terrified alters can participate safely. Quite often, a DID patient has an alter who is expert at handling crises, and the patient can authorize us to call on this alter for help should it become necessary.

Dissociating patients who are less in touch with their anxiety (covert DID and DD–NOS patients, as well as those with severe PTSD) will usually give us concrete suggestions that are appropriate to their level of self-understanding. Often, they will point to a behavioral sign of nervousness, such as leg shaking, and advise us to allow them a test break whenever we see their leg jiggle. As in therapy, using a person's natural coping system supports the sense of safety of the person as a whole.

In calming our own anxieties, it is extremely helpful to keep in mind that, in DID, the presenting patient is also an alter. One alter's viewpoint of another is not necessarily objective, especially if there has not been much direct communication between them. Alter personalities perceived by the "host" as dangerous may turn out to be valuable and cooperative test participants once we recognize their role in the system. A careful DID assessment can do much to clarify the healthy coping skills of supposedly "dangerous" self-aspects. This is why Kluft's dictum that the helping professional maintain a uniformly respectful attitude toward all alters and not play favorites applies to testing as much as it does to therapy (see Chapter Nine).

Although the safety concerns of DID testees present a unique challenge to test procedure, they simply reflect a variation on issues that are central for all chronically traumatized patients: shame, fear, and loss of control. The calm, emotionally neutral but warm attitude and work focus that are basic to the assessor's role do much to diminish these concerns. In remaining stable and unflustered by the patient's behavior, we provide testees with a sense of safety, with a stability of relatedness that mitigates their shame, and with a task focus that supports their self-control.

Flashbacks are often the greatest source of safety risk during testing. Flashbacks and intensely upsetting associations to test stimuli are common phenomena in DID and other traumatized patients. They can occur on any cognitive or personality measure because these upsetting reactions are not dependent on the general qualities of the test, but rather on the patient's unique associations to elements of the test.

The DID patient may respond to a test picture by acting as if she or he is again experiencing a traumatic event (*flashback*) or may react with fear and confusion to a simple cognitive measure that happens, by its verbal or visual qualities, to trigger a traumatic association (*traumatic overlay*). Because these patients are often unaware of the stimuli that provoke their anxiety and are also often unable to perceive their affect until it reaches intolerable and uncontrollable levels, flashbacks and traumatic overlays can come as frightening shocks to both patient and tester. Moreover, unlike the psychotic patient whom they often superficially resemble, DID patients recognize the inappropriateness of their responses and react with considerable shame to them.

For example, one DID patient who remained relatively calm and organized during her personality testing suddenly became terror stricken and dysfunctional when shown the toy blocks of a simple puzzle test (the Wechsler Block Design Test). When asked to describe what was happening to her, the patient shamefacedly explained that she was seeing herself once again locked in her toy box, as she had been as a child, with only her blocks for company. Evidently freed by her verbalization of this past trauma, this patient asked to continue with the task and was able perform at a satisfactory level.

Flashbacks, traumatic memories, and sudden emotional surges can be handled and minimized during testing by simple procedures that parallel basic DID treatment techniques. We can reground patients in reality by asking them to look at us and to attend to our voice. Even better, we can anticipate and monitor these problems by regularly asking testees how they are doing throughout the testing. This monitoring also encourages patients to attend to low levels of their affect so that they, and we, can take steps to handle their feelings before they become too extreme. When we verbally recognize that our DID testees did complete a test even though they were upset, we diminish their sense of internal and external victimization. As the above example shows, discussing a flashback or emotional outburst after it has occurred sometimes enables DID patients to connect present and past experience and may free them to respond more effectively.

Supportive safety techniques also mitigate the traumatic countertransference of the tester. In helping patients deal with safety issues and their attendant feelings of shame and loss of control, assessors temper their own sense of being terrible people who are torturing patients with their tests.

Maintaining the Test Structure

JANET

One day after a brief test break, I returned to my office to find my DID patient, Janet, curled up in a fetal position in a corner of the room. She did not respond to my questions or to my efforts to resume the testing. Apparently, Janet had switched to a mute child alter during the break. I quietly commented on her behavior and, without touching her or in any way reinforcing her helplessness, asked her whether she could get help from older alters so that we could understand what was going on. I then took my seat and indicated that I would wait until she felt able to continue. After a brief interval, Janet sat up, smiled, and calmly said she was ready to resume testing. She later told me that she was proud of herself for being able to risk this one overt switch during the testing and that she was especially pleased she came out of the switch by herself, with awareness of what had happened. Janet thanked me for not touching her, "because that would have really frightened us." What had appeared to be a regression or manipulative behavior was instead an expression of a new freedom and control in Janet's mind.

DID patients inevitably investigate the tester's consistency and flexibility. Like Janet, at times they do this forcefully. More often, however, the testing of the tester occurs in subtle ways such as by requests for unusually frequent breaks or for small changes in test procedure.

As I have come to better understand the distinctive testing behaviors of DID patients, I have moderated my initial attitude that I must maintain an invariant test structure. I think that DID patients usually not only test our ability to maintain or lose our structure but even more so they observe our ability to behave flexibly and sensitively within the safety of our structure. This is what they have most missed in growing up. I find that it works best if I take a stand on issues essential to the testing while showing my readiness to modify minor points.

For example, I will insist it is essential for testees to finish a long and unpleasant test but will accede to their request to sit on the floor while completing the task. Unlike borderline and antisocial patients, DID testees will respond to this flexible structure with increased task focus and will not push the issue further.

THE TEST BATTERY

With the process of understanding and working effectively with the dissociative disordered testee established, I move to a description of a test battery for these patients. I will begin with a discussion of some specialized tests for measuring dissociation. I will then describe how the tester and therapist (sometimes one and the same person, sometimes two people) can make use of information from a traditional test battery that has been modified to account for dissociative phenomena.

Measures of Dissociation

A few selected tests are specifically designed for measuring dissociation. Undoubtedly, the most researched, most translated, and most clinically useful test of dissociation in adults is Eve Carlson and Frank Putnam's Dissociative Experiences Scale (DES). It is probably also the most misunderstood test in the field.

To put these statements in perspective, let me describe the nature and purpose of the DES. This is a brief, twenty-eight-item self-report measure that takes about ten minutes to complete. Testees rate a series of dissociative symptoms on a frequency scale ranging from zero to one hundred and showing the percentage of time they have a particular dissociative experience when they are not under the influence of alcohol or drugs. The total score is an average response to all items (the sum of scores divided by the number of items).

In addition to giving a score, the DES is also helpful on the more qualitative, clinical level when it is used as an interview measure. After the DES is completed, the tester can go through the items and ask patients to give concrete examples of experiences they endorsed at particularly high rates. Thus, we can get a picture of the meaning of dissociative experiences for the individual patient.

DES items are grouped into three categories. *Amnestic dissociation* items include experiences such as (1) finding oneself somewhere without knowing how one got there and (2) not being able to remember important events in one's life, such as one's wedding or graduation. *Depersonalization* and *derealization* experiences involve distorted perceptions of oneself and the world. These items tap phenomena such as (1) looking in the mirror and not recognizing oneself and (2) feeling like one is looking at the world through a fog. *Absorption* and *imaginative involvement* phenomena include (1) staring into space and not being aware of the passage of time and (2) becoming so involved in a daydream that it seems real.

In a recent multicenter study of the DES with more than one thousand psychiatric inpatients, a cutoff score of thirty correctly identified 74 percent of those patients who had DID and 80 percent of those who did not have DID. With its brevity, simplicity, and effectiveness, it is not surprising that the DES is a popular measure.

The down side of the DES comes from its misuse. The DES is only a screen; it cannot, in itself, establish a DID diagnosis. After all, DID is not simply a severe form of dissociation; it is qualitatively different from other dissociative and posttraumatic disorders. In other words, no matter how high the score, we should never conclude that this score confirms that the patient has DID. We can only say that we have cause to suspect that the patient may have a dissociative disorder and that we need to investigate our hypothesis further.

This qualification is especially important because the chances are very great that a patient who gets a score of thirty does not have DID. Carlson calculates that the chances of *incorrectly* diagnosing someone with DID because that person gets a score of thirty or more on the DES is over 80 percent!

The apparent discrepancy between the diagnostic effectiveness of the DES in research and clinical settings occurs because DID is a relatively rare disorder. This rarity makes it likely that most people with high DES scores will not have DID. The high potential for overdiagnosis of DID is an important point to keep in mind as we examine DID markers on any test. It is particularly likely that we will have difficulty distinguishing DID patients from those with severe PTSD who also show dissociative symptoms.

How, then, should the DES be used? It is a perfect measure for the frequent times that the assessor or the referring therapist suspects dissociation may be a part of the clinical picture. The DES is a time- and cost-effective way to get some initial information on this hunch to decide whether we ought to delve further into the matter.

The DES is also a perfect first step in a more extensive DID evaluation because it alerts both tester and testee to possible dissociative symptoms that can be clarified with further questioning. Because dissociation is an automatic reaction that has been used by many patients since early childhood, patients often need a tool like the DES to help them attend to their dissociative reactions and to think about these essentially nonconscious, nonverbal experiences in verbal terms.

When using the DES as an interview tool, I find it best to ask the patient for concrete, everyday examples of highly endorsed items. This tactic allows me to evaluate whether the patient is showing classic dissociative symptomatology or whether the high score reflects a misunderstanding of the problem, malingering, or other nondissociative phenomena. I try to frame my requests for details on the dissociative process as though I am asking about skills, rather than faults, because this tack stimulates the nonshameful curiosity of the patient about his or her own mental processes. I may inquire how the patient does behavior X or turns the behavior on and off, explaining that I am asking because not everyone can do X. Asking about the first time the patient remembers doing X often helps pinpoint early traumatic triggers when amnesia renders the patient's history sparse. The following is an example.

LOUISE

Louise was referred for a DID assessment by her individual therapist after she began having separate personalities. The therapist was concerned about the potentially disorganizing and iatrogenic effects of Louise's participation in an incest survivor group that included a number of dissociative disordered patients and where members spoke at length about their "hurt inner child."

Louise got a score of fifty-seven on the DES. When asked to give specific, everyday examples of items, her responses were vague and often did not seem to indicate dissociation. For example, her description of amnesia involved having disagreements with her siblings over what had occurred in the family, rather than dissociative amnesia. What did emerge from her DES descriptions was an intense and painful identity confusion. For example, Louise said she never recognized herself in the mirror because she never had any idea what she looked like. The identity confusion was apparent across all of Louise's tests. Her diffuse and conflicted self-experience had evidently enabled Louise to identify with the internal confusion and struggles of the dissociative disordered members in her therapy group. After further evaluation and discussion with her therapist, Louise received a diagnosis of borderline personality disorder.

Measures of Dissociation for Other Age-Groups. The DES is meant to be given to adult patients—that is, individuals who are eighteen years and older. Fortunately, we now have a reliable and valid measure of dissociation for children, Frank Putnam's Child Dissociation Checklist (CDC-Version 3.0). The CDC is a twenty-item report scored by a parent or another adult who is very familiar with the child's behavior. The rater simply circles items as *not true, sometimes true,* or *very true* of the child.

The CDC covers distinctive dissociative behaviors that are "quietly" maladaptive and thus are often overlooked in children. These include *dissociative amnesias,* such as the child getting easily lost while going to familiar places or thinking it is morning when it is actually afternoon. Other subtle dissociative signs include *rapid shifts in characteristics,* such as the child showing hour-to-hour variations in skills, and *spontaneous trance states,* including frequent daydreaming in school.

The CDC also taps more overtly disturbing dissociative symptoms that may be misdiagnosed as signs of severe psychosis or conduct disorder. These include *hallucinations,* such as the child claiming he or she hears voices; *identity alteration,* such as the child insisting on being called by different names and referring to him- or herself in the third person; and *aggressive and sexual behavior,* such as unusual sexual precocity and deliberate self-injury. As with the DES, the CDC is meant as a screen for dissociation, not as a diagnostic measure for childhood DID.

At this point, no validated measure of adolescent dissociation is available. This is a problem from both a clinical and preventive perspective because DID is understood to stabilize and become resistant to change by late adolescence. The Adolescent Dissociative Experiences Scale (A-DES), by Judith Armstrong, Frank Putnam, and Eve Carlson, is a new measure; it is not yet validated and so should not be used as a diagnostic screen. The A-DES can, however, be used as a part of a clinical interview to help explore dissociative phenomena occurring from late latency to early adulthood (approximately ten to twenty-one years of age). The thirty test items are scored by the adolescent on a ten-point scale ranging from *never* to *always.* Questions cover the DES topics of *dissociative amnesia, absorption/imaginative involvement,* and *depersonalization/derealization.* Items also focus on issues that are central to adolescent dissociation: experiences of *passive influence,* such as feeling that something inside of you is making you do something you don't want to do; *dissociated identity*, such as feeling that your past is a puzzle and that some of the pieces are missing; and *dissociated relatedness*, such as finding that your relationships with your friends change suddenly and you don't know why.

Structured Interviews for Dissociation. Marlene Steinberg's Structured Clinical Interview for *DSM-III* and *DSM-IV* Disorders (SCID-D) and Colin Ross and associates' Dissociative Disorders Interview Schedule (DDIS) are two validated structured interviews that allow the assessor to make a DID diagnosis.

The DDIS is a 131-item interview with a simple yes/no format that takes about forty minutes to complete. In addition to providing information on a DID diagnosis, it also surveys a variety of associated phenomena, including childhood abuse, somatic complaints, and paranormal experiences. The relative ease of administration and the brevity of the DDIS make it the interview of choice when time and training opportunities are at a premium.

The SCID-D allows for diagnostic discrimination among the five DSM dissociative disorders: *Dissociative Amnesia, Dissociative Fugue, Depersonalization Disorder, Dissociative Identity Disorder,* and *Dissociative Disorder–Not Otherwise Specified.* The more than 250-item interview can take ninety minutes or more to administer. The interviewer must have experience in identifying the verbal and nonverbal signs of the five dissociative symptoms explored by this test: *amnesia, depersonalization, derealization, identity confusion,* and *identity alteration.*

The SCID-D can be extremely useful in cases in which complex diagnostic issues have arisen. As with any diagnostic structured interview, it is possible for patients to consciously conceal, manufacture, or overemphasize symptoms on the SCID-D. These possibilities are lessened by two SCID-D procedures: (1) interviewees must give concrete details of each symptom they report and (2) interviewers must make a careful assessment of dissociative symptoms exhibited by the patient during this anxiety-provoking interview. The SCID-D interview structure is also helpful in guarding against the overdiagnosis of DID because the format and scoring ensure that patients will not be labeled as DID simply on the basis of their exhibiting moderate dissociative symptomatology or a sense of identity confusion. Consider the following example.

JULIA

Julia was referred for testing by her therapist, who had extensive experience with DID. Julia's almost continual "spacing out" during the therapy hour led the therapist to suspect that her patient was suffering from a severe dissociative disorder, possibly DID. In her assessment, as in her treatment, Julia showed little interest in talking about her spacing out.

On the SCID-D, she did not endorse items concerning amnesia or identity alteration; thus, it was highly unlikely she was suffering from DID. Julia perked up, however, when asked questions about depersonalization. In an animated flood of words, she described an almost constant sense of feeling that part of her body was outside herself. Her efforts to communicate with her divided body elicited the bouts of spacing out. Julia was then able to trace the onset of her depersonalization to an early traumatic incident that had a profound effect on her and her family. She told the tester she had never bothered to discuss her depersonalization experiences in therapy because it simply had never occurred to her that not everyone feels detached from their bodies!

Cognitive Assessment

Cognitive evaluation is often an important part of the DID assessment because it can shed light on crucial questions of differential diagnosis. An intelligence test such as the Wechsler Adult Intelligence Scale-Revised (WAIS-R IQ) can clarify whether or not the patient has a formal thought disorder consistent with a psychotic condition. Many symptoms of DID, such as hearing voices or feeling that one's actions are controlled by others, mimic psychosis. Although it may be possible for someone to be both psychotic and DID, psychotic-like dissociative phenomena are caused by such processes as flashbacks and alter interference, not true psychosis. Thus, the DID patient's IQ testing should not show signs of severely disturbed reasoning or reality testing.

Indeed, in a sample of over one hundred DID and DD–NOS inpatients at Sheppard Pratt Hospital, we found these patients' WAIS-R IQ results to be remarkably unremarkable. Scores ranged from mildly retarded to superior on this test, with an average in our group of precisely one hundred. No ability or area of thinking was found to be generally superior or damaged in this sample. In the more severely disorganized of these patients, the IQ was extremely helpful in ruling out psychotic conditions.

Dissociation interferes with memory and behavioral control and often causes perplexingly inconsistent cognitive performance. Thus, DID patients can often present complex diagnostic questions concerning dissociative disorder or neurological dysfunction. The IQ test, along with more specific cognitive testing (such as a memory scale), can be used to determine the presence or absence of a learning, memory, or attention-deficit disorder.

Because the cognitive and memory problems of DID patients are triggered by psychological issues, not neurological dysfunction, these patients generally perform adequately on cognitive measures. They may also give multiple responses to questions that illustrate their ability to simultaneously think at lower and advanced cognitive levels, something not found in simple brain damage.

The WAIS-R IQ can also be analyzed on a qualitative level for treatment planning. An examination of the pattern of cognitive strengths and weaknesses shown on the test allows the assessor to identify the situations that impede or facilitate the patient's adaptive reasoning. IQ testing can help clarify the unique triggers that elicit brief cognitive disorganization in the individual DID patient.

When doing a qualitative analysis of the DID patient's cognitive functioning, it is important to remember that the IQ test is not a bland activity for traumatized people. Asking how praise and punishment are alike (WAIS-R Similarities) or arranging a series of pictures to show a man stealing the clothing of a woman who is swimming nude (WAIS-R Picture Arrangement) are not necessarily neutral tasks. The alternately stressful and non-stressful material of the IQ, however, can provide the means for exploring the skills of the various alters in the DID patient's coping system. For example:

D E E N A

Deena, a generally quiet and submissive fourteen-year-old DID patient, was embattled with Diana, a "bad" alter given to bouts of seemingly unprovoked aggressive behavior. Deena complained of blurred vision during an IQ test on a subsection that measured attention to visual detail (WISC-R Picture Completion). Interestingly, she got a perfect score on that measure. Afterward, she told the tester that Diana had given her the answers to this subtest. After the test results were shared with the patient and her therapist, they were able to consider the possibility that the aggressive Diana was actually a clear-seeing alter who could anticipate potentially harmful social interactions. The IQ test was central in transforming Diana's role from Deena's enemy into her protector. Once Diana could verbally communicate within the self-system, her need to aggressively protect the other alters quickly ended.

Personality Assessment

Different kinds of personality assessments are useful when testing for levels and types of dissociation.

Structured Personality Tests. A number of tests of general psychopathology are termed "structured" because they consist of questions that are answered in basic yes/no format. I will focus here on the Minnesota Multiphasic Personality Inventory-2 (MMPI-2) because it is the most widely used and extensively researched of these tests.

The MMPI-2 is made up of 550 questions that allow for scoring on ten clinical scales measuring such symptoms as depression, hypochondriasis, paranoia, and mania. In addition, the test has four validity scales and a number of subscales that tap important attitudes, such as the tendency to exaggerate one's problems or to deny one's difficulties. The length of the test and its yes/no format make it a very stressful measure for most DID patients. The MMPI-2 often arouses intense internal arguments over responses, causing the patient to have troubling somatic symptoms such as headaches and nausea. This effect makes it especially important that the measure be given after a testing alliance has been established.

One reason that the MMPI-2 is such a popular and practical instrument is the availability of computerized scoring and interpretation programs for the test that incorporate information from the vast MMPI research database. Generally, these programs do not take into account the new PTSD and dissociation research literature. Thus, the DID assessor must be prepared to modify computer interpretations so that they appropriately reflect what is known about the effects of trauma and dissociation on personality functioning. With such modifications, the MMPI-2 can be a useful addition to the DID assessment battery.

Of primary importance in understanding the MMPI-2 results of DID patients is that the majority of these patients show an elevated score on the F scale. The F scale is a validity scale usually viewed as an indicator that the patient is fabricating symptoms ("faking bad"). An examination of the items of the F scale, however, shows that it is made up of many dissociative symptoms, such as being bothered by hearing "very queer things," and trauma-connected experiences, such as experiencing severe family discord. In fact, the MMPI research on traumatized groups (for example, combat war veterans) consistently finds that an elevated F scale is characteristic of these populations.

It appears, then, that the best way to interpret F scale elevations in most DID patients is as a signal of their truly unusual and disorganizing experiences. When a patient's F scale is extremely elevated, an examination of additional test data (such as other MMPI validity indicators, other test results, the question of secondary gain) can help the assessor make a final decision about the validity of the test findings.

The research literature on the MMPI-2 clinical scale scores of DID patients does not point to a single, unique test pattern. The most common finding is elevation on scales F and Eight (which also contains many dissociative items). An F-Eight pattern is found in patients who are multisymptomatic or disorganized for a variety of reasons, from schizophrenia to prolonged stress. Thus, we cannot distinguish DID from other severe disorders on the basis of the MMPI alone. Examining the pattern of clinical symptoms, however, can yield information that is useful from a treatment standpoint. Here's an example:

JOHN

John, who had been in treatment for two years, was referred for testing to clarify his present DID diagnosis and to help in treatment planning. John's testing showed active PTSD and DID. The test also highlighted, however, his angry acting out (scale Four) and his tendency to blame others for his own difficulties (scale Six). These data fit with John's other test results. They suggested that although John had surely been victimized in the past, he was now invested in viewing himself as a helpless victim in the present. He tended to externalize problems, to rationalize his own mistakes, and to have little empathy for other people's viewpoints. This finding helped

John and his therapist consider the possibility that his need to focus on past traumas was, in part, a defensive maneuver designed to distract himself from facing painful present-day responsibilities.

Projective Personality Tests. *Projective tests* are measures with little external structure that allow the testees a great deal of choice in how to respond. The very vagueness of the task encourages testees to "project" their own ways of organizing reality onto the tests and thus bring into relief their basic adaptational style. Projective tests are generally used to confirm, rather than establish, diagnosis. Most important, these tests tell us about patients' internal conflicts, interpersonal assumptions, and personality strengths and weaknesses, information essential to treatment planning and outcome assessment. In this section, I discuss the role of the Thematic Apperception Test (TAT) and the Rorschach Inkblot Test, the two most commonly used projective tests, in clarifying the personality functioning of DID patients.

The Thematic Apperception Test (TAT) consists of twenty black-and-white cards depicting people and scenes. The testee is asked to make up stories to a series of these pictures, describing the thoughts and feelings of the characters and their interactions. At Sheppard Pratt, we have found several cards (1, 2, 3BM, 6GF, 7GF, 8BM, 9GF, 11, 12F, 13MF, 15, and 16) to be particularly useful in eliciting meaningful narratives from female patients. When working with traumatized and dissociative disordered patients, I also find it valuable to end the test by handing the patient the remaining pile of cards and requesting that he or she write a story to the card of his or her choice. The medium of writing to a personally meaningful picture often calls forth a central life theme, one the patient has found difficult to define in memory and to declare in speech.

The prime utility of the TAT is its ability to highlight the patient's relational world. From the standpoint of DID, this ability not only means that the TAT gives us data on the patient's relationships with external others but also helps us understand the relationships within the patient's alter world. The following case example illustrates this latter point.

KATIE

Katie, a DID patient, was hospitalized in an effort to deal with her increasingly severe self-cutting, which was of mysterious origin. Her embattled alter system provided a wide range of "suspects" for this behavior. In several TAT stories to cards depicting two female figures, Katie described physical fights in which well-behaved and loving women were trying to protect themselves from selfish, aggressive women. Interestingly, the supposedly gentle and caring heroines were accomplishing their self-protection by such murderous methods as strangling and stabbing. These stories were extremely helpful in uncovering the dynamics of Katie's self-cutting in that they made it likely that her cutting was not the action of the so-called aggressive alters. Katie, the quiet host, confirmed that it was she who cut. She did so to control assertive alters who made her afraid or angry when they attempted to gain control of her body.

The stories of DID and other traumatized patients are distinctive in that they center on themes of fear, harm, and safety seeking. Dissociative coping mechanisms are clearly illustrated in stories in which heros avoid stress by changing their state of awareness and by compartmentalizing their experience. For example, they may "go away" in the mind and "not be there" or achieve longer-lasting state change by sleep and death. Interpersonal conflicts may be dissociatively resolved through sudden, unmotivated changes in characters' behaviors, goals, or feelings. Often, DID patients will express their sense of having separate identities by giving two different stories to a single card or by identifying several characters as being the same person.

Finally, the TAT can also help us recognize strengths in DID patients. By examining the range of relationships and coping mechanisms depicted in their stories, the assessor can isolate coping strengths and capacities for interpersonal cooperation that may lie hidden beneath the patient's disorganized presentation. Even a single story in which the hero is helped by another or in which the possibility of hope exists points to a foundation on which therapeutic work can proceed.

The Rorschach Inkblot Test as scored by the Exner Comprehensive System has a considerable body of reliability and validity data. The testee is asked to respond to ten photographs of inkblots by describing what they could represent. As is clear from this description, the aim of the Rorschach is not at all obvious. The scoring system, which is based not so much on *what* the testee sees, but on *how* the response is formed, is equally subtle. As a result, the Rorschach is often viewed as an ideal projective measure that enables one to examine elements of the patient's personality that are not subject to conscious awareness or simple behavioral observation.

The use of the Rorschach to study DID has a long history, beginning with the seminal work of Milton Erickson and David Rapaport. I do not summarize the body of research data here; rather, I focus on what the general Rorschach literature on traumatized and dissociative disorder patients has to tell us about the personality functioning of DID patients. Much of the new information presented here comes from Armstrong and Loewenstein's Multiple Personality Disorder Assessment Research Project at the Sheppard Pratt Hospital, where we now have data on the Rorschachs of more than one hundred such patients.

The Rorschachs of DID patients tend to be similar to those of PTSD patients in that both groups give responses descriptive of traumatic events. Armstrong's Traumatic Content Index, a combination of Blood, Anatomy, Morbid, and Aggressive responses, is more elevated in DID patients than in other pathological groups. Unlike PTSD patients, however, who tend to oversimplify their experience, DID patients view things in a complex fashion (High Blends, low Lambda).

The dominant coping style of DID patients is highly internalizing (Introversive). These people deal with stress by thought, delay of action, and obsessive compartmentalization of experience. They tend to avoid affective arousal and are emotionally constricted (low affective ratio, FC greater than CF). They do not have a formal thought disorder (nonsignificant Schizophrenia Index). These characteristics are markedly unlike the borderline, "hysteric," antisocial, schizophrenic, and bipolar patients, whom they are often said to resemble.

Also unlike those of the above-mentioned patients, DID Rorschachs tend to show underlying personality strengths. DID patients have a well-developed capacity for insight (FD) and complex and accurate views of people (low M-, presence of at least one COP).

Finally, the presence of mildly to moderately disturbed thinking (elevated special scores) points to something clinicians need to be aware of as they help these patients understand their past: DID patients' understanding of events is not always accurate; rather, their memories may reflect elements of a divided reality, as well as the fears and confusions that naturally surround traumatic experiences.

Together with the information from Rorschach test scores, a qualitative analysis of responses and accompanying test behaviors can give helpful treatment insights. For example, the Rorschach can give data about the degree to which the patient's dissociative defenses are overwhelmed (D scores) and the source of the present stress (content and sequence analysis). These data can help the therapist in making decisions about treatment pacing and whether the present treatment is working to stabilize the patient.

The following set of Rorschach responses to Card VII, a card that generally elicits benign perceptions of women, is an illustration of the rich and practical clinical information the Rorschach can provide on DID patients. These responses were given by a patient described as "treatment resistant":

> "Human bones with bugs and worms crawling inside." (The patient puts the card down and then picks it up, as if exploring despite her disgust.) "One part of this doesn't fit . . . unless somebody was murdered and that was a murder weapon . . . but that's worse." (The patient begins to rock and cover her face.) "I was thinking of pelvic bones. . . ." (She suddenly laughs, and her whole demeanor changes.) "Oh! There's two Indian women."

We can see in this sequence of responses that this patient is facing a stalemate typical of dissociators. She struggles between living in a disconnected world that is frightening because it doesn't make sense and making connections between ideas that are too awful to contemplate.

This Rorschach sequence also beautifully captures the defensive benefits of alter switching. In the abrupt transition that occurs at the end of this patient's chain of associations, we see an alter system working to limit painful knowledge and to preserve the person's capacity to think like people who live in a "safe" world.

∾

The new ideas that DID brings to testing does not mean that assessors need to discard their standard test methods. Rather, diagnosing DID requires us to consider additional ways of looking at test data. In particular, test responses that appear to be contradictory and discrepant with other information about the patient ought not to be ignored, deemphasized, or viewed as an index of deception. Contradictory test performance is in many ways the hallmark of a divided personality.

I have described a standard battery supplemented by brief screening measures and structured interviews for DID that enables the tester to evaluate the presence and extensiveness of dissociation. Methods for eliciting and monitoring the input of dissociated self-states are also outlined. Unlike other patients with self-fragmentation, DID patients tend to show notable strengths on psychological tests. Thus, their test results can usually be distinguished from those of patients with neurological disorders, thought disorders, and affective disorders.

A competent and useful DID assessment requires that the tester keep up to date with the new and growing test literature on PTSD, dissociative disorders in general, and DID in particular. Without such a background, the assessment is likely to miss or misdiagnose dissociative symptomatology when it appears.

Traditional testing, when not informed by the new findings on traumatized and dissociating patients, is, on the one hand, likely to misdiagnose patients with DID. On the other hand, the relative rarity of DID makes the danger of overdiagnosis considerable. As with other complex developmental disorders, the diagnosis of dissociative disorders requires the converging input of information from several sources. Test data are an essential part of that input, but they should always be used in conjunction with observational, treatment, historical, and other supporting data to make a definitive diagnosis.

NOTES

P. 7, *Colin Ross and associates:* Ross, C. A., Ellason, B. A., & Fuchs, D. (1992). Axis I and Axis II comorbidity of multiple personality disorder. In B. G. Braun & E. B. Carlson (Eds.), *Proceedings of the Ninth International Conference on Multiple Personality and Dissociative States*. Chicago: Rush Presbyterian Hospital.

P. 9, *the PTSD test literature:* Levin, P. (1993). Assessing posttraumatic stress disorder with the Rorschach projective technique. In J. P. Wilson & B. Raphael (Eds.), *International handbook of traumatic stress syndromes* (pp. 189–200). New York: Plenum Press.

P. 19, *Undoubtedly, the most researched:* Bernstein, E. M., & Putnam, F. W. (1986). Development, reliability, and validity of a dissociation scale. *Journal of Nervous and Mental Disease, 174,* 727–735.

P. 20, *In a recent multicenter study:* Carlson, E. B., Putnam, F. W., Ross, C. A., Torem, M., Coons, P., Dill, D., Loewenstein, R. J., & Braun, B. G. (1993). Validity of the Dissociative Experiences Scale in screening for multiple personality disorder: A multicenter study. *American Journal of Psychiatry, 150,* 1030–1036.

P. 21, *Carlson calculates that the chances:* Carlson, E. B., & Armstrong, J. G. (in press). Diagnosis and assessment of dissociative disorders. In S. J. Lynn & J. W. Rhue (Eds.), *Dissociation: Theoretical, clinical, and research perspectives.* New York: Guilford Press.

P. 22, *a reliable and valid measure of dissociation for children:* Putnam, F. W., Helmers, K., & Trickett, P. K. (1993). Development, reliability, and validation of a child dissociation scale. *Child Abuse and Neglect, 17,* 731–740.

P. 23, *The Adolescent Dissociative Experiences Scale (A-DES):* Armstrong, J. G., Putnam, F. W., & Carlson, E. B. (1993). *The Adolescent Dissociative Experiences Scale.* Unpublished scale, Sheppard and Enoch Pratt Health System, Baltimore, MD.

P. 24, *Marlene Steinberg's Structured Clinical Interview:* Steinberg, M. (1992). *The Structured Clinical Interview for DSM-IV Disorders.* Washington, DC: American Psychiatric Press.

P. 24, *Colin Ross and associates' Dissociative Disorders Interview Schedule (DDIS):* Ross, C. A., Joshi, S., & Currie, R. (1990). Dissociative experiences in the general population. *American Journal of Psychiatry, 147,* 1547–1552.

P. 25, *An intelligence test:* Anastasi, A. (1988). *Psychological testing.* New York: Macmillan.

P. 28, *I will focus here on the Minnesota Multiphasic Personality Inventory-2 (MMPI-2):* Butcher, J. N. (1990). *Use of the MMPI-2 in treatment planning.* New York: Oxford University Press.

P. 29, *In fact, the MMPI research:* Engels, M., Moisan, D., & Harris, R. (1994). MMPI indices of childhood trauma among 110 female outpatients. *Journal of Personality Assessment, 63,* 135–147.

P. 30, *the Thematic Apperception Test (TAT):* Tomkins, S. S. (1972). *The Thematic Apperception Test: Theory and technique of interpretation.* New York: Grune & Stratton.

P. 30, *the Rorschach Inkblot Test:* Exner, J. E. Jr. (1993). *The Rorschach: A comprehensive system. Vol 1: Basic foundations* (3rd ed.). New York: Wiley.

P. 32, *The use of the Rorschach to study DID:* Erikson, M. H., & Rapaport, D. (1980). Findings on the nature of the personality structure in two different dual personalities by means of projective and psychometric tests. In E. C. Rossi (Ed.), *The collected papers of Milton Erikson* (Vol. 3, pp. 271–291). New York: Irvington.

P. 32, *The Rorschachs of DID patients:* Armstrong, J. G. (1991). The psychological organization of multiple personality disorder as revealed in psychological testing. *Psychiatric Clinics of North America, 14,* 533–546.

P. 32, *Armstrong's Traumatic Content Index:* Armstrong, J. G., & Loewenstein, R. J. (1990). Characteristics of patients with multiple personality and dissociative disorders on psychological testing. *Journal of Nervous and Mental Disease, 178,* 448–454.

P. 35, *As with other complex developmental disorders:* Armstrong, J. G. (1994). Reflections on multiple personality disorder as a developmentally complex adaptation. In *Psychoanalytic study of the child* (pp. 340–364). New Haven: Yale University Press.

2

DISSOCIATION, PSYCHOTHERAPY, AND THE COGNITIVE SCIENCES

Daniel J. Siegel

Writing a chapter on a cognitive science approach to the treatment of Dissociative Identity Disorder (DID) is a challenge. How can I share with you, the reader, a way to be with another person in psychotherapy that is informed by a variety of disciplines, including anthropology, computer science, linguistics, neuroscience, and philosophy, and by computer scientists, philosophers, neuroscientists, and anthropologists?

The professional journey I have taken up to this point reflects this attempt to integrate perspectives from a number of disciplines. From biology through pediatrics to child psychiatry, I have always been fascinated with ways of understanding people. As a psychiatric trainee, I was frustrated with the limited views of a diagnostic formulary approach to human lives. I entered child psychiatry and pursued studies in child development, attachment theory, memory, and narrative in hopes of finding a scientific way of understanding human subjectivity.

What has emerged from this journey is a perspective derived from developmental and cognitive sciences that I find especially helpful in treating individuals with DID. The approach stems from both clinical work with traumatized individuals who have dissociative disorders and academic studies from the cognitive sciences.

In other writings, I have summarized views on cognitive science and psychiatry and on memory and trauma. These works were, by convention, communicated with impersonal, highly referenced ideas. You may find them useful as a scientific resource for this chapter, which is designed to be both more personal and clinically user friendly.

THE RELATIONSHIP BETWEEN PATIENT AND CLIENT

Let's begin by considering the psychotherapy setting. Let's first examine the client from a cognitive science perspective.

Some people say that the human brain is the most complex thing in the universe—and why shouldn't they? Enclosed in the skull are billions of neurons, each of which connects to an average of thousands of other neurons. These neurons form various architectural layers, including local circuits, subcortical nuclei, cortical regions, and systems. In general, the neurons connect in a "neural network," rather than in a linear (or serial) fashion. The activity of the brain is thought to occur via the neural activation patterns that take place in the neural net. This set of networklike activations is called *parallel distributed processing (PDP)*.

Most brain activity is outside of "consciousness" or phenomenal awareness. In fact, most of what becomes conscious is usually linear or serial: thought processes, focal attention, autobiographical memory, storytelling, and language reception and production. Thus, the majority of brain activity is parallel, but somehow we are aware of and produce serial "thinking."

Hot and Cold Cognition

Before returning to the therapy office to see how the ideas of consciousness and parallel processing influence our therapist-patient interactions, a few words on "hot" and "cold" cognition are in order. When we as therapists try to understand the interactions between parent and child and between therapist and patient, we need an understanding of both hot and cold cognition.

Ideas such as memory processes, mental models (or schemata), metacognition (processing cognitive processes or thinking about thinking), and attention have been studied by cognitive psychologists for decades. These scientists have attempted to be precise in their work, and they generally have avoided studies of emotions. Thus, these concepts are called "cold" cognitions, as opposed to the "hot" cognitive concepts of emotion, state of mind, and affect regulation. The subjective experience of an individual is shaped by deep, developmentally influenced, hot emotional/cognitive processes and the more "logical," cold cognition. All of these processes directly shape thought and reasoning.

Back to the therapist's office. There sits the patient, watching the therapist. A thought comes to consciousness, a bodily state enters awareness, and emotion floods her. (I use *she* for the patient, *he* for the therapist for a semantic reference point to avoid confusion). Let's try to understand this "experience" from a very basic perspective. It is safe to say that what a person experiences comes from the activities of his or her neural network patterns. So what? Well, here is, for me, the exciting part. There are ways of understanding how early life experiences shape the structure and function of the brain. Experiences such as emotional neglect, insecure attachments, loss, or trauma may produce specific cognitive patterns (both hot and cold). Let me give you an example.

The mind/brain can be in a certain "state of mind" that can include dominant emotional tone, behavioral response patterns, memory accessibility, and schemata or mental models. In infants, states of mind change rapidly and abruptly (for example, laughing to crying to smiling within minutes). It is a developmental achievement to have smooth transitions across states. If a parent provides conflictual behaviors (at one time being available emotionally; at another time being threatening), the infant may use state of mind shifts to adapt to this inconsistent set of behaviors from the same caregiver. One state of mind may include a sense of security, along with recall of close times and an "internal working model" of security to the "accessible parent," and this memory evokes an "approach response." Later, the now abusive parent activates a different state of mind with the dominant emotion of fear, a response pattern of withdrawal, memory recall of previously frightening times, and a model of attachment that may be disorganized (the attachment figure is the source of terror, rather than of safety).

As many authors have noted, people with DID have reports of early, chronic trauma as children. In addition to the actual physical aspects of abuse being traumatizing, the perpetuation of abrupt state transitions may also be developmentally damaging. The establishment of "cognitive barriers" that prevent access across mental states appears to be a fundamental aspect of the development of DID.

Now back to the office. The therapist says, "Good afternoon." The patient looks at the therapist and says, "Good afternoon." As with any relationship, each person perceives the other through the filter of prior experiences and present expectations. Referred to as "transference" by psychotherapists, this filter can be useful in aiding patients in psychotherapy. If the patient has DID, what is the nature of this perceptual filter? As with any individual, one's state of mind influences many things, including perceptual bias and accessibility of memory. If the patient perceives the therapist as an authority figure, the meaning of that perception may vary across states. What will she be aware of? Consciousness may be blocked across states of mind. Thus, her subjective experience of the therapist will vary greatly and depend on the history of that particular state.

Suppose the therapist presents the open-ended request: Tell me about your childhood. What will the patient say? What will she think? What will she remember? What is involved in the act of remembering? What determines how memory influences the stories we tell one another? After all, what the patient is about to tell is a story driven, in part, by her memory and influenced, in part, by her perception of the therapist's expectations.

With a patient who has DID, this process may be particularly complex. For example, one alter personality state may perceive you, the therapist, as being comforting and open. That alter may be motivated to tell you what it knows about experiences as a child. Another alter, feeling suspicious of your intentions, may attempt to block the first alter's recounting or even to take executive control of the body. This internal process may be experienced by the patient as confusion or anxiety. You may perceive this moment as the patient's hesitation or reluctance. The story that emerges may reflect both the divided access to memory and the patient's mixed motivations toward becoming vulnerable to you.

MEMORY, NARRATIVE, AND DISSOCIATION

Stories are a fundamental part of human cognition called *narrative*. Narrative is the telling of a sequence of events. The narrative mode of thought begins early in child development and is an important way that children perceive and make sense of the world. Narrative takes into account the teller and the listener and can thus be considered a form of discourse. Perspectives include first and third person and past, present, and future and may include statements about intentions and inner emotional states. Thus, they contain the components of time, space, logic, self, and other.

For children, narratives can be co-constructed with their parents; this task allows for the joining together in the telling of a story. A similar process, "memory talk," between parent and child focuses on the parent's interest in the views and inner experience of the child. Narrative both establishes a sense of meaning for a child and is a shared process between parent and child that can shape the degree of importance of the content of memory. Thus, the social discourse process of storytelling is influenced by social factors (teller's expectation of listener's needs), relationship factors, imagination, and elements of memory. For a patient with DID, there may have been numerous forms of prohibition against revealing what she remembers. These may have taken the form of overt threats (if she "tells the secrets"), punishment, denial, or ignoring at times of disclosure. A lack of genuine interest in the child's internal world, including contents of memory, would further inhibit this social mnemonic process.

Memory is inextricably linked to other cognitive processes, including development, consciousness, mental models, metacognition, emotions, and state of mind. The following basic principles of memory may be a helpful reference guide.

1.　*Memory is a process.* There is no closet in the brain in which a memory is stored like photographs in an album. Remembering, like other cognitive processes, is thought to be a product of the interactions of complex networks of nerve cells in the brain. Remembering can be thought of as the activation of a neural net profile that represents the things being recalled. Thus, memory can be thought of as a verb, not a noun. Remembering thus activates potential patterns established by prior experiences. For a patient with DID, alter states may have different potential patterns that can be activated. The process of reinstatement of a memory in a patient with DID will thus be highly dependent on her state of mind (personality state) at the time of retrieval of a memory.

2.　*Memory is reconstructive,* not reproductive. Both the process of encoding an event (perceiving the external stimuli, internally responding to it, and registering these into some form) and retrieving it (reactivating the neural net profile representing these encoded elements) are products of neural processing. These various stages of processing are influenced by active mental models or schemata that link together perceptual biases, associated memories, emotions, and prior learning. The details remembered may be accurate, though incomplete. The details may be biased by postevent questioning. In a patient with DID, this reconstructive process will be influenced by the alter's particular mental models and memory accessibility. Her perception of your expectations may also influence the way the elements of a memory are reassembled. A different alter, with its own unique perceptual biases, models, and memory access, may thus reconstruct a different story about the same event.

3. *Memory and consciousness are not the same.* Memory is not a unitary thing. At least two forms of memory depend on different brain structures. Some forms of remembering involve conscious awareness; others do not. Thus, the mind can store information that is not easily accessible to consciousness but that can influence behavior. Most of "cognition" is nonconscious. This state helps explain numerous phenomena in DID, including flashbacks, intrusive images, interalter conversations, and actions or feelings that lack a sense of self.

4. *Memory involves monitoring processes* that assess the origin and accuracy of a memory. Memory includes both experiential and correspondent dimensions of subjective recollections. *Experiential* refers to the sense of conviction an individual has regarding the accuracy of a memory. *Correspondent* refers to the correlation between the recalled information and the actual experience. These two features may be somewhat independent under certain conditions (for example, hypnosis, brain injury, intensive postevent questioning) and in certain individuals. For DID, source monitoring may be distorted in a developmentally adaptive way. For example, memories of traumatic events may be attributed to "other people's experiences." A sense of self and time may be separated from autobiographical memory such that a patient with DID is aware of an event as a fact lacking in emotional response.

5. *Memory and narrative are not identical.* The language-based output of telling a story about an event is an approximation of retrieving information in memory and is influenced by the social context of the storyteller and story listener. Thus, encoding, storage, and retrieval are often followed by the recounting of a story to another person; this recounting may be driven by both memory retrieval processes and social factors. Attachment experiences early in life may influence the way people remember and how they tell their autobiographical story.

For example, a patient with DID may reveal distinct autobiographical styles and content across alters. One alter's life story may be idealized yet lack specific memories. Another alter may insist that it does not recall any aspect of its childhood. Its life story is devoid of a child history and may begin in early adulthood. Yet another alter's story may indicate awareness of past trauma and envision the self as a victim with responsibility for past abuse but without ability to influence present or future life events. Each alter has its own story to tell.

6. *The development of memory, though residing in the brain, is profoundly influenced by interpersonal experiences.* Early remembering is enhanced by parent-child interactions that involve shared construction of stories about remembered events. Inhibition of this memory talk may be a part of memory disturbances in childhood trauma. For the patient with DID, your interest as a therapist in her internal experience and life story may be a central factor in facilitating developmental change. By providing a safe environment in which whatever the patient is able and willing to explore is supported and heard, a new process within the patient can be catalyzed. As the prohibitions against an open connection between memory and autobiographical narrative are lifted, the patient can gain a new internal freedom and behavioral flexibility before unknown.

7. *Trauma may uniquely affect memory* at the various levels of processing, including encoding, storage, retrieval, and recounting. Cognition and interpersonal experiences during and subsequent to trauma may uniquely affect the ways memories for these events are processed and later accessed.

The study of memory has resulted in the conceptualization of different "systems" or "processes" leading to two very different forms of memory. These forms have been described as implicit (procedural, or early memory) versus explicit (declarative, or late memory; see Figure 2.1). Although these various terms may not always overlap, I use the terms *implicit* versus *explicit* memory in this chapter for the sake of simplicity.

Early	Late
Procedural	*Episodic/Semantic*
Nondeclarative	*Declarative*
Implicit	*Explicit*
A behavioral (and possibly emotional and somato-sensory) form of memory devoid of the subjective internal experience of recalling, of self, or of past.	A form of memory requiring conscious aware-ness and the subjective sense of recollection and, if autobiographical, of self and pastness.

Figure 2.1
**Some Roughly Synonymous Terms for at
Least the Two Major Forms of Memory**

Implicit memory is the way the brain encodes an experience and then influences later behavior without requiring conscious awareness (see Figure 2.2). Thus, the skill of riding a bicycle can be demonstrated even if a youngster has no recall of when he or she learned to ride. This is implicit memory without explicit recall. Implicit memory may also include emotional, perceptual, and/or somatic sensations derived from past experiences but without a sense of their origins in the past. Implicit memory may be fundamental to repeated patterns of maltreatment and to transference phenomena in the DID patient.

Take, for example, a patient with DID who was abused by a parent. Implicit memory for a given abused alter may include behavioral reactions to flee, avoidance of trusting authority figures, intense fear, and somatic memories of being beaten. As these implicit memories are reinstated without a sense of something being remembered, the patient will experience them as "here and now" processes that will greatly influence her feelings toward you and therapy in general.

Explicit memory is directly accessible to conscious awareness and can usually be expressed with words. This expression can

Implicit:	Does not require focal attention for encoding
	Can be encoded, stored, and retrieved independent of hippocampal formation (H.F.)
Explicit:	Requires focal attention for encoding
	Initially requires hippocampal formation (H.F.) for encoding and retrieval
	Later retrieval may not require the H.F. and may be due to "cortical consolidation," in which a days to weeks to months process of automatic rehearsal makes memories permanent in the cortex.

Figure 2.2
Fundamental Features of Memory

include both memory for facts (semantic memory in Ernst Tulving's original model) and for personally experienced events ("episodic" memory). Episodic or autobiographical memory has the unique features of self and time, which distinguish it qualitatively from memory for facts, which may have no sense of when a fact was learned. For example, a patient may have a semantic (factual) memory of her mother having beaten her. This fact may be dissociated from an episodic (autobiographical) memory of a specific episode in which a sequence of events can be recalled. Patients with DID have frequent dis-associations of episodic from semantic memory.

There is physiological evidence for this distinction. The medial temporal lobe memory system, including the hippocampus and related brain structures, is thought to be essential for the processing of explicit memories. Hypnotic amnesia, surgical analgesia, benzodiazepines, and a neurological illness or injury demonstrate the presence of implicit memory and explicit memory systems (see Figure 2.3). That memories involve not only sequences of events (story) but also the objects themselves that make up an event (memory) has strong implications for the

Childhood amnesia

Organic amnestic syndrome (for example, Korsakoff's)

Benzodiazepine effects

Hypnotic amnesia

Surgical anesthesia

Divided attention phenomena

Possible conditions:

Posttraumatic stress disorder

Dissociative disorders

Figure 2.3
Conditions Associated with Dis-Associations Between
Implicit (Intact) and Explicit (Impaired) Memory

treatment of DID. For not only must the conscious memory of a trauma be worked through, but also the emotionally charged object in the memory needs to be addressed.

Defining DID

The impact of acute or chronic trauma on a child substantially influences cognitive development. How do the experiences and emotions of terror, betrayal, and pain affect the child's development of a personal memory system? How does the prohibition (via threats or the effort to preserve family relationships) against talking openly about these experiences affect their encoding and subsequent accessibility to retrieval? How do possible impairments in explicit encoding during a traumatic experience impair subsequent cortical consolidation and narrativization? Trauma may thus impede the normally associated functions of implicit (behavioral, emotional, somatic, and perceptual) and explicit memory with autobiographical narrative and self-reflection (metacognition).

How do these trauma-specific impacts on memory processes influence other developmental domains? It has been hypothesized that several processes may occur in a child in response to repeated trauma that may directly affect memory. Intentional efforts to block a memory from consciousness is called *suppression*. As suppression is repeated frequently, it may become an automatic process called *repression*. A different adaptive process is called *dissociation*. This process is thought to block the initial explicit encoding of a memory. Alter states of a consciousness (such as in an alter personality) or divided attention (as in consciously focusing attention away from a traumatic stimulus) may produce such a blockage in encoding. Later conscious access to a memory of a dissociated experience will be impaired. Implicit memory (behavioral, emotional, somatic, perceptual) may be distorted but intact.

For a patient with DID, both repression and dissociation may be present to various degrees with different alters. Other psychological defenses that influence memory are fantasy, play, projection, projective identification, and denial; they are active following trauma during childhood. How do these processes affect the adult's memory of childhood? These issues need to be understood further in order to pursue scientifically informed clinical and forensic work with patients diagnosed with DID. Although a few studies empirically support the idea of blocked recall during adulthood of childhood trauma, more research is needed to clarify and validate the reality of this clinical finding. Other authors question the validity of "delayed recall," the notion of repression, and of DID itself.

Returning to our focus on the two people sitting in a therapy office: one is a therapist, one a patient with DID. Each person has a body with brain/neurons and a history of prior experiences and relationships. What can happen between these two individuals that can lead to deep emotional transformations? For the patient with DID, relatively rigid segregations in usually associated functions can lead to marked discontinuity in consciousness. These segregations have been adaptive to past severely conflictual relationships and abusive experiences.

One view of clinical dissociation is that it is a dis-association of usually associated cognitive functions. The simplest example is that of memory: one can view posttraumatic amnesia as a separation of usually synchronous implicit and explicit memory. Thus, conscious access to a prior traumatic event is impaired (blocked explicit memory called *Dissociative Amnesia*), but emotional (fear), behavioral (startle, avoidance), and somatosensory (flashbacks, intrusive images) components of implicit memory are relatively intact, albeit highly charged (see Figure 2.4). Other dis-associations include the distortion of a sense of self and time, which are fundamental aspects of explicit autobiographical memory.

A. Blocked awareness

   May be "dissociative amnesia" with impaired explicit processing and/or "repressive amnesia" with blocked access of retrieval from LTM.

B. Specific avoidant behaviors

   Intact learned behavioral response

   Intact implicit memory not requiring conscious awareness or experiential sense of recalling

C. Intrusive elements

Hyperarousal/startle	Intact implicit memory
Hypervigilance	Intact implicit memory
Hyperamnesia	Partially consolidated explicit memory
Nightmares	Blocked explicit processing and cortical consolidation
Flashbacks	Intact metamemory capacity but misidentification of source

Figure 2.4
**Some Suggested Elements of Memory
in Posttraumatic Conditions**

Cognitive barriers may segment specific functions into repeated clusters characteristic of states of mind: mental models, emotional tone and regulation, behavioral response patterns, memory (implicit, explicit), and even autobiographical narrative (see Figure 2.5). You would thus see this segmented clustering in a patient with DID as having alternate states or "personalities" that have enduring patterns of these grouped cognitive functions. One alter's life story and lifestyle may be quite distinct from another's. Reviewing the history of each state's life can be helpful at revealing the emotionally adaptive reason for the present segmentations.

But how can one person "really" have several personalities? The answer is—she doesn't. Each of us can achieve distinctive states of mind that activate the basic cognitive functions described above. What differs for patients with DID is that (1) they have not been given the opportunity to develop relatively smooth transitions across states, (2) the segregation of states was developmentally adaptive because it helped the child cope better, and (3) its maintenance is important in the present to avoid functional chaos. This means that if a child is biologically capable of state segregation and is not provided with state transition assistance in the form of affect regulation and attunement (which is fundamental to social referencing wherein a child tunes in to parents' emotional states for guidance), the establishment of dissociation as an adaptive structural mechanism may occur. Continued conflictual relationships and traumatic experiences can then perpetuate the use of these initially adaptive mechanisms.

Diagnosing DID

Maintaining clinical neutrality balanced with empathic support, patient advocacy, and awareness of vulnerability to suggestion is a challenge for all of us. I believe that this fine line is walkable, however, especially when one is armed with a cognitive science background. For example, the inability of a patient to recall her family during childhood is a finding present in the approximately

DID:

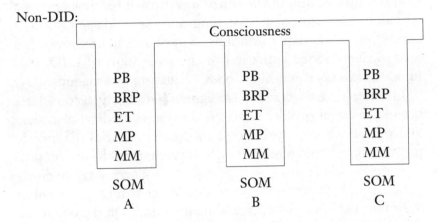

Non-DID:

Figure 2.5
A Diagrammatic View of State of Mind Function in
DID and Non-DID ("Normal") Controls

Note: This diagram illustrates that states of mind are clusterings of specific cognitive functions, such as perceptual biases and behavioral response patterns. The difference illustrated here is that a person with DID has a blocked access to consciousness across different states. In DID the history of a particular state also remains segregated.

10 percent of the nonclinical U.S. adult population classified as having a "dismissing" attachment. As far as we can tell by studies of attachment theory, these individuals were not abused. It is more likely that they grew up in emotionally distant homes, with little attunement or affective connection. More on this later. The point here is: do not jump to premature conclusions of physical abuse and a diagnosis of DID based purely on hunches.

So, armed with therapists' neutrality and an empathic stance of patient advocacy, you find that this patient has signs of dissociation. She complains of features of PTSD, of classic dissociation symptoms, and in the office has intra-interview amnesia with demonstration of a "switching process" and suggestion of abrupt but subtle state transitions. Now what? Before reviewing a cognitive science approach to the treatment of DID, it is important to say something about evaluation and diagnosis.

In a complete psychiatric assessment, you need to consider a broad variety of problem areas as diverse as medical disorders and relationship disturbances. In the differential diagnostic process, you should attempt to avoid premature closure on possible diagnostic entities, such as mood disorders, anxiety disorders, thought disorders, neurological disorders, personality disorders, factitious disorder, and malingering. On the one hand, time and energy are well spent at this stage of evaluation to avoid erroneous diagnoses or missed diagnoses and prolonged, misguided therapeutic interventions. On the other hand, one must "believe in dissociation in order to see it." Not considering the diagnosis—either because of ignorance or forgetfulness—can lead to frustrated therapeutic efforts.

PSYCHOTHERAPY AND DISSOCIATIVE IDENTITY DISORDER

With this background, we can now dive into specific approaches to the psychotherapy of individuals with DID. The principles described on the following pages may also be integral to other models of therapy, but they form the basis of a cognitive sciences approach. These principles are

- The core self: agency, coherency, affectivity, and continuity
- Affect regulation and self
- Attachment: secure base and safe haven
- Consciousness, mental models, and states of mind
- Metacognition, awareness of thinking
- Memory and narrative
- Traumatic memories and their resolution
- Body and mind
- The experiential role of the therapist
- Choice and continuity: healing and the whole person

The Core Self: Agency, Coherency, Affectivity, and Continuity

Daniel Stern's conceptualization of basic developmental aspects of the core self in infancy examines the central role of four features. *Agency* is the infant's experiencing of the initiation of action as being within the self. Infants gain an increasingly complex capacity for motor agency as they develop. *Coherency* is the developing sense of connection of the infant to bodily and perceptual sensation. This somatosensory experience allows the infant to feel an integrated sense of his or her body and the surrounding world. *Affectivity*, or range of internal emotional states, is another fundamental part of the infant's sense of self. Experiencing a range of emotions and learning to regulate these varied internal states and to communicate them externally are all a part of the infant's affectivity. Finally, the infant's sense of history across these three domains gives him or her a sense of *continuity* of self.

Although Stern does not apply these aspects of self to DID or to childhood trauma, one can see their central utility. Childhood trauma can be seen to impair the development of each of these four senses of a core self. In relationship with another human being, especially one who may be in a position of trust, the abused child may experience her motor activity (agency) being forcefully constrained. Her somatosensory perception (coherency) may be bombarded with frightening or painful stimuli. The fear, terror, rage, betrayal, anxiety, shame, and confusion that can be inherent in childhood trauma may severely affect her affectivity. Her capacity to experience uncomfortable emotions and to learn, by sensitive and supportive social experiences, how to regulate them may be markedly impaired.

If dissociative adaptations are available, the child may attempt to maintain attachment, minimize her incapacity to function, and make some "sense" out of the world by dissociative mechanisms. This alteration in continuity of consciousness across states of mind permits a segmentation of experience that can keep awareness of repeated trauma isolated. This compartmentalization of consciousness, memory, emotion, mental models, and behavioral response patterns achieves a discontinuity that may be adaptive in cases of ongoing child abuse. This internal adaptation, however, by its essence, impairs the development of a sense of core continuity.

Psychotherapy aims to facilitate the development of these core senses of self. The overriding goals are to help a patient achieve a sense of choice in life (agency) in which she can freely elect to have somatosensory experiences, including sexuality (coherency), and have a full range of emotions, including uncomfortable ones, that do not incapacitate her (affectivity). The choice to be aware of present experiences and to recall past ones as needed is a fundamental aspect of her growing sense of continuity. The development of these aspects of a core self is at the center of therapeutic work.

Thus, you may get a sense that the patient's overall sense of a core self is underdeveloped and fragile. A given alter may have a more highly developed core identity. However, the rigidity with which that alter may cling to this separation from other alters and the fear of collapse if awareness, feelings, or memories are shared reflects the person as a whole system's damaged sense of a core self. It is helpful to respect this fragility and to avoid overestimating the "system's" strengths and readiness for intensive work. The process of changing cognitive barriers is a huge developmental task. Developing these various senses of a core self is fundamental to the therapy process and takes time. "The slower you go, the faster you'll get there" is a helpful reminder to not push the system too quickly.

The process of psychotherapy can facilitate the development of a core sense of self in numerous ways. Supporting the patient's right to choose what she does with her body and what she does with her life catalyzes a sense of agency. Focusing on the patient's relationship with her body, in the past and in the present, is important. Historical adaptations may have led her to dissociate her body as a "separate self" such that painful (and pleasurable) feelings are inaccessible to many states. The gradual working through of traumatic experiences can allow for a new connection to the body, which permits this development of a sense of coherency.

Overwhelming emotions are common in traumatized children. You as the therapist can facilitate the patient's tolerance of painful emotions and the acquisition of new skills to regulate them. Such facilitation will aid in the development of a freer affective core self. As past traumas are shared and as present life experiences are explored, the patient will gain a new sense of a historical self. The developing sense of agency, coherency, and affectivity across time, combined with this emerging autobiographical story, will allow a patient to begin to develop a core sense of continuity.

Affect Regulation and Self

Some authors consider the regulation of affect to be a central defining characteristic of self. Emotions are the content and process of communication between infant and parent. They are a central ingredient to feeling interpersonally "connected" or understood. Emotions thus facilitate a sense of belonging to others. Communication across a range of emotions of both negative and positive tone can allow the child familiarity and comfort with a spectrum of internal emotional states and their external expression. Social referencing is the way children use the emotional state of their parents to determine how they should emotionally respond to ambiguous situations.

The development of a capacity to regulate and tolerate emotions is a fundamental process in the psychotherapy of patients with DID. A given alter or "state" will often have a limited repertoire of emotions. The adaptive historical significance helps us understand why this is so for a particular alter. In therapy this understanding can help guide your interventions. Remember, social referencing to the parent helps the child learn to tolerate emotions. Similarly, the patient, now developing a therapeutic attachment, will be using your emotional response to help guide her present experience. Your awareness of your own emotions as a therapist is important—and will be distinctly evoked as you relate to different alters.

A helpful technique is to gently "push the envelope" of tolerance of the alter. I find it helpful to know the history of a given alter and the meaning of a present experience in the historical context before I proceed with this technique. Following is an example:

An alter whose life has been to be angry at abusers and to scare them away (by physically damaging her own body) says she feels only anger. After "tuning in" to her feelings, I ask about her relationship with the other alters. She says they hate her—and she hates them. They want her to die.

I feel sad—and sense a sadness in her covered up by bravado and anger. I say, "I feel sad. I wonder if that gets lonely." A tear comes to her eye, and she says, "No. They're disgusting and mean—and they hate me."

I say, "It must be so hard to have your parents hurt you and have these inside states say they hate you—especially when all you were trying to do was protect everyone." More tears come. The "angry alter" now says, "There was nothing else I could do."

I say, "You tried your hardest to get them to stop—and were being angry—carrying all the anger for everyone, trying to hurt the body. None of that got them to stop." More tears.

I say, "I wonder if it's time for you to not be the only one who is able to carry the anger. It is sad that the others have been so frightened of you and that they won't have anything to do with you. How lonely that must be."

She says, with tears, "I feel so sad."

This example illustrates the process of identifying a state's emotional tone and dominant, permissible affect. Then, within the narrated historical context, one can explain the developmental situation that led to this configuration. The present reaction to the isolation—for the alter "out front" and the others—can then be explored emotionally and allow for a gentle expansion of emotional tolerance. This tolerance can be both with a given alter and across barriers to other states.

A core experience for DID patients in therapy is the learning of new capacities for tolerating uncomfortable and unfamiliar affects within a given state of mind. Interstate access to a range of emotions permits both permeability across barriers, as well as interalter communication. In therapy sessions, I attempt to have alters discuss their emotional state (for example, sadness). I often ask them to explore other emotions as well (for example, anger, fear, need for comfort). As alters gain the capacity to tolerate and eventually regulate a greater range of their internal emotional states, the ongoing need for compartmentalization will become significantly less.

Attachment: Secure Base and Safe Haven

The developmental importance of attachment is central in the treatment of individuals with DID. Cognitive science can inform attachment theory by illuminating ideas about mental models and states of mind that form the core of a developmental view of object relations theory. Attachment theory suggests that caregivers serve as figures who provide a predictable source of nurturance and comfort. The repeated experience of need satisfaction with an attachment figure as a source of safety leads to an internal model of a "secure base." This sense of security allows infants to grow, explore, and play. In times of distress, the attachment figure can provide a "safe haven" where the infant can go for safety. Under healthful circumstances, this sense of security will shape the internal working models, or attachment schemata, of individuals in relation to others. In the worst case, the only "safe haven" available to the child becomes some fantasy.

If attachment figures fail to provide predictable, soothing behaviors, attachment may not be secure. If, in addition, attachment figures are the source of frightening and/or frightened behavior (the opposite of what an infant's attachment requires), the infant may develop a disorganized form of attachment. Disorganized attachment may be a predisposing factor leading to dissociative disorders. If a parent is at times frightening and at times neutral or nurturing, the infant may develop mutually conflictual mental models for a given attachment figure. To maintain attachment, the state of mind (including mental models) triggered by a given parental set (for example, frightening) may need to be kept distinct from that for other sets (for example, nonthreatening). One can see how the need and capacity to compartmentalize states of mind and their cognitive components (emotions, memory, mental models, behaviors) can lead, with chronicity, to the development of DID. The acquisition of "unitary identity" is a developmental achievement. DID can be seen as a deviant developmental pathway driven by interpersonal adaptations.

As the therapist, you will be serving a vital function in patients' development. For patients with DID, each alter may have a specific internal working model of attachment. The transference, or perceptual biasing filter, that a given alter experiences you with will thus vary between alter states. Attachment theory is equally relevant for the therapist. Your countertransference will correspondingly vary across alters.

For example, one alter may evoke in you a feeling of idealization and vulnerability. The alter may be naive to being betrayed and have a segmented sense of hopefulness, need for affection, and longing. Another alter may evoke in you a sense of being hated and feeling fearful that you will betray the patient in some way. This alter may be very aware of being hurt by parental figures in the past and may be very wary of your therapeutic zeal. Your own emotional responses can be vital to your understanding of the therapeutic relationship and to the patient's intrapsychic experiences.

As therapy proceeds, the challenge is to provide a predictable environment of safety and empathic attunement so fundamental to secure attachment relationships. To foster this, you as the therapist can rely on a framework of the essential features of secure attachments. These include being emotionally available, interested in and perceptive of the emotional needs of the patient; being consistent; and being effective at addressing the emotional needs. None of us, as parents or as therapists, are perfect. Breaks in emotional attunement are inevitable in both parenting and therapy. The repair (or reconnection) after these unavoidable breaks is crucial for a secure attachment. As therapy unfolds, you will be a safe haven for the patient to go to in distress. Also, with time, your interactions will be internalized and your facial image will serve an emotional regulating function, soothing the patient in your absence. As with other healthy attachment relationships, the coherent internal working model of a secure attachment can allow child and patient alike to develop a sense of a secure base and an ability to be more out in the world.

As this healing relationship develops, the patient may be ready to deal with the conflictual mental models of her own caregivers—the models that may have been segmented into separate alters. Grief over the loss of an idealized attachment figure often occurs. Within the safety of her relationship with you, this mourning can yield a liberation and remove the need for continued compartmentalization.

Consciousness, Mental Models, and States of Mind

The complex topic of consciousness reaches a new height in attempts to understand DID. "Discontinuity of consciousness across states of mind" is a phrase concisely summarizing DID. As Figure 2.5 illustrated, division of consciousness is the hallmark of DID, not so much the capacity to have differing states, which is normal for all people.

Although you will be speaking with language (verbal and nonverbal) to the awareness of the patient, it is helpful to remember that the alter "out in front" is receiving data that then may be accessible to any—or all—of the other alters. Thus, it is not only ill-advised, but usually impossible, to "keep secrets" intentionally between alters.

The subjective experience of a given alter may be that it is unaware of others, or it may be aware of others' listening in or that others are sharing consciousness and even making internal—or external—commentary. Whatever the patient's stated awareness, it is safe to assume that there are parallel listeners, at least, if not on-line "senders" of information. Thus, a dynamic exists among alters that is fundamental to their functioning and the "decision" as to who comes out in front to either "take the heat" or "bail out."

For example, if you are talking about a past traumatic event, one alter may be consciously unaware of certain details. If you say, "I wonder if anyone else can help you fill in the missing pieces," information can be sent directly to the "on-line alter."

This new information may be especially distressing because it may never have been processed by that state before and thus may be shocking. Care must be taken in assessing the readiness of alters to know about the existence or memories of other alters. I find it helpful to give them (the whole person) permission to discuss whatever they are ready to—and, for those who are not ready, to be able to not listen in at this time. For resolution of trauma, though, it may be essential at some point that there be no required amnestic barriers across alters. Thus, everyone may need to know about things at some time.

A technique that is very helpful, especially early in therapy, is to give messages throughout the system. This can be accomplished by saying, "I need for everyone to listen." The parallel processor seems very capable of hearing this alert message and relaying it to all states of mind.

Metacognition, Awareness of Thinking

The brain's capacity to represent and be aware of its own processes permits insight and awareness of the subjective nature of human experience. Metacognition includes the development of the ability to have an appearance-reality distinction. This development involves both representational diversity (what I think may be different from what someone else thinks) and representational change (what I think today may be different from what I think about the same thing tomorrow). The realization that one mind can have different emotions simultaneously toward the same person is also an achievement of metacognitive development.

Children develop these capabilities and can communicate them between the ages of three and eight. Young children exposed to abuse or other frightening behaviors may be particularly vulnerable to these experiences because of their metacognitive immaturity. A child at this age may thus have particular difficulty processing confusing parental/adult behaviors and have to segment his or her experiences to make sense of them. Thus, an immature capacity for metacognition can be established and maintained for years to come.

You as the therapist may encounter alters who demonstrate particularly immature states of metacognition. This immaturity may reflect both arrested development and the need to avoid reflection that would produce incapacitating anxiety. With the therapeutic alliance established, you can begin catalyzing metacognitive development as the therapy encourages self-reflection, which before may have been defensively inhibited. Thinking about their own thinking, feeling, and unconscious should be introduced with sensitivity. Exploring new ideas about feelings toward a significant other, such as that a child is not guilty of bringing on abuse, that a child can have mixed emotions toward the same caregiver, and that views of a given person can evolve over time, are each examples of therapeutic metacognition.

I find it helpful to regularly reflect on the process of thinking, feeling, and relating with my patients. This reflection serves several purposes. These shared reflections, for me, communicate a sense of our collegial relationship that diversifies and strengthens the therapeutic relationship. It is a kind of "journey," in a metacognitive realm, that helps carry communication to a fuller level. Furthermore, the nature of the talking itself catalyzes the development of these metacognitive capacities. For example, after the patient has emotionally explored a past relationship, I might say, "When I think about how you had to have such different feelings for the same person, it makes me realize how much your mind must have had to struggle to keep on communicating with him." Then she pauses and says, "When I think about that, it makes me shudder and think of my brother. How different I am now!"

As therapy evolves, the patient's evolving metacognitive abilities to reflect will serve as a facilitator to communication between her and you and between her various states of mind.

Memory and Narrative

As discussed above, memory and narrative are inextricably linked in the development of memory in childhood. Narrative includes a listener and a teller and thus can be thought of as a form of discourse. Genres of narrative include schemata and fictional and autobiographical stories.

One view of DID is that alters have distinct autobiographical narratives and autobiographical themes. The compartmentalization of models for self or other, memories, emotional tone, and behavioral response patterns thus may yield narratives quite distinct among alter personalities. This finding is reflected in the distinct self-images and a sense of history and worldview described by different alters.

Numerous authors view autobiographical narrative as the essence of a sense of self. This meaning-making process can involve self-reflection and can be driven both by specific episodic memories and by mental models of the self and others. Thus, narratives are products of the mind's need to make sense of or tell a story about the events in one's life. This serial, sense-making process may select from the huge amount of autobiographical memory still in parallel form. Thus, "narrativizing" is an example of the brain's mechanism of extracting a serial representation from a parallel set of processes.

Your clinical awareness of the central role of narrative in defining the self can help provide a potentially useful therapeutic stance. Each alter has a story to tell. For a given alter, the coherency of the story may reflect its meaning to the sense of "self." Thus, the theme or gist of the narrative can reveal much about the organizing mental models. Themes such as being the "betrayed one," the "loved one," or the "angry one" can help provide insight into the alters' self-concepts and narrative structures.

A useful therapeutic technique when the timing is right is to outline a "narrative chart" in which each alter involved in a given emotional theme (for example, anger) or period (for example, over the summer) or experience can be described. Time of being born, reason for coming into being, emotional/interpersonal goals, techniques used to achieve these goals, and present life experience can be charted for each alter. Accessing these thematic items can help both patient and therapist to make sense of how each alter holds particular roles and has a piece of a larger history. This understanding can be a first step toward alter communication. An example follows:

At a point of impasse in a two-year therapy, I suggested that the patient and I review part of a chart we had made a few months earlier. It became clear that two alters had not been charted yet and that they had been "yelling" at each other about what was going on in therapy during the past week. In charting their individual histories, it became clear that each had the theme of self-destructive behaviors that were used to repel an abusive parent at particularly crucial moments in the patient's youth. These two alters were now isolated from the others in discussions of "what to do with anger." Their anger, it seems, was classified by the others as "sick," and they were banished from participation with the others, who had found an "anger coalition" to try to deal productively with anger.

By having the chart and expanding it by including these two alters, they were given a sense of "belonging" to the whole. This inclusion catalyzed several weeks of exploration of their shame at having been self-destructive and the fear of repeating these behaviors. The impasse was overcome, and the patient's relief and subsequent progress were striking.

Traumatic Memories and Their Resolution

Dissociative phenomena—such as amnesia, derealization, distorted sense of self and time, intrusive imagery, flashbacks, and made feelings, thoughts, and actions—could also be thought of as intact implicit memory in the absence of explicit processing (see Figure 2.4). Conscious awareness of traumatic events would thus lack a sense of "pastness" or "self" or even that something is being recalled. Activation of implicit memories could be triggered by either trauma-specific external or internal stimuli (for example, a car backfiring, a sense of betrayal). An example of this form of adaptation during trauma follows:

A patient was raped at ten years of age by a group of school boys. During the rape, she focused her attention on a picture of a waterfall on the wall. She had had prior traumatization and had developed dissociative defenses for more than five years prior to this tragic event. When this traumatic event was over, she got dressed, stumbled her way back home, and was scolded for being disheveled and late from school.

Twenty years later, the patient was frightened of groups of schoolboys she saw from her apartment window. She found herself drawing pictures of waterfalls and feeling numb. The night prior to a therapy session, after a date had been overly aggressive verbally with her, she took a three-hour shower. In the session, she looked dazed. I asked her what was going on. She said she couldn't remember. She told me about the shower. I asked her, striving for a neutral approach, to "tell me about the shower." She said that all she could think about was "waterfalls, waterfalls, water . . ." She dissociated, or "switched," into a small girl eager to play. I suggested that something was too frightening to pursue and that that was O.K. But—and I wanted "everyone to listen"—she seemed quite upset and dazed by something that had happened. When she was ready, someone could come out and we could talk about how to figure out what had happened.

The condensed set of subsequent sessions went like this: Quite a lot of distress took place across alters—about "not telling"—that others inside and I could and should not know. It was fine to like waterfalls, and we should just look into that. After some preparation and evidence from numerous alters that they needed to talk, it was agreed that some would listen and that the ones who couldn't would be "taken care of" by some helpful parental figures inside.

By starting at the beginning and going to the end of an experience, the recounting process can begin to make sense out of a confusing set of feelings, images, and bodily sensations. In this example, the patient had an alter that clung to the image of the waterfall, but others came forward to tell their different experiences. At numerous moments in the session, the patient experienced the bodily reaction, emotions of fear and terror, and the perception of attackers in the room as if the rape were happening at that moment. This aspect of traumatic resolution, the abreaction or bringing together of sensations as if the event where happening in the present, may be essential for resolution to occur.

As the patient experiences these elements, you as therapist bear witness to her trauma and serve to reflect with her almost simultaneously how painful and frightening the trauma was. As details of the events are experienced and reenacted, the various perceptual modalities, spatial context, and emotional reactions are brought together for what may be the first time. As this dissociated memory is assembled (not reassembled), the emotional reactions of the past can be explored. These can include a sense of responsibility and guilt and a sense of betrayal, terror, and rage. The bodily, perceptual, and emotional elements are explored step-by-step.

As the event is told and as the recounting includes its termination and the patient's ultimate survival, it is important to reflect on the patient's present reactions to those events from the past. This reflection of the past event may be a totally new process, and one that helps transform these previously implicit-only dissociated traumatic memories into an implicit/explicit form.

What I have proposed is that flashbacks, intrusive images, bodily sensations, fear responses, and avoidance behavior are all aspects of an "implicit only" dissociative traumatic memory profile. Dissociative amnesia can be thought of as an impaired explicit memory, and implicit memories arise without an explicit context to understand them.

In this patient's case, her focus of attention on the waterfall allowed her (in that alter state) to not explicitly process the other aspects of the traumatic event. Waterfalls and showers thus became associated with a "not knowing" state of mind. As the sessions later revealed, the date's verbal aggression created an internal state of fear and betrayal that paralleled emotionally the fear and betrayal she felt from her schoolmates. The shower was her attempt to "not know." The series of therapeutic abreactions allowed her to resolve this traumatic memory. She was able to reflect on it in the present and try to make sense of how it has affected her life. As this implicit-only form of memory became available to reflect on and to explicitly process, it then became a part of her developing autobiographical narrative. Since this series of sessions, this patient has never again had a recurrence of her intrusive posttraumatic stress symptoms around this event.

Accessing traumatic memories, planning for therapeutic abreaction, and carrying out the necessary working-through process should not be rushed. Although these processes may be essential for effective therapy for DID, their premature and overzealous use can produce negative therapeutic outcomes. It is crucial to establish a strong therapeutic alliance and to focus on present life situations, including relationships and the need for safety, before beginning uncovering work. Many experienced clinicians also advise establishing good interalter communication prior to memory work in order to use the resources of the patient during future times of significant distress and disorientation. Direct trauma work must take place within an established therapeutic relationship.

Body and Mind

For centuries scholars have pondered the distinctions between soma and psyche. Recent views of brain development and function suggest that the subjective experience of mind can be understood by the normal activations inherent in brain activity. The very structure of the neuronal interconnections both determines brain activity and is shaped by interpersonal experiences. The parts of the brain involved in emotions and their regulation are directly linked to input from perceptual and bodily sensation circuits. We need input from our bodies and emotions to perform numerous cognitive processes, including reasoning. The bodies of patients with DID have often been a source of vulnerability and pain as a focus of physical or sexual abuse. Premature physiological arousal and conflictual relationships may lead to precocious sexuality, which, in turn, may lead the patients to feel that their bodies are a source of shame or betrayal. For these reasons, you may find your patient to be, in certain states especially, quite profoundly disconnected from her body.

This disconnection certainly produces difficulties with sexuality and physical affection. Furthermore, this segmenting of bodily function and sensation away from other mental activity, although an adaptive response, can actually block the vital somatic data from emotional processing. In therapy this emotional paralysis should be observed and noted by you before being directly addressed with the patient. It is important to not overwhelm a patient's adaptive defenses before they are ready to have alternative coping mechanisms.

In individuals with isolation of the body, sensations and actions may be profoundly frightening and a source of dread and shame. These emotions, as with other derivatives of traumatic adaptation, should be gently but steadily explored. Helping the patient gain intimate connection to her body can provide the missing elements of a balanced emotional life.

The Experiential Role of the Therapist

This chapter began with a scene of two individuals sitting together in a room. We focused on the subjective experiences for the person in the role of patient. I believe that psychotherapy, especially with traumatized individuals, requires a deep cognitive/emotional experience on the part of both patient and therapist. The cold cognitive processes of attention, memory, mental models, metacognition, and narrative can serve as a rational framework with which to follow and chart the course of psychotherapy. This map is vital to finding your way through some often confusing and frightening details of experiences.

For example, viewing an unresolved traumatic memory as impaired explicit processing permits a rational approach to therapeutic abreaction. Catalyzing this explicit processing of a traumatic event is a central objective in this model. This "intellectual" framework, however, is only part of the essence of the therapy.

The relationship between you and the patient is also fundamental to the healing process. The therapist plays many roles: teacher, attachment figure, psychoanalyst, supportive ally, and developmental facilitator. In each of these roles, the therapist "bears witness" to the evolution of the patient's emerging self as historical events are recounted, as present life situations are revealed, and as future paths are charted. The patient's progression from passive recipient of life events to the scribe for historical recounting to the proactive author of her autobiography is facilitated by the therapist's many roles.

These massive developmental changes and emotional experiences within the patient occur within your therapeutic relationship. To allow them to occur, you must provide many of the elements that were not available to her as a child. Therapy requires a safe, predictable environment. Boundaries of space and time must be clearly defined and respected. It is your job as therapist to provide all of these roles and nurturance in a setting where the patient's needs are explored but the therapeutic boundaries are maintained. It is sad how often one hears in consultation about seemingly well-intended therapists whose misguided zeal led them to have endlessly long sessions, meetings outside the office, transgressions of therapeutic roles (for example, becoming a patient's friend), or becoming themselves so emotionally involved that they lose their required therapeutic objectivity.

Balancing hot and cold cognitive processes is as much a matter for ourselves as for our patients. As therapists we must be emotionally involved in the therapy. In the role of attachment figure, our attunement requires our own hot cognitive processing of deep emotional issues. It is painful to bear witness to the pain our patients have experienced. These various roles are deeply moving for us, as well as for our patients.

It is an artful balance, however, to be emotionally involved and to maintain a therapeutic objectivity that helps facilitate our emotional processing. The key here is that the purpose of the therapeutic relationship is the therapy of the patient, not of the therapist. If you become numb to your own historical issues or emotional blind spots, however, this distancing will also impair the work. Although students may be particularly open to their own dynamics, here is an example of a blind spot that was dangerous.

A supervisee was treating a DID patient who was struggling with some profoundly conflictual grief issues after the death of an abusive mother. The student seemed to favor the angry alters and to ignore the pain of the saddened ones. He also seemed oblivious to the sadness hidden beneath the anger. A suicidal crisis emerged when the patient had intense internal distress about this conflict. Supervision of the trainee led to the uncovering of his own ambivalence about a close relative who had committed suicide six months earlier. Thus, the trainee's unresolved emotional issues were unintentionally but directly impeding the therapy of the patient. Eventually, the student therapist was able to work through his own issues enough to stop "playing favorites" and be attuned to the many layers of the patient's grief. Therapeutic progress resumed.

Thus, it is crucial that each of us be open to our own emotional experiences and developmental histories. This awareness and willingness to be open to our own issues can then allow our full participation as therapists in a therapeutic relationship with patients. My own life is deeply affected by this work and by these relationships. By being emotionally involved in the process, I am able to maintain my focus on therapeutic goals for the patients. Ironically, inability or unwillingness to be emotionally available seems to be a risk factor for therapeutic stagnation. Emotional involvement with a patient that produces therapeutic boundary violations can replicate early betrayal experiences. Thus, it is crucial to find the experiential role that allows us to be involved as therapists with the patients' needs and to create and maintain the therapeutic environment of safety and predictability that remains fully in focus.

Choice and Continuity: Healing and the Whole Person

So much of what went wrong in the early experiences of individuals with DID is that things were done to them and arrested development ensued. I think our role is to provide an opportunity for an individual to experience a relationship in which her development is enhanced, rather than inhibited. Part of this enhancement is in providing a sense of dignity and choice. The idea that therapists "fuse" or "integrate" patients seems counterproductive. More helpful, I think, is the view that therapy can offer patients the ability and therefore the right to choose, if they want, to allow their development to continue.

Ongoing dissociation is, in fact, retraumatizing to patients' core sense of coherency, affectivity, agency, and continuity. Therapy can provide an opportunity to gain coherency with the body, to tolerate a wider range of emotions, to become the center of one's own initiative, and to have a coherent (though initially painful) autobiographical continuity. Reflecting on past experience, present life situations, and future plans can facilitate these changes.

By providing a safe and comforting therapeutic alliance, the barriers across states of mind can become more permeable and less rigid, such that the investment in separateness may become less intense. Both implicit and explicit memories may become accessible across states. The patient may find a time when nondissociative defenses become more accessible than continued, traumatizing dissociation. When eventually the patient may feel ready to dissolve these cognitive barriers, she may find that the barriers have become so permeable as to make the transition seem a non-event. Other patients may find a ritualized "breaking down of the Berlin Wall" to help the transition.

A new, core sense of self can emerge as previously divided states yield to the thrust toward continuity. The emotional connection of the therapist to the patient and to the process, as with the parents who help facilitate the exploration of a securely attached child, allows for the patient to feel the emotional strength to try a new way of life. The increased flexibility of mental models and accessibility of memories allow for the patient to become the author of her autobiography. Continuity of consciousness across states in the present, accessibility to awareness of past events, and freedom to choose future action can facilitate the developing sense of a historical self.

Through the intricate process of this facilitated development, the patient with DID can begin to make sense out of her disruptive inner lives. She can become free to live with choice and dignity. This process is both profoundly challenging and rewarding. Both individuals sitting in the therapy office are deeply affected by the process. We as therapists bear witness to the pain that for so long was shouldered alone, buried in dissociative isolation. Growth takes time. It is a privilege to be able to join in her journey of growth and liberation.

My hope is that this chapter can provide elements of a cognitive sciences framework that may help shed some light on the direction and details of this journey. Informed by a variety of disciplines, we can use fully our ideas and our emotions to help guide the way.

NOTES

P. 40, *In other writings, I have summarized views:* Siegel, D. (1995a). Memory, trauma, and psychotherapy: A cognitive sciences view. *Journal of Psychotherapy Practice and Research, 4*(2) 93–122; Siegel, D. (1995b). Perception and cognition. In B. Kaplan & W. Sadock (Eds.), *Comprehensive textbook of psychiatry* (6th ed., pp. 277–291). New York: Williams & Wilkins.

P. 40, *These neurons form various architectural layers:* Edelman, G. (1992). *Bright air, brilliant fire.* New York: Basic Books.

P. 40, *This set of networklike activations:* Morris, R.G.M. (Ed.). (1989). *Parallel distributed processing: Implications for psychology and neurobiology.* New York: Clarendon Press.

P. 40, *Most brain activity:* Kihlstrom, J. F. (1987). The cognitive unconscious. *Science, 237,* 1445–1452.

P. 40, *most of what becomes conscious:* Dennett, D. C. (1991). *Consciousness explained.* Boston: Little, Brown.

P. 40, *Ideas such as memory processes:* Posner, M. I. (Ed.). (1989). *Foundations of cognitive science.* Cambridge: MIT Press.

P. 41, *These scientists have attempted to be precise:* Johnson-Laird, P. N. (1983). *Mental models: Towards a cognitive science of language, inference, and consciousness.* Cambridge, MA: Harvard University Press.

P. 41, *There are ways of understanding how early life experiences:* Schore, A. (1994). *Affect regulation and the origin of the self.* Hillsdale, NJ: Erlbaum.

P. 41, *The mind/brain can be in a certain "state of mind":* Horowitz, M. J. (1987). *States of mind* (2nd ed.). New York: Plenum Press; Horowitz, M. J. (Ed.). (1991). *Person schemas and maladaptive interpersonal patterns.* Chicago: University of Chicago Press.

P. 41, *One state of mind may include a sense of security:* Main, M. (1991). Metacognitive knowledge, metacognitive monitoring, and singular (coherent) vs. multiple (incoherent) models of attachment: Findings and directions for future research. In P. Marris, J. Stevenson-Hinde, & C. Parkes (Eds.), *Attachment across the life cycle* (pp. 127–154). New York: Routledge.

P. 42, *As many authors have noted, people with DID:* Kluft, R. P. (Ed.). (1985). *Childhood antecedents of multiple personality.* Washington, DC: American Psychiatric Press; Putnam, F. (1989). *Multiple personality disorder: Diagnosis and treatment.* New York: Guilford Press.

P. 43, *The story that emerges may reflect:* Nissen, M. J., Ross, J. L., Willingham, D. B., Mackenzie, T. B., & Schacter, D. L. (1988). Memory and awareness in a patient with multiple personality disorder. *Brain and Cognition, 8,* 117–134.

P. 43, *Stories are a fundamental part of human cognition:* Bruner, J. S. (1986). *Actual minds, possible worlds.* Cambridge, MA: Harvard University Press.

P. 43, *The narrative mode of thought begins early in child development:* Nelson, K. (1989). *Narratives from the crib.* Cambridge, MA: Harvard University Press.

P. 43, *For children, narratives can be co-constructed:* Nelson, K. (1993). Events, narratives, memory: What develops? In C. A. Nelson (Ed.), *Minnesota Symposium in Child Development: Memory and emotion* (pp. 1–24). Hillsdale, NJ: Erlbaum.

P. 44, *The following basic principles of memory:* Siegel, D. (1995a). Memory, trauma, and psychotherapy: A cognitive sciences view. *Journal of Psychotherapy Practice and Research, 4,*(2), 93–122.

P. 44, *Remembering, like other cognitive processes:* Squire, L. R. (1987). *Memory and brain.* New York: Oxford University Press.

P. 44, *Memory is reconstructive, not reproductive:* Neisser, U. C. (Ed.). (1982). *Memory observed: Remembering in natural contexts.* New York: W. H. Freeman.

P. 44, *The details may be biased by postevent questioning:* Ceci, S., & Bruck, M. (1993). Suggestibility of the child witness: A historical review and synthesis. *Psychological Bulletin, 113*(3), 403–439.

P. 45, *Some forms of remembering involve conscious awareness:* Schacter, D. L. (1989). On the relation between memory and consciousness: Dissociable interactions and conscious experience. In H. L. Roediger & F.I.M. Craik (Eds.), *Varieties of memory and consciousness: Essays in honor of Endel Tulving* (pp. 355–390). Hillsdale, NJ: Erlbaum.

P. 45, *Most of "cognition" is nonconscious:* Greenwald, A. G. (1992). New look 3: Unconscious cognition reclaimed. *American Psychologist, 47*(6), 766–779.

P. 45, *Memory involves monitoring processes:* Johnson, M. K. (1991). Reflection, reality monitoring, and the self. In *Mental imagery: Proceedings of the Twelfth Annual Conference of the American Association for the Study of Imagery* (pp. 1–12). New York: Plenum Press.

P. 45, *Memory includes both experiential and correspondent dimensions:* Pettinati, H. M. (Ed.). (1988). *Hypnosis and memory.* New York: Guilford Press.

P. 45, *Attachment experiences early in life:* Main, M. (1991). Metacognitive knowledge, metacognitive monitoring, and singular (coherent) vs. multiple (incoherent) models of attachment: Findings and directions for future research. In P. Marris, J. Stevenson-Hinde, & C. Parkes (Eds.), *Attachment across the life cycle* (pp. 127–154). New York: Routledge.

P. 46, *Early remembering is enhanced by parent-child interactions:* Fivush, R., & Hudson, J. A. (Eds.). (1990). *Knowing and remembering in young children.* New York: Cambridge University Press.

P. 46, *The study of memory has resulted:* Squire, L. R. (1992a). Declarative and non-declarative memory: Multiple brain systems supporting learning and memory. *Journal of Cognitive Neuroscience, 4*(3), 232–243.

P. 47, *Implicit memory is the way:* Schacter, D. L. (1992). Understanding implicit memory: A cognitive neuroscience approach. *American Psychologist, 47*(4), 559–569.

P. 47, *This expression can include both memory for facts:* Tulving, E. (1985). How many memory systems are there? *American Psychologist, 40,* 385–398.

P. 48, *Episodic or autobiographical memory:* Rubin, D. (Ed.). (1986). *Autobiographical memory.* New Haven, CT: Yale University Press.

P. 48, *The medial temporal lobe memory system:* Squire, L. R. (1992b). Memory and the hippocampus: A synthesis from findings with rats, monkeys, and humans. *Psychological Review, 99*(2), 195–231.

P. 49, *Trauma may thus impede:* Siegel, D. (1995a). Memory, trauma, and psychotherapy: A cognitive sciences view. *Journal of Psychotherapy Practice and Research, 4*(2), 93–122.

P. 50, *several processes may occur in a child:* Terr, L. (1991). Childhood traumas: An outline and overview. *American Journal of Psychiatry, 148,* 10–20.

P. 50, *As suppression is repeated frequently:* Kihlstrom, J. F., & Baurhardt, T. M. (1993). The self-regulation of memory: For better and for worse, with and without hypnosis. In D. M. Wegner & J. W. Pennebaker (Eds.), *Handbook of mental control.* Englewood Cliffs, NJ: Prentice Hall.

P. 50, *A different adaptive process is called dissociation:* van der Kolk, B. A., & van der Hart, O. (1989). Pierre Janet and the breakdown of adaptation in psychological trauma. *American Journal of Psychiatry, 146,* 1530–1540.

P. 50, *Although a few studies empirically support:* Briere, J., & Conte, J. (1993). Self-reported amnesia for abuse in adults molested as children. *Journal of Traumatic Stress, 6*(1), 21–31; Herman, J., & Schatzow, E. (1987). Recovery and verification of memories of childhood sexual trauma. *Psychoanalytic Psychology, 4*(1), 1–14; Williams, L. M. (1992). Adult memories of childhood abuse: Preliminary findings from a longitudinal study. *The Advisor, American Professional Society on the Abuse of Children, 5*(3), 19–21.

P. 50, *Other authors question the validity:* Holmes, D. S. (1991). The evidence of repression: An examination of sixty years of research. In J. L. Singer (Ed.), *Repression and dissociation* (pp. 85–102). Chicago: University of Chicago Press; Loftus, E. F. (1993). The reality of repressed memories. *American Psychologist, 48*(5), 518–537; Piper, A. (1994). Multiple personality disorder. *British Journal of Psychiatry, 164,* 600–612.

P. 50, *For the patient with DID, relatively rigid segregations:* Nissen, M. J., Ross, J. L., Willingham, D. B., Mackenzie, T. B., & Schacter, D. L. (1988). Memory and awareness in a patient with multiple personality disorder. *Brain and Cognition, 8,* 117–134.

P. 51, *The simplest example is that of memory:* Siegel, D. (1995a). Memory, trauma, and psychotherapy: A cognitive sciences view. *Journal of Psychotherapy Practice and Research, 4*(2), 93–122.

P. 54, *She complains of features of PTSD:* Putnam, F. (1989). *Multiple personality disorder: Diagnosis and treatment.* New York: Guilford Press.

P. 55, *Daniel Stern's conceptualization:* Stern, D. N. (1985). *The interpersonal world of the infant.* New York: Basic Books.

P. 57, *Some authors consider the regulation of affect:* Schore, A. (1994). *Affect regulation and the origin of the self.* Hillsdale, NJ: Erlbaum.

P. 60, *Attachment theory suggests that caregivers:* Main, M., Kaplan, N., & Cassidy, J. (1985). Security in infancy, childhood, and adulthood: A move to the level of representation. In I. Bretherton & E. Waters (Eds.), Growing points of attachment theory and research. *Monographs of the Society for Research in Child Development, 50*(1–2, Serial No. 209) 66–104.

P. 60, *The repeated experience of need satisfaction:* Bowlby, J. (1969). *Attachment and loss: Vol. 1. Attachment.* New York: Basic Books.

P. 60, *If, in addition, attachment figures are the source:* Main, M., & Hesse, E. (1990). Parent's unresolved traumatic experiences are related to infant disorganized attachment status: Is frightened or frightening parental behavior the linking mechanism? In M. T. Greenberg, D. Cicchetti, & E. M. Cummings (Eds.), *Attachment in the preschool years: Theory, research, and intervention* (pp. 161–182). Chicago: University of Chicago Press.

P. 60, *Disorganized attachment may be a predisposing factor:* Liotti, G. (1992). Disorganized/disoriented attachment in the etiology of dissociative disorders. *Dissociation, 5,*(4), 196–204.

P. 61, *with time, your interactions will be internalized:* Schore, A. (1994). *Affect regulation and the origin of the self.* Hillsdale, NJ: Erlbaum.

P. 62, *The complex topic of consciousness:* Marcel, A., & Bisiach, E. (Eds.). (1988). *Consciousness in contemporary science.* New York: Oxford University Press.

P. 62, *Whatever the patient's stated awareness:* Li, D., & Spiegel, D. (1992). A neural network model of dissociative disorders. *Psychiatric Annals, 22*(3), 144–147.

P. 63, *Metacognition includes the development:* Flavell, J. H., Green, F. L., & Flavell, E. R. (1986). Development of knowledge about the appearance-reality distinction. *Monographs of the Society for Research in Child Development, 51*(1), 212.

P. 65, *Narrative includes a listener and a teller:* Britton, B. K., & Pellegrini, A. D. (Eds.). (1990). *Narrative thought and narrative language.* Hillsdale, NJ: Erlbaum.

P. 65, *Numerous authors view autobiographical narrative:* Bruner, J. S. (1986). *Actual minds, possible worlds.* Cambridge, MA: Harvard University Press; Dennett, D. C. (1991). *Consciousness explained.* Boston: Little, Brown; Kegan, R. (1982). *The evolving self.* Cambridge, MA: Harvard University Press.

P. 66, *Dissociative phenomena, such as amnesia:* Siegel, D. (1995a). Memory, trauma, and psychotherapy: A cognitive sciences view. *Journal of Psychotherapy Practice and Research, 4*(2), 93–122.

P. 68, *This aspect of traumatic resolution:* Freud, S. (1958). Remembering, repeating, and working through. In S. Freud, *Complete psychological works* (Standard edition, Vol. 12). London: Hogarth Press. (Original work published 1914)

P. 68, *What I have proposed is that flashbacks:* Siegel, D. (1995a). Memory, trauma, and psychotherapy: A cognitive sciences view. *Journal of Psychotherapy Practice and Research, 4*(2), 93–122.

P. 68, *Recent views of brain development:* Schore, A. (1994). *Affect regulation and the origin of the self.* Hillsdale, NJ: Erlbaum.

P. 70, *We need input from our bodies and emotions:* Damasio, A. R. (1994). *Descartes' error: Emotion, reason, and the human brain.* New York: Putnam.

3

MODELS OF HELPING
The Role of Responsibility

Catherine G. Fine

The attitude one holds toward "responsibility" in the cause and correction of mental illness determines, to a large extent, the style of intervention used in treatment. This is no less true for the treatment of dissociative identity disorder (DID)—and, in fact, may be more influential in this case. In this chapter I will review therapeutic approaches to the DID patient in the context of the evolving field of dissociative disorders and then examine various models of therapy in treating DID, especially those stemming from attitudes toward therapeutic responsibility. I will explore the distribution of personalities across these models to anticipate prognosis, level of intervention, and outcome so that an *optimal fit* can be achieved.

The formal and appropriate inclusion in the *DSM-III* (1980) of a category of posttraumatic conditions that has been documented for centuries marks the beginning of a resurgence of interest in dissociative conditions. Although dissociative disorders held a prominent place in the French and German medical texts of the nineteenth century, the emergence of Freudian conceptualizations of trauma overshadowed the earlier psychodynamic work of Janet, Charcot, and others, from which Freud formulated his theories of unconscious influences on conscious activities. As early as 1848, Antoine Despine, who described the first scientific treatment of DID, worried that important findings of the day regarding dissociation would go underground and be forgotten. For more than a century, this prophesy came to pass.

The rediscovery of dissociative conditions in the mid 1970s was prompted by a few pioneers (Wilbur, Kluft, Braun) who not only seemed to listen to their patients and resist efforts to fit patients into rigid categories and treatment protocols but also were willing to explore scientific discovery through paradigmatic shifts in thinking. These trailblazers were able to shift their established diagnostic considerations and treatment paradigms to new ones that would better explain their clinical observations, anticipate appropriate treatment goals, and manage the course of the therapy. Since then, the number of publications on dissociative disorders has risen exponentially, with each contributor reviewing, integrating, and rearranging the initial findings of the 1970s and 1980s to meet his or her patients' needs and to fit each respective clinician's style.

Therapeutic pluralism, approaching treatment through a variety of methods and orientations, was met with some successes and many failures. Yet, like the phoenix relentlessly rising from the ashes, new approaches to therapy for the DID patient were driven by professional interactions and continued attention to the patient. Out of this rich learning experience, Richard Kluft has succinctly derived several fundamental principles of treatment that need to be both respected and fully integrated into the successful therapy model for dissociative disorders irrespective of the theoretical orientation of the therapist (see Chapter Nine). Additionally, Kluft weighs pragmatic aspects of treatment in the light of necessary therapeutic interventions and their consequences on the therapy dyad.

The therapist who is knowledgeable in the treatment of dissociative disorders and informed about the pragmatics of treatment is understandably proactive, rather than solely reactive to occurrences in and out of treatment. Because the therapy dyad is functioning within a dissociative field, the stance of the therapist with regard to the dissociative condition pervades each reaction to and from the therapist. Each intervention addresses not only the immediate therapy concerns but also an awareness of the nature of the dissociative phenomena as the overriding feature from which all other symptoms are derived. Therefore, appropriate respect for the quality of each therapeutic interaction is helpful. The therapist's stance in the treatment of dissociative disorders is best expressed as an approach to the patient informed by issues of proper responsibility, appropriate negotiations of boundaries, as well as a clear appreciation of transference-countertransference exchanges.

The therapist's implicit model of helping fundamentally influences the therapeutic relationship. Phil Brickman's sociopsychological model is specifically concerned with styles of helping and their implications for the therapy. This model enlightens therapists as to their approach in a way that best takes into account the impact of dissociation on both the thinking and affect of the patient with DID. An awareness of these models assists the therapist to achieve a healthy distance from the concrete thinking of DID patients, their trance logic, as well as the ongoing impact of projection, projective identification, and primary process thinking. Rectification of these fundamental distortions, essential for eventual integration of all of the personalities, will be affected by both the therapist's belief of what constitutes help and what the DID patient finds helpful. Another way of stating the problem is to ask, "Who is responsible and in what way for the giving and receiving of help in therapy?" This is a particularly burning question for DID patients who function in multiple realities and who tend to disown their feelings, behaviors, and thoughts and to blame others for them.

THE NATURE OF THERAPEUTIC RESPONSIBILITY

Before exploring specific models of responsibility as applied to therapy, and specifically to DID, two aspects of therapeutic responsibility must be introduced: the relationship of cause and effect in psychosocial dysfunction and the meaning of responsibility in treatment.

Cause, Effect, and Therapeutic Responsibility

Unlike the laws of physics, for which a specific effect can be seen as resulting from a specific and related cause, considerations of cause and outcome surrounding the issue of therapeutic responsibility are not in direct relation to one another. They are mediated by complex issues such as blame and control. Therefore, a conceptual framework in which blame and control can be explicitly explored will be helpful to further elucidate attribution of responsibility. This framework, in turn, will influence how one asks for and receives help, as well as how someone gives help.

Therapists need to be clear about their understanding of how they will and will not give help (what their responsibility is and isn't). They need to explore with patients each other's understanding of responsibility in the therapeutic alliance. This exploration should begin fairly early in the treatment process in an effort to correct distorted notions surrounding "whose therapy is it anyway." For the DID patient, clarifications and confrontations will continue as all personalities enter treatment more formally and test the therapeutic boundaries. Each part of the mind will need to commonly agree on what constitutes both its individual and the joint responsibility in therapy.

If personalities collude to avoid a common thrust or if the common thrust is not along the lines of a healthy, productive, sane treatment outcome, then that therapist and patient have not come to a compelling, safe understanding of what constitutes treatment, and *thus no treatment is possible.*

What Does Responsibility in Treatment Mean?

Brickman contends that, at least initially, controlling one's behavior is more important than understanding the underlying cause of events. Most therapists would agree that patients who do not achieve behavioral control are unlikely to make therapeutic gains. This statement is particularly relevant for the DID patient who has an ongoing struggle with modulation of affect and who sometimes gives in to acting out a conflict behaviorally, rather than verbalizing it. From the onset of therapy, practitioners must be respectful of the basic ground rules of treatment. Whether the patient has been in treatment before for DID or whether the diagnosis of DID has just recently been made, the beginning phases of any new therapy need to focus on establishing the treatment frame, delineating the boundaries, and setting up a therapy situation in which feelings can be explored yet not impulsively acted on.

The conceptual framework for attribution of responsibility proposed by Brickman can aid therapist and patient alike to describe, explore, and implement a meaningful and workable treatment relationship to assist DID patients in containing their overwhelming affects, recognizing their multiple transferences, and negotiating therapy boundaries. This framework is particularly helpful in containing therapeutic work that evolves in a dissociative field.

Brickman's four models of helping (discussed in the following sections) assist therapists in noticing what they believe about the issues of control and blame and subsequently in helping therapists better explore these issues with their DID patients. Yet, considerations of blame and control will need to be taken up not only with the patient as a whole but also with each individual personality. The therapist will want to assess which model each personality subscribes and then explore its therapeutic validity, considering the stated treatment goal. For example, it will be essential that personalities of a DID patient who say they are ready to do abreactive work not be working within a helping model that is likely to lead them to retraumatization.

MODELS OF RESPONSIBILITY

Although Brickman's models apply to all social interactions, in this chapter I will present their applicability to therapeutic interactions with the DID patient. The four models of responsibility are *moral, medical, enlightenment,* and *compensatory*, each with different views as to the cause and correction of one's illness (see Table 3.1).

The Moral Model

In the moral model, people are responsible for problems and solutions. They are responsible for both creating and solving their problems. Patients are responsible for their actions and can take steps to correct their problems. Excessive consumption of alcohol, for example, is seen as a sign of weak character, and to stop drinking, alcoholics need to exercise willpower. With dissociative disorders, DID individuals would need to recognize that they need help; they not only would have to seek out therapy but also would need to pursue a therapy that is likely to recognize or aid them in recognizing the extent of their dissociative symptoms, as well as a therapy geared to integration of all parts of the mind. This stepwise process implies a certain amount of persistence, discernment, and appropriate judgment; all can be quite challenging for the DID individual.

Within the moral model, supportive help involves reminding people of how responsible they are for their own fate and how important and necessary it is that they help themselves. Although people who subscribe to the moral model assume responsibility for the cause of the problem, their focus is predominantly future oriented. They not only concentrate on present solutions for future applications but also embrace looking away from the past.

The value of the moral model is that it compels people to take an unequivocal stance toward their lives. If people do not like the way things are, they should recognize that they are responsible for changing them and should start changing them.

One problem associated with the moral model is it can lead its subscribers to blame the victim. It may strike an all-too-familiar chord for the often masochistic DID patients, who may blame themselves for their suffering or even do self-harm as a penance. Alternatively, the moral model may lead its adherents

Table 3.1
Models of Responsibility in the Helping Professions

Model:	Patient Responsibility for Problem's Cause	Correction
Moral	+	+
Medical	-	-
Enlightenment	+	-
Compensatory	-	+

to subscribe to narcissistic omnipotence as a way of life—or, in the case of the DID patient, some personalities would rigidly bind to such a belief and misguidedly posit that because they are responsible for all things, all things are possible. Finally, the moral model is one of loneliness. Success comes by one's own doing and failure by one's own incapacity.

Ellis's rational-emotional therapy and Frankl's existential therapy are typical examples of therapies that subscribe to the moral model. For example, Ellis theorizes that how people feel does not come from attitudes learned from parents, spouses, or friends, but rather from the person's tendency to overintensify and overpersonalize his or her outlook. The patient's responsibility is to recognize his or her misconstrued viewpoint and to realize how this contributes to his or her dysphoria and what distortions underlie them. The therapist's role is to recognize the distortions and to vigorously confront the patient in an ongoing manner while the patient is exhorted to change.

The Medical Model

In the medical model, people are held responsible for neither the origins of their problems nor the solutions to their problems. It is called medical model because modern Western medicine embodies this belief in its training of physicians. Drugs and surgical interventions can target specific complaints with minimal input from the patient. In the medical model, the patient is seen as the passive recipient of a solution based on someone else's judgment. Here, people see themselves and are seen by others as incapacitated.

This model illustrates that the people who can change the circumstances of the individual are outside the person who experiences the problem. The helpers are responsible for prescribing the solution (for example, bed rest, medication).

One advantage of the medical model is that it allows people to ask for and accept help without being blamed; after all, they are not really spiritually weak, they are simply ill. The same symptoms that may be punished under another model would receive treatment under the medical model. Another advantage is that DID patients do not have to "keep a stiff upper lip"; they can find a compassionate arena for the acknowledgment of their distress and possibly reacquire lost hope.

With this renewed aspiration, however, may endure a false belief surrounding the immediacy of the relief. Is it not common to hear the DID patient say something that expresses the attitude: "You're the doctor. You do something for me!" When compared with a psychiatrist, a nonphysician psychotherapist is sometimes spared this "sick role" motif surrounding the mistaken belief that medication will make IT all better—whatever IT is imagined to be. But the psychotherapist may be magically delegated the task of knowing the history without being told (especially the aspects of their lives the patients themselves do not remember), of understanding the unspoken, and of responding correctly and with due empathy to the "crumbs" of information imparted by DID patients. Clearly, the myth of the "doctor who will make the hurt go away" remains in many personalities, particularly ones that feel helpless and depleted.

Thus, an added predicament with the medical model is that it fosters dependency. For instance, the more the patients believe they are ill (as opposed to having deficiencies in social learning), the more they will be dependent on mental health practitioners.

The patient empowers the professional helper with the skills to not only find solutions but also enforce them. The therapist becomes Big Brother, Big Daddy, or Big Mama—at best an externalized superego—and as such, the patients risk losing the ability to fend for themselves. Of course, this is in no way ignoring or minimizing the fact that some mental disorders have clear and strong biological components and need ongoing medical intervention to diminish crises; in those cases, dependency is not a risk based on a psychological construct, but rather a statement of reality.

A therapeutic modality that risks lending itself at times to the medical model is psychoanalysis. The *psychoanalytical model* would support the belief that human nature, parental failures, and the rigid demands of civilized society may produce neurotic problems. Change is produced through analyzing defenses made conscious through the patient's relationship with the analyst, defenses made apparent through transference(s) of the major emotional patterns from the patient's life onto the therapist. A former DID patient of mine who had been twice analyzed (according to her, successfully) typically expected me to analyze her dreams, to interpret her writings and drawings, and to verify and validate her memories—because that was my job! I wondered whether this expectation also implied that I had to do her abreactions.

The pure medical model not augmented by more ongoing and responsible engagement by the patient with the therapist risks leaving the DID patient in a position of vulnerability and with a sense of helpless complacency for too long.

The Enlightenment Model

In the enlightenment model, people are blamed for causing their problems but are not believed responsible for solving them. This model emphasizes "enlightening" the participants about the authentic character of their problems. They are instructed as to how difficult the solutions will be; the implication, of course, is that they will not accomplish their stated goals on their own because, had it been that simple, they would have done it already. The model requires people to accept a negative self-image, as well as the help of others on others' terms. Brickman proposes that "people who subscribe to this model see themselves as (at the very least) responsible by their past behavior, and sometimes as guilty or even sinful, and consequently still suffering" or paying the piper for their past misadventures. If they ended up where they are now, it is their own fault.

The solution becomes compliance with the harsh or compassionate regimen provided by agents who represent the moral force of the community. According to the enlightenment model, this solution exists outside the individual's control and is a function of the good graces of the helpers. The agent of change is a higher force and power, or a group that has seen the light. Alcoholics Anonymous is one of the more thriving examples of the enlightenment model. It requires newcomers to take responsibility for their past—rather than to blame parents, job, and spouse—and to admit to their own inability to control their behaviors.

The problem with the enlightenment model is that people's lives can get reconstructed around a symptom. Additionally, the support system of people adhering to this model can be other people with similar problems. The benefit of feeling heard and understood by someone who has "been there" is soon overshadowed by the realization that the enlightenment model patient not only struggles with his or her own issues but also then has to grapple with the fallout from his or her support system's difficulties as well—because those who comprise the support system have at least the same difficulties as the patient requiring support. Finally, this model empowers the "ministry" and the "minister," rather than the individual who is struggling.

Needless to say, this is a disastrous model for the person with DID to subscribe to if he or she intends to modify the pathological dissociative defenses, rather than just "put one foot in front of the other" for the present moment. The enlightenment model feeds the DID patient's old distorted beliefs that often reflect negative self-statements from the past, fed by confession of deeds (which the patient may or may not have done) and associated regret. The unpredictability of the help, according to this view, recapitulates the DID patients' unstable childhood environment.

Indeed, the DID patient will have difficulty predicting the mind-set of some support group members. The DID patient may not duly appreciate when other group members will be available for backing or when they will need sustenance themselves. Moreover, DID patients in no way need a "minister" or other authority figure implanted in their lives now that they are no longer children. Authority figures in the past rendered the DID child powerless and helpless; they depotentiated the child. Therefore, the enlightenment model for patients with DID runs the risk of feeding a repetition compulsion that may be so familiar it may go unnoticed.

Additionally, if the DID patients project the authority figure role onto the therapist, they will be "walking on eggshells." They may feel the need to please the therapist, and their idea of pleasing the therapist may never allow the expression of any powerful negative emotion to arise; their ability to ever address the negative transferences that are sure to arise is thus limited.

The Compensatory Model

In the compensatory model, people are not blamed for their problems but are still held responsible for solving them. People are seen as requiring help to overcome obstacles. Impediments and original drawbacks are not believed to have been brought on by them. It is understood, however, that they need special help from others to find solutions. Therapists who subscribe to this model see themselves as resources that the person does not have. But the responsibility for *using* this help is on the recipient!

According to the compensatory model, recipients of help are perceived by others as deprived or suffering, not from their own deficiencies, but rather from the failure of the social and familial environment to provide for them. For the DID patient, the therapist who subscribes to this model may think the patient was deprived in childhood of the opportunity to access the support, love, and caring that every child deserves—and needs for proper development. The therapist believes that the family did not protect the child from overwhelming life experiences, either through passive neglect or active attack. Yet further, the social system in childhood and the mental health system in adulthood are seen as failing the patient. Therefore, DID therapists may mobilize their skills on behalf of their patients, at least for a time, until the appropriate resources have been acquired so that the patients can then become responsible for their own fate.

The value of the compensatory model is that it focuses the subscribers on *solutions,* rather than belabors endlessly the issue of cause and blame. The DID patient lives in multiple realities, and many of these realities focus on the past, on causes rather than solutions. It is important to keep in mind that, in the past, the DID patient was hopeless, helpless, and abandoned. Through conscious and unconscious flashbacks, many patients with DID believe that nothing has changed since their childhood. They ignore or are unable to grasp the difference between current events "feeling" catastrophic and "being" catastrophic. Consequently, this lack of future orientation, combined with an intense involvement in the past, increases the inner struggle in patients whose personalities at the onset of treatment are unlikely to know how to mobilize the psychological tools necessary to their improvement. The personalities based in the past may be cognitively or emotionally fixated. As they move out of their traditional modus operandi, they may bring to the problem solving a sense of helplessness, betrayal, and lack of control and thus hinder elucidating any predicament.

The likely inadequacy of the compensatory model is that those who see themselves as continually having to solve problems they did not create are likely to feel a great deal of pressure in their lives. Patients with DID commonly have personalities that are either actively working in treatment or strenuously keeping the overall patient functioning in day-to-day life and consequently become depleted and exhausted because they feel that they are carrying the load for the others. Therapists may therefore need to intervene to either support the work of these alters and engage other personalities in a similar endeavor or interpret their masochism and eventually engage other personalities to support the ones that are overwrought.

When working with DID patients, therapists must strive to avert the parallel processing so common in these patients (see Siegel, Chapter Two). But a mixture of failed transient identification, combined with the sheer exhaustion in working with these patients, can lead to therapists' countertransferential reaction based on "fixing the problem," rather than on helping the patient figure out how to fix the quandary. As time passes and as this destructive scenario replays itself, the therapists themselves can develop signs of secondary posttraumatic stress disorder (PTSD). Another deficiency of the compensatory model is that the subscriber may end up with a paranoid view of the world, with thoughts shifting from "I have to solve the problem" to "*Only* I can really solve the problem; otherwise everyone else would not be turning to me for the solution."

A model of therapy that embodies the assumptions of the compensatory model is found in cognitive therapy. The role of the cognitive therapist (as seen from this compensatory model) is one of collaborative exploration and support in reviewing and confronting maladaptive thinking and overwhelming affects and sensations. The initial task and responsibility of the cognitive therapist is to model how to explore problems and to guide interventions. Eventually, that responsibility will be turned over to the patients, who will be expected to monitor their own performance and to reinforce themselves appropriately.

MODELS OF RESPONSIBILITY APPLIED TO THE THERAPEUTIC ENCOUNTER

The above review of models of responsibility as applied to therapy in general and to therapy with the DID patient in particular allows us to focus more specifically on how to proceed in our own treatment of DID in the light of such models. Yet, such considerations need to be viewed not only from the perspective of the therapist but also from the standpoint of the patient, and in the case of DID, across personalities.

Perspective of the Therapist

In my experience, the only viable model of responsibility for the therapist working with DID patients is to enter the therapeutic encounter with the compensatory model in mind. Recall that this model views the patients as not responsible for the *cause(s)* of their problems, but as responsible for the *solution(s)* to their problems.

It will not be sufficient for the therapists who chose to consider this model on a purely intellectual level to nod in agreement with a "well, that makes sense" stance. If this model were as obvious as it appears at first blush, there would be fewer boundary violations, less overinvolvement of patient and therapist, and fewer derailments of the therapeutic process. Therefore, therapists would need to review with honesty (and possibly disarming directness) the belief system that they subscribe to in practice, rather than in theory. Only then can appropriate adjustments be made.

Such a paradigm is embodied in my *tactical integration perspective* in the work with DID. This is a dynamically informed cognitive model geared at containing overwhelming experiences as it helps stabilize external behaviors in the present and uncover past traumas. It is a model in which learning from past experiences is more important than abreacting them and in which abreactions are negotiated in a fractionated way as affect tolerance increases. Integration is achieved more as a by-product of work previously done than as a necessary end product or torch held out to the world.

Perspective of the DID Patient

The DID patient often embraces treatment with caution and a great degree of circumspection—but not always surrounding the most helpful issues. For example, I remember being interviewed by a DID patient who was contemplating treatment and who was more interested and concerned about the view from my window (trees were considered dangerous and not to be trusted) than she was about what therapy entailed or the qualifications of the therapist.

DID patients as non-unified individuals have parts of the mind focused on separate and sometimes very different concerns at treatment onset. The beliefs of the personalities diverge in many respects, including on what constitutes help, what they are responsible for in the treatment situation, and what they can expect from the therapist. They tend not to follow one particular model of responsibility, but—rather to no one's surprise—they follow (or attempt to follow) many models with varying success. The preferred model of responsibility may depend on the individual personality's belief system about that issue. Therefore, at treatment onset, personalities are scattered across the four models discussed in this chapter. This dispersal means that the uninformed or acting-out DID patient has one chance in four to begin his or her work with the appropriate model of helping or responsibility in treatment.

Distribution of Personalities Across the Models

Various personalities within the patient may adhere to different models of responsibility. Some may be helpful for therapeutic development; others may hinder. Whatever their implicit assumptions regarding cause and cure, understanding the view of responsibility held by various alters will go far in assisting in successful treatment. Below I consider a few examples to elucidate this point.

The compensatory model tends to be embraced by host personalities who are motivated for treatment and who have either learned to negotiate some of the pre-treatment affective storms or are affectively detached and minimally symptomatic. Protector personalities, whether adult, adolescent, or child, can use this model effectively.

The medical model is preferred by the depleted host personalities who have given up on trying to be strong, competent, and effective. They often think they have failed in their role within the personality system and may be failing to keep the whole individual functioning. They are often guilt-ridden and somewhat neurasthenic. The medical model also fits the needs of helpless-feeling child personalities, as well as angry, deprived adolescent personalities who protest while they secretly long to be taken care of. Some abuser personalities who disown any active emotional connection to the rest of the system of personalities enter into the medical model paradigm through an attitude of: "It's their problem, not mine."

The enlightenment model seems to be favored by abuser personalities who are less detached than sadistic. They may report being quite proud that they caused the problem—confusing internal and external reality, taking credit from circumstances not of their own making and then sitting back and enjoying the fallout.

The moral model may be espoused by caretaker personalities and some protectors who are more focused on outcome. These personalities are often willing to take responsibility for anything and everything if they are able to orient the system toward looking for solutions, rather than focusing on the past. Looking toward the future may help them keep an affectively detached stance from the traumas of the earlier years.

The above examples are in no way exhaustive or a complete description of distribution of personalities across models of responsibility. Rather, they are an attempt to describe some relevant observations in hopes that therapists will become more sensitive to them in their own cases.

IMPLICATIONS FOR TREATMENT

With respect to these models of responsibility, an early task of the therapist is to uncover which model a DID patient implicitly assumes. To accomplish this, the therapist will need to initially stabilize the patient and then begin to access the various parts of the mind. Whether through formal mapping of the personalities or in following "hot" affective or cognitive themes as personalities emerge, the therapist not only will attend to the stated needs, wants, and fears of the assorted personalities but also must notice the model of responsibility to which each personality subscribes.

If the examined personality focuses on the compensatory model, the therapist will support that personality's continued alliance with it. If it is not the compensatory model, the therapist may begin to gently but consistently question and challenge the validity of some beliefs that advance a less than helpful stance. The DID therapist would at this stage have a stance that is more intervening than purely exploratory.

As treatment progresses, the therapist should notice that an increasing number of personalities are abiding by the beliefs of the compensatory model. This acceptance may not be stated directly, but rather may be played out by the patient's diminished dependency and decreased projections on the therapist. Additionally, it might be expected that the personalities' alliance with the compensatory model foretells of impending integrations when like-minded personalities begin their abreactive work.

Monitoring the deviation in alliance from a medical, enlightenment, or moral model to a compensatory model may mark a shift in treatment trajectory in which previously noncommitted or ambivalent personalities finally get to work. Therefore, therapists could oversee the evolution of prognostic indicators across the personalities by attending to the degree of allegiance to the compensatory model. Favorable treatment outcome will necessarily depend on the patient's dedication to a model of helping that promotes mastery and self-efficacy.

NOTES

P. 81, *The formal and appropriate inclusion:* American Psychiatric Association. (1980). *Diagnostic and statistical manual of psychiatric disorders* (3rd ed.). Washington, DC: Author.

P. 81, *place in the French and German medical texts of the nineteenth century:* Ellenberger, H. F. (1970). *Discovery of the unconscious.* New York: Basic Books.

P. 81, *As early as 1848, Antoine Despine:* Fine, C. G. (1988). The work of Antoine Despine: The first scientific report on the diagnosis and treatment of a child with multiple personality disorder. *American Journal of Clinical Hypnosis, 31,* 32–39.

P. 82, *scientific discovery through paradigmatic shifts in thinking:.* Kuhn, T. S. (1970). *The structure of scientific revolutions* (2nd ed.). Chicago: University of Chicago Press.

P. 82, *Therapeutic pluralism:* Kluft, R. P. (1988). Today's therapeutic pluralism [Editorial]. *Dissociation, 1,* 1–2.

P. 82, *professional interactions and continued attention to the patient:* Kluft, R. P. (1991). Multiple personality disorder. In A. Tasman & S. M. Goldfinger (Eds.), *American Psychiatric Press review of psychiatry* (Vol. 10, pp. 161–188). Washington, DC: American Psychiatric Press.

P. 82, *is functioning within a dissociative field:* Loewenstein, R. J. (1993). Posttraumatic and dissociative aspects of transference and countertransference in the treatment of multiple personality disorder. In R. P. Kluft & C. G. Fine (Eds.), *Clinical perspective on multiple personality disorder.* Washington, DC: American Psychiatric Press.

P. 83, *Phil Brickman's sociopsychological model:* Brickman, P., Carulli-Rabinowitz, V., Karuza, J., Coates, D., Cohn, E., & Kidder, L. (1982). Models of helping and coping. *American Psychologist, 37*(4), 368–384.

P. 87, *rational-emotional therapy:* Ellis, A. (1962). *Reason and emotion in psychotherapy.* Secaucus, NJ: Citadel.

P. 87, *Existential therapy:* Frankl, V. (1992). *Man's search for meaning: An introduction to logotherapy. (4th ed.).* Boston: Beacon Press.

P. 90, *people who subscribe to this model:* Brickman, P., et al. (1982), pp. 368–384.

P. 93, *is found in cognitive therapy:* Beck, A. T. (1976). *Cognitive therapy and the emotional disorders.* New York: International Universities Press.

P. 94, *Such a paradigm is embodied:* Fine, C. G. (1991). *Treatment stabilization and crisis prevention in the treatment of multiple personality disorder.* Philadelphia: Saunders.

4

MEDICATIONS IN THE TREATMENT OF DISSOCIATIVE IDENTITY DISORDER

Moshe S. Torem

The purpose of this chapter is to provide the reader with an overview of the various psychotropic medications that may be used in the treatment of patients with dissociative identity disorder (DID), as well as guidelines for their use and discussion of their benefits and potential side effects.

No one specific medication or combination of medications can cure patients with DID. The use of psychotropic medication, however, can be quite helpful by providing any of the following benefits:

1. Reduce the intensity of debilitating symptoms, such as anxiety, panic, depression, poor concentration, flashbacks, nightmares, insomnia, and poor impulse control

2. Improve the patient's mental state and readiness to benefit from psychotherapeutic interventions

3. Provide the benefit of psychopharmacological interventions in patients who have the comorbidity of DID along with another

Acknowledgment: Dr. Torem wishes to thank Marilyn Funk, senior secretary, for her valuable assistance in typing the manuscript for this chapter.

psychiatric disorder, such as major depression, bipolar mood disorder, panic disorder, and obsessive-compulsive disorder

I agree that the primary treatment for patients with DID is individual psychotherapy. This treatment has been supported by the writings of Richard Kluft, Bennett Braun, Philip Coons, Frank Putnam, Colin Ross, James Spira, and others. I believe, however, that a comprehensive multimodal approach is more effective. Such an approach of psychotherapy integrates psychodynamic, behavioral, existential, cognitive, and biological modalities. The relationship between patient and therapist is of paramount importance in creating an alliance whereby the patient is empowered to make choices, to report on the use or misuse of medication, and to participate in evaluation of the desired outcome, whether it be the alleviation of symptoms, the improvement in functioning with the activities of daily living, or the high aspiration for personal growth and existential/spiritual fulfillment.

MEDICATIONS AND PSYCHOTHERAPY

General Considerations

In their training, physicians traditionally are exposed to the idea that medications are an integral part of general clinical practice. Nonmedical therapists need to educate themselves on the special meaning and use of psychotropic medications and their place in the overall treatment of patients with DID.

The outcome of using any psychotropic medication is highly influenced by the relationship between the patient and the treating physician, as well as by the patient's advanced expectations regarding the desired result of drug therapy. This interplay has been scientifically recognized and has been termed the *placebo effect*. It includes expectations of outcome as perceived by the patient as well as by the physician, and not the direct influence of the active chemical ingredient in the prescribed drug. This effect is so important that it has become a standard in the efficacy evaluation of new drugs to include double-blind studies so that neither the patient nor the prescribing physician knows which drug is the placebo and which contains the active chemical ingredient being tested. The placebo effect occurs regularly when a patient uses medication. It may enhance the direct therapeutic effect of the chemical ingredient in the medication; this is the *positive placebo effect*. The placebo effect may diminish the therapeutic efficacy of the chemical ingredient in the prescribed medication; this is the *negative placebo effect*. At times, the negative placebo effect can be so powerful that it not only eliminates any potential therapeutic effect of the chemical ingredient but also produces undesirable side effects. These findings were published by Frederick Evans, Arthur Shapiro, and Arthur Shapiro and Louis Morris.

The purpose of the prescribing physician is to do anything possible to enhance the positive placebo effect and thus maximize the therapeutic efficacy of the prescribed medication. Enhancing the positive placebo effect involves the use of the patient's positive transference relationship to the physician, the patient's belief that the prescribed medication will have the desired therapeutic effect, and the patient's belief in the curative powers of the physician. On the physician's side, enhancement involves the belief in his or her own skills and knowledge in treating the patient's condition, the belief that the prescribed medication will work in a positive therapeutic manner, and the belief that the specific patient receiving the prescribed medication will benefit from the medication and that there is hope for healing, therapeutic progress, or at least symptom relief.

I believe that any time patients swallow the prescribed medication, they symbolically incorporate and internalize their image of the physician, as well as the nature of their relationship, including what took place in the previous session. This internalization when the medication is swallowed is extremely important to remember because the very relationship with the prescribing clinician is an essential part of practicing effective pharmacotherapy. Well-trained, seasoned psychiatrists know this and, therefore, spend at least twenty to thirty minutes and, at times, up to an hour with a patient even when the patient's primary therapist is a nonphysician who does not prescribe medication. Moreover, I believe that the nonphysician therapist can enhance the efficacy of the prescribed medication by positively endorsing the prescribing psychiatrist's therapeutic knowledge, experience, and skills in the field of dissociative disorders and previous successes with other patients. Additional members of the team may influence this process in hospital and clinical settings. These team members include the nurse and the nursing assistant, as well as the occupational therapist, art therapist, social workers, and pharmacist, who may endorse the efficacy and positive therapeutic expectations of the prescribed medication and the positive reputation of the prescribing physician or may criticize and question the wisdom of using the prescribed medication.

All of the above-mentioned factors may explain the extreme variability of outcome results in using psychotropic and other medications in patients with DID as well as other psychiatric disorders.

Specific Considerations

Patients with DID deserve specific considerations in using psychopharmacotherapy. The following points are important to remember:

1.   Patients with dissociative disorders usually have a history of trauma and may have a tendency to express their unresolved issues around the trauma by repeating and reenacting the traumatic issues in their relationship with the physician. This transference in itself may involve an expectation that the physician only look and behave in a nice way but, in fact, he or she may end up hurting the patient just as the patient was hurt in the past. David Spiegel called this phenomenon the *traumatic transference*, originating from the double-binds to which the patient was

exposed when growing up. The physician must be aware of such psychodynamics and their potential to sabotage and undermine any therapeutic intervention, including pharmacotherapy.

2.   Patients with dissociative disorders frequently dissociate during the session and may have amnesia to certain parts of or the whole session. This dissociation may interfere with the patient's compliance with and understanding of the proper use of the prescribed medication, the purpose for using it, and the potential side effects.

3.   It is important to recognize that alter personality states, even though hidden, obscure, and not directly involved in the therapeutic dialogue with the physician, may still sabotage and undermine the therapeutic outcome of the prescribed medication. This subversion may take place in a variety of ways, such as hiding the medication from the patient, enhancing undesirable side effects, taking higher than prescribed doses, skipping certain doses, or mixing alcohol when it is forbidden.

4.   Patients with DID may at times be highly suggestible and could use what Martin Orne termed *trance logic*. In this state of mind, the patient's thinking is rather concrete, incorporating suggestion in a literal form.

5.   In working with patients who have DID, the prescribing physician may face the phenomenon of one personality state being depressed, anxious, or even psychotic and requiring pharmacotherapy with a specific medication. Other personality states, however, may be in a relaxed and neutral state of mind and not need any medication. The dilemma for the physician is choosing the most appropriate and efficacious therapeutic intervention. Should the medication be prescribed for the patient as a whole only when the specific symptoms are shared by all the personalities, or is it legitimate to prescribe medication only when the dominant personality states suffer from certain dysfunctional symptoms?

6.   The issue of comorbidity deserves special attention. Many patients with DID may also suffer from other primary psychiatric disorders, such as major affective disorders, anxiety disorders,

Attention-deficit Hyperactivity Disorder, alcoholism, and Obsessive-Compulsive Disorder, as well as a variety of personality disorders, such as Borderline Personality Disorder, Narcissistic Personality Disorder, Histrionic Personality Disorder, Dependent Personality Disorder, and Avoidant Personality Disorder. I believe it is legitimate to use pharmacotherapy for a DID patient who has comorbidity with another psychiatric disorder. The medication is then prescribed for target symptoms originating from a secondary psychiatric diagnosis.

7.   The phenomenon of dissociation in itself is often associated with a variety of physical signs and symptoms, such as changes in heart rate, increased perspiration, rapid breathing, increase or decrease in blood pressure, blurred vision, numbness, intestinal hyperperistalsis, constipation, diarrhea, urinary frequency, urinary urgency, dry mouth, headaches, and dizziness. All of these may be difficult to differentiate from potential side effects of a given medication or a coexisting medical illness.

8.   A variety of medications frequently used in the general practice of medicine may act as triggers for dissociative episodes. For example, the over-the-counter decongestant Sudafed; the antihypertensive nifedipine; anti-inflammatory agents, such as ibuprofen; cortical steroids, such as dexamethasone; antibiotics, such as norfloxacin and ofloxacin; and antiparkinsonian agents, such as benztropine (Cogentin) are frequently associated with rapid heartbeat and shortness of breath, which may act as dissociation triggers.

Efficacy of the Medications

Richard J. Loewenstein provides some basic guidelines for the use of rational psychopharmacology in the treatment of patients with DID. He mentions several ground rules. The first ground rule is that the use of medications for DID patients must be understood in the context of the total treatment of DID. He points out the importance of establishing clear reasoning for the expected benefits of a medication and of having clinical criteria for assessing whether the medication is beneficial. The second ground rule emphasizes that most problems in the treatment of DID patients are not solvable with medication and have to be addressed in a broader context of psychotherapeutic intervention in a trustful therapist-patient relationship. Loewenstein's third ground rule has two parts: (1) one must attempt to treat symptoms in DID that are valid psychopharmacological targets and (2) one must target symptoms that are present across the whole person, and not those localized in separate alter personalities.

Richard Kluft points out that the presence of valid medication-responsive symptoms are very important before the decision to use medication is enacted. Nonpharmacological interventions have to be used for the same symptoms to enhance the potential positive response from the psychotropic medications. The physician prescribing the medication should have a trustful relationship with the patient and understand the patient as a whole, including the history of previous experiences with psychotropic medications. Some clinical trials have reported partial success in individual cases with dissociative disorders using a variety of medications, such as antidepressants, benzodiazepines, beta-blockers, clonidine, or low-dose neuroleptics.

Loewenstein and associates reported on a systematic study of pharmacotherapy for patients with DID. The authors reported moderate improvement with the use of clonazepam (Klonopin) in some PTSD symptoms and five DID patients in an open-label nonblind clinical trial. The patients showed sustained improvement over six to twelve months in the continuity of sleep, severity of nightmares, and flashbacks. The patients maintained a stable clonazepam dose, and scant abuse was noted.

Braun reported on the efficacy of clonidine and high doses of propranolol for the treatment of hyperarousal, anxiety, poor impulse control, disorganized thinking, and rapid switching in patients with dissociative disorders.

PHARMACOTHERAPY FOR
SPECIFIC TARGET SYMPTOMS

Even though I believe in treating the person as a whole, physicians ought to agree with their patient on specific goals for the medications and choose specific target symptoms to alleviate or reduce in intensity.

Anxiety and Anxiolytic Medications

Anxiety is a very common symptom in patients with dissociative disorders. It may be expressed with a sense of subjectiveness, restlessness, the feeling that some disastrous event may take place, loss of control, agitation, and a variety of physical symptoms, such as shortness of breath, blurred vision, urinary frequency, urinary urgency, diarrhea, tension headaches, poor concentration, dyspepsia, and parasthesias (peripheral numbness).

The following groups of medications can be used for the control of anxiety: benzodiazepines, sedative antihistamines, buspirones, beta-blockers, and small doses of certain neuroleptics.

Benzodiazepines. Benzodiazepines are relatively safe anxiolytic medications. They can be classified into three major subgroups: short acting, intermediate, and long acting (see Table 4.1). The two drugs in the short-acting subgroup—midazolam (Versed) and triazolam (Halcion)—are not recommended for use with dissociative disorders. From the intermediate subgroup, the most often used have been lorazepam (Ativan) and alprazolam (Xanax). From the long-acting subgroup, the most commonly used have been clonazepam (Klonopin), diazepam (Valium), chlordiazepoxide (Librium), and clorazepate (Tranxene). Generally speaking, all benzodiazepines are well absorbed from the intestine after oral administration. No significant correlation has

Table 4.1
Benzodiazepines: Comparative Equivalent Doses

Alprazolam (Xanax)	0.5 mg
Chlordiazepoxide (Librium)	25.0 mg
Clonazepam (Klonopin)	0.25 mg
Diazepam (Valium)	5.0 mg
Lorazepam (Ativan)	1.0 mg

been found between plasma concentration and clinical effects, so plasma level monitoring has no clinical benefit. The duration of action is determined mainly by the distribution, and not by the rate of elimination. The major metabolism of these medications is done in the liver through microsomal oxidation and demethylation. Patients with liver disease may have trouble metabolizing these medications.

Potential side effects: Relatively, these medications are very well tolerated and have few side effects, which disappear with dose adjustment. The most common side effects are too much sedation, fatigue, drowsiness, nystagmus, anterograde amnesia (most likely with high-potency agents), and confusion and disorientation (mostly in elderly patients). In some patients. paradoxical agitation may take place in the form of insomnia, hallucinations, nightmares, and rage reactions. All of these are likely to occur in patients with a previous history of aggressive behavior.

Withdrawal: Abrupt discontinuation of a benzodiazepine may produce the following symptoms:

1. *Withdrawal* occurs in one or two days in the short-acting subgroup, three or four days in the intermediate subgroup, and five to ten days in the long-acting subgroup. Common symptoms include insomnia, agitation, anxiety, changes in perception, dysphoria, gastrointestinal distress, and even such severe reactions as hallucinations, seizures, and coma.

2. *Rebound* occurs hours to days after medication withdrawal. Symptoms of anxiety may be similar or more intense than those originally reported by the patient.

3. *Relapse* symptoms may occur weeks to months after the medication is discontinued, and the symptoms are similar to the original anxiety present prior to the use of the medication.

Withdrawal protocol: To withdraw patients from benzodiazepines, use an equivalent dose of diazepam (Valium) as a substitute (for equivalent doses, see Table 4.2) according to the following protocol:

- Reduce diazepam by ten milligrams daily until a total daily dose of twenty milligrams is reached.
- Then continue to reduce by five milligrams daily to an end point of total abstinence.
- Consider propranolol (Inderal) to aid in the withdrawal process.
- Alprazolam (Xanax) requires a special protocol that includes the following steps:

Reduce alprazolam by 0.5 milligrams per week; quicker withdrawal may result in delirium and seizures.

Carbamazepine in therapeutic doses may aid in the withdrawal process.

An alternative to the above method is to substitute alprazolam (Xanax) with an equal dose of clonazepam (Klonopin) in divided doses and then decrease the clonazepam by one milligram per day.

Special precautions for all benzodiazepines:

Do not use on patients with sleep apnea disorders.

Administer with extreme caution to patients who perform hazardous tasks requiring mental alertness and physical coordination.

Table 4.2
Benzodiazepine Trade Names and Dose Ranges

Generic Name	Trade Name	Usual Adult Dose Range (mg/day)	Adult Single Dose Range (mg)
Alprazolam	Xanax	0.5–6	0.25–1
Chlordiazepoxide[1]	Librium	15–100	5–25
Clonazepam	Klonopin	1.5–10	0.5–2
Clorazepate	Tranxene	7.5–60	3.25–22.5
Diazepam[1]	Valium	2–60	2–10
Flurazepam[2]	Dalmane	15–30	15–30
Halazepam	Paxipam	60–160	20–40
Lorazepam	Ativan	2–6	0.5–2
Oxazepam	Serax	30–120	10–30
Prazepam	Centrax	20–60	10–20
Quazepam[2]	Doral	7.5–30	7.5–30
Temazepam[2]	Restoril	15–30	15–30
Triazolam[2]	Halcion	0.125–0.5	0.125–0.5

[1]Also available for parenteral administration. Diazepam is available for IV administration in 5 mg/ml syringes. Lorazepam is available for IM administration in 2 and 4 mg/ml syringes.

[2]FDA-approved for use as a hypnotic.

Benzodiazepines lower the tolerance to alcohol, and high doses may produce mental confusion similar to alcohol intoxication.

Physical and psychological dependence, tolerance, and withdrawal symptoms may be produced by all benzodiazepines. These are correlated with the dose and the duration of use.

Abrupt withdrawal following prolonged use may produce seizures.

Toxicity:

Overdose with these medications is rarely fatal if taken alone. However, they may be lethal when the overdose is taken in combination with other drugs, such as alcohol and barbiturates. Symptoms of overdose may include hypotension, depressed breathing, and coma.

Pregnant women must be cautioned that benzodiazepines freely cross the placenta and may accumulate in the fetus.

Data regarding teratogenicity are inconclusive.

Special instructions to patients:

Consumption of caffeinated beverages may counteract the therapeutic effects of the prescribed medication.

The dose should be maintained as prescribed. Do not increase the dose without consulting your physician.

Driving a car or operating other machinery should be avoided until a response to the drug is determined.

Avoid the use of alcohol; it may enhance the effects of these medications, as well as alcohol side effects.

Avoid abrupt stopping of these medications.

Drug interactions:

Caffeine may counteract sedation and increase insomnia.

Cimetidine may decrease the metabolism of benzodiazepines.

Antihistamines may increase central nervous system (CNS) depression, as well as cause coma and respiratory depression in high doses.

Barbiturates may cause the same drug interactions as antihistamines.

Alcohol may cause the same drug interactions as antihistamines.

Estrogens (including oral contraceptives) may decrease the metabolism of a benzodiazepine and thus increase its plasma level, as well as its duration in the body.

Propoxyphene (Darvon) may decrease the metabolism of benzodiazepines.

Comparing various benzodiazepines:

1. Alprazolam (Xanax)

   It reaches a peak plasma level within one to two hours of administration.

   Half-life elimination is reached between nine and twenty hours.

   It is rapidly and completely absorbed by most patients. Increasing the speed of absorption can be achieved by using it sublingually.

   It is effective in patients with panic attacks and as an adjunct in the treatment of depression.

   Dosing: The starting dose is 0.25 milligrams three times a day (t.i.d.); the usual daily dose is 1 to 5 milligrams per day; the maximum daily dose is 10 milligrams per day.

   Note special precautions on withdrawal.

   It decreases Stages I, IV, and REM sleep and increases Stage II sleep.

2. Chlordiazepoxide (Librium)

   25 milligrams of Librium is equivalent to 0.5 milligrams of Xanax.

   Peak plasma level is reached through oral administration in one to four hours.

   Elimination half-life is four to twenty-nine hours of the parent drug and twenty-eight to one hundred hours of the active metabolites.

   Oxazepam (Serax) is one of Librium's active metabolites.

   Avoid using by intramuscular (IM) injections because the absorption is erratic and unpredictable.

   Most commonly used in patients with alcohol withdrawal in preventing delirium tremens (DTs).

Ampacids decrease the absorption rate from the gastrointestinal tract.

Dosing: The starting dose is 5 milligrams t.i.d.; the usual daily dose is 15 to 100 milligrams per day; and the maximum daily dose is 300 milligrams per day.

3. Clonazepam (Klonopin)

0.25 milligrams of Klonopin is equivalent to 0.5 milligrams of Xanax or 25 milligrams of Librium.

Clonazepam is quickly and completely absorbed through the intestine and reaches a peak plasma level within one to four hours. However, it has a slow onset of activity.

Elimination half-life is nineteen to sixty hours.

It has no active metabolites.

It has strong anticonvulsant effects.

It is commonly used for the treatment and prevention of panic attack and is also effective in patients in a manic episode.

It is effective in controlling aggressive behavior and the symptoms of akathisia.

4. Diazepam (Valium)

5 milligrams of Valium is equivalent to 0.5 milligrams of Xanax or 0.25 milligrams of Klonopin or 25 milligrams of Librium.

It has a rapid onset of action and reaches peak plasma level within one or two hours of oral administration.

Elimination half-life is fourteen to seventy hours for the parent drug and thirty to two hundred hours for its metabolites.

It is metabolized in the liver and has active metabolites, such as oxazepam (Serax) and temazepam (Restoril).

Males have a shorter half-life and higher clearance rate than females.

Chronic use causes accumulation in fat tissue.

Heavy smoking is associated with higher clearance.

It is especially effective as an anticonvulsant, for alcohol withdrawal, akathisia, and as a muscle relaxant.

It decreases Stages I, IV, and REM sleep.

5. Lorazepam (Ativan)

1 milligram of Ativan is equivalent to 0.25 milligrams of Klonopin or 0.5 milligrams of Xanax or 5 milligrams of Valium or 25 milligrams of Librium.

It is well absorbed with oral administration, including sublingually.

Peak plasma level is reached within two hours by oral administration, within forty-five to seventy-five minutes by intramuscular (IM) injection, within five to ten minutes intravenous (IV) injection, and within sixty minutes with sublingual administration.

Elimination half-life is eight to twenty-four hours.

It has no active metabolites.

The action of onset is slow.

Dosing: The starting dose is 0.5 milligrams two times a day (b.i.d.); the usual daily dose is 2 to 6 milligrams per day; the maximum daily dose is 10 to 20 milligrams per day.

It is a good muscle relaxant.

It is effective for akathisia and acute dystonia.

It causes significant anterograde amnesia, which does not correlate directly with the sedative potency.

Withdrawal symptoms appear sooner than with long-acting drugs.

It decreases Stage I and REM sleep and increases Stage II sleep.

Tip: Alprazolam (Xanax) and clonazepam (Klonopin) are relatively more potent when dealing with panic and somewhat less potent with dealing with generalized anxiety.

Sedative Antihistamines. In this group, I mention two examples: hydroxyzine (Atarax, Vistaril) and diphenhydramine (Benadryl).

These medications do have some anti-anxiety effects but no muscle-relaxing features. There is no potential abuse or habituation. They *do* have some antiemetic features.

1.   *Hydroxyzine (Atarax, Vistaril)* has few side effects. Its sedation, when used for longer periods of time, loses its effect because patients develop tolerance. The starting dosage is ten milligrams t.i.d.; the usual dose is twenty-five milligrams; and the maximum dose is four hundred milligrams per day. It is considered a very safe medication.

2.   *Diphenhydramine (Benadryl)* is available over the counter in the United States in a variety of cough syrups and decongestant agents. However, it depresses REM sleep in doses of fifty milligrams and higher. The starting dosage is twenty-five milligrams b.i.d.; the usual daily dosage is twenty-five milligrams four times a day (q.i.d.) or every four to six hours as circumstances may require (p.r.n.); and the maximum dose is five hundred milligrams per day. Side effects and toxicity include drowsiness and dry mouth, and possible urinary retention in high doses. This medication should be avoided in patients with asthma, glaucoma, emphysema, chronic pulmonary disease, and shortness of breath. Alcohol should be avoided because it will increase the drowsiness.

Buspirone (BuSpar). Buspirone is a relatively new selective anxiolytic medication that is not a benzodiazepine. It has no anticonvulsant features, is not a muscle relaxant, and does not develop any tolerance or habituation. It is believed to work on the central nervous system by decreasing the noradrenergic and dopaminergic activity. Long administration of buspirone may cause a down-regulation of the serotonin Type II receptors. This medication is specifically effective when sedation is desired without causing any psychomotor impairment in functioning. Patients with a history of alcohol and substance abuse benefit from buspirone, rather than from benzodiazepines. It has also been used for the augmentation of antidepressant medications, and some patients claim that when taken in doses of forty to eighty milligrams per day, it also has its own antidepressant effect. Buspirone may also potentiate anti-obsessional effects of fluoxetine, sertraline, or paroxetine.

The usual starting dosage is five milligrams b.i.d; the usual daily dosage is ten milligrams t.i.d; the maximum dose is sixty to eighty milligrams per day.

Clinical efficacy begins within one or two weeks of administering the usual dose of thirty milligrams per day. This medication is not useful on an as-needed basis. The maximum effect is usually seen in three or four weeks from the onset of administration. Food may reduce the rate of absorption. Peak plasma takes place between 0.7 and 1.5 hours. Elimination half-life is one to eleven hours. The drug has one active metabolite.

Potential side effects and toxicity: The following side effects have been reported with buspirone: headaches, dizziness, light-headedness, fatigue, numbness, and upset stomach. Withdrawal effects have not been reported. There is no cross-tolerance with benzodiazepines, barbiturates, or alcohol.

Buspirone is a relatively safe medication, and no deaths have been reported in people who overdose on it. Toxic effects in cases of overdose include dizziness, nausea, and vomiting. Safe use during pregnancy has not been determined. Both buspirone and its metabolites, however, are excreted in the mother's milk.

Drug interactions:

1. *Haloperidol (Haldol):* This drug may be inhibited in its metabolism when given in combination with buspirone, and thus plasma levels may stay higher for a longer time.

2. *Antidepressants:* Fluoxetine and monoamine oxidase inhibitors (MAOIs), when used in combination with buspirone, may cause high blood pressure and also potentiate anti-obsessional effects.

3. *Diazepam (Valium):* Buspirone may cause an increase in the serum level of Valium.

Tip: The anti-anxiety effects of buspirone are gradual; signs of improvement may begin within seven to ten days after starting the medication and reach a peak of improvement in two to four weeks.

Beta-Blockers. Beta-blockers, such as propranolol (Inderal), are most effective in the treatment of the autonomic symptoms of anxiety. This medication blocks the beta-adrenergic receptor sites and thus prevents the natural neurotransmitters of norepinephrine and epinephrine from taking effect. Since the 1960s, these medications have been used for the treatment of anticipatory anxiety, such as performance during tests, public speeches, interviews, and in the theater. The starting dosage of Inderal is 10 milligrams t.i.d.; the usual daily dosage is 20 milligrams t.i.d.; the maximum dose is 240 milligrams per day. Braun reported on the experimental use of higher doses of Inderal in patients with DID to reduce rapid switching. The control of anxiety, however, is not a primary indication and does not appear in the *Physicians Desk Reference (PDR)*, nor is it specifically approved by the Food and Drug Administration (FDA) for this specific purpose.

Bradycardia, hypotension, light-headedness, dizziness, and occasionally fainting are side effects. The drug may also cause mental depression.

Neuroleptics. Some patients with severe anxiety (to the point of agitation) respond better to small doses of sedative neuroleptics, such as perphenazine (Trilafon), two milligrams t.i.d. up to four milligrams q.i.d.; thioridazine (Mellaril), ten milligrams t.i.d. up to twenty-five milligrams q.i.d.; and chlorprothixene (Taractan), ten milligrams t.i.d. up to fifty milligrams q.i.d. Some patients with very severe agitation respond to an IM injection of droperidol (Inapsine) in the form of 2.5 to 5.0 milligrams, producing sedation and sleep lasting between one and three hours, following which the patient wakes up relaxed, with no agitation.

Depression

Depression associated with feelings of helplessness, hopelessness, futurelessness, and anhedonia is a common symptom in patients with dissociative disorder. Some patients may have the comorbidity of a major depression, a dysthymic disorder, or bipolar disorder. These should be treated accordingly as indicated in the standards of practice for mood disorders.

Antidepressant medications are currently available in the following groups: tricyclic antidepressants, monoamine oxidase inhibitors (MAOIs), selective serotonin reuptake inhibitors (SSRIs), and miscellaneous antidepressants.

In selecting an antidepressant medication, I use the following guidelines:

Safety. Safety is of paramount importance to emphasize the fact that some patients with dissociative disorders can be very impulsive and act out on an instant urge in a self-destructive way. Providing the patient an antidepressant medication that potentially can be overdosed must be considered in terms of the medication's safety profile. The wider the gap between the therapeutic dose and the toxic lethal dose, the safer the medication. In that sense, the tricyclic antidepressants and the MAOIs are the least safe; the new generation of antidepressants, such as the SSRIs, are the safest; and such medications as trazodone (Desyrel) and bupropion (Wellbutrin) are significantly safer than the tricyclics, but not as safe as the SSRIs.

Symptom Profile. Some patients who exhibit depression may slow down and withdraw emotionally and physically, have increased sleep (hypersomnia), increased eating (hyperphagia), generalized fatigue, and low energy level. This subgroup of patients responds well to antidepressant medications that not only alleviate the patients' moods but also have an energizing effect by suppressing the appetite and decreasing the patients' need to sleep. Medications in that group are fluoxetine (Prozac), paroxetine (Paxil), bupropion (Wellbutrin), protriptyline (Vivactil), and to a lesser extent, desipramine (Norpramin) and tranylcypromine (Parnate). Another subgroup of patients experiences depression association with psychomotor agitation and restlessness. Such patients also experience insomnia, anxiety, poor appetite at times associated with weight loss, and a feeling of aimless energy. These patients respond better to antidepressants that have a sedating effect to improve their sleep and reduce their level of anxiety and agitation. The medications in this group are trazodone (Desyrel), amitriptyline (Elavil), doxepin (Sinequan), trimipramine (Surmontil), and maprotiline (Ludiomil).

Side Effect Profile.

1. *Anticholinergic:* Some patients are particularly sensitive to anticholinergic side effects, such as dry mouth, blurred vision, constipation, sweating, and delayed micturition (urinary retention). This sensitivity may be related to the patient's occupation or personal sensitivities and preferences. Antidepressants highly potent in their anticholinergic side effects are amitriptyline (Elavil), clomipramine (Anafranil), doxepin (Sinequan), maprotiline (Ludiomil), and amoxapine (Asendin). Antidepressants with the fewest anticholinergic side effects are desipramine (Norpramin), nortriptyline (Pamelor), trazodone (Desyrel), fluoxetine (Prozac), sertraline (Zoloft), and paroxetine (Paxil).

2. *Cardiovascular side effects:* Orthostatic hypotension, dizziness, tachycardia, and cardiac arrhythmias are not uncommon with antidepressant medications. Antidepressants with the fewest cardiovascular side effects are fluoxetine (Prozac), sertraline (Zoloft), paroxetine (Paxil), and nortriptyline (Pamelor). Antidepressants with a highest frequency for cardiovascular side effects are amitriptyline (Elavil), clomipramine (Anafranil), and imipramine (Tofranil).

3. *Extrapyramidal side effects:* Amoxapine (Asendin) is the antidepressant most commonly related to these specific side effects because of a metabolite resembling the neuroleptic drugs.

4. *Epileptic seizures:* These have been reported with maprotiline (Ludiomil) in doses above 225 milligrams per day and in bupropion (Wellbutrin) in doses of 450 milligrams per day and higher.

5. *Weight gain:* The issue of weight gain is extremely sensitive in U.S. culture. Many patients will not take medications associated with weight gain. Antidepressants associated with a weight gain of ten pounds or more are amitriptyline (Elavil), doxepin (Sinequan), and maprotiline (Ludiomil). Those associated with the least weight gain are fluoxetine (Prozac), sertraline (Zoloft), paroxetine (Paxil), bupropion (Wellbutrin), protriptyline (Vivactil), and tranylcypromine (Parnate).

Concomitant Medical Conditions. Some patients suffer from narrow angle glaucoma, which is relatively well managed with eyedrops. Such patients should not be given antidepressants that have anticholinergic effects; these medications may exacerbate a state of acute glaucoma, requiring emergency intervention. Other patients may have benign hypertrophy of the prostate gland, which makes them more sensitive to developing urinary retention with medications that have anticholinergic effects.

Previous Experience with a Certain Antidepressant. Patients who have had a positive previous experience with a certain antidepressant prefer to use it again if faced with the choice of taking one. Prescribing clinicians should be sensitive to this issue and inquire about the patient's previous experience with certain antidepressants. A simple guideline is, What worked before has a good chance of working again. The opposite of that is also true. The patient's negative experience with a certain antidepressant will diminish the chances of its efficacy even if everything else is compatible.

Previous Familiarity with a Certain Antidepressant. Some patients are familiar with positive efficacy of certain antidepressants taken by a family member or friend or from their own reading about it. Such information should be elicited from the patient because it potentiates the positive placebo effect and improves the chances of a positive therapeutic outcome, provided the rest is compatible and there is no contraindication.

Timing. Many antidepressants can be given in one dose that will be sufficient for twenty-four hours. Most patients with insomnia will benefit from a once-a-day dose given at bedtime, thus promoting sleep, in addition to the antidepressant effects. This timing will also increase the patients' compliance in using the medication.

Patient Choice. Some patients with dissociative disorders detest being controlled and dictated to by medical professionals or by any other authority figures. It is extremely important to incorporate the patient's need for empowerment and mastery into the prescribing skills of the physician. I ask my patients to choose their own schedule of medication, whether it's before meals or after meals, in a once-a-day dose or in divided doses, provided everything else is equal. This choice increases a patient's sense of partnership in the decision process and improves the chances for cooperation in taking the prescribed medication.

Age. Elderly patients are more sensitive to hypotensive side effects of any medications, including antidepressants. Therefore, they should be given antidepressants with the fewest hypotensive side effects and be educated about ways of preventing orthostatic hypotension.

Cost. An antidepressant's high cost beyond the patient's economic affordability will reduce the chances of the patient's cooperation in taking the prescribed medication. Physicians should be sensitive to the issue of cost and educate themselves about the financial impact a specific medication may have on the patient's budget. This issue should be included in the discussion with the patient prior to choosing a specific antidepressant.

For information on specific daily doses of antidepressant medications, see Table 4.3.

Flashbacks and Poor Impulse Control

Flashbacks and poor impulse control are quite common in patients with dissociative disorders. The following medications provide some relief from the intensity of these symptoms: per-

Table 4.3
Antidepressants and Various Doses Per Day

Generic Name	Trade Name	Starting Dose (mg per day)	Usual Dose (mg per day)	Maximum Dose (mg per day)
Nortriptyline	Pamelor	10–25	75–100	150
Amitriptyline	Elavil	10–75	100–150	300
Imipramine	Tofranil	10–50	100–150	300
Protriptyline	Vivactil	5–10	30–45	60
Trimipramine	Surmontil	25–50	100–150	300
Doxepin	Sinequan	25–50	100–150	300
Amoxapine	Asendin	50–100	100–200	600
Maprotiline	Ludiomil	25–50	75–125	225
Fluoxetine	Prozac	10–20	20–40	80
Sertraline	Zoloft	25–50	100–150	200
Paroxetine	Paxil	10–20	20–40	50
Trazodone	Desyrel	25–75	100–250	600
Bupropion	Wellbutrin	75–100	150–300	450
Tranylcypromine	Parnate	10–20	20–40	60

phenazine (Trilafon), chlorprothixene (Taractan), haloperidol (Haldol), and droperidol (Inapsine). It's important that such medications be used with great caution and in low doses. Once the symptom has been significantly reduced, every attempt should be made to decrease and discontinue the specific neuroleptic medication used. Droperidol (Inapsine) is available only by injection for IM or IV use. In dissociative patients, it should be used only as an IM injection in extreme states of high agitation with flashbacks, confusion, and destructive acting out. Inapsine has been found very helpful in doses of 2.5 to 5 milligrams every four to six hours. The therapeutic response takes place within fifteen to thirty minutes. Many patients fall asleep and then wake up in a different state of mind more relaxed, mature, and appropriate. For specific daily doses of the above medications, see Table 4.4.

Table 4.4
Neuroleptics and Various Doses Per Day

Generic Name	Brand Name	Starting Dosage	Commonly Used Dose	Maximum Dose
Perphenazine	Trilafon	2 mg t.i.d.	4 mg/d	24–30 mg/day
Chlorprothixene	Taractan	10 mg t.i.d.	25 mg q.i.d.	300 mg/day
Haloperidol	Haldol	1 mg t.i.d.	3 mg q.i.d.	20 mg/day
Droperidol	Inapsine	1.25 mg q.i.d.	2.5 mg q.i.d.	15 mg/day

Rapid Switching

Rapid switching is not easy to control. Braun reported on the use of Inderal, as well as Klonopin, with limited success in reducing rapid switching. My experience involves the use of Inderal in doses of 60 to 240 milligrams per day, as well as Klonopin in doses of 6 to 16 milligrams per day. The success rate improves with the use of hypnotherapeutic centering techniques.

Two patients had a moderate response to the use of the antiepileptic and mood stabilizer carbamazepine (Tegretol) in doses of one hundred milligrams t.i.d. up to two hundred milligrams q.i.d. Therapeutic serum levels for carbamazepine should be in the range of four to twelve milligrams per liter.

Sleep Apnea and Nocturnal Myoclonus

In recent years, I have experienced more than a dozen patients with DID who have been in long-term psychotherapy, have worked through many of their unresolved issues, and in the face of various medications, have continued to suffer from insomnia, as well as daytime symptoms of dissociation, amnesia, confusion, flashbacks, repetitive headaches, and depression. A thorough history, including information from the patient's spouse, as well as other relatives, revealed nighttime snoring, as well as leg jerking. This information resulted in a special referral to the Sleep Lab for a nighttime polysomnogram, which revealed the diagnosis of obstructive sleep apnea, at times in combination with nocturnal myoclonus. The obstructive sleep apnea is apparently not uncommon in DID and PTSD patients. It interferes with the completion of healthy sleep cycles, including REM sleep, and it reduces oxygen saturation and thus causes the brain to suffer from brief periods of hypoxia. This sleep pattern results in the patient's having chronic sleep deprivation, as well as daytime symptoms, including daytime sleepiness and poor concentration. Effective therapy for these cases involves treatment with a C-PAP (continuous pressurized air perfusion) machine or BI-PAP (bi-level pressurized air perfusion) machine. In addition, patients diagnosed with nocturnal myoclonus were successfully treated with small amounts of Klonopin (up to three milligrams at bedtime) or small amounts of Sinemet in doses ranging from one tablet of 25/100 at bedtime to 50/200 at bedtime. Improvement in the patient's quality of sleep at night resulted in a dramatic improvement in the patient's daytime symptoms, including many of the dissociative symptoms mentioned above, as well as in the patient's level of daytime functioning.

This information suggests that dissociative symptoms in patients with DID, as well as other aggravating symptoms, may be of multiple origins and may require a multimodal approach for successful treatment. It also points out that many DID patients may have comorbidity with other psychiatric disorders, as well as medical disorders.

NEW MEDICATIONS

The following medications have recently been released by the FDA for use with a variety of psychiatric conditions and may also be helpful in patients with DID: fluvoxamine (Luvox), naltrexone (ReVia), nefazodone (Serzone), risperidone (Risperdal), and venlafaxine (Effexor). Table 4.5 provides basic information regarding the drugs' primary indication, postulated mechanism of action, and various appropriate doses.

Table 4.5
New Drugs: Names and Dose Ranges

Generic (Trade) Name	Indication	Average Adult Dose Range (mg)	Adult Single Dose Range (mg/day)
Fluvoxamine (Luvox)	OCD	100–200	50–300
Naltrexone (ReVia)	Alcoholism/ Narcotic Dependence	50–100	25–150
Nefazodone (Serzone)	Antidepressant	200–300	200–600
Risperidone (Risperdal)	Antipsychotic	2–4	2–8
Venlafaxine (Effexor)	Antidepressant	100–125	75–225

Fluvoxamine (Luvox)

Fluvoxamine (Luvox) is an SSRI. In that sense, it is quite similar to others in the SSRI group, such as fluoxetine (Prozac), sertraline (Zoloft), and paroxetine (Paxil). Even though the medication is particularly indicated in the treatment of patients with obsessive-compulsive disorder, it also has antidepressant features similar to the other SSRIs. So far, I have limited experience in the use of this medication but have found it helpful in DID patients who have ruminating thoughts and various obsessions and compulsions, as well as in cases of DID patients who have a concurrent diagnosis of obsessive-compulsive disorder. It may be important to note here, however, that fluvoxamine inhibits the activity of cytochrome P450 isozymes 1A2, 2C9, and 3A4, thereby slowing the metabolism of other medications taken concurrently by the patient. It delays the clearance and increases serum concentration of the following drugs: alprazolam (Xanax), propranolol (Inderal), terfenadine (Seldane), and astemizole (Hismanal), and some of the tricyclic antidepressants. DID patients who concurrently suffer from drug addiction and are receiving methadone treatment may have increased plasma concentrations of methadone if they concurrently take fluvoxamine.

In addition, fluvoxamine and MAOIs should not be taken within two or three weeks of each other.

Naltrexone (ReVia)

Naltrexone (ReVia, which means "to live again") has been found helpful in DID patients who suffer from concurrent diagnoses of alcohol dependence and opiate addiction. This medication is an opiate antagonist, and animal studies have shown that opiate antagonists will decrease the animal drinking of alcohol and craving for opiate-type drugs. In 1990, Braun reported on some success in the use of naltrexone (ReVia) in the treatment of DID patients. Braun believes that some of the DID patient's symptoms can be understood in terms of the brain's addiction to its own internal opiates (the beta endorphins). Beta endorphins may be stimulated for increase in higher amounts at the time of repeated abreactions and repeated self-injurious behavior, which, according to Braun, are analogous to a drug addict dependent on opiates. Braun reported on a trial of naltrexone (ReVia) for the control of such self-injurious behaviors as self-mutilation, bingeing and purging, compulsive sexuality, and compulsive exercising. However, this was a nonblind trial. So far, I have had no experience in my practice with the use of this medication. Its place in efficacy in the treatment of DID patients remains to be seen by further research.

Nefazodone (Serzone)

Nefazodone (Serzone) is chemically related to trazodone (Desyrel). It is an antidepressant and works by blocking the reuptake of norepinephrine (NE), serotonin, and dopamine (DA). One effect of nefazodone is somnolence, so it is best taken at bedtime and perhaps as an effective drug in the treatment of insomnia because it does not interfere with the patient's REM sleep. My experience in using this new drug with DID patients is limited; however, it may have a special place in the treatment of DID patients who suffer from depression associated with severe insomnia because this drug does not reduce the patient's REM sleep and, in fact, according to a study by Ann Sharpley and her colleagues, may increase REM sleep.

Risperidone (Risperdal)

Risperidone (Risperdal) is a new neuroleptic classified as an atypical antipsychotic medication and is claimed not to have any extrapyramidal or tardive dyskinesia side effects. Apparently, its mechanism of action may be mediated by blocking the receptors for dopamine Type 2 (D) and serotonin Type 2 receptors. It also blocks alpha 1 and alpha 2 adrenergic receptors, as well as histaminergic receptors. My clinical experience with Risperdal in DID patients has been limited to several severe cases dominated by symptoms of rapid switching, severe flashbacks, and other PTSD intrusive symptoms, such as severe anxiety, panic, and agitation. A dosage of 0.5 to 3.0 milligrams b.i.d. was found to be highly effective in diminishing flashbacks, nightmares, agitation, and rapid switching. I have heard similar reports on the success of this medication for DID patients with the above symptoms from other clinicians, such as Dr. James Chu, from McLean Hospital in Boston, and Dr. Richard Wolin, from Buffalo, NY.

Further research and clinical trials need to be done to better assess the efficacy and usefulness of this medication with DID patients.

Venlafaxine (Effexor)

Venlafaxine (Effexor) is a new antidepressant whose mechanism of action is believed to be the inhibition of reuptake of serotonin and norepinephrine. It is also a weak inhibitor of dopamine reuptake. Chemically, it is unrelated to tricyclics or other known antidepressant agents. The drug is reported to have no anticholinergic side effects. It should not be used in conjunction with

MAOIs. Venlafaxine is metabolized in the liver by the cytochrome $P_{450}IID_6$ system, so any drugs that inhibit the effectiveness of this system will increase the plasma of venlafaxine. The major side effects of this medication are nausea (37 percent), headaches (25 percent), and somnolence (23 percent). The usual dosing begins with 25 milligrams t.i.d., gradually increasing to a maximum dose of 225 milligrams per day. My experience with this medication in DID patients is limited, and I have reserved its use for DID patients who suffer from depression as a major dysfunctional symptom and who have not responded to other well-known antidepressants. For further information on venlafaxine (Effexor), I refer the reader to an excellent paper by Stuart Montgomery.

❧

It is important to remember the following points in using medications with patients with DID:

1. *Treat the person, not the illness.* I believe that effective therapy of a DID patient involves the whole person, and not just DID or any other disease. The person should be treated, not a disease.

2. No one specific medication or medication combination cures the core symptoms of dissociative disorders.

3. Medications are used as an aid in reducing the intensity of some symptoms, alleviating other symptoms, and helping the patient better use psychotherapy.

4. In cases in which the psychotherapy and the pharmacotherapy are provided by two different clinicians, it is vital for these clinicians to make every effort to work together as a cooperative team to improve the therapeutic response to prescribed medications.

5. Patients with dissociative disorders are not immune to other psychiatric diagnoses, such as bipolar or unipolar mood disorders, panic disorder, obsessive-compulsive disorder, nocturnal myoclonus, or others that do respond quite well to

pharmacotherapy. In cases in which comorbidity does exist, pharmacotherapy should be considered and used.

6. Safety should always be of the highest priority. In suicidal patients with a history of overdoses, the administration of medication should be given cautiously and preferably in an inpatient setting.

7. Taking medication from a caring and empathic physician, making it an experience of mastery for the patient, increases the positive therapeutic outcome.

8. More research is needed in this area of psychopharmacotherapy to determine which combinations of medication administration are the ones that have the best therapeutic outcome in specific patients.

9. Michael Gainer and I have found that a subgroup of patients diagnosed with DID also had a comorbidity of sleep apnea. The proper treatment of the sleep apnea significantly reduced the dissociative switching and amnesia during the day.

NOTES

P. 100, *Richard Kluft:* Kluft, R. P. (1984). Aspects of the treatment of multiple personality disorder. *Psychiatric Annals, 14,* 51–55; Kluft, R. P. (1985). The treatment of multiple personality disorder (MPD): Current concepts. In F. F. Flach (Ed.), *Directions in psychiatry* (pp. 1–10). New York: Hatherleigh; Kluft, R. P. (1989). Playing for time: Temporizing techniques in the treatment of multiple personality disorder. *American Journal of Clinical Hypnosis, 32,* 90–97.

P. 100, *Bennett Braun:* Braun, B. G. (1986). *The treatment of multiple personality disorder.* Washington, DC: American Psychiatric Press.

P. 100, *Philip Coons:* Coons, P. M. (1986). Treatment progress in 20 patients with multiple personality disorder. *Journal of Nervous Mental Disorder, 174,* 715–721.

P. 100, *Frank Putnam:* Putnam, F. W. (1986). The treatment of multiple personality: State of the art. In B. G. Braun (Ed.), *Treatment of multiple personality disorder* (pp. 175–198). Washington, DC: American Psychiatric Press;

Putnam, F. W. (1989). *Diagnosis and treatment of multiple personality disorder.* New York: Guilford Press.

P. 100, *Colin Ross:* Ross, C. A. (1989). *Multiple personality disorder: Diagnosis, clinical features, and treatment.* New York: Wiley.

P. 101, *Frederick Evans:* Evans, F. J. (1985). Expectancy, therapeutic instructions, and the placebo response. In L. White, B. Tursky, & G. E. Schwartz (Eds.), *Placebo: Theory, research and mechanism* (pp. 215–228). New York: Guilford Press.

P. 101, *Arthur Shapiro:* Shapiro, A. K. (1960). A contribution to a history of the placebo effect. *Behavioral Science, 5,* 109–135; Shapiro, A. K. (1968). Semantics of the placebo. *Psychiatric Quarterly, 42,* 653–696.

P. 101, *Arthur Shapiro and Louis Morris:* Shapiro, A. K., & Morris, L. A. (1978). The placebo effect in medical and psychological therapies. In S. L. Garfield & A. E. Bergin (Eds.), *Handbook of psychotherapy and behavior change* (2nd ed.; pp. 369–410). New York: Wiley.

P. 102, *David Spiegel:* Spiegel, D. (1986). Dissociation, double-binds, and posttraumatic stress. In B. G. Braun (Ed.), *The treatment of multiple personality disorder* (pp. 61–77). Washington, DC: American Psychiatric Press.

P. 103, *Martin Orne:* Orne, M. T. (1959). Hypnosis: Artifact and essence. *Journal of Abnormal Psychology, 58,* 277–299.

P. 104, *Richard J. Loewenstein:* Loewenstein, R. J. (1991). Rational psychopharmacology in the treatment of multiple personality disorder. *Psychiatric Clinics of North America, 14,* 721–740.

P. 105, *Richard Kluft:* Kluft, R. P. (1985). The treatment of multiple personality disorder (MPD): Current concepts. In F. F. Flach (Ed.), *Directions in psychiatry* (pp. 1–10). New York: Hatherleigh.

P. 105, *benzodiazepines, beta-blockers, clonidine, or low-dose neuroleptics:* Barkin, R., Braun, B. G., & Kluft, R. P. (1986). The dilemma of drug therapy for multiple personality disorder. In B. G. Braun (Ed.), *Treatment of multiple personality disorder* (pp. 107–132). Washington, DC: American Psychiatric Press; Braun, B. G. (1990a). Unusual medication regimens in the treatment of dissociative disorder patients: Part I. Noradrenergic agents. *Dissociation, 3,* 144–150; Fichtner, C. G., Kuhlman, D. T., Gruenfeld, M. J., et al. (1990). Decreased episodic violence and increased control of dissociation in a carbamazepine-treated case of multiple personality. *Biological Psychiatry, 27,* 1045–1052; Loewenstein, R. J., Hornstein, N., & Barber, B. (1988). Open trial of clonazepam in the treatment of posttraumatic stress symptoms in MPD. *Dissociation, 1,* 3–12; Ross, C. A. (1989). *Multiple personality disorder: Diagnosis, clinical features, and treatment.* New York: Wiley.

P. 105, *Loewenstein and associates:* Loewenstein, R. J., Hornstein, N., & Barber, B. (1988). Open trial of clonazepam in the treatment of posttraumatic stress symptoms in MPD. *Dissociation, 1,* 3–12.

P. 105, *Braun reported on the efficacy of clonidine:* Braun, B. G. (1990a). Unusual medication regimens in the treatment of dissociative disorder patients: Part I. Noradrenergic agents. *Dissociation, 3,* 144–150.

P. 115, *some patients claim:* Jacobsen, F. M. (1991). Possible augmentation of antidepressant response by buspirone. *Journal of Clinical Psychiatry, 52,* 217–220.

P. 116, *Braun reported on the experimental use:* Braun, B. G. (1990a). Unusual medication regimens in the treatment of dissociative disorder patients: Part I. Noradrenergic agents. *Dissociation, 3,* 144–150.

P. 122, *Rapid switching is not easy to control:* Braun, B. G. (1990a). Unusual medication regimens in the treatment of dissociative disorder patients: Part I. Noradrenergic agents. *Dissociation, 3,* 144–150.

P. 122, *hypnotherapeutic centering techniques:* Torem, M. S., & Gainer, M. J. (1993, March). *The center core: Imagery for experiencing the unifying self.* Paper presented at the American Society of Clinical Hypnosis Thirty-Fifth Annual Scientific Meeting, New Orleans.

P. 123, *patient's level of daytime functioning:* Dr. Michael Gainer and I reported on these findings at the November meeting of the International Society for the Study of Dissociation in Chicago, as well as in the *ISSD Newsletter* (1994). Dr. Richard Kluft, who was present at our presentation in Chicago, reported that he, too, had had several DID patients who concomitantly suffered from sleep apnea and whose daytime symptoms were significantly improved following appropriate treatment with C-PAP.

P. 124, *Fluvoxamine (Luvox) is an SSRI:* For further information on this new medicine, refer to Griest, J. H., Jefferson, J. W., Kobak, K. A., et al. (1995). Efficacy and tolerability of serotonin transport inhibitors in obsessive-compulsive disorder. *Archives of General Psychiatry, 52,* 53.

P. 125, *Braun reported on some success in the use of naltrexone (ReVia):* Braun, B. G. (1990b). The use of naltrexone in the treatment of dissociative disorder patients. In B. G. Braun (Ed.), *Seventh International Conference on Multiple Personality and Dissociative States* (p. 20). Chicago: Rush University Department of Psychiatry.

P. 126, *study by Ann Sharpley and her colleagues:* Sharpley, A. L., Walsh, A. E. S., & Cowen, P. J. (1992). Nefazodone—a novel antidepressant—may increase EM sleep. *Biological Psychiatry, 31,* 1070–1073.

P. 126, *from other clinicians:* J. Chu, personal communication, 1995; R. E. Wolin, personal communication, 1994.

P. 127, *excellent paper by Stuart Montgomery:* Montgomery, S. (1993). Venlafaxine: A new dimension in antidepressant pharmacotherapy. *Journal of Clinical Psychiatry, 54*(3), 119–126.

FOR FURTHER READING

Barkin, R., Braun, B. G., & Kluft, R. P. (1986). The dilemma of drug therapy for multiple personality disorder. In B. G. Braun (Ed), *Treatment of multiple personality disorder* (pp. 107–132). Washington, DC: American Psychiatric Press.

Braun, B. G. (1986). *The treatment of multiple personality disorder.* Washington, DC: American Psychiatric Press.

Braun, B. G. (1990a). Unusual medication regimens in the treatment of dissociative disorder patients: Part I. Noradrenergic agents. *Dissociation, 3,* 144–150.

Braun, B. G. (1990b). The use of naltrexone in the treatment of dissociative disorder patients. In B. G. Braun (Ed.), *Seventh International Conference on Multiple Personality and Dissociative States* (p. 20). Chicago: Rush University Department of Psychiatry.

Coons, P. M. (1986). Treatment progress in 20 patients with multiple personality disorder. *Journal of Nervous and Mental Disorders, 174,* 715–721.

Evans, F. J. (1985). Expectancy, therapeutic instructions, and the placebo response. In L. White, B. Tursky, & G. E. Schwartz (Eds.) *Placebo: Theory, research and mechanisms* (pp. 215–228). New York: Guilford Press.

Fichtner C. G., Kuhlman, D. T., Gruenfeld, M. J., et al. (1990). Decreased episodic violence and increased control of dissociation in a carbamazepine-treated case of multiple personality. *Biological Psychiatry, 27,* 1045–1052.

Griest, J. H., Jefferson, J. W., Kobak, K. A., et al. (1995). Efficacy and tolerability of serotonin transport inhibitors in obsessive-compulsive disorder. *Archives of General Psychiatry, 52,* 53.

Jacobsen, F. M. (1991). Possible augmentation of antidepressant response by buspirone. *Journal of Clinical Psychiatry, 52,* 217–220.

Kluft, R. P. (1984). Aspects of the treatment of multiple personality disorder. *Psychiatric Annals, 14,* 51–55.

Kluft, R. P. (1985). The treatment of multiple personality disorder (MPD): Current concepts. In F. F. Flach (Ed.), *Directions in psychiatry* (pp. 1–10). New York: Hatherleigh.

Kluft, R. P. (1989). Playing for time: Temporizing techniques in the treatment of multiple personality disorder. *American Journal of Clinical Hypnosis, 32,* 90–97.

Loewenstein, R. J. (1991). Rational psychopharmacology in the treatment of multiple personality disorder. *Psychiatric Clinics of North America, 14,* 721–740.

Loewenstein, R. J., Hornstein, N., & Barber, B. (1988). Open trial of clonazepam in the treatment of posttraumatic stress symptoms in MPD. *Dissociation, 1,* 3–12.

Montgomery, S. (1993). Venlafaxine: A new dimension in antidepressant pharmacotherapy. *Journal of Clinical Psychiatry, 54*(3), 119–126.

Orne, M. T. (1959). Hypnosis: Artifact and essence. *Journal of Abnormal Psychology, 58,* 277–299.

Putnam, F. W. (1986). The treatment of multiple personality: State of the art. In B. G. Braun (Ed.), *Treatment of multiple personality disorder* (pp. 175–198). Washington, DC: American Psychiatric Press.

Putnam, F. W. (1989). *Diagnosis and treatment of multiple personality disorder.* New York: Guilford Press.

Ross, C. A. (1989). *Multiple personality disorder: Diagnosis, clinical features, and treatment.* New York: Wiley.

Shapiro, A. K. (1960). A contribution to a history of the placebo effect. *Behavioral Science, 5,* 109–135.

Shapiro, A. K. (1968). Semantics of the placebo. *Psychiatric Quarterly, 42,* 653–696.

Shapiro, A. K., & Morris, L. A. (1978). The placebo effect in medical and psychological therapies. In S. L. Garfield & A. E. Bergin (Eds.), *Handbook of psychotherapy and behavior change* (2nd ed., pp. 369–410). New York: Wiley.

Sharpley, A. L., Walsh, A. E. S., & Cowen, P. J. (1992). Nefazodone—a novel antidepressant—may increase EM sleep. *Biological Psychiatry, 31,* 1070–1073.

Spiegel, D. (1986). Dissociation, double-binds, and posttraumatic stress. In B. G. Braun (Ed.), *The treatment of multiple personality disorder* (pp. 61–77). Washington, DC: American Psychiatric Press.

Torem, M. S., & Gainer, M. J. (1993a, March). *The center core: Imagery for experiencing the unifying self.* Paper presented at the American Society of Clinical Hypnosis Thirty-Fifth Annual Scientific Meeting, New Orleans.

Torem, M. S., & Gainer, M. J. (1993b, April). *Treatment of MPD: A systems approach.* Paper presented at the Eighth Regional Conference on Trauma, Dissociation, and Multiple Personality, Akron, OH.

Torem, M. S., & Gainer, M. J. (1994). Sleep and dissociation: New findings. *ISSD News, 12*(4), 8.

PART TWO

OUTPATIENT INTERVENTIONS

C H A P T E R

5

TREATMENT OF EARLY ONSET

Gary Peterson

There is growing awareness that, like several other disorders, Dissociative Identity Disorder (DID) begins in childhood and manifests in varying ways during one's life. Many children with DID-like symptoms are difficult to diagnose because symptoms in youth often vary from the expected adult form. In addition, treatment of dissociative disorders in children and adolescents is complicated by social, legal, and developmental issues. Clinicians must modify the treatment strategies for DID in youths to take into account issues including current safety, cognitive development, psychosexual role development, and home and school environment.

In this chapter, I will review some historical and theoretical issues related to DID in youths and discuss general principles of treatment. I will also describe treatment techniques to resolve problems that occur commonly when treating patients with DID.

THEORETICAL PERSPECTIVE

For the past century, the role of abuse and dissociation in the development of psychopathology has risen and fallen in awareness and popularity. In this section, I will outline early and current theories on the development of dissociative disorders. I will also present a way of understanding the subjective sense of consciousness for alternate personality states or "alters."

History, Incest, and Dissociation

Pierre Janet (1859–1947), building on the work of others such as Puysegur and Bertrand, studied patients with amnesia, fugue, and what would come to be known as alternate personality states. He realized that traumatic events could precipitate the splitting off of memories and feelings. He called this phenomenon *dissociation*. He was able to show that traumatic memories made conscious could relieve the dissociative symptoms.

Janet's contemporary, Sigmund Freud (1856–1939), in "The Aetiology of Hysteria," postulated incest as a basis for neurosis. He wrote: "It seems to me certain that our children are far more often exposed to sexual assaults than the few precautions taken by parents in this connection would lead us to expect. . . . it is to be expected that increased attention to the subject will very soon confirm the great frequency of sexual experiences and sexual activity in childhood." His assertion brought scornful rejection from his mentors and peers. Subsequently, he repudiated his own observations and reinterpreted as fantasies the painful disclosures of his patients.

Sandor Ferenczi is a third contemporary, born in 1873. Ferenczi is one of the least recognized of the great contributors to psychoanalytic theory. He may have been the first to postulate the connection between incest and DID. Shortly before his death in 1933, he presented to the 1932 Weisbaden International Psycho-Analytical Association Congress his paper "Confusion of Tongues Between Adults and the Child," in which he wrote:

> A typical way in which incestuous seductions may occur is this: an adult and a child love each other, the child nursing the playful fantasy of taking the role of mother to the adult. . . . [W]ith pathological adults, especially if they have been disturbed in their balance and self-control by some misfortune or by the use of intoxicating drugs, they mistake the play of children for the desires of a sexually mature person or even allow themselves—irrespective of any consequences—to be carried away.
>
> When the child recovers from such an attack, he feels enormously confused, in fact, split—innocent and culpable at

the same time—and his confidence in the testimony of his own senses is broken. . . . If the shock increases in number during the development of the child, the number and the various kinds of splits in the personality increase too, and soon it becomes extremely difficult to maintain contact without confusion with all the fragments, each of which behaves as a separate personality yet does not know of even the existence of the others.

Ferenczi died the following year, his theoretical contribution to trauma theory almost forgotten.

Current Models for the Development of DID

Authors in recent literature on DID have supported a wide variety of etiologic bases, including spiritual, physiological, psychological, sociological, and trauma-based theories. Within the field of trauma disorders today is a general acceptance of two similar but independently derived models for the development of DID. These models suggest that (1) if a person with an innate ability to dissociate is subjected in early childhood to what are perceived as severe or overwhelming stresses and (2) if the environment is unable to absorb the resulting distress or to otherwise comfort the child, then (1) the splitting off of the memory of the stressful events can occur and (2) in the most severe cases, DID will develop. Therefore, during childhood the stage is set for the development of clinical DID in childhood, adolescence, or adulthood. This developmental view forces us as therapists to consider that DID is fundamentally a child and adolescent disorder, only recognized when it reaches its fullest, most debilitating form usually manifested in early adult life (age late twenties to early thirties).

These trauma models for the development of DID are supported clinically by reports of the chaotic environment and distressing histories of these children and adults. Only carefully designed large-scale prospective studies, however, will be able to determine the ultimate validity of these theories.

Levels of Consciousness

People with DID have incomplete internal communication between internal self-perceived self states now called identities, personality states, or simply "alters." Incomplete communication includes having one-way and two-way amnesia between alternate personality states. The self state, which is in control of the body most of the time and presents itself for therapy, is called the "host" personality state. The "host" is a part of the mind that usually knows the least of all the personality states about what is occurring in the "internal world" of the alters. When an alter does not have control of the body, it is usually amnestic for what happens in the environment. Many or all of the other well-developed alters can usually be aware of the world outside the mind, the world the therapist lives in, when the host personality state is in control of the body. One-way amnesia occurs when an alter such as the host has no awareness of events when another alter is "out."

Another difficulty in interalter communication is that the alters are at times not available to the alter that is controlling the body. How can one conceptualize the activities of alters not in contact with the conscious mind? I have observed that although alternate personality consciousness appears to lie along a continuum, it can be understood as having three "levels" of experience: awake, asleep, and dead (see Figure 5.1).

When the alter is *awake*, it is directly in contact with the outside or external world through bodily senses. The awake alter can experience the world in two modes: *out* and *not out*. When the alter is awake and out, it has executive control of the body. In this state, it is most likely to observe itself as having distinct height, hair color, facial features, and size different from other alters. In the beginning phase of therapy, the host alternate personality state is likely to have no awareness of external situational occurrences when another alter is out (not co-conscious). As therapy proceeds, co-consciousness becomes more common among alters. An alter can choose to take control of only a por-

AWAKE ← → ASLEEP ← → DEAD

OUT ← → NOT OUT	ACTIVE ← → INACTIVE

Figure 5.1
Alternate Identity "Levels of Consciousness"

tion of the body, such as the hand to write, hit, or hold. In this case, the alter is out for that part of the body.

When the alter is awake and not out, it observes the external world through the senses and may influence the behavior and feeling state of the alter that is out. The alter that is not out, however, is not in primary control of the body. This mode of influencing behavior is particularly common in children; for them it appears that alters primarily manipulate the host personality state and the body through commands and other indirect means such as sharing or "bleeding" feeling states to the host.

The alter is *asleep* when it has no direct contact with the external world. It has no awareness of bodily sensations or direct control of the body. Days, months, or years can pass with an alter at this level. In this state, the alter rejuvenates itself for its next excursion to the outside world.

While asleep, the alter has two modes: *active* and *inactive*. While active and asleep, the alter is able to communicate with other alters. Early in therapy, alters that are active and asleep are usually unable to contact the out host personality state. As therapy progresses and as the host develops co-consciousness when other alters are out, alters develop the ability to be in contact with the host in this state. In this state, the alter experiences itself as being "in my room" or other place that alters frequently report or that can be set up during the course of therapy.

While inactive and asleep, the alter has no perception of processing or interacting with other personality states. The alter may describe this state as being "out of it." The alter may experience no thinking, no activity, and no planning.

The third level of consciousness is *dead*. The alter and all other identities experience the dead alter as nonexistent.

In general, the closer to being out, the easier it is for an alter to describe its experiences and the internal world activities to other people. Alters are reluctant or find it difficult to describe experiences while inactive.

During therapy the patient and the therapist may discover another system of identities that the alters have had no previous knowledge of. This discovery may occur when an alter from the familiar system crosses an internal barrier and finds itself in another subsystem of the mind. This experience can be confusing, disorienting, or frightening. After the alter returns to the familiar system, it may be aware of having a peculiar experience but may not be able to explain it well. This is an experience distinct from the dead alter that has no awareness whatsoever of any experience during the period of "death."

Alter death may occur at any time without warning. It is marked by the system of alters losing all contact with the dead alter. Unlike when an alter is "on vacation," during death remaining alters have no indication or awareness of the whereabouts of the missing alter. Alter death is distinguished from fusion (the coming together of alters, sometimes referred to as *integration*) in that, during death, remaining alters experience no increased range of emotion, no recovered memories, and no sense of joining with another part of the mind. Alter death is confirmed by the return of the alter and by its relating its self-experience of nonexistence being dead.

The host and other personalities can experience the death of an alter as an extremely dysphoric event. An alter may remain dead for a long interval, even through the course of therapy. It's unclear whether suggestions or notes to the system or dead alter have any direct effect on the return of the alter. When an alter returns from being dead, it may feel extremely weak and have impaired memory and sense of strength and/or power. Over time, the previously dead alter may regain its predeath self-perception, power within the system, and memory for past events.

Death of alters as perceived by the remaining alters may be experienced as permanent by the patient, such as reported by the patient in *The Three Faces of Eve*. In the case of "Eve," it is not clear whether this "permanent death" of alters was an artifact of therapy or a function of the organization of the mind of the patient. There is no reason to believe that a part of the mind has been destroyed in alter death, so in general we can expect the dead alters to resurrect.

Principles of Treatment

I turn now to treatment principles for dissociative disorders with emphasis on young DID patients. Practical solutions for common therapeutic quandaries are outlined.

Therapeutic Principles

Treatment principles for adults with DID are the starting place to guide the treatment of DID youngsters. Treatment of children is more complicated than the treatment of adults, however, for several reasons:

- The clinician must consider the patient in the context of cognitive development and age-appropriate behavior.
- Each child lives within the universe of the family constellation. Words and behaviors within the family may have a significance different from the general social meaning, and the therapist must learn the child's context to facilitate effective therapy.
- The therapist must coordinate with a wide variety of people, including parents, extended family members, teachers, social service workers, allied therapists, physicians, and other experts. The therapist must gather information from these

sources, translate it into a form meaningful to therapy, and then apply it.

- If the child is secretly still being abused, the therapy will not unfold in an understandable, helpful manner. The patient will remain symptomatic, and the helping professional will be befuddled.

Several clinicians have written on treating child and adolescent dissociative disorders. From any of these works, the reader can glean valuable insight into the treatment of dissociative children. Compare the treatment flow for adults with DID as described by Putnam to an outline of treatment flow for children by Kluft (Table 5.1). You can see that although the major components are incorporated into each, Kluft's child outline focuses on the early tasks.

Kluft's description of treatment flow begins with "First do no harm." This is an important principle, and one we as therapists need to keep in mind as we propose each intervention. All treatments, from individual psychotherapy to hospitalization, can have detrimental effects. We must be alert to the potential side effects, as well as benefits, for each intervention.

When working with the young patient with DID, the therapist must remain alert for ongoing family-based trauma. Three cases in point:

An eighteen-year-old female had been in hospital for almost a year when weekend home visits began, thus preparing patient and family for the patient's return to home. After each home visit, the patient would severely regress. The therapist carried out a detailed alter-by-alter exploration of weekend activities. After much resistance, one alter revealed an ongoing sexual relationship between the patient and her father. She had carefully guarded against revealing the incest until she was eighteen years old in order to protect her father from criminal prosecution.

A twelve-year-old boy had exhibited grand mal seizurelike symptoms at school. Only after a series of crises, careful following of the parental reports, and an interview confronting the parents' behavior was it discovered that the mother was suffering from undiagnosed DID.

An eleven-year-old boy with DID had an extremely resistant family. The father agreed to bring the boy to therapy only after we involved social services and obtained a court order. A few weeks before the expiration of the court order, the boy told his therapist he had (mentally) destroyed his system of personalities and his experience of an internal world by exploding them with dynamite. The boy totally lost contact with his internal system. His experiences were further buried, rather than coming to narrative memory. By exploding his internal system, he experienced his alters as "dead." He has not returned to therapy in the intervening year and a half.

Length of Treatment

Treatment may last from a few sessions to several months. Kluft states, "It is clear that with controlled, protected and active treatments child DID patients usually recover unity rather rapidly." Unfortunately, it is often difficult to establish a "controlled, protected and active" treatment. Commonly, these children who are living at home are in a chaotic, confusing environment, sometimes without protection from exposure to the alleged perpetrator of sexual abuse, from the physically and psychically abusing parent, or from witnessing violence in the home. The child living outside the home is bombarded with conflicts of loyalty to one or another parent or, in the case of foster care, the instability of changing foster homes and of having other foster care children in and out of the home during crisis placement. Sadistically abused children may require therapy for many years.

Table 5.1

Comparing Treatment Approaches for Adults and Children with DID

Tasks of Therapy with DID Patients	Stages of Treatment (for adults) (Putnam, 1989a)	Suggested Therapeutic Approaches (for children) (Kluft, 1986)
Safety, an overriding principle: The relative vulnerability of children leads us to explicitly state the need for therapists to be vigilant for children's safety.		First do no harm.
Diagnosis: Diagnosis is necessary to guide the therapy. In adults information usually comes directly from the patient. In children information comes from the patient, parents, and others (for example, school personnel, physician, siblings).	Making the diagnosis Initial interventions (meet alter personalities, gather some history, and develop a working relationship with the personality system)	Assessment and documentation
Beginning therapy: With children, assurance of protection is an explicit goal; the child may not reveal ongoing abuse. Usually, adults can inform the therapist of current dangers directly. In both groups, get the alters to contract for cooperation. With children obtain agreements such as protection from self-harm and which alter will be "out" at school. With adults contract for restraint of substance abuse, self-injurious behavior, and promiscuity.	Initial stabilizations (contracting with specific alters and the personality system as a whole in order to control what were previously uncontrollable behaviors)	Establish protection of the patient and the treatment. Introduce an active stance into the therapy sessions. Explore consciously available history, experiences, feelings, and perceptions in an atmosphere of empathic acceptance.

Understanding the dissociative paradigm: Encourage adults to let the family understand their behavior. With children it is critical that parents understand the dissociative process so that they can make the appropriate responses.	Acceptance of diagnosis (This can be an ongoing issue throughout therapy.)	Help the patient achieve a preliminary comprehension of circumstances.
"Integration process": Technically, "integration" includes the whole experience of alters getting to know about each other and becoming cooperative with each other.	Development of communication and cooperation (among alters) (This is ongoing until final fusion of alters.)	Reconciliation of the personalities
Trauma experience transformation: Shifting the trauma experience from amygdala emotion-mediated to hippocampal narrative-mediated memory. Usually done with play therapy in children and dialogue and abreactive replays of the experience in adults.	Metabolism of trauma (Should begin only after stabilization is successful.)	Abreaction Working through and grief work
Fusion: This is the coming together of alters as one, usually done in stages. Natural, nonhypnotic, nonritual fusion is the preferred mode, most common with children.	Resolution and integration (Some may elect to terminate therapy and remain with DID.)	Integration and fusion
Postfusion follow-up: Follow-up is necessary in both age-groups in order to help the patient learn and consolidate new coping skills. Therapists new to DID may overlook the importance of this step. Exposure to new stresses may reopen the dissociative adaptive mechanism.	Development of postresolution coping skills (Integrated patients have been stripped of their primary psychological defense, dissociation, and have precious little to replace it as protection against the stresses of everyday life.)	Postintegration treatment Periodic follow-up

For dissociative children in a safe environment, recovery from dissociative symptoms is frequently not a major issue during therapy. In our mental health clinic setting, most of the youngsters who have clear symptoms consistent with DID (missing time, voices inside their head that can answer questions during interview, not remembering behaviors that the voices admit to doing, being forced by the voices to do things against their will) will report a marked diminution of auditory and visual hallucinations from the first clinical interview discussing these voices. These hallucinatory experiences may not return until a time of crisis. In short, although dissociative symptoms may resolve quickly, diminution of symptoms does not necessarily mean the child no longer has DID. This is not unlike DID in adults, for which the more "classic symptoms" may be apparent only sporadically.

As with other factors related to DID, such as finding the presence of an inner self helper, the phenomenon of rapid resolution of voices in youngsters seems to be clinician specific. Some clinicians report that only rarely do the hallucinatory experiences of the patient rapidly, spontaneously resolve.

Because of these factors, during brief therapy dissociative symptoms may diminish and patients may benefit for specific problems. In some reported cases, youngsters fully resolved the dissociative disorder. In general, however, ongoing therapy is most often required for anyone who had developed a DID coping style—children being no exception.

Individual Therapy

Therapy with dissociative children is initiated and carried out much in the same way as all therapy with nondissociative traumatized or abused youngsters. As with nondissociative children, young children often use play therapy well. Older children and adolescents may do best with interpersonal "talk therapy" and adjuncts such as art, journaling, sand tray play—even puppet dialogue if appropriate. And some special considerations are especially apropos for dissociation problems. The key to the remission of internal strife and suffering from the trauma experience appears to be the transformation of the experience of traumatic events as mediated by the amygdalae into a narrative memory of traumatic events mediated by the hippocampus. In shifting from the parallel process of implicit, nondeclarative memory into explicit, declarative memory, the traumatized person can modulate the experience and have the transformed experience put into the perspective of the person's other life experiences. For therapists new to dissociative disorders, consultation or supervision can be critical to successful case resolution and is highly recommended.

For the child who clearly has DID, using the treatment flow described by Putnam (see Table 5.1) along with techniques for traumatized children should take the therapist a long way toward resolving the trauma. Initial tasks should include stabilizing the system through interalter contracts to decrease violent, disruptive, self-destructive behaviors and to optimize schoolwork through cooperation and the sharing of information.

Ideally, only the most academic alter would be out at school, and other alters would be observing, learning along with the academic alter. Agreements can be reached in which disturbing, disruptive alters will tone down their influence during class, perhaps in exchange for time "out" after the school day is over.

On average, the alters in children are less familiar with each other, compared with alters in adults. In adults the alters often share a mutual internal world and established opinions of one another. In children, however, it is much more common that the alters know little or, occasionally, nothing about each other. Alters in children generally do not speak with each other about the host personality state, as is so common in adults. The alters in children generally speak directly with the host personality state. Therefore, introducing alters to one another in early treatment of children is an especially salient task.

Most children and adolescents with dissociative problems do not have DID. Rather, many young patients present with problems consistent with other disorders. Symptoms may include trancelike states, missing blocks of time, and hearing voices. Dissociative disorder-not otherwise specified (DD-NOS) is the resulting diagnosis. Perhaps in the future (after publication of *DSM-V*), these youngsters will carry a diagnosis of dissociative disorder of childhood. Clinicians experienced in therapy with abused youths may sometimes find themselves at a loss when treating abused non-DID dissociative youngsters. When alter personalities are not available but dissociative features are prominent, the therapist may want to use ego-state-oriented therapies. Two ego-state-oriented therapies that the clinician might chose are ego-state therapy and transactional analysis.

Ego-state therapy focuses on the dissociative phenomenon and is accomplished with the use of hypnosis. The theory does not theoretically limit or define the nature or number of specific ego states. *Ego states* are described as personality segments or organized systems of behavior and experience bound together and separated from other such states. The goal of therapy is to increase cooperation and to decrease conflict between ego states. The technical process of ego-state therapy usually involves a hypnotic induction followed by a dialogue between two ego states of the patient. No evidence suggests that such therapy creates separate alters. Instead, it fosters interaction between aspects of the entire mind.

Transactional analysis (TA) is an ego-state-oriented therapy developed by psychiatrist Eric Berne in the 1950s and 1960s. It became popular as a "pop psychology" in the 1970s. In TA an *ego state* is defined as "a consistent pattern of feeling and experience directly related to a corresponding consistent pattern of behavior." Although TA theory was not developed through use of a dissociation paradigm, the theory does include such concepts as ego-state "contamination" (mistaking one ego state for another) and ego-state "exclusion" (shutting out, not giving access to an ego state); these can be considered dissociative phenomena. TA theory does not call for the use of hypnosis and is usually combined with gestalt therapy techniques developed by Fritz Perls. It has led to the development of powerful theory and therapy styles such as "redecision therapy."

Family Interventions

Work with families can vary according to needs and may vary from family education to clearly family therapy. These decisions are made similarly to the way they are made when the identified patient has a disorder other than a dissociative disorder.

Interactions with and support of the family can take place in many ways. DID and dissociative problems are familial and intergenerational phenomena. On the basis of their strengths and freedom from pathology, the parents may or may not be incorporated into the therapy process.

Because the therapist is in the room with the child for usually only an hour a week, it is incumbent on the therapist to incorporate the family, especially the parent figures, into the treatment process. The parents should be informed about the nature of dissociative disorders and alerted to the continual vulnerability of the child to dissociative reactions.

The therapist should clearly, openly, and nonjudgmentally explore family interactions for punishment style and potential abuse. This exploration includes informing the parents up front of the therapist's mandate to report suspected abuse. In addition to the general family history gathered during the opening phase of treatment, specific questions about problems with dissociation in family members should be asked. The child may have learned this coping style from a parent.

Inform the family of the potential roller-coaster unfolding of therapy and, with the assent of the patient, keep the parents informed as to the nature of progress. School-age children will generally feel completely comfortable with their parents knowing about their interalter world and how they are influenced by the alters. The family will need assurance that the child is not "crazy" and that he or she has a good chance of making substantial gains in therapy—with the help of the family. Adolescents are more aware of the societal association of hearing voices with "being crazy." They generally know that most other adolescents do not hear voices. They want to be like their peers in this and many other ways. Therefore, discussing hearing voices is usually more disconcerting for an adolescent than it is for a child.

Parents serve as observers for changes in their child's behaviors. They can be asked to keep a log of trance, disremembered, and other behaviors. This information can be gathered at the beginning of the session, and the therapist can explore the experience of these observations with the patient. Not infrequently, the therapist may suggest that a parent have a psychiatric evaluation. Parents should be encouraged to take care of themselves so that they are able to care for their children. The therapist may use the analogy of the emergency oxygen supply announcement given by flight attendants: first put on your own oxygen mask, and then you can help your children put on theirs.

A nonabusing family may help the ritualistically abused child if the family can move away from the community. Changing residence may decrease exposure to triggers and vulnerability to harassment by the previous abusers. Most families, however, do not have the ability to set up a new residence without great sacrifice; this inability induces more stress in the family system.

Group Therapy

Socialization is a vital learning component for child development, and it is a major purpose of most child groups. Therefore, group therapy is encouraged for dissociative children who can tolerate the group environment. Activity groups may be appropriate for younger dissociative children, and social process groups can help older children and adolescents.

Although group therapy for adult DID patients in mixed disorders groups can be highly problematic, children's groups should be less so. Because childhood alters are usually not so distinct or clamoring for recognition as compared with those of adults, the likelihood that a child with DID will be disruptive to a mixed disorders group is less than for an adult with DID. Significant regressions and even full-blown tantrums are not uncommon in children's activity groups. Therefore, the shifting to a young child alter is not as likely to be noticed in a children's group.

Danger lurks for abused, dissociative children who enter a sex abuse group. To fit in and to be accepted by the group, the host or an alter identity of a child may prematurely disclose the child's abuse and be left with a sense of exposure, shame, and horror at what it has done. This feeling could result in regression both in therapy and within social settings. The group therapist must wisely modulate the speed and nature of the child's self-disclosure, taking into account the child's strengths and vulnerabilities. Abused dissociative children in groups should always have an individual therapist available to them so that the children can dissipate anxiety and process group therapy experiences outside the group.

Expressive Therapies

When available, expressive therapies (art, music, movement) can be a superb adjunct to individual and family therapy interventions. Children can express their feelings and gain a sense of empowerment through the successes these modalities provide. Care should be taken for the allied therapist to relay back to the individual therapist the nature of the material and the progress being made. The child reluctant to deal with issues of abuse may be less resistant to expressing feelings in these therapies than in individual therapy, where the child knows that he or she may be expected or urged to disclose or discuss the "bad things" that have happened (see Dawson and Higdon, Chapter Eight).

Hypnotherapy

Hypnosis is a technique used to facilitate the flow of therapy. Hypnotic paradigms can be used during any phase of therapy. In the only paper published on the use of hypnosis with childhood

DID, the author described using hypnosis for diagnosis or treatment with each one of five juvenile patients.

Problems, however, are inherent in using hypnotic techniques with dissociative youths. Sadistically abused children may have been subjected to hypnosis by perpetrators, and the children may experience formal hypnosis techniques as reabuse. Children may not understand the concept that their hypnotic response is of their own free will because their experience is that of responding to the therapist's instructions. Therefore, the children may think they are being "controlled" by the therapist during the hypnosis process.

Children and adolescents are, as a group, more hypnotizable than are adults, and they have a greater degree of dissociative experiences. Hypnosis-based interventions, therefore, can be used with youngsters without the explicit use of hypnosis.

Although the formal use of hypnosis is not commonly needed in the treatment of dissociative children and adolescents, for a therapist, knowledge of the hypnotic paradigm is essential. Every clinician treating dissociative patients should be trained in hypnosis. Without hypnosis training, the therapist cannot fully comprehend the nature of the experiences of the DID patient. When the hypnosis trainee realizes he or she can induce in him- or herself many of the experiences reported by the DID patient, the cloudy mystique of the DID phenomena diminishes, and the therapist can more easily understand the patient's experiences. The therapist will also be able to facilitate controlled switching and to communicate more effectively with the patient.

Unique problems arise with the use of hypnosis for evaluations for abuse. In many jurisdictions, the use of hypnosis to uncover trauma compromises the testimony during legal proceedings.

Hospitalization

Children with DID usually enter hospital because of self-destructive and aggressive symptoms, rarely for their recognized dissociative symptoms. But as clinicians increasingly recognize

dissociative symptoms, more children will be diagnosed with these disorders.

As with any disorder, hospitalization of a dissociative child is a crisis for the family and the child alike. Whenever possible, avoid it. The child may perceive being away from home and family as a traumatic experience. To cope with this crisis of hospitalization, the patient may develop a new "model patient" alter, or existing disruptive alters may take a "vacation" from monitoring and influencing the host personality state and outside activities; the result is a dissociative-symptom-free patient. In my experience, youths with dissociative disorder diagnoses from a referring clinician are discharged without a dissociative disorder diagnosis.

As with other youths, dissociative children and adolescents commonly enter hospital for dangerous, self-destructive, or aggressive behaviors, perhaps because of voices telling them to kill themselves or others. Hostile alters take over behavior and cause what appears to be impulsive action. During therapy, hospitalization may also be required, albeit rarely, to address a newly discovered or particularly resistant aggressive alter at a time when the patient fears that the alter's emergence will result in an attack on the therapist.

The child's whole mind system or a substantial number of alters may feel depressed, in which case antidepressant medication should be considered. Monitor carefully the timing of relief of symptoms. Depression may lift prior to the initiation of medication because the prehospital environmental stresses have been dissipated. Depression may lift immediately on initiation of antidepressants because of the suggestibility of the patient.

Have specific goals for hospitalization. At discharge, document which goals have been met, which haven't been met, and why they haven't. This record will help guide reentering outpatient therapy. Whenever possible, include the outpatient therapist in the hospitalization process. Child and adolescent inpatient units are usually sophisticated programs, highly complex, and discipline interdependent. When the outpatient therapist cannot be the therapist in hospital because of hospital privilege constraints or

the therapist's lack of time, knowledge, or inclination, the hospital staff can still use the therapist's knowledge of the child's and the family's dynamics. The therapist is the best person to help the staff predict how well or poorly the patient and the family will likely adapt to the program. The therapist can help the staff prepare backup contingencies should the family fail to follow through.

Specialized dissociative inpatient programs for children and adolescents are extremely rare. If admitting to a nonspecialty unit, the child's therapist should inform and educate the nursing and other staff as to the nature of dissociative disorders, including the potential problems in group therapy and the varied responses to psychotropic medication. Be prepared for staff splitting and for anger at the ward therapist/psychiatrist because of the strain on the staff that the dissociative patient's unexpected, perplexing behavior produces.

The therapist should have the patient ready for the milieu at the end of the therapy hour. Use Kluft's rule of thirds—the first third to get into the work, the second third to do the work, and the last third to close the work down and process. The "work" may be as emotional as processing trauma or as intellectual as negotiating with alters for certain behaviors.

Do not insist that staff accept the diagnosis of DID. Some staff will come around as they experience the patient. Some staff will never conceptualize the case using the dissociative domain. (See Kluft, Chapter Nine, for more on hospitalization for dissociative disordered patients.)

Psychotropic Medication

Those with dissociative disorders benefit primarily through a psychodynamically aware interpersonal approach in individual therapy. The judicious use of psychotropic medication, however, can be an important adjunct. Although no controlled outcome studies use psychotropic medication for either child or adult DID patients, numerous case reports and open trials indicate that psychotropic medication can be of help in treating adult

DID. If we use the paradigm of DID as a prolonged posttraumatic stress disorder (PTSD), we can glean some rough guidelines for medication intervention.

Child psychiatrists frequently have to prescribe medication "off label": they prescribe for an age or disorder not approved by the Food and Drug Administration (FDA). They often prescribe medication according to the research literature for purposes that may never be approved by the FDA. If challenged in court, they would have to defend their use of the medication on (1) the common use of the drug for that purpose and age within the community and (2) child psychopharmacology research studies. Remember to document informed consent from the parents and assent by the child.

The patient's active participation in the choice of class of medication, the specific medication within the class, and initial dose can be important. Children are highly suggestive, and every effort should be made to put the placebo effect to good use. For DID patients, try to ensure that all available parts of the mind support the use of medication. Child alters usually go along with the decisions of older alters. Giving the young patient a role in medication decisions will decrease the likelihood of setting up a daily or more frequent struggle between the child and the parents trying to administer the medication.

One clinical trial for the use of psychotropic medication for PTSD in children has been published. This was an A-B-A design showing the efficacy of the beta-blocker propranolol. Several controlled clinical trials of the use of antidepressants for PTSD in adults have been conducted, but none for children or adolescents. Antidepressants have been shown to decrease symptoms of depression and sleep disturbance in adults with PTSD. In addition, a recent study indicates that fluoxetine (Prozac) can diminish avoidance symptoms in PTSD adults. Other medications have been less well studied. Results with lithium have been equivocal, as have results with anticonvulsants.

Use of stimulant medication such as methylphenidate (Ritalin) in hyperactive children with dissociative problems has not been systematically studied. Clinically, however, these children seem to partially respond. This finding is consistent with the fact that stimulants help both people with and without attention deficit disorder to concentrate. The benefit of stimulants appears to sustain during the period of medication administration; this finding suggests a physiological effect, rather than a placebo effect.

Antianxiety medication can temporarily help the patient become more relaxed and is often used in conjunction with other medication. Many dissociative patients, however, have had problems with drug or alcohol abuse; thus, the use of benzodiazepines should be prescribed with caution.

The use of neuroleptics with adults with DID is equivocal. The medication does not appear to decrease the dysphoric experience of hearing the alters' voices. Prescribing neuroleptics can disrupt a potential therapeutic alliance between the alters and the therapist/psychiatrist because of the perception by the alters that the purpose of the medication is to make the voices (the alters) "go away." In this case, alters experience the taking of medication as an attempt by the clinician to kill or otherwise destroy them. An example:

A nineteen-year-old woman recently told me that her voices were most distressing at the time she took her neuroleptic medication. She said her psychiatrist prescribed the major tranquilizer to make the voices go away. As she held the pill, the voices would scream loudly, "Don't do it! Don't do it!" She added that the voices told her the psychiatrist was trying to kill her.

In children and adolescents, the use of a low-dose, low-potency neuroleptic such as thioridazine (Mellaril) may be useful to decrease anxiety and, incidentally, the dysphoria-inducing voices. As with any neuroleptic, however, the possibility of developing tardive dyskinesia is present. The patient and the family should be fully informed of the possibility of tardive dyskinesia prior to starting and during the course of medication administration.

Neuroleptic medication should never be prescribed "to make the voices go away." Rather, they should be prescribed to "help you feel more relaxed and to be able to sleep more soundly." Recently, two of my female adolescent dissociative patients have reported that taking a low-dose, low-potency neuroleptic helped them feel "like people again."

PRACTICAL SOLUTIONS TO COMMON PROBLEMS

My clinical experience with young DID patients has led to some rather imaginative solutions to problems that cannot be solved in such a direct way with nondissociative patients. Many of these problems are common to a large proportion of dissociative cases. Discussed below are some of the common and interesting situations my patients have resolved by using their strengths to reframe, negotiate, and develop effective solutions to perplexing difficulties.

Interalter Confidentiality

Sometimes highly contended in the treatment of those with DID is the issue of interalter confidentiality. When dealing directly with alters early in therapy, the alters may tempt the therapist to collude with one alter to withhold important historical or clinical information from another (usually the host) personality. The alter divulging the information may present a convincing argument against sharing the information internally. This alter may claim that the host is too weak to accept the information or that the information will induce trauma in other alters. Psychodynamically, however, withholding internal secrets may be analogous to withholding family secrets during childhood. Maintaining family secrets may have been (and may still be) a key factor in the continued perpetration of abuse.

Some therapists have expressed strong arguments in favor of respecting the alter's request for interalter confidentiality. They think it is their responsibility to learn the mind's secrets in order to help the patient. Agreeing to this interalter secret keeping, however, is fraught with problems. Some alters may be capable of maintaining a literal, eidetic recollection of sessions, and therapists are usually not capable of precise recollection of session details. If the therapist divulges "secret" information to another alter, the disclosing alter might claim a breach of trust on the part of the therapist and thus divert or perhaps disrupt therapy. Commonly, the protective, secret-keeping alter is overprotective of the host. This may be because of the protective alter's accepted role, or it may be related to a fear that if the secret is divulged to the host, the alter will be less powerful, distinct, or special.

One way to deal with interalter confidentiality, maintaining safety, and not breaching trust is to use the following guidelines:

- Discuss the issue of confidentiality—sequentially and collectively—with the host and other alters as they are met.

- Address the reality that the therapist cannot, over time, remember specific details that the alter has requested be kept secret.

- Be open about the interest of developing and maintaining a sense of trust and about the likelihood that the divulging alter would feel betrayed if the therapist accidently discussed an internal secret with another alter.

- Tell the alter that the therapist will discuss with other alters any information divulged to the therapist as he or she deems clinically relevant and useful. If the proditorious alter thinks the host is not ready to hear disturbing information, the alter may withhold that information. At a later time, when the host can deal with it, the secret may be divulged.

As a matter of routine, you can elect to end each session in a summary with the host personality. If the host is not co-conscious, ask the host whether it wants feedback or observations from the therapist. If an alter senses it has prematurely divulged information to the therapist, it can take control of the mouth or give a message to the host to decline discussing the session.

• Respect the decision of the patient's response. If the host declines to discuss the session, ask how that decision was made. You will be able to determine whether the divulging alter has made the decision not to inform the host and can build on this secrecy issue in future sessions.

Using this procedure accomplishes several tasks: (1) freeing the therapist from having to remember which points of information are "secrets," (2) openly addressing the issues of fallibility of the therapist, (3) encouraging distressing information to be discussed, and (4) setting in place an automatic self-monitoring by the patient as to how quickly sensitive information is shared among alters.

Suicidal Impulses and Alters' Cognitive Development

Self-deprecatory auditory hallucinations and commands to kill oneself are not uncommon symptoms in persons with DID. The presenting or host personality may suffer from hearing these persecutory voices. The host personality may develop a sense of overwhelming hopelessness at the recurrent driving dictates to destroy oneself and may feel impelled toward self-injury. An understanding of the cognitive development of the perpetrating alternate personality can play a role in the treatment process resulting in the elimination of internal suicidal commands.

The voices that the host personality hears are usually voices of alternate personalities. As the therapist explores the personality system, the perpetrating alter often readily identifies itself. Alternate personalities have varying degrees of knowledge, awareness, and sophistication about diverse aspects of life. Not uncommonly, they will have a Piagetian preoperational level of cognitive development on the subject of death. For instance:

SALLY AND JANE

Sally, the angry alter, would frequently tell Jane, the host personality, to kill herself. Sally was angry that Jane usually succeeded in keeping Sally from taking control of the body. Sally believed that if Jane died, Sally would be able to take over. Sally proclaimed, "I would be number one!" On questioning, it became apparent that Sally did not understand the permanency of death, the nature of the body when dead (no heartbeat or breathing, other organs do not function, body changes color). In this case, education of the naive alter was in order. Sally did not initially believe the information, but she accepted that I believed the permanency of death. With this information and a negotiation between Sally and Jane to give Sally more time in control of the body and to encourage Sally to ask for what she wants (of Jane) more directly, the suicide commands from Sally diminished dramatically.

To summarize these guidelines:

- Identify the alter perpetrating the suicidal commands.
- Learn what is the self-perceived role of this alter and "join" with the alter in the understanding of what a hard job it is to carry out this role.
- Explore the motivation for the suicide "threats." Sometimes the motivation is as simple as wanting "time out" and being frustrated by the host personality. Often, the motivation has to do with a disparaging, deprecating attitude toward the host personality or a sense that the host should die because he or she is so miserable. (Later, the therapist may uncover that this

deprecation has to do with the perpetrating alter's own sadness and grief that has been projected onto the host.)

- Establish a contract between alters to decrease the suicidal hallucinations in exchange for something the perpetrator alter wants. The host personality may agree not to resist the emergence of the persecutory alter at mutually agreeable times and situations.

- Request that the perpetrating alter ask directly for what it wants of the other alters, offering the support of the therapist during the initial negotiations.

- Never condone self-destructive behaviors.

- Seek less damaging alternatives.

- Have as many alters as are willing be aware of the agreements between alters. This awareness increases understanding and lends support for success for the agreement as a more united will develops.

Pain Control

Although headaches and other somatic complaints in children with DID are less frequent and less severe than in adults with DID, pain symptoms can be problematic in youths. When a DID patient with severe headaches is seen by a neurologist, the common diagnosis is "mixed tension/migraine headaches," and amitriptyline (Elavil) is often prescribed. In addition, physicians frequently prescribe sumatriptan (Imitrex) injection, with limited relief for the patient.

When a recurrent somatic symptom has no measurable physical cause, then examining the mind for a solution is warranted:

- Ask through the host personality whether an alter or alters are involved with the pain. Often, the answer will be affirmative. If the alters do not know, then you may want to give some examples and temporal connections, such as experiencing increased headaches when alters switch. By careful analysis and by talking directly with influential alters, you may discover that headaches often occur when one or another of the alters is angry or irritated with the host. If this is the case, you can explain the association to each alter and request that the responsible alter be more direct.

- Suggest that the alter be more assertive and verbally clear as to what is bothering it and what it wants. The host identity's role is to listen to the pain-initiating alter to try to understand the alter's point of view and to work toward a compromise. You may find that the host's irritation and anger can likewise inflict physical discomfort on other alters without the host ever knowing it was the cause of the problem.

- Encourage the host not to use analgesics for pain when other methods are possible. Analgesics, even intramuscular morphine, can be ineffective in controlling the alter-induced algetic episodes:

MARGARET

Margaret reported that she would periodically arrive at the hospital emergency room with severe headaches. She would get intramuscular morphine. When I asked whether it helped, she replied, "Yes, it helped. It would make me go to sleep, and I would wake up the next day without a headache." As an alternative to her trip to the emergency room for opiates, she was able to markedly diminish her headaches by working with other alters in the fashion described above.

Sleep Problems

Sleep difficulties can occur for myriad reasons, including depression, anxiety, poor sleep hygiene, alcohol or drug abuse, and organic problems such as hyperthyroidism. Yet, when encountering a DID patient with sleep problems, it is probable that the sleep disturbance has something to do with trauma and the identity system. Sleep problems often involve an alter reexperiencing trauma or wanting to be in control of the body when others won't let it.

Here is a simple approach to confirm whether the problem is alter-related and to alleviate the problem:

- Inquire through the host personality whether a specific alter is involved with the sleep problem. The answer is almost invariably yes.

- Ask through the host (or directly to the alter that has been asked to come out) what is causing the sleep problem. Your specific intervention comes from the answer to this inquiry.

- Often, the part of the mind causing the sleep disturbance is not aware of the importance of sleep to the body. If that is so, have another alter educate the sleep problem alter or inform the alter yourself as the therapist and therefore an expert on sleep needs.

- Assign the alter to go to the library and read about the importance of sleep. If the sleep problem alter cannot read, recruit an older, literate alter to read the information to it. As an alternative, you can ask another alter to give or "lend" the illiterate alter the ability to read so that the illiterate alter can get the information directly from the written source. Incidentally, the illiterate alter may wish to retain its reading ability, something you will want to support.

- The goal of this exercise is to find a solution to the sleep problem alter's needs that will maintain sleep integrity. If the alter wants time out, negotiate with the others how this may be done. You may need to overcome the trepidation of other alters about the wisdom or safety of the plan. You can teach the alter how to telescope time so that five minutes in control of the body seems like five hours or five days.

- Convince the alter not to do reexperiencing of trauma during sleep time. As a temporizing exercise, the alter can plan to reexperience it during waking hours or do the reexperiencing deep inside the mind. Ultimately, you want the alter to work through and dissipate the emotional pain associated with the trauma.

- You may get resistance from other alters to trauma reexperiencing during waking hours because the terrifying feelings bleed across alters and cause considerable distress. You may be able to convince the system that this alter's processing will take precedence during therapy time and get agreement from the sleep problem alter to encapsulate the experience between therapy sessions.

Nocturnal Enuresis

Late-onset bed-wetting in a person with DID occurs occasionally. When it does, and if no organic reason is found for the symptom, it is often because an infant alter is taking control of the body during sleep. The alter comes out at night because that is the time when other alters' defenses are down. The other alters may not be aware of the enuretic behavior until the body wakes up feeling wet and cold.

Sometimes, the infant alter is wetting for the sheer pleasure of the warm feeling of comfort that happens in the few moments of the urination period. If that is the case, teach the patient that these sensations can be taken into the internal world. Tell the infant, through an older alter, that it can reproduce the feeling internally within the mind as often as it would like. Have the infant alter (while not in control of the body) practice generating the warm, comfortable feeling during the therapy session. Solicit a volunteer alter to see to the infant's needs and to report to the therapist if they want further assistance.

JACK

Jack is a seventeen-year-old boy with four distinct alters. During one session, his parents were very upset because he had again begun to wet his bed, a symptom he had not had since shortly after entering therapy a year and a half before. During the session, through information from the alters, Jack found out that his two-year-old alter, which had been activated by increasing focus on past traumas during the therapy hour, was giving itself comfort by experiencing the warmth of urine on his body while in bed. The infant abandoned control of the body when the urine began to cool. Through practice during the session, the infant was able to induce the same sensation without taking control of the body.

Calling on a "Mute" Alter

Communication by alters can take many forms, including using direct speech; sending words to the personality that is out; controlling the mouth, breathing apparatus, and vocal cords of the body; writing; drawing; and using ideomotor responses. Early in therapy, however, it is not uncommon to come across an alternate personality that is resistant, reluctant, or even unable to talk. The alter may be mute or deaf. The noncommunicative alter may be a preverbal infant, an animal, or an anthropomorphic inanimate object. For each of these alter forms, the process toward open communication can be the same.

The first task is to uncover which part of the mind has the closest relationship with the mute alter. This task is usually done through the host personality asking the parts of the mind and coming up with a response. If there is no answer, be patient. It will come unless the host is still in extremely poor communication with the alters, in which case the prerequisite work is to increase interalter communication.

After you know which alter is closest to the mute alter, request they open a channel through that alter to the host. Ask whether it is willing to translate the thoughts, feelings, and attitudes of the mute alter. When you get an affirmative response, ask through that alter whether the mute alter would like to communicate with you. A dialogue can then begin. If the mute alter does not want to communicate, ask why and do what you can to decrease the alter's objections or apprehensions. As you show respect to the mute alter's attitudes and views, the alter will soon naturally come to communicate through its own "voice" to the host. At this time, you can request, with the assent of the other alters, that the alter come into control of the body and speak directly with you.

Remember, these alters are not used to speaking their thoughts to others and probably are not very comfortable with being in control of the body. Be patient and understanding; the alter can rapidly gain assurance and become a part of the therapeutic "team" of alters.

Did You Ask?

DID is a condition of self-perceived autonomous mind states. To retain the perception of distinct selves, by necessity all memories and perceptions of these states of consciousness (and unconsciousness) must be distinct and simultaneous, and internal information barriers must be set up in order for these perceptions of distinction to be maintained. It is logical, however, that the information of a previously "in control of the body" self-state [read "alter"] may rest somewhere else in the mind even though inaccessible to the currently conscious self-state.

When working with someone with DID, it is an unnecessarily paternalistic temptation for the therapist to provide the information that is unavailable to the conscious self-state. This temptation frequently comes about late in the session when the non-co-conscious host returns to control the body. The therapist's impulse may be to fill in the gaps if the host is interested in knowing what happened (see "Interalter Confidentiality" on page 157). The therapist who provides the information without first inviting the patient to search the mind is missing an opportunity for the patient to experience success in information retrieval. An analogy is for an individual to unnecessarily support an infant or an elderly person in ambulation. In the case of Jack with enuresis as described above, the next time he wet, he asked, "Why?" of the alters and developed a soothing ritual by an adolescent alter that he reported to me the next session.

As the patient gets used to searching the mind for information during the therapy session, this exercise can be generalized to situations occurring outside the therapy hour. A mark of progress is the point at which the patient comes into the consultation room, talking about a crisis that has happened since the last session.

The therapist knows a bridge has been crossed when the patient's answer to the question, "Did you ask (the others inside what was going on)?" and the answer comes back, "Yes, and this is what they said. . . ." By this time, the patient generally has resolved the crisis with the information received or is ready to work through it in the session, with the therapist's guidance.

Therapist supervisors and consultants will notice a similar phenomenon with their trainees. As a trainee gains experience with dissociative patients, he or she will increasingly have asked the patient for the answer prior to supervision. Inexperienced therapists often buy into the patient's perception of separate parts and may forget they are working with only one mind that has protectively and (if the patient wishes) temporarily segmented itself.

CAUTIONS AND LIMITS OF THE APPROACH

A major caveat in working with dissociative children and adolescents is the issue of safety, including ongoing abuse. These youngsters live in a microsociety influenced heavily by family historical and current dynamics. Either through fear or because of family mores, they might not tell the truth about what is happening in the home. An example of this occurred a few years ago at a local hospital in which an eighteen-year-old DID patient had her one-year anniversary of hospitalization and was about to be discharged. When she came back from home visits, however, she would regress terribly. One of the patient's alters soon revealed to her therapist that she was having sex with her father each time she would go on pass.

Premature divulging of trauma experiences is a common occurrence for patients working with inexperienced therapists.

Therapists new to the area of abuse or dissociation should obtain consultation or supervision on the first few cases to decrease the mistakes and to help move therapy along. Child and adolescent therapists are encouraged to treat a few adult cases early in their learning so that they can understand the final form of the disorder. These therapists are especially well equipped to treat dissociative disorders because of their experience in withholding judgment and in having to project themselves into the child's imaginative world when treating nondissociative young patients.

All therapists working with dissociative patients should have training in hypnosis. Otherwise, the therapist will be missing critical tools to help the therapy progress.

No controlled clinical trials have been undertaken in the treatment of DID. We as therapists have only our clinical experience, the experience of other therapists, and good judgment to guide our way down the path of this new therapeutic approach of knowingly working with the will and cooperation of segments of the mind in an internal effort to decrease boundaries and increase communication.

SHORT-TERM MANAGED CARE

Crisis interventions can be managed in short-term care. The overall treatment of childhood DID, however, does not lend itself well to short-term therapy. Even if, on discovering the dissociative process, there is a rapid decrease in hallucinatory experiences, self-destructive behaviors, and other maladaptive behaviors, the work of ego strengthening, developing internal support and cooperation, and evolving alternative coping skills is paramount for the long-term well-being of the child. One approach to managed care treatment certification is to obtain approval for an "episode" based on the most troubling symptoms at the time. Children and adolescents with DID usually qualify for several diagnoses at any one time. With good documentation, careful symptom description, and judicious choice of diagnoses, treatment may be extended to accommodate the needs of the patient.

∽

Ground is just now being broken toward the understanding of dissociative disorders in childhood. In this chapter, I have touched on both theoretical and practical issues in the development and treatment of early-onset DID. However gratifying it may be that therapists across the country arrive independently at similar treatment approaches, we as therapists are only beginning to understand how we can help these children use the power of their minds to understand themselves, to use their resources to the best of their ability, and ultimately to heal themselves.

NOTES

P. 135, *manifests in varying ways during one's life:* American Psychiatric Association. (1980). *Diagnostic and statistical manual of mental disorders* (3rd ed.). Washington, DC: Author, p. 305; Peterson, G. (1990). Diagnosis of childhood multiple personality disorder. *Dissociation, 3,* 3–9.

P. 136, *traumatic memories made conscious could relieve the dissociative symptoms:* Putnam, F. W. (1989b). Pierre Janet and modern views of dissociation. *Journal of Traumatic Stress, 2,* 413–429.

P. 136, *sexual activity in childhood:* Freud, S. (1962). The aetiology of hysteria. In J. Strachey (Ed. and Trans.), *The standard edition of the complete psychological works of Sigmund Freud* (Vol. 3, p. 207). London: Hogarth Press. (Original work published in 1896)

P. 137, *does not know of even the existence of the others:* Ferenczi, S. (1955). Confusion of tongues between adults and the child [Originally: The passions of adults and their influence on the sexual and character development of children]. In M. Balint (Ed.), *Final contributions to the problems and methods of psycho-analysis* (pp. 161–165). New York: Brunner/Mazel. (Original work published in 1933)

P. 137, *including spiritual, physiological, psychological, sociological:* Stern, C. R. (1984). The etiology of multiple personalities. *Psychiatric Clinics of North America, 7,* 149–159.

P. 137, *trauma-based theories:* Ross, C. A. (1989). *Multiple personality disorder: Diagnosis, clinical features, and treatment.* New York: Wiley.

P. 137, *two similar but independently derived models:* Ross, C. A. (1989). *Multiple personality disorder: Diagnosis, clinical features, and treatment.* New York: Wiley.

P. 137, *for the development of DID:* Braun, B. G., & Sachs, R. G. (1985). The development of multiple personality disorder: Predisposing, precipitating, and perpetuating factors. In R. P. Kluft (Ed.), *Childhood antecedents of multiple personality* (pp. 37–64). Washington, DC: American Psychiatric Press; Kluft, R. P. (1984b). Treatment of multiple personality disorder: A study of 33 cases. *Psychiatric Clinics of North America, 7,* 9–29.

P. 137, *reports of the chaotic environment:* Fagan, J., & McMahon, P. P. (1984). Incipient multiple personality in children. *Journal of Nervous and Mental Disease, 172,* 26–36.

P. 137, *distressing histories of these children:* Hornstein, N. L., & Tyson, S. (1991). Inpatient treatment of children with multiple personality/dissociative disorders and their families. *Psychiatric Clinics of North America, 3,* 631–648.

P. 137, *and adults:* Putnam, F. W., Guroff, J. J., Silverman, E. K., Barban, L., & Post, R. M. (1986). The clinical phenomenology of multiple personality disorder: A review of 100 recent cases. *Journal of Clinical Psychiatry, 47,* 285–293.

P. 138, *three "levels" of experience:* Peterson, G. (1988). Developmental concepts and annihilation in multiple personality [Summary]. *Proceedings of the Fifth Annual International Conference on Multiple Personality/Dissociative States, 55.*

P. 141, *The Three Faces of Eve:* Thigpen, C. H., & Cleckley, H. (1957). *The three faces of Eve.* New York: McGraw-Hill.

P. 141, *Treatment principles for adults with DID:* Braun, B. G. (Ed.). (1986). *Treatment of multiple personality disorder.* Washington, DC: American Psychiatric Press; International Society for the Study of Dissociation. (1994). *Guidelines for treating dissociative identity disorder (multiple personality disorder) in adults.* Skokie, IL: Author; Kluft, R. P. (1984a). Aspects of the treatment of multiple personality disorder. *Psychiatric Annals, 14,* 51–55; Kluft, R. P. (1984b). Treatment of multiple personality disorder: A study of 33 cases. *Psychiatric Clinics of North America, 7,* 9–29; Putnam, F. W. (1989b). Pierre Janet and modern views of dissociation. *Journal of Traumatic Stress, 2,* 413–429.

P. 142, *Several clinicians have written on treating child and adolescent dissociative disorders:* Fagan, J., & McMahon, P. P. (1984). Incipient multiple personality in children. *Journal of Nervous and Mental Disease, 172,* 26–36; Hornstein, N. L., & Tyson, S. (1991). Inpatient treatment of children with multiple personality/dissociative disorders and their families. *Psychiatric Clinics of North America, 3,* 631–648; Kluft, R. P. (1985a). Childhood multiple personality disorder: Predictors, clinical findings, and treatment results. In R. P. Kluft (Ed.), *Childhood antecedents of multiple personality* (pp. 167–196). Washington, DC: American Psychiatric Press; Lewis, D. O. (1991). Multiple personality. In M. Lewis (Ed.), *Child and adolescent psychiatry: A comprehensive textbook* (pp. 707–715). Baltimore, MD: Williams & Wilkins; McMahon, P. P., & Fagan, J. (1993). Play therapy with children with multiple personality disorder. In R. P. Kluft & C. G. Fine (Eds.), *Clinical perspectives on multiple personality disorder* (pp. 253–276). Washington, DC: American Psychiatric Press; Silberg, J. L., Stipic, D., & Taghizadeh, F. (in press). Dissociative disorders in children and adolescents. In J. Noshpitz (Ed.), *Handbook of child and adolescent psychiatry.* New York: Basic.

P. 142, *with DID as described by Putnam:* Putnam, F. W. (1989a). *Diagnosis and treatment of multiple personality disorder.* New York: Guilford Press.

P. 142, *an outline of treatment flow for children:* Kluft, R. P. (1986). Treating children who have multiple personality disorder. In B. G. Braun (Ed.), *Treatment of multiple personality disorder.* Washington, DC: American Psychiatric Press.

P. 142, *Kluft's description of treatment flow begins with "First do no harm":* Kluft, R. P. (1986). Treating children who have multiple personality disorder. In B. G. Braun (Ed.), *Treatment of multiple personality disorder.* Washington, DC: American Psychiatric Press.

P. 143, *Treatment may last from a few sessions:* Fagan, J., & McMahon, P. P. (1984). Incipient multiple personality in children. *Journal of Nervous and Mental Disease, 172,* 26–36; Kluft, R. P. (1985a). Childhood multiple personality disorder: Predictors, clinical findings, and treatment results. In R. P. Kluft (Ed.), *Childhood antecedents of multiple personality* (pp. 167–196). Washington, DC: American Psychiatric Press; Kluft, R. P. (1985b). Hypnotherapy of childhood multiple personality disorder. *American Journal of Clinical Hypnosis, 27,* 201–210; Kluft, R. P. (1986). Treating children who have multiple personality disorder. In B. G. Braun (Ed.), *Treatment of multiple personality disorder.* Washington, DC: American Psychiatric Press.

P. 143, *to several months:* Weiss, M., Sutton, P. J., & Tuecht, A. J. (1985). Multiple personality in a 10-year-old girl. *Journal of the American Academy of Child Psychiatry, 24,* 495–501.

P. 143, *Kluft states, "It is clear:* Kluft, R. P. (1986). Treating children who have multiple personality disorder. In B. G. Braun (Ed.), *Treatment of multiple personality disorder.* Washington, DC: American Psychiatric Press, p. 94.

P. 146, *"classic symptoms" may be apparent only sporadically:* Kluft, R. P. (1987b). Unsuspected multiple personality disorder: An uncommon source of protracted resistance, interrupting psychoanalysis. *Hillside Journal of Clinical Psychiatry, 9,* 100–115; Kluft, R. P. (1991a). Clinical presentations of multiple personality disorder. *Psychiatric Clinics of North America, 3,* 605–630.

P. 146, *finding the presence of an inner self helper:* Adams, M. A. (1988). Internal self helpers of persons with multiple personality disorder. *Dissociation, 2*(3), 138–143; Allison, R. B. (1974). A new treatment approach for multiple personalities. *American Journal of Clinical Hypnosis, 17,* 15–32.

P. 146, *youngsters fully resolved the dissociative disorder:* Kluft, R. P. (1985a). Childhood multiple personality disorder: Predictors, clinical findings, and treatment results. In R. P. Kluft (Ed.), *Childhood antecedents of multiple personality* (pp. 167–196). Washington, DC: American Psychiatric Press.

P. 146, *traumatized or abused youngsters:* Donovan, D. M., & McIntyre, D. (1990). *Healing the hurt child.* New York: W. W. Norton; James, B. (1989). *Treating traumatized children.* Lexington, MA: Lexington Books.

P. 146, *young children often use play therapy well:* Gorman, J. N. (1972). Dissociation and play therapy: A case study. *Journal of Psychiatric Nursing, 10*(2), 23–26.

P. 147, *put into the perspective of the person's other life experiences:* van der Kolk, B. A. (1994). *Trauma and memory I: The dissociative defense* [Videotape]. Ukiah, CA: Cavalcade Productions.

P. 147, *the treatment flow described by Putnam:* Putnam, F. W. (1989b). Pierre Janet and modern views of dissociation. *Journal of Traumatic Stress, 2,* 413–429.

P. 147, *techniques for traumatized children:* Donovan, D. M., & McIntyre, D. (1990). *Healing the hurt child.* New York: W. W. Norton; James, B. (1989). *Treating traumatized children.* Lexington, MA: Lexington Books.

P. 147, *cooperation and the sharing of information:* Gould, C., Graham-Costain, V., Peterson, G., & Waterbury, M. (1993). *Treating dissociation in children* [Videotape]. Ukiah, CA: Cavalcade Productions.

P. 148, *a diagnosis of dissociative disorder of childhood:* Peterson, G. (1991). Children coping with trauma: Diagnosis of "dissociation identity disorder." *Dissociation, 4,* 152–164; Peterson, G., & Putnam, F. W. (1994). Preliminary results of the field trial of proposed criteria for dissociative disorder of childhood. *Dissociation, 7,* 212–220.

P. 148, *ego-state therapy:* Watkins, H. H., & Watkins, J. G. (1993). Ego-state therapy in the treatment of dissociative disorders. In R. P. Kluft & C. G. Fine (Eds.), *Clinical perspectives on multiple personality disorder.* Washington, DC: American Psychiatric Press.

P. 148, *transactional analysis:* Berne, E. (1966). *Transactional analysis in psychotherapy.* New York: Grove Press.

P. 148, *Ego states are described as personality segments:* Federn, P. (1952). On the distinction between healthy and pathological narcissism. In E. Weiss (Ed.), *Ego: Psychology and the psychoses* (pp. 323–364). New York: Basic Books.

P. 148, *separated from other such states:* Watkins, H. H., & Watkins, J. G. (1993). Ego-state therapy in the treatment of dissociative disorders. In R. P. Kluft & C. G. Fine (Eds.), *Clinical perspectives on multiple personality disorder.* Washington, DC: American Psychiatric Press.

P. 148, *consistent pattern of behavior:* Stewart, I., & Joines, V. (1987). *TA today: A new introduction to transactional analysis.* Chapel Hill, NC: Lifespace, p. 329.

P. 149, *"redecision therapy":* Goulding, M., & Goulding, R. (1979). *Changing lives through redecision therapy.* New York: Brunner/Mazel.

P. 149, *Interactions with and support of the family:* Benjamin, L. R., & Benjamin, R. (1992). An overview of family treatment in dissociative disorders. *Dissociation, 5,* 236–241.

P. 149, *dissociative problems are familial:* Braun, B. G. (1985). The transgenerational incidence of dissociation and multiple personality disorder: A preliminary report. In R. P. Kluft (Ed.), *Childhood antecedents of multiple personality* (pp. 127–150). Washington, DC: American Psychiatric Press.

P. 149, *and intergenerational phenomena:* Coons, P. M. (1985). Children of parents with multiple personality disorder. In R. P. Kluft (Ed.), *Childhood antecedents of multiple personality* (pp. 37–64). Washington, DC: American Psychiatric Press.

P. 149, *learned this coping style from a parent:* Peterson, G., & Boat, B. W. (1992, June). *Working with families of MPD patients: Costs and benefits.* Paper presented at the Fourth Annual Eastern Regional Conference on Abuse and Multiple Personality, Alexandria, VA.

P. 150, *mixed disorders groups can be highly problematic:* Buchele, B. J. (1993). Group psychotherapy for persons with multiple personality and dissociative disorders. *Bulletin of the Menninger Clinic, 57,* 362–370.

P. 150, *recognition as compared with those of adults:* Kluft, R. P. (1985a). Childhood multiple personality disorder: Predictors, clinical findings, and treatment results. In R. P. Kluft (Ed.), *Childhood antecedents of multiple personality* (pp. 167–196). Washington, DC: American Psychiatric Press.

P. 151, *a superb adjunct to individual and family therapy:* (see Chapter Eight, this volume.)

P. 151, *the use of hypnosis with childhood DID:* Kluft, R. P. (1985b). Hypnotherapy of childhood multiple personality disorder. *American Journal of Clinical Hypnosis, 27,* 201–210.

P. 152, *more hypnotizable than are adults:* London, P., & Cooper, L. M. (1969). Norms of hypnotic susceptibility in children. *Developmental Psychology, 1,* 113–124.

P. 152, *a greater degree of dissociative experiences:* Putnam, F. W., Helmers, K., & Trickett, P. K. (1993). Development, reliability, and validity of a child dissociation scale. *Child Abuse and Neglect, 17,* 731–742.

P. 152, *the testimony during legal proceedings:* (see Chapter Seven, this volume.)

P. 153, *more children will be diagnosed with these disorders:* Hornstein, N. L., & Tyson, S. (1991). Inpatient treatment of children with multiple personality/dissociative disorders and their families. *Psychiatric Clinics of North America, 3,* 631–648.

P. 154, *The judicious use of psychotropic medication:* Loewenstein, R. J. (1991). Rational psychopharmacology in the treatment of multiple personality disorder. *Psychiatric Clinics of North America, 3,* 721–740.

P. 154, *psychotropic medication can be of help in treating adult DID:* Loewenstein, R. J. (1991). Rational psychopharmacology in the treatment of multiple personality disorder. *Psychiatric Clinics of North America, 3,* 721–740.

P. 155, *guidelines for medication intervention:* van der Kolk, B. A. (1993). Biological basis of PTSD. *Primary Care, 20,* 417–32.

P. 155, *efficacy of the beta-blocker propranolol:* Famularo, R., Kinscherff, R., & Fenton, T. (1988). Propranolol treatment of childhood posttraumatic stress disorder, acute type. *American Journal of Diseases of Childhood, 142,* 1244–1247.

P. 155, *antidepressants for PTSD in adults:* Davidson, J. (1992). Drug treatment of PTSD. *British Journal of Psychiatry, 160,* 309–314; Davidson, J., Kudler, H., Smith, R., Mahorney, J. L., Lipper, S., Mannett, E., Saunders, W. B., & Cavenar, J. O. (1990). Treatment of posttraumatic stress disorder with amitriptyline and placebo. *Archives of General Psychiatry, 47,* 259–266.

P. 155, *diminish avoidance symptoms in PTSD adults:* van der Kolk, B. A., Drey-fuss, D., Michaels, M., Shera, D., Berkowitza, R., Fisler, R., & Saxe, G. (1994). Fluoxetine in posttraumatic stress disorder. *Journal of Clinical Psychiatry, 55,* 517–522.

P. 155, *results with anticonvulsants:* Davidson, J. (1992). Drug treatment of PTSD. *British Journal of Psychiatry, 160,* 309–314.

P. 156, *both people with and without attention deficit disorder:* Rapoport, J. L., Buchsbaum, M. S., Weingartner, H., Zahn, T. P., Ludlow, C., & Mikkelsen, E. J. (1980). Dextroamphetamine: Its cognitive and behavioral effects in normal and hyperactive boys and normal men. *Archives of General Psychiatry, 37,* 933–943.

P. 156, *problems with drug or alcohol abuse:* Hornstein, N. L., & Putnam, F. W. (1992). Clinical phenomenology of child and adolescent dissociative disorders. *Journal of the American Academy of Child and Adolescent Psychiatry, 31,* 1077–1085; Putnam, F. W., Guroff, J. J., Silverman, E. K., Barban, L., & Post, R. M. (1986). The clinical phenomenology of multiple personality disorder: A review of 100 recent cases. *Journal of Clinical Psychiatry, 47,* 285–293.

P. 157, *the issue of interalter confidentiality:* Peterson, G. (1993, October). Interalter confidentiality. *Dissociation Notes,* p. 2. (Available from NCTSSD, P. O. Box 3693, Chapel Hill, NC 27515)

P. 159, *not uncommon symptoms in persons with DID:* Putnam, F. W. (1989a). *Diagnosis and treatment of multiple personality disorder.* New York: Guilford Press.

P. 159, *the elimination of internal suicidal commands:* Peterson, G. (1993, July). Suicidal impulses and alters' cognitive development: A treatment strategy. *Dissociation Notes,* p. 2. (Available from NCTSSD, P. O. Box 3693, Chapel Hill, NC 27515)

P. 160, *cognitive development on the subject of death:* Kane, B. (1979). Children's concept of death. *Journal of Genetic Psychology, 134,* 141–153; Peterson, G. (1988). Developmental concepts and annihilation in multiple personality [Summary]. *Proceedings of the Fifth Annual International Conference on Multiple Personality/Dissociative States, 55.*

P. 161, *less severe than in adults with DID:* Kluft, R. P. (1985a). Childhood multiple personality disorder: Predictors, clinical findings, and treatment results. In R. P. Kluft (Ed.), *Childhood antecedents of multiple personality* (pp. 167–196). Washington, DC: American Psychiatric Press.

P. 166, *inaccessible to the currently conscious self-state:* Peterson, G. (1994, January). "Did you ask?" *Dissociation Notes,* p. 2. (Available from NCTSSD, P. O. Box 3693, Chapel Hill, NC 27515)

FOR FURTHER READING

Adams, M. A. (1988). Internal self helpers of persons with multiple personality disorder. *Dissociation, 2*(3), 138–143.

Allison, R. B. (1974). A new treatment approach for multiple personalities. *American Journal of Clinical Hypnosis, 17,* 15–32.

American Psychiatric Association. (1980). *Diagnostic and statistical manual of mental disorders* (3rd ed.). Washington, DC: Author.

American Psychiatric Association. (1987). *Diagnostic and statistical manual of mental disorders* (3rd ed., rev.). Washington, DC: Author.

American Psychiatric Association. (1994). *Diagnostic and statistical manual of mental disorders* (4th ed.). Washington, DC: Author.

Benjamin, L. R., & Benjamin, R. (1992). An overview of family treatment in dissociative disorders. *Dissociation, 5,* 236–241.

Berne, E. (1966). *Transactional analysis in psychotherapy.* New York: Grove Press.

Braun, B. G. (1984). The role of the family in the development of multiple personality disorder. *International Journal of Family Psychiatry, 5,* 303–313.

Braun, B. G. (1985). The transgenerational incidence of dissociation and multiple personality disorder: A preliminary report. In R. P. Kluft (Ed.), *Childhood antecedents of multiple personality* (pp. 127–150). Washington, DC: American Psychiatric Press.

Braun, B. G. (Ed.). (1986). *Treatment of multiple personality disorder.* Washington, DC: American Psychiatric Press.

Braun, B. G., & Sachs, R. G. (1985). The development of multiple personality disorder: Predisposing, precipitating, and perpetuating factors. In R. P. Kluft (Ed.), *Childhood antecedents of multiple personality* (pp. 37–64). Washington, DC: American Psychiatric Press.

Buchele, B. J. (1993). Group psychotherapy for persons with multiple personality and dissociative disorders. *Bulletin of the Menninger Clinic, 57,* 362–370.

Chu, J. A., & Dill, D. L. (1990). Dissociative symptoms in relation to childhood physical and sexual abuse. *American Journal of Psychiatry, 147,* 887–892.

Coons, P. M. (1985). Children of parents with multiple personality disorder. In R. P. Kluft (Ed.), *Childhood antecedents of multiple personality* (pp. 37–64). Washington, DC: American Psychiatric Press.

Davidson, J. (1992). Drug treatment of PTSD. *British Journal of Psychiatry, 160,* 309–314.

Davidson, J., Kudler, H., Smith, R., Mahorney, J. L., Lipper, S., Mannett, E., Saunders, W. B., & Cavenar, J. O. (1990). Treatment of posttraumatic stress disorder with amitriptyline and placebo. *Archives of General Psychiatry, 47,* 259–266.

Dawson, P. L., & Higdon, J. F. (1996). Chapter Eight, this volume.

Dell, P. F., & Eisenhower, J. W. (1990). Adolescent multiple personality disorder: A preliminary study of eleven cases. *Journal of the American Academy of Child and Adolescent Psychiatry, 29,* 359–366.

Donovan, D. M., & McIntyre, D. (1990). *Healing the hurt child.* New York: W. W. Norton.

Earl, W. L. (1991). Perceived trauma: Its etiology and treatment. *Adolescence, 26,* 97–104.

Fagan, J., & McMahon, P. P. (1984). Incipient multiple personality in children. *Journal of Nervous and Mental Disease, 172,* 26–36.

Famularo, R., Kinscherff, R., & Fenton, T. (1988). Propranolol treatment of childhood posttraumatic stress disorder, acute type. *American Journal of Diseases of Childhood, 142,* 1244–1247.

Federn, P. (1952). On the distinction between healthy and pathological narcissism. In E. Weiss (Ed.), *Ego: Psychology and the psychoses* (pp. 323–364). New York: Basic Books.

Ferenczi, S. (1955). Confusion of tongues between adults and the child [Originally: The passions of adults and their influence on the sexual and character development of children]. In M. Balint (Ed.), *Final contributions to the problems and methods of psycho-analysis* (pp. 156–167). New York: Brunner/Mazel. (Original work published 1933)

Freud, S. (1962). The aetiology of hysteria. In J. Strachey (Ed. and Trans.), *The standard edition of the complete psychological works of Sigmund Freud* (Vol. 3, pp. 189–221). London: Hogarth Press. (Original work published 1896)

Gorman, J. N. (1972). Dissociation and play therapy: A case study. *Journal of Psychiatric Nursing, 10*(2), 23–26.

Gould, C., Graham-Costain, V., Peterson, G., & Waterbury, M. (1993). *Treating dissociation in children* [Videotape]. Ukiah, CA: Cavalcade Productions.

Goulding, M., & Goulding, R. (1979). *Changing lives through redecision therapy.* New York: Brunner/Mazel.

Hornstein, N. L., & Putnam, F. W. (1992). Clinical phenomenology of child and adolescent dissociative disorders. *Journal of the American Academy of Child and Adolescent Psychiatry, 31,* 1077–1085.

Hornstein, N. L., & Tyson, S. (1991). Inpatient treatment of children with multiple personality/dissociative disorders and their families. *Psychiatric Clinics of North America, 3,* 631–648.

International Society for the Study of Dissociation. (1994). *Guidelines for treating dissociative identity disorder (multiple personality disorder) in adults.* Skokie, IL: Author.

James, B. (1989). *Treating traumatized children.* Lexington, MA: Lexington Books.

Kane, B. (1979). Children's concept of death. *Journal of Genetic Psychology, 134,* 141–153.

Kluft, R. P. (1984a). Aspects of the treatment of multiple personality disorder. *Psychiatric Annals, 14,* 51–55.

Kluft, R. P. (1984b). Treatment of multiple personality disorder: A study of 33 cases. *Psychiatric Clinics of North America, 7,* 9–29.

Kluft, R. P. (1985a). Childhood multiple personality disorder: Predictors, clinical findings, and treatment results. In R. P. Kluft (Ed.), *Childhood antecedents of multiple personality* (pp. 167–196). Washington, DC: American Psychiatric Press.

Kluft, R. P. (1985b). Hypnotherapy of childhood multiple personality disorder. *American Journal of Clinical Hypnosis, 27,* 201–210.

Kluft, R. P. (1985c). The natural history of multiple personality disorder. In R. P. Kluft (Ed.), *Childhood antecedents of multiple personality* (pp. 197–238). Washington, DC: American Psychiatric Press.

Kluft, R. P. (1986). Treating children who have multiple personality disorder. In B. G. Braun (Ed.), *Treatment of multiple personality disorder.* (pp. 79–105). Washington, DC: American Psychiatric Press.

Kluft, R. P. (1987a). The parental fitness of mothers with multiple personality disorder: A preliminary study. *Child Abuse & Neglect, 11,* 273–280.

Kluft, R. P. (1987b). Unsuspected multiple personality disorder: An uncommon source of protracted resistance, interrupting psychoanalysis. *Hillside Journal of Clinical Psychiatry, 9,* 100–115.

Kluft, R. P. (1991a). Clinical presentations of multiple personality disorder. *Psychiatric Clinics of North America, 3,* 605–630.

Kluft, R. P. (1991b). Hospital treatment of multiple personality disorder: An overview. *Psychiatric Clinics of North America, 3,* 695–720.

Kluft, R. P. (1993). Basic principles in conducting the psychotherapy of multiple personality disorder. In R. P. Kluft & C. G. Fine (Eds.), *Clinical perspectives on multiple personality disorder* (pp. 19–50). Washington, DC: American Psychiatric Press.

Kluft, R. P. (1996). Chapter Nine, this volume.

Lewis, D. O. (1991). Multiple personality. In M. Lewis (Ed.), *Child and adolescent psychiatry: A comprehensive textbook* (pp. 707–715). Baltimore, MD: Williams & Wilkins.

Loewenstein, R. J. (1991). Rational psychopharmacology in the treatment of multiple personality disorder. *Psychiatric Clinics of North America, 3,* 721–740.

London, P., & Cooper, L. M. (1969). Norms of hypnotic susceptibility in children. *Developmental Psychology, 1,* 113–124.

Malenbaum, R., & Russell, A. T. (1987). Multiple personality disorder in an eleven-year-old boy and his mother. *Journal of the American Academy of Child and Adolescent Psychiatry, 26,* 436–439.

McMahon, P. P., & Fagan, J. (1993). Play therapy with children with multiple personality disorder. In R. P. Kluft & C. G. Fine (Eds.), *Clinical perspectives on multiple personality disorder* (pp. 253–276). Washington, DC: American Psychiatric Press.

Peterson, G. (1988). Developmental concepts and annihilation in multiple personality [Summary]. *Proceedings of the Fifth Annual International Conference on Multiple Personality/Dissociative States, 55.*

Peterson, G. (1990). Diagnosis of childhood multiple personality disorder. *Dissociation, 3,* 3–9.

Peterson, G. (1991). Children coping with trauma: Diagnosis of "dissociation identity disorder." *Dissociation, 4,* 152–164.

Peterson, G. (1993, July). Suicidal impulses and alters' cognitive development: A treatment strategy. *Dissociation Notes,* p. 2. (Available from NCTSSD, P. O. Box 3693, Chapel Hill, NC 27515)

Peterson, G. (1993, October). Inter-alter confidentiality. *Dissociation Notes,* p. 2. (Available from NCTSSD, P. O. Box 3693, Chapel Hill, NC 27515)

Peterson, G. (1994, January). "Did you ask?" *Dissociation Notes,* p. 2. (Available from NCTSSD, P. O. Box 3693, Chapel Hill, NC 27515)

Peterson, G., & Boat, B. W. (1992, June). *Working with families of MPD patients: Costs and benefits.* Paper presented at the Fourth Annual Eastern Regional Conference on Abuse and Multiple Personality, Alexandria, VA.

Peterson, G., & Putnam, F. W. (1994). Preliminary results of the field trial of proposed criteria for dissociative disorder of childhood. *Dissociation, 7*, 212–220.

Putnam, F. W. (1989a). *Diagnosis and treatment of multiple personality disorder.* New York: Guilford Press.

Putnam, F. W. (1989b). Pierre Janet and modern views of dissociation. *Journal of Traumatic Stress, 2*, 413–429.

Putnam, F. W. (1991). Dissociative disorders in children and adolescents: Developmental perspective. *Psychiatric Clinics of North America, 3*, 519–532.

Putnam, F. W. (1993). Dissociative disorders in abused children: Behavioral profiles and problems. *Child Abuse & Neglect, 17*, 39–45.

Putnam, F. W., Guroff, J. J., Silverman, E. K., Barban, L., & Post, R. M. (1986). The clinical phenomenology of multiple personality disorder: A review of 100 recent cases. *Journal of Clinical Psychiatry, 47*, 285–293.

Putnam, F. W., Helmers, K., & Trickett, P. K. (1993). Development, reliability, and validity of a child dissociation scale. *Child Abuse & Neglect, 17*, 731–742.

Rapoport, J. L., Buchsbaum, M. S., Weingartner, H., Zahn, T. P., Ludlow, C., & Mikkelsen, E. J. (1980). Dextroamphetamine: Its cognitive and behavioral effects in normal and hyperactive boys and normal men. *Archives of General Psychiatry, 37*, 933–943.

Riley, R. L., & Mead, J. (1988). The development of symptoms of multiple personality disorder in a child of three. *Dissociation, 1*, 43–46.

Ross, C. A. (1989). *Multiple personality disorder: Diagnosis, clinical features, and treatment.* New York: Wiley.

Silberg, J. L., Stipic, D., & Taghizadeh, F. (in press). Dissociative disorders in children and adolescents. In J. Noshpitz (Ed.), *Handbook of child and adolescent psychiatry.* New York: Basic.

Smith, W. (1996). Chapter Seven, this volume.

Stern, C. R. (1984). The etiology of multiple personalities. *Psychiatric Clinics of North America, 7*, 149–159.

Stewart, I., & Joines, V. (1987). *TA today: A new introduction to transactional analysis.* Chapel Hill, NC: Lifespace.

Thigpen, C. H., & Cleckley, H. (1957). *The three faces of Eve.* New York: McGraw-Hill.

van der Kolk, B. A. (1993). Biological basis of PTSD. *Primary Care, 20*, 417–32.

van der Kolk, B. A. (1994). *Trauma and memory I: The dissociative defense* [Videotape]. Ukiah, CA: Cavalcade Productions.

van der Kolk, B. A., Dreyfuss, D., Michaels, M., Shera, D., Berkowitza, R., Fisler, R., & Saxe, G. (1994). Fluoxetine in posttraumatic stress disorder. *Journal of Clinical Psychiatry, 55,* 517–522.

Watkins, H. H., & Watkins, J. G. (1993). Ego-state therapy in the treatment of dissociative disorders. In R. P. Kluft & C. G. Fine (Eds.), *Clinical perspectives on multiple personality disorder* (pp.277–299). Washington, DC: American Psychiatric Press.

Weiss, M., Sutton, P. J., & Tuecht, A. J. (1985). Multiple personality in a 10-year-old girl. *Journal of the American Academy of Child Psychiatry, 24,* 495–501.

6

AN OUTLINE FOR PSYCHOANALYTICAL TREATMENT

Stephen S. Marmer

The name of the disorder discussed in this book has changed over the years, from Gmelin's exchange personalities in 1781, through split personality and dual personality to dissociated personality in *DSM-I*, hysterical personality and dissociative type in *DSM-II*, multiple personality disorder (MPD) in *DSM-III* and *III-R*, and now dissociative identity disorder (DID) in *DSM-IV*. The names have changed, but the patients and the phenomenon have remained the same. Or have they? Has our theoretical and clinical approach shaped the presentation of our patients? Let me set the stage for my discussion by briefly presenting my first MPD/DID patient from 1971.

While in the first months of my psychiatry residency at UCLA, a female patient presented with what we thought was a "hysterical" movement disorder, with tremor and pseudoseizures. We did the typical extensive and expensive university neurological workup, which was negative. It soon became clear that, in addition to her movement symptoms, the patient would also go into spontaneous dissociated states. I treated her as a *DSM-II* Hysterical Neurosis, Conversion Type, for fourteen months, taking her through suicidal crises, marital difficulties, estrangement from her mother, and ambivalence over children. She gave a history of a traumatic child-hood, with a serious surgery at age eighteen months and suspicions of parental abuse, but with nothing else definitive. During the four-teenth month of treatment, while I was out of town, she appeared twenty-four hours late for an appointment with the colleague who was covering for me. Because she was confused and suicidal, he hos-pitalized her. When I returned a few days later, I noticed she appeared to be more "spaced-out" than usual. After an hour-long psychotherapy session spent discussing her depression she declared that she was very tired and had a bad headache. She put her head down for a moment, and when she lifted it again, I thought I was in the room with another person. "Hello," she said. "Hello," I answered. "Who are you?" "I'm Buffy," she replied, introducing her multiplicity openly for the first time. As I came to realize during the next few days, I had been seeing Buffy and Janet alternate with my patient, Martha, many times, noting unexplained idiosyncrasies but not understanding them as multiple personalities.

Fortunately, I had wonderful supervisors (Louis "Jolly" West, Eugene Mindlin, and Robert Stoller), who not only were superb psychiatrists and outstanding teachers but also were well placed administratively. This latter fact helped protect me during my treatment of a patient with a controversial diagnosis. Together, they taught me the approach I used with my first patient and have influenced all my work since.

Prior to the explosion of renewed interest in MPD/DID in 1984, it was believed that this was a rare diagnosis. Like Martha, most such patients, when they did appear, presented with a small number of alter personalities. Some patients were thought to have "dual" personalities. Although these patients had a history of sex-ual or physical abuse, the specific link to childhood trauma was not then considered to be definitive; some concern was even expressed about the mixture of fact and fantasy in those memo-ries. "Classical MPD" patients, such as Eve and Sybil, were understood as the diagnostic prototype, whereas subtler (and what we now know as more typical) presentations of this condition more frequently went unrecognized. By 1984 the field changed dramatically. After that time, patients with MPD/DID appeared more commonly, were recognized as having many more personalities (alters), and aroused entirely new controversies.

That year saw the publication of a host of articles on MPD/DID and the convening of national and international meetings on the subject. The intellectual currents that produced this explosion were decisive for the direction of the field during the next decade. Leadership came from clinicians working in the field of hypnosis (see Smith, Chapter Seven). Their approach resonated with the strong interest in child advocacy and with a growing awareness, fostered by experience with veterans of Vietnam, of the effects of trauma. With few exceptions, clinical settings, rather than research or academic ones, were drawn to this topic and this patient group. The number of psychoanalysts contributing to the field of MPD/DID in those days can probably be numbered in single digits. Psychoanalysis, however, is arguably the most powerful theory of the mind and still might be understood as the "basic science" of almost all schools of psychotherapy.

My interest in psychoanalysis presented a dilemma for me because I have a strong professional identity as a psychiatrist, a strong clinical identity as a psychoanalyst, and a strong interest in dissociation and trauma. If I was not to develop a multiple professional identity disorder of my own, I had to seek a way to integrate these different approaches. Freud had been part of a commission looking into the behavior of Austrian soldiers after World War I and strongly supported the concept of traumatic neurosis. He and Breuer, in the 1890s, had treated dissociative patients whom they described in their *Studies in Hysteria*. In *The Ego and the Id*, written in 1923, Freud explicitly referred to DID:

> We cannot avoid giving over our attention for a moment longer to the ego's object identifications. If they obtain the upper hand and become too numerous, unduly powerful, and

incompatible with one another, a pathological outcome will not be far off. It may come to a disruption of the ego in consequence of the different identifications, becoming cut off from one another by resistances. Perhaps the secret of the cases of what is described as multiple personality is that the different identifications seize hold of consciousness in turn.

I introduce this quotation to show that psychoanalysis still has much to say about the theory and treatment of DID. If psychoanalytic understanding is missing from psychotherapy, the treatment is at risk of being superficial, and the therapeutic alliance is at risk of turning into reenactment.

PSYCHOANALYTIC CONCEPTUALIZATIONS

An approach to treatment can be ad hoc, or it can have a theoretical foundation. In my own work with DID patients, I try to integrate what is known about trauma with the structure of personality that is known from psychoanalysis. The absence of psychoanalytic understanding in this field has led to some simplistic notions of treatment. Outlined here is an initial effort to correct this deficiency.

Trauma, Conflict, and Deficiency

Although emphasis has been placed on the role of initial trauma in the development of DID, other important considerations can also be elucidated from a psychoanalytic tradition. These include the principles of *conflict* and *deficiency*.

Trauma. The literature on DID reports that more than 90 percent of patients with this disorder remember a history of childhood physical and/or sexual abuse. Although the veracity of such memories has been under attack, most workers in this area still emphasize trauma as the etiological agent in DID.

Trauma refers to two sorts of injuries. *Physical and sexual traumas* have a major corporeal element that makes them easier to identify. *Psychological trauma* refers to emotional distress caused by fear of separation, punishment, or disapproval of an important other person (object) or to the fantasy of physical or emotional harm. I have seen many patients with DID for whom the psychological trauma seemed sufficient to account for their symptoms. Although it would be a major error to dismiss reports of physical or sexual abuse as fanciful, my own experience has shown that it is not essential in the history of such patients to have corporeal trauma. In the debate about the accuracy of childhood memories of corporeal abuse, the role of noncorporeal psychological trauma has been relatively neglected. (I will return to the subject of trauma and its link with dissociation later in this chapter.)

However much trauma plays a role in DID, it cannot be the sole important factor. If a pedestrian is hit by a car that is traveling at ninety miles per hour, we can be satisfied that trauma alone was the agent of destruction. In cases of DID, we must look also to the two other ingredients present in all mental conditions and to the alignment of all three in the life history of the patient.

Conflict. By *conflict*, I refer to anxiety, ambivalence, depression, or distress over having internally contradictory feelings, wishes, or "commands." Traditionally, the oedipal situation produced the major neurotic conflict: the little boy loved his mother and wanted her undivided love and attention. At the same time, he also loved his father. He recognized that his mother also loved his father and that exclusive possession of the mother meant pushing the father aside. Realizing that the father was mightier than he, the little boy feared the father's wrath and conceptualized the wrath in the form of a fantasy that the father would castrate him.

The "successful" solution to the oedipal conflict was to renounce the desire for exclusive possession of the mother and to resolve ambivalence toward the father by loving him and identifying with him. Thus, the boy would want to become like the father and find a woman like the mother. "Unsuccessful" resolutions of this conflict are many. They might find the boy projecting his fear of the father onto all future authority figures; the boy might want to win the father's love by becoming more like the mother, thus seeking the sexual love of a man; he might renounce his aggression and become passive; he might be the prisoner of severe jealousy; and he might disconnect from all attachments, finding the inevitable ambivalence of relationships intolerable. Although there are many other variations to this theme, the point here is that, in normal development, some issues are hard for children to resolve. Those issues may leave residual conflicts in the best of upbringings. When mild or moderate psychological trauma is added, the conflicts become greater still.

The distinctive nature of DID is to sequester these conflicts in alter personalities. Feelings of pleasure regarding sexuality might be represented by a sexual alter, whereas feelings of guilt, dread, repulsion, and the like might each be assigned a separate and different alter. Sometimes there are heterosexual alters, asexual alters, homosexual alters, and alters that punish the sexual ones. It should not be presumed, however, that each alter is a pure culture of one point of view. Not only does the patient as a whole experience conflict, but so too can individual alters. I have found in supervision that this alter conflict is often overlooked. Furthermore, the depth and breadth of conflict is essential to understand and work with during the phases of treatment when the patient is divided and after "integration" as well. It would be incorrect to assume that, after integration, all conflict has been resolved.

Deficiency. Deficiency has become an area of increasing interest, especially for followers of Kohut's work. Just as the child needs vitamins and minerals, not just sufficient calories, for proper nutrition, people need proper emotional ingredients. If a person misses out during childhood on proper mirroring and proper empathy or if his or her frustrations are not managed properly, the person will be unable to develop a coherent self necessary for self-comfort and to give the person stability throughout the rest of his or her life. These ingredients are thought to be especially deficient in cases of Narcissistic Personality Disorder and Borderline Personality Disorder. My clinical experience shows that many patients with DID also suffer from significant deficiency of this sort.

This deficiency state has prompted some authors to regard DID as a self-psychological disorder. Others see it as a disorder of insufficient self-coherence, with alters serving the purpose of internal transitional objects or internal depictions of fantasied self-objects. To understand how alters serve as self-objects requires a brief digression.

Classical psychoanalysis concerned itself with the development of motivation and the expression and inhibition of that motivation. Its theory of motivation was expressed in the scientific metaphor of the day as "instinctual drives." Freud originally posited two such drives—the drive toward self-preservation and the sexual drive—that were in competition with each other. The self-preservation drive, had it been developed further, might well have led to an early psychoanalytic psychology of the self. Perhaps in response to having been attacked for his theory of sexuality, Freud emphasized the development of libido theory. When these two drives failed to explain such things as masochism and traumatic dreams, Freud recast his instinct theory in terms of libido (which included both sexuality and self-preservation) and the unfortunately named "death instinct" (which included aggression, repetition, and the search for quiescence). I will return to this theme later, but for our purposes here, it is important to note that the drives and the defenses against them and fantasies about them preoccupied classical psychoanalysis.

From the late 1950s through the present, Balint, Winnicott, Bowlby, Fairbairn, Guntrip, and Kohut each discovered that inadequate nurturing could have a decisive effect on the shaping of the individual in ways that would reappear in his or her relationships and in the transference. Patients who suffer from DID have disturbances in nurturing and empathy that shape their presentation. DID is generally regarded as a disorder-with-good-prognosis illness, but if there is considerable deficiency along with trauma, the prognosis will be worse and the treatment will take a different turn. For such patients, building psychic structure becomes a critical task from the outset. The general willingness of a straightforward trauma patient to tell his or her story does not apply in cases in which deficiency plays a large role.

DID as a Disorder of Defense

Perhaps it seems obvious today, but it is worth repeating that DID is a syndrome of defense. The individual who presents with DID does not have many people living within one body. Every alter personality is a mental construct: a defense created by the patient to preserve him- or herself from a piece of mental content that is thought to be too threatening or unbearable. This issue goes back to the very earliest days of psychoanalysis. Charcot and Janet believed that trauma in susceptible individuals caused *hysteria*, their term for what we would now call a dissociated response. In the 1890s, Freud determined that the trauma itself did not cause the illness; rather, the defense against remembering or reexperiencing the trauma constituted the illness. In much the same way, we might think of hypertension as the kidney's defense against inadequate blood flow.

Under the simpler trauma theory, symptoms were either direct representations or straightforward symbols of the traumatic event. Remembering the trauma, or decoding the relationship between the trauma and the symptom, would bring about cure. This remembering is not unlike those patients who want to spend all of their time focusing on "remembering the abuse." Under the defense theory, different alters are complicated mental constructs used by the patient to keep different thoughts and feelings separated. Therefore, merely "learning about the abuse" is not sufficient. Learning about the styles of defenses, their interrelationship, and the fantasies embedded in them becomes just as important (in some cases, more important) than extracting the abuse history.

Roy Schafer has taught that defenses are not simply mechanisms designed to keep something out; they are also elaborate stories and fantasies. Defenses must not be looked at as the enemies of the work, to be overcome so that the really good stuff can emerge. Instead, they are part of the way the patient constructs his or her world—internal and external. Careful attention to the defensive style of the various alters, as well as to the way the defenses work together or against each other within the alter system, must be central to treatment. Even if we as therapists could eliminate all dissociative defenses instantly and painlessly, we would not be curing the patient, for we would be missing the understanding of the style with which they have managed their affects and perceptions, their self-concept and their understanding of the world. We would also be missing an understanding of the effects of having lived with dissociation during preceding years.

Splitting, Dissociation, and Repression

The defenses thought to predominate in DID are *splitting* and *dissociation*. These terms have been used in a confusing and imprecise manner, however, in both psychoanalysis and psychiatry. It is worthwhile to pause here for a clarification on the way I understand and use these terms.

Splitting. Freud used the term *splitting* in three ways. Sometimes he meant something akin to pathological ambivalence, in which the individual found himself or herself unable to reconcile profoundly contradictory feelings or urges. At other times, he meant something akin to isolation, in which the affect connected to a thought was separated from the ideational content.

At still other times, he meant the division of the self to accommodate different views of reality. Followers of Melanie Klein use splitting in the first sense—the division of others in the world into good and bad versions and the inability to reconcile or unite them into so-called whole objects that possess both good and bad attributes simultaneously. The DID literature uses splitting in the third sense—of internal divisions within the self to allow different realities to coexist. The literature on Borderline Personality Disorder uses splitting in all three ways but emphasizes the first and second versions.

Splitting is not always pathological. All babies start their development by using "passive splitting" to differentiate experience according to whether it feels good or feels bad. Their stage of cognition and perception allows only this rather basic sorting of events and images of other people (known in psychoanalysis as "objects," to contrast them with the "subject" of the experience). Somewhere around the middle to end of the first year, probably coinciding with the appearance of "stranger anxiety," infants move to "active splitting," exerting active mental processes to keep apart good objects and good self from the bad objects and bad self. They need to do this for two important developmental reasons. You know it is easier for a single bad experience to ruin an otherwise good day, than for a good experience to redeem an otherwise bad day. How much more so for a small child who does not have a large database of experience or a sophisticated worldview? To maintain a sense of goodness in the world (a good self and a good object), babies need to protect good experiences from contamination by seemingly more powerful bad ones. At the same time, babies lack sufficient maturity for a sense of object constancy. That comes a few years later. Sometime toward the end of the Mahler's object constancy phase, which coincides roughly with the oedipal period, the normal child transforms a mostly splitting hierarchy of defenses to a mostly repression hierarchy of defenses. In so doing, the child can relate to himself or herself as a person with both good and bad traits and can see that the world contains whole objects that contain both good and bad elements. Without passive and active splitting, the child would be burdened by the weight of his or her bad experiences. In cases of traumatic childhood, such a weight could be crushing. No wonder that children with over-whelming and traumatic histories rely so dearly on the use of splitting.

For such traumatized children, we find splitting not only in the sense of dividing good and bad experience but also in the sense of maintaining two or more incompatible views of reality. If the "bad" is sufficiently overwhelming, the child finds that ordinary "good versus bad" splitting doesn't work. In such cases, fantasy identities and fantasy realities have to be constructed. "I am not the child who is being abused. There is another child who looks like me and has my name who is the one being abused." Or, "It is not my parents who are beating me or molest-ing me. My parents are a different set of people." Or, "I did not have a disturbing thing happen in the middle of the night. I was just fine. I can go to school or play with my friends and don't have to think about what happened to that other child who was in my bed last night when my parent came in." This sort of split-ting saves children from more serious mental breakdown but at the price of discontinuity of identity and perception.

Dissociation and Repression.　Two other terms used in a variety of ways are *dissociation* and *repression*. Some writers regard them as essentially the same; other writers make various distinctions between them. I think it is more useful to see them as different processes. Dissociation is an earlier and more primitive defense relied on by many mammals and reptiles. Repression is more advanced and requires the presence of a more highly developed consciousness.

Repression is a defense by which mental contents already in sec-ondary process are removed from awareness. Developmentally, repression comes into its own after object constancy is attained. *Dissociation*, in contrast, is a more primitive and earlier defense that operates under the rules of primary process. When thoughts, memories, or affects are removed from consciousness through dissociation, the "operating system" of primary process allows for displacement, condensation, and symbolization. When a patient with DID presents with alter personalities that are male and female, old and young, wise and innocent, past and present, without being burdened with a feeling of contradiction, we see the primary process aspects of dissociation in action.

In this computer age, it may be useful to think of primary process and secondary process as two different operating systems for managing mental files. *Primary process* is the older system and is based on visual and tactile perceptions. We see primary process in action every day in dreams. *Primary process* stores mental content by connotation; it is pictorial and impressionistic; thoughts are fluid; attention moves freely from topic to topic; ingredients of an idea can be disassembled and reassembled easily or moved around and transformed. The concept of linear time moving inexorably in one direction does not hold in primary process. Instead, time can be run forward, backward, or in a rearranged sequence. *Secondary process* is the newer system, based on auditory and verbal perceptions and organizations. *Secondary process* stores mental content by denotation; it is strongly bound to words; attention moves in linear chains from one topic to another; time moves in one direction, from past, through present, to future. Loosely speaking, primary process is more like poetry, secondary process more like prose; primary process more Platonic, secondary process more Aristotelian; primary process more "right brained," secondary process more "left brained."

By virtue of the way dissociation and splitting work together, patients with DID organize their symptoms. This particular alignment of defenses leaves them, so to speak, in a "waking dream." If merely repression and not dissociation were at work, simply making what was unconscious conscious would be helpful. But in the case of patients with DID, the very things that are dissociated are themselves stuck in primary process. They must be translated and then transformed into secondary process, not just simply remembered. Much unhappiness on the part of patients and therapists results from this failure to appreciate the work that the defenses demand. Treatment that seeks either forced "integration" before working through defenses or overly rapid recovery of memories without respect for the utility of the defenses against remembering invites great trouble.

The Identity Problem in DID

What is the central feature of DID? Is it dissociation? Is it splitting? Is it trauma and child abuse? I assert that the central issue is identity. I have worked with many patients who lacked one or more of the *DSM* criteria for DID but who still seemed to have the essence of the disorder embodied in the multiplicity of their identity.

Generally, *DSM* arguments are of only passing importance to psychoanalysis, but in this case the change of name from Multiple Personality Disorder to Dissociative Identity Disorder gives us a chance to reconsider the essence of the condition. If it is dissociation, and if DID is to be grouped under the general rubric of dissociative disorders, I believe that our understanding of it will be slanted away from the critical realm of identity. Although many DID patients have a lot in common with PTSD patients, others have much in common with those suffering from identity diffusion and from transsexualism and with those whose identities are not typical or even catalogued as disorders, such as spies, double agents, con artists, impersonators, and actors.

Once again, the field's emphasis on trauma to the neglect of conflict and deficiency, on memory to the neglect of defense, and on integration for its own sake rather than as a by-product of self-discovery skews therapeutic attention away from important issues of identity. I elaborate on the topic of identity, especially from the point of view of object relations and transitional object relatedness, in the following sections dealing directly with technique.

APPLYING THE THEORY TO TREATMENT

In this section, I address some main elements of a psychoanalytically based treatment of DID. I must clarify that it is rare to be able to do something approaching pure psychoanalysis with such patients, but my approach relies very heavily on the psychoanalytic approach. That approach is traditionally grouped under the headings of therapeutic alliance, transference and countertransference, interpretation, resistance, and working through.

Therapeutic Alliance

The most important step in treatment is the establishment of the therapeutic alliance. In a sense, this work is never completed during the course of psychotherapy. Setting up the therapeutic alliance starts with an acceptance that you are dealing with a whole person who presents in a divided and fragmented form. To restore the patient to wholeness requires that you see every component of that total person as necessary to his or her development. It also requires an atmosphere of safety and consistency for both therapist and patient.

At the beginning, I want patients to know that to get well they will need honesty, courage, and perseverance. If they bring those ingredients, they will get from me consistency and endurance. My immediate availability is less important than whether I will be able to stick with them to the finish. They must not use me all up in the first six weeks of treatment; recovery from DID is more like a marathon than a sprint. Therefore, I may not always be available to them at the exact moment of their distress between sessions. If they wish to do so, they may leave messages for me, which I will listen to and return when I can and when I think it is appropriate. However, I will also be working during the day with other patients whose needs in their own eyes are just as worthy.

I strive to treat all alters, even destructive and obnoxious ones, with respect. I regard them all as Purple Heart veterans of a terrible struggle; all are entitled to a place of honor. In so doing, I try to create a climate in which every alter and every part of the patient can feel safe participating in the therapy. I also want to show the patient that all parts of him- or herself need to be understood and accepted (even if we ultimately want some parts to become more mature). I sometimes say, "Just as every mouth needs teeth, every person needs an effective aggressive side."

In the early post-1984 DID era, it was commonplace for therapists to seek the patient's internal self-helper alter and to conduct the treatment by using that alter as a co-therapist. This procedure errs on the presumption that such helper alters really know as much as they claim and neglects that they, too, are defensive constructions that need to be understood on their own terms and not exploited for our needs—even our legitimate therapist needs. They are helpful as allies only to the extent that we not play favorites or indulge the fantasy that they are really internal co-therapists.

It is important that both parties feel safe. For me safety means that boundaries are respected—mine and the patient's. It should go without saying that, during psychotherapy, sexual conduct between the treating therapist and the patient should never occur. Sadly, I have been an expert witness in too many cases in which this rule has been violated. I believe in minimum physical contact of any kind between treating therapist and patient. The hug that comforts one child alter may be viewed as a rape by another; the handshake that one alter seeks may be an evil symbol to another. Because it is essential to help the patient move from imagistic primary process to verbal secondary process, I emphasize words and talking in my treatment. Even if the patient is incapable of putting ideas and feelings into words at the beginning, it is a goal of treatment to attain that ability. However, I work with whatever other media the patient needs to express himself or herself, including drawings, sculpture, music, diaries, movies, and pantomime, as long as whatever is produced is subject to verbal inquiry and to word interpretations. As a rule, nonverbal expressions have been created before the sessions and are discussed and analyzed during the sessions.

Patients sometimes experience fugue states during a session, and I am understanding of their need to hide under a table or behind a chair or to crouch in a corner. If a patient is in a dissociated condition at the end of a session and cannot easily be brought out of it, I let him or her stay in the waiting room for a while to regroup. If this action becomes a regular pattern, however, it needs to be reconsidered. Patients are not glued to the chair or to the couch, but they are not allowed to redecorate my office, whether the process is artistic or destructive.

In the first weeks of treatment, patients have a right to know certain basic things about me: my training, my experience, my style and philosophy of work. I am fairly visible in my community in both psychiatric and community arenas, so it is difficult to maintain complete anonymity, but the details of my personal life are not areas where the patient is welcome. Neither are they welcome in my home. I have had only one experience of a patient following me after working hours. Such things need to be dealt with immediately and may be grounds for discontinuing the therapy if they cannot swiftly be understood and curbed.

Because I try to treat DID on an outpatient basis, I generally see patients three times per week. Certain patients need more time than that; few need less. Most patients I have treated can use hour-long sessions productively. Occasionally, patients may need longer sessions. If, after the first few weeks of therapy, a patient is making frequent phone calls to me between sessions, I generally regard that as indication to increase the number of sessions per week.

Financial arrangements are complex with DID because, in many cases, the illness interferes with the ability of the patient to obtain the funds for treatment. I do not accept barter for therapy. The few times I was persuaded to try it with non-DID patients ended unhappily. Any fee must be at a level at which neither party feels exploited. There are many good reasons for giving DID patients reduced fees, but the demanding nature of the work requires that the therapist be free of resentment, and usually this translates into a fee. I also set my schedule so that I can have a life of my own outside the office. It is important not to sacrifice the quality of one's own life or to create future patients in your spouse or children in the course of saving the lives of one's patients.

Frequently, patients ask me about recommendations for reading on DID. I discourage this. I want the field of the therapy to be as uncontaminated as possible. I would prefer not to have to worry about whether a particular symptom or story was shaped by another patient, a movie, a book, or even a scientific article. In general, I am unenthusiastic about support groups for DID, as I have found that often they support the illness more than they support the recovery, and they provide fertile ground for stories and histories to intermix.

Cases brought to me for consultation most often founder on the therapeutic alliance. This is the zone in which the treatment will succeed or fail. It provides a safety net, the ability for both you and the patient to have faith in the future when everything seems to be going badly. It provides the opportunity for the patient to hate you and to come back the next day without feeling like trying to kill you or himself or herself.

This alliance is not something you can create in the first two weeks of treatment and not worry about. It is more like living in a house: the roof will need fixing one rainy season and then the water heater will blow up; you'll need a new refrigerator, and then the dishwasher will crash; then someone will throw a rock through the window, and you'll have to replace that. It needs constant maintenance and repair.

Force yourself to review on a regular basis, What is the state of the therapeutic alliance? Have I done anything to damage our alliance? Is the patient doing anything to damage our alliance, such as coming to sessions intoxicated? These and other questions must be part of a regular checklist for self-supervision.

Transitional Object Relatedness

To this point, most of my thoughts on the therapeutic alliance have been fairly generic. The psychoanalytic concept that contributes most to the therapeutic alliance is that of the transitional object. Winnicott coined the term "transitional object" and had a very sophisticated notion of it. He said that the transitional object is the state of relatedness between the mother, the teddy bear, and the thumb. It is typically thought of as the blanket that Linus carries around with him in the "Peanuts" cartoon. However, it is far more than that. It is a state of mind that all human beings need in order to help themselves through separation. Its ultimate fulfillment in psychological terms is the coherent self, which is one's permanent transitional object if one is lucky enough to be healthy to the degree that one has it. It is what all people carry with them at all times. In childhood, people usually use material objects for transitional relatedness, but the need for and use of transitional phenomena do not end in childhood or reach their limits in material things. Imaginary companions provide transitional relatedness. Religion, political ideology, science, and music fulfill transitional relatedness needs by exerting a soothing influence that helps people feel less isolated in the universe.

DID patients suffer much trauma in childhood, often at the hands of those whom they count on for love. If a parent or other important person either engages in trauma or colludes with it, the result for the child is that he or she is not sufficiently comforted. In this respect, DID patients lack comforters. To survive, they must create their own comforters by turning to themselves and their alters. Because they can't make a coherent self, they make a polyfragmented self or selves, and they use their alters for the same purposes that non-DID children would use transitional objects, except that in normal childhood, transitional objects are a way station on the road to establishing a coherent self, and in DID, patients are stuck with their alters.

In psychoanalytic psychotherapy with DID patients, the therapist becomes a transitional object in two senses. First, you become the first individual with whom each and every part of the patient has a relationship; you thus become the patient's first constant object—first lighthouse, first North Star—that he or she has ever had. You also become the first consistent person who is an ongoing reality for all of the patient's alter states. DID patients need that experience to organize themselves. Second, the patient takes you in, each alter differently at first, initially as a whole collection of transitional objects, but ultimately as a major transitional object they will hold within them. Followers of Kohut and self psychology may be more comfortable calling the internalized representation of the therapist a "self-object." My theoretical differences with this are important but too subtle and complex for this chapter. From a practical point, I would not want to quarrel with this alternative terminology. We fulfill that function for DID patients and all of their alters. Ultimately, they come to understand that they share a valuable experience around which they can begin to reorganize themselves.

The reason I place so much emphasis on the therapeutic alliance is that these patients, on the face of it, don't have a natural inclination to form a therapeutic alliance. More typical neurotic patients will have had enough good mothering early on that they have well-developed receptor sights for a therapeutic alliance. They have had enough times when they've been picked up, when they've been held, when they've been contained, when their emotions have been processed by someone else and returned back to them, to have a prototype or template for this kind of experience. In contradistinction, dissociative patients with a very heavy dose of trauma combined with a lot of deprivation are less ready to form a therapeutic alliance. They are deeply yearning for it, with a profound need but also an enormous difficulty in feeling safe in such a situation. Often, they have not known anyone who will not enter into a seduction if they're being seduced, someone who will not enter into abuse if they are vulnerable or abusive. Just as they have too much memory (as in a fugue or flashback) and too little memory (as in dissociation and repression), such patients also have too much affect and not enough affect. When they are in a reenactment, they are flooded with emotion; when they are in a dissociated state, they don't have enough contact with emotions. Constancy in the therapeutic alliance on the part of the therapist is extremely important and often leaves a very narrow optimal zone within which to work.

Mapping from the Perspective of the Therapeutic Alliance

Seen from the perspective of the therapeutic alliance, getting to know the overall dimensions of the patient takes on a new aspect. The first phase of treatment does consist of getting to know the functional purpose and characterological style of the different dissociative states, whether full-fledged DID or another related dissociative disorder. This getting-to-know is not the same thing, however, as cognitive mapping. I prefer to call it "acquainting yourself with the overall architecture of the person." It is more like walking through a building than actually sitting down with the blueprints. The very act of getting-to-know creates a therapeutic joint enterprise and enhances the therapeutic alliance. For the first time ever, all parts of the patient are allowed to be heard. This interalter communication also sows the seeds for undermining the therapeutic alliance as they become competitive with one another.

Thus, the therapeutic alliance becomes a feedback spiral in which conditions that deepen it create new issues that threaten it, the analysis of which strengthens it again, and so forth. I do not generally write out poster boards of a patient's "map" because I regard this tactic as an unnecessary reification that countermands my overall strategic goal of getting the patient to experience the self as ultimately unitary. Seeing the various alters as different states or functions matches my therapeutic goals and encourages the patient to become more attached to the therapy than to the unique separateness of various alters. Concrete mapping tends to strengthen the territoriality and chauvinism of each alter toward its own symbolic "flag" and "national anthem."

The therapeutic alliance can be said to enter a higher phase of development when you and the patient, parts and all, are able to identify mutual goals. Here, you reach the point where the patient can begin to understand consequences of his or her behavior and take responsibility for his or her actions. Inevitably, the therapeutic alliance starts in a context of transference—generally a mixture of eagerly wished-for positive trusting transference and dangerously guarded-against negative transference.

Transference and Countertransference

Transference and *countertransference* are used in various ways by different authors. *Transference* is the phenomenon of experiencing a current real relationship through the lens of a significant prior one, usually unconsciously. It is a displacement onto a new situation of the emotions and fantasies developed during an older situation. When transference becomes the dominating feature of a patient's mental life and when the patient's central issues are repeatedly reexperienced within the treatment context, this is called a *transference neurosis*. *Countertransference* originally referred to the emotions unconsciously evoked in the therapist in response to the patient's transference. Later, it became connotatively understood as the reactions by the therapist toward the patient that undermine the treatment alliance. Later still, it was understood as the responses in the therapist stimulated by the projections or projective identifications of the patient. Without getting too technical, projective identification refers to the emotions the patient needs the therapist to feel when the patient cannot feel them directly, or when the patient needs to treat the therapist in such a way as to evoke a feeling the patient is unable to express.

Transference and countertransference also illustrate that what a person can't remember or say aloud is often remembered in the form of reenactments. Thus, the transference becomes a major reenactment by which the therapist can learn crucial things about a patient's past and inner lives.

As Judith Armstrong states in Chapter One, with a DID patient, transference is always present on at least three levels: the patient as a whole, the patient as a complex system, and the patient feeling entirely like the part-self alter presenting to the therapist at a given moment. At every stage of the treatment, and in every session, the patient is presenting issues on three levels simultaneously.

The patient as a whole may be bewildered, may be indulging in magical fantasy wishes that you can solve his or her problem without any help or pain from the patient. Often, the patient as a whole suffers from a metaphorical expressive aphasia. The patient has experiences and doesn't recognize the links between those experiences; the patient cannot conceptualize, let alone articulate, them. At such times, the whole patient may become enormously frustrated and have rage attacks such as we see in patients who have poststroke expressive aphasia.

At the same time, the patient is a complex system with competing and often canceling affects, desires, memories, and attitudes toward treatment. While this is going on, the patient may be in the thrall of one particular among many alters, each of whom may have a different reaction to the therapist.

Such patients may be reexperiencing trauma all the time. After they begin treatment, they find you asking them to let their anesthesia wear off. From their point of view, both in the therapeutic alliance and in the transference, the minute they come into the treatment, you're torturing them. Thus, there is bound to be inherent ambivalence, with positive and negative transference elements co-existing simultaneously.

There is a story of a man who meets an old friend on the train and insists that the friend be a guest in his home. The friend protests, preferring to stay in a hotel, but eventually gives in. After a wonderful week of business and friendship, the guest is about to leave when the host presents him with a bill three times larger than what the hotel would have charged. When the guest protests, the host suggests that they take the matter to the town judge. After each man explains his position, the judge determines that the guest must pay in full before leaving to return to his hometown. Dejectedly and with great disillusion about their friendship, the guest ponders how to pay this unexpected bill; suddenly, his host tears up the receipt and says, "You owe me nothing." "But you took the case before the town judge, and he agreed with you," said his friend. "What were you trying to do? Why did you put me through all this if you were going to tear up the bill?" The host replied, "I just wanted to show you what an idiot we have for a judge in this town." This story illustrates what happens in a transferential relationship in which the patient is unable to tell his or her story. The patient has to reenact it within the transference, often with shifting role assignments.

Sometimes the patient is the abused child and the therapist is the abuser. Sometimes the therapist is the rescuer to the abused child and sometimes is the passive onlooker who should have rescued the child but did not or could not. At other times, the patient is the abuser to the therapist as child victim. Often, these role assignments shift from session to session or even within a single session. Sometimes the roles will be represented within the patient's system. Some alters will want to be rescued or parented by the therapist; some alters will want to destroy the therapist, seen transferentially as the parent or even as the weak and vulnerable parts of the patient.

Once there is a general knowledge of how the patient's system works, the therapist can often track these shifting dramas. Sometimes the picture is so obscure that only the countertransference responses of the therapist offer a clue as to what is going on. A common phenomenon is that of *parallel dissociation*, in which the therapist feels the disconnectedness the patient cannot otherwise describe in words. Sometimes a countertransference reaction of deadness or difficulty linking and tracking is the only clue available to alert the participants of the dynamics of what is occurring. Here, it is especially important that the therapist retain the twin attitudes of open and empathic involvement and calm, serene, "above the fray" professionalism. Many dissociative patients, however, interpret calm professionalism not as the reassuring presence of a safe person, but as the weakness or indifference of a person who should have been able to rescue them. Here again, it is on the strength of the therapeutic alliance that the unfolding of the transference depends.

Some alter configurations are more appealing to many therapists than other alter groups. So-called self helpers, internal wise gurus, and pseudo co-therapists often become favorite alters for novice therapists. It should never be assumed that such alters know as much about the system as they claim; nor should the therapist ever be seen as playing favorites. First, it has been my experience that aggressive alters are generally more helpful in the long run than self helper alters. Second, the patient must learn to accept and deal with all of his or her parts, and if the therapist plays favorites, this will convey the message that some alters have a lesser place in the total system. Third, it is a mistake to make any alter feel as though it was not welcome in the treatment.

An especially difficult aspect of the transference is that the patient may be on several emotional and cognitive levels of development within a single session. The critical thing to keep in mind is that the patient is re-creating elements in the transference in lieu of verbal remembering. It is also important to note, however, that merely remembering is not enough. I will return to this topic in the section "Working Through, or How Does Therapy Cure?" but in the transference we learn about the patient's character structure, get to experience firsthand the nature of the patient's distortions, have to endure a spectrum of abusive experiences and seductions, and observe and track the accuracy of the patient's reporting.

As Alice Brand-Bartlett, Bonnie Buchele, and Ira Brenner have stated in recent workshops, transference in patients with DID is made more difficult by the fact that it is symbolized differently from the transference in neurotic patients. Whereas the whole patient can sometimes see that a transference storm is a drama he or she has contributed to, the complex system and the alter present in the moment cannot. For them it is really happening in a very concrete way. At such moments, interpretations of transference are feeble. Transference interpretation requires that the patient be capable of distinguishing past from present, concrete from abstract, and cause from effect. But only within that difficult transference vortex can the patient acquire these perspectives. Working within the transference, therefore, requires great patience from the therapist and great perseverance from the patient.

Working Through, or How Does Therapy Cure?

In prepsychoanalytic days, it was believed that trauma in susceptible individuals caused hysteria—or what we would now call dissociative disorders. Patients were thought to have suffered from unremembered trauma that was being expressed in various symptoms. The "cure" was to get them to remember their forgotten trauma. This nineteenth-century theory was also popular in 1984 when DID was rediscovered. It still forms the basis of theory for many therapists and patients. "Getting the memories out" through hypnosis, Amytal, art or play therapy, as well as by talking, is thought of by many as a necessary step toward cure.

In 1895, Freud broke through that simple formula by asserting that it was not the trauma itself that caused the symptoms, but rather the defense against the experience of remembering and feeling the trauma. This statement moved the therapeutic arena into the workings of the patient's mind and allowed Freud to explain how symbolism, fantasy, wish, and trauma blended in special combinations unique to each patient. In this theory, working with the defenses, especially the effort to replace more primitive defenses with more mature ones, became the way to reach cure.

Another view that was both old-fashioned and modern is that if trauma caused psychopathology, corrective emotional experience would cure it. Franz Alexander was the advocate of this theory, although its roots were in the so-called moral therapy of the late eighteenth and early nineteenth centuries, as was depicted in the film *The Madness of King George*. A variation of this theory without its more overt manipulative tone can be detected in Self Psychology, with its reliance on mirroring, twinning, affective atunement, and empathy. This is a more sophisticated version, in that it locates the restorative experience within the transference, rather than in overt real-world actions. Those overt actions had their day in DID when many in the field advocated various versions of so-called reparenting.

I believe that, by its nature, a psychoanalytic approach is supportive and corrective insofar as it offers consistency, continuity, empathy, reliability, and the willingness to see the treatment as a marathon in which both patient and therapist cross the finish line. What patients have lacked in safe objects that would be open to them without aggression or seduction is offered in this approach. If we as therapists hug them, give them bottles, or hold their hands, we are reenacting with our patients, not correcting their trauma or deficiency states.

My preferred view is that traumatic states are mediated by the presence or absence of personal narrative. The nature of traumatic memory is that it is encoded in a more primary process way that is easily subject to dissociation. In *Beyond the Pleasure Principle*, Freud noted that trauma can so overwhelm stimulus barriers that the individual is overwhelmed. In response, the individual enlists a triad of defenses: dissociation, repetition, and aggression. The traumatized person dissociates and seeks quiescence in the form of the "nirvana principle," engages in repetition of the trauma in the form of disturbing dreams or relationships that re-create abuse, and is left with a superabundance of aggression that may be expressed against others or the self.

These phenomena certainly appear in patients afflicted with DID. In the course of treatment, patients also get more memory than they can handle and more affect than their self-schema can process. By history they have learned that they can't rely on the stability or benevolence of the world. To deal with this fact, they dissociate and create their own worlds with their own *dramatis personae*. Simple remembering will not make them better, and they are unable to accept the kindness of the therapist without suspicion. Besides, the hug that comforts one alter may be experienced as an intrusion by another.

The approach to a cure may be found in the theories of Roy Schafer. The organizing effect of narrative, of verbally organized personal history, binds the disturbing affect and blends memory with an awareness of the present. Primary process, with its mostly pictorial images, its ability to have past, present, and future all flow into each other in all directions, fuels dissociative alter systems. Secondary process, with its mostly word-associated ideas, its reliance on cause and effect, its unidirectional time line, is a system that needs things to make sense. Although we can never change the facts of a person's life, we as therapists have the ability to organize their feelings and memories into a narrative and thus influence its meaning.

In this paradoxical sense, the future can cause the past. Trauma in our patients was made more unbearable by virtue of its meaninglessness. In dissociation the associational linking is missing. Autobiographical narrative provides that linking associational path. It simultaneously provides the sense that all parts of the patient belong to that autobiography.

Such a narrative is not merely a linear recounting of facts. It is discovered by the data of the transference experience that both patient and therapist share in real time. By its very nature, such a narrative, which links past experience to transference drama, also heightens awareness of the rules of consequence and helps the parts of the patient feel allegiance toward each other.

Often, an alter will not realize the effect of its behavior on the welfare of other alters. Frequently, an alter will believe that whatever it is experiencing is 100 percent of reality, for that alter is not present when other alters experience other things. Thus, a suicidal alter may think there is no hope because its total existence is despair. Another alter may not be concerned with danger because its total existence is having fun. A coherent narrative leads the patient to see that no alter can assume that it has the only valid perspective, for none are around 100 percent of the time. If they were, they would not have DID.

Freud's term for the part of the treatment that needed more than mere interpretation was *working through*. The use of narrative for working thorough is illustrated in a brief story by Eli Wiesel.

> When the great Rabbi Israel Baal Shem-Tov saw misfortune threatening his people, it was his custom to go into a certain part of the forest to meditate. There he would light a fire, say a special prayer, and the miracle would be accomplished and the misfortune averted. Later, when his disciple, the celebrated Magid of Mezritch, had occasion, for the same reason, to intercede with heaven, he would go to the same place in the forest and say, "Master of the Universe, listen! I do not know how to light the fire, but I am still able to say the prayer," and again, the miracle would be accomplished.
>
> Still later, Rabbi Moshe-Leib of Sasov, in order to save his people once more, would go into the forest and say, "I do not know how to light the fire, I do not know the prayer, but I know the place and this must be sufficient." It was sufficient and the miracle was accomplished. Then it fell to Rabbi Israel of Rizhyn to overcome misfortune. Sitting in his armchair, his head in his hands, he prayed. "I am unable to light the fire and I do not know the prayer. I cannot even find the place in the forest. All I can do is to tell the story, and this must be sufficient."
>
> And it was sufficient.

As psychotherapists we cannot give our patients a different childhood. Even our best intentions will not erase their trauma or neglect. And we cannot reparent them. We cannot remember for them. What we can do is help them tell their story. If it is a story based on what we discover in the transference, processed and retold in the context of a therapeutic alliance, it will be sufficient.

Strategic Integration

In the course of creating a coherent narrative, we as therapists help patients discover their unity of experience. Integration is held by most therapists to be a desirable goal—sometimes a necessary goal. Approaches to integration differ. For some, a blended board of directors that cooperate efficiently is sufficient integration. For others, tactical interventions that bring alters together are emphasized. In this theory, integration is approached as a series of stages, often thought of as serial.

For example, alter A may be integrated with alter B, and the resultant alter AB can then be integrated with alter C, or perhaps alter CD, if they had been integrated earlier. Sometimes similar or like alters are integrated to reduce population explosion among alters. Sometimes different or unlike alters are integrated to give them necessary skills. Such integration can be on a trial basis, facilitated by hypnosis or some other image technique. Sometimes various ceremonies can be held to encourage alters to merge.

Strategic integration, as I understand it within this psychoanalytic outline, takes a different approach. From this perspective, patients are divided because their knowledge and affects are too disturbing to be experienced in a nondissociative way. As the treatment progresses, all alters are participating in the same enterprise with the same therapist. They are working on the same narrative history construction. I look for signs that emotions are being experienced across dissociative barriers. I try to facilitate movement of all alters to more advanced and mature developmental positions. As the treatment progresses, the patient begins to see that the behaviors of one alter affect the options of all alters.

For example, if one alter likes to smoke, other alters will have a cough and a sore throat. If one alter needs to binge, another alter will be upset over how it looks. If one alter is reckless sexually, another alter may need to seek treatment for a sexually transmitted disease. Accounting for his or her experience in therapy with a therapist who is constant across all alters leads the patient to develop affective permeability across dissociative barriers. If the dynamic issues that generated the dissociation are addressed, they will generally fall away of their own weight. If alters across the system know each other's histories and feel each other's feelings, their investment in separateness melts. Sometimes patients don't realize that integration is taking place, but the therapist can recognize it when an angry alter becomes tearful, a sad, pathetic alter becomes annoyed, or a manic, substance-abusing party alter worries about consequences.

Borderline Personality Disorder and DID

Perhaps DID is more of a spectrum disorder than the literature acknowledges. One way to look at this is to explore some of the similarities between Borderline Personality Disorder (BPD) and DID.

Many authors regard DID as a subset of BPD. David Fink and I have argued that these are two distinct conditions that in certain cases can be comorbid in the same patient. We have concluded that BPD dissociation is different from DID dissociation. The former is more dreamy, "spaced out," or absent; the latter is a complex hierarchy of nuanced states, each of which contains a strong fantasy element. BPD has more of a "low tech" defensive organization; DID has a more "high tech" structure. BPD patients have "unstable instability"; DID patients have "stable instability," which can be predicted once the overall architecture of the system is understood. BPD patients have great difficulty soothing themselves and may turn to others with alternating idealization and devaluation in the process of attempting to use objects for soothing. DID patients are much better at self-soothing; indeed, their alter system may be understood as an elaborate attempt to do just that. BPD patients use splitting in the sense of polarization of good and bad. DID patients split their identity. BPD patients know who they are but not what they are. The DID patient is a collection of whos, each knowing clearly what it is. BPD structure is more like a building with a single large room: when the heat is on, the room becomes too hot; when the air conditioning is on, the room becomes too cold; swings between extremes prevail. The DID patient is more like a bank vault or high-security archive with many tiny compartments for storing secrets and valuables. A cold room and a hot one may exist simultaneously side by side.

It may be that the patients who require more structured therapeutic interventions, more tactical maneuvers, more direct techniques, and periods of hospitalization are those who have more BPD features. Indeed, it may be that a single recommended treatment for DID is inadequate until there is greater specificity of subtypes of the disorder.

Dreams

Dreams are used for diagnosis, prognosis, and as part of my theory of the dynamics of DID. The psychoanalytic theory of dreams holds that every day a person gathers new data and that every night the person sorts those data during dreams. These data, called *day residue*, mingle with other connotatively linked material during the primary process data sort that occurs during sleep. If an image from the day residue is being put into a file cabinet bursting with papers, some of those papers will fall to the floor during filing. When they are picked up, they may represent wishes, memories, and emotions that are loosely related to the day residue and that can be combined under the primary process rules of displacement, condensation, and symbol formation. When the person wakes, the jagged edges of the mostly visual dream is smoothed out into a verbal story. In dreams, one can be one's current age and talk with people from one's childhood who appear exactly as they did then. One can be transformed from human to animal, from male to female or vice versa; one can be both absent and present. Seen from this perspective, DID behaves much like a waking dream. In fact, if you approach the presentation of a patient with the concept that he or she is living a waking dream, many of the phenomena of DID will seem less exotic, and the relationship to the transference will become clearer.

Dreams have also helped me make diagnoses. For example:

This patient would behave strangely whenever she was drinking. My consultation task was to determine whether the patient had an alcohol-related pathological intoxication with personality changes or had DID with an alcoholic alter. She had a dream in which she was leading her high school drill team, and every time she looked to the front, another one of her selves standing behind her in the group would create mischief. This dream helped me conclude that the correct diagnosis was DID and that her drinking came after, rather than before, her dissociations.

Dreams illustrating the dynamics of a patient are present across all diagnoses. For example:

A patient with DID once presented me, over a two-week period, with a series of dreams that we discovered were the symbolic representations of an abuse scene from the perspective of several alters. The dreams in question were all highly symbolic, but each was dreamed in a different style. Noting that one dream was a still life, another was filled with vivid colors, another with movement and sound, still another with surrealistic phenomena, and a final one with action, danger, and injury, we were able to understand and analyze the defensive and cognitive organization of her various alters.

That same patient demonstrated in her dreams that we were nearing termination phase. Earlier in treatment, she had had a dream in which she saw herself on a hospital gurney and saw me sticking acupuncture needles into her vocal chords. In the pretermination dream, three mice were living harmoniously near room 813. She had often represented her personalities as mice, but never before in harmony and cooperation. Her father had died on August 13, a date she had "forgotten" or confused in earlier times.

Memories, False Memories, and Ritual or Cult Abuse

Memories are a controversial aspect of treatment for DID. My position is that a credulous stance is essential for the therapeutic alliance to take hold. You must believe in your patient for the patient to connect with you. At the same time, none of us were witnesses to events in the past. We are therefore more like historians than detectives when we try to make sense out of the combination of symptoms, narrative, and transference we encounter in our patients.

As a general rule, a psychoanalytic approach will be less intrusive, less "suggestive," and more open to the possibility that all memory—in patients across the spectrum and in people who never become patients—is a blend of accurate recording, an admixture with related events and memories, emotions, wishes, and fantasies. I hold that everything a patient says may be an accurate depiction of real events in the historical past. At the same time, all mental processes are subject to unconscious influence from within the person and to a degree of social influence from without. Care taken in avoiding suggestion, and a willingness to hold belief and skepticism simultaneously in your mind, create a climate that makes the productions of the patient safer to rely on.

Much of the controversy about false memories would never have arisen if our field had not oversold its findings. Likewise, a patient in therapy will generally find it difficult to pursue getting well and getting even at the same time. For that reason, I have been unenthusiastic about lawsuits against alleged abusers of decades ago. Such lawsuits interfere with treatment by diverting energy and attention away from the internal work the patient needs. They also offer new opportunities for others to use the lawsuit for new abuse. There is much to be said for the old cliché, "Living well is the best revenge."

By the same token, I believe that advocates of the position that there is no such thing as repressed memory or that false memories are a frequent phenomenon of psychotherapy are overstating their case. Many of us have had patients who were able to get objective confirmation of their memories, either in the form of hard evidence or by way of acknowledgment by their former abusers.

What do you do when a patient reports memories of abuse to the alleged abuser and that party asks you whether you believe your patient? I hold that we must believe in our patients while making it clear that we have a therapist's belief, not a lawyer's or judge's belief. The "rules of evidence" for psychotherapists and for lawyers, judges, and police officers are different. At the same time, we must carefully sift through the transference to see what it tells us about the patient and his or her veracity.

Legal clouds that hang over a treatment setting can interfere with therapeutic progress. Therapists need to combat the impulse to fear their patients or the relatives of their patients. A path toward therapeutic clarity is to keep the focus on the patient, on the therapeutic alliance, and on the transference. (This applies to treatment cases; the expert witness role calls for other considerations beyond the scope of this chapter.)

With respect to memories of ritual abuse and cults, I remain a credulous skeptic. I know that unspeakably horrific things have actually occurred in our time that were disbelieved by many when they heard early reports. My own experience with patients has been that most ritual and cult memories have turned out to be displacements of abuse closer to home. Projecting it onto an outside group has often been a defense. Yet, colleagues whom I respect assure me that they have had patients whose stories are entirely credible. For now, I am content to remain confused.

∾

Here are some final points to keep in mind:

- DID is a disorder of defense. Patients use dissociation and splitting to keep out of awareness any memories and emotions that would otherwise be overwhelming to them.
- DID has elements of trauma, conflict, and deficiency. The field has tended to overemphasize trauma in its effort to correct the neglect of trauma in prior eras. A psychoanalytic approach gives weight to all three areas.
- DID is as much an identity disorder as it is a dissociative disorder. Patients with DID live in a waking dream, governed by the rules of primary process.
- The defense mechanisms of dissociation and splitting are prominent in DID. Dissociation differs from repression in key respects.
- Treatment of DID relies on forming a solid therapeutic alliance in which all alters are invited as honored members. Therapists must avoid playing favorites among alters. Although patients must be met where they are, alters should not be taken at face value.
- The therapist is a transitional object for the patient, thus providing the first experience all alters share. This becomes the first step toward strategic integration.
- Critical information is learned in the transference and by careful monitoring of the countertransference. Transference can help clarify the credibility of memories, as well as provide an ever-shifting dramatic re-creation of the critical developments and characters in the life of the patient.
- Patients get better during the process of working through, with the help of narrative reorganization of their previously

dissociated experiences. We can never change past events, but we can create new meaning.

- Strategic integration takes the approach that the patient is a whole person who has a complex structure that may manifest itself in dissociated ways. Encouraging the development of a greater band width of affect across dissociative barriers eventually dissolves the need for separateness. Tactical maneuvers can be used sparingly in such an approach.

- DID may be a disorder with different subtypes, each of which might benefit from different techniques. Comorbidity with BPD may necessitate more active interventions, including hospitalization.

- Memories are data that may be linked to actual events but that may also be affected by unconscious internal influences as well as external social ones. Keeping the focus on treatment and recovery will help keep both patient and therapist from getting off the track.

NOTES

P. 185, *We cannot avoid giving over our attention*: Freud, S. (1955). The ego and the id. In J. Strachey (Ed. and Trans.), *The standard edition of the complete psychological works of Sigmund Freud* (Vol. 19, pp. 3–29). London: Hogarth Press. (Original work published 1923)

P. 210, *When the great Rabbi Israel Baal Shem-Tor*: Wiesel, E. (1966). *The gates of the forest*. New York: Holt, Rinehart & Winston.

7

THE USE OF HYPNOSIS IN DIAGNOSIS AND TREATMENT

William Smith

Hypnosis is simply a technique. Yet, if used within a therapeutic paradigm by psychotherapists thoroughly trained in the therapeutic application of hypnosis, it can be an extremely effective therapeutic tool. It is especially useful when used in diagnosis and intervention for patients with dissociative disorders. In this chapter, I describe how inducing a dissociative state can be curative for dissociative disorders, and especially for patients with Dissociative Identity Disorder (DID).

DID is currently defined as the existence of two or more distinct personality states that alternate in taking full control of the person's behavior. Generally regarded as a product of repetitive, severe traumas in childhood, DID is essentially an adaptive effort gone awry. Dissociative defenses ultimately result in a failure of the normally integrative functions of memory and consciousness. Important elements of experience and identity are sequestered

---

This chapter is a compilation of two articles by the author: The section entitled "The Use of Hypnosis Diagnosis" was taken from pages 338–340 of Allen, J. G., & Smith, W. H., (1993). Diagnosing dissociative disorders. *Bulletin of the Menninger Clinic, 57*(3), 328–343. The other sections have been taken from Smith, W. H. (1993). Incorporating hypnosis in the psychotherapy of patients with multiple personality disorder. *Bulletin of the Menninger Clinic, 57*(3), 344–354. The articles have been altered slightly to correspond to the style used in this book. Reprinted by permission.

out of the mainstream of consciousness, become organized as alternate selves, and reemerge in situations reminiscent of the earlier traumas. The pathology, secondary to reliance on dissociative defenses, ranges from mild to severe and may include depression, sleep and eating disorders, substance abuse, sexual dysfunction, self-mutilation, somatoform and conversion disorders, and widespread characterological disturbances. The clinical presentation of such individuals is highly variable, and the underlying dissociative pathology may not be easily apparent.

USE OF HYPNOSIS IN DIAGNOSIS

Direct contact with an alter personality is the only definitive way of confirming a diagnosis of DID. As a sort of controlled dissociation itself, hypnosis can influence the dissociative barriers and allow alters to "come out." In many DID cases, hypnosis is unnecessary; alters will emerge if simply asked. But if time is short and there is still some doubt, hypnosis can be an invaluable tool.

Patients with dissociative disorders are invariably highly susceptible to hypnosis, relying as they do on defensive strategies that can be thought of as similar to self-hypnosis. After inducing a trance state, the therapist asks the patient "if there is another thought process, part of the mind, part, person, or force that exists in the body." Another approach is to ask about disremembered behaviors—for example, "I'd like to talk to the part (or side) that cut Mary's arm."

Hypnotic interviewing does not invariably evoke alters even when they exist. DID is not ruled out by unproductive hypnotic interviewing; one or more uncooperative alters may not allow communication to occur. But when alters are accessed, another level of diagnostic inquiry may begin, that of "mapping the system." To get a sense of the alters and their relationship to each other, each alter is interviewed and the circumstance of its creation ascertained. The current adaptive or destructive role each alter plays in the overall system should also be determined. This aspect of diagnosis should proceed only after a consistent treatment frame has been established and the patient has been taught how to use hypnotic techniques for affect modulation and self-soothing. And even then, care must be taken. Exploring the traumatic origins of the alters may be retraumatizing and must proceed gradually.

Cautions and Concerns

What are some other concerns when using hypnosis? One is that DID might be caused by hypnotic interviewing. Is it possible that a highly hypnotizable individual might "produce" a new personality in response to a clinician's implicit or even explicit suggestion that one exists? It is true that phenomena resembling DID can be produced through hypnosis. Indeed, Watkins's ego-state therapy actually exploits the capacity many people have for experiencing different aspects or sides of themselves for therapeutic purposes. It is also true that once a patient is in treatment, the patient's dissociative processes that have culminated in alters may continue and produce more.

But there is no evidence that judicious interviewing can actually create the complex dissociative pathology seen in DID. Clinicians who lack experience with DID should use hypnosis with caution, however, because highly hypnotizable people may produce phenomena resembling DID. Care must also be taken to avoid making a diagnosis based on hallucinations or anesthesias that could persist as symptoms.

Therapists with patients who have dissociative symptoms exhibiting amnesia may desire hypnotic interviewing to determine whether unremembered traumas have caused their problems. Occasionally, the patients themselves ask for the procedure. Sometimes recurrent dreams or fragments of memories seem to suggest early abuse, and hypnosis is sought to bring whatever is on the edge of awareness into full consciousness.

There are several important cautions to such investigations. First, the recovery of traumatic memories may be retraumatizing and may exacerbate rather than relieve the patient's distress.

Even if the patient is generally functioning at a high level and does not suffer regression, the revelation may trigger anxiety, guilt, and depression. Second, what is "revealed" may not be the truth the patient is seeking. Hypnosis increases many people's ability to recall more about the past, but the accuracy of such memories is suspect. Hypnotically facilitated recall is subject to the same distortions as—and maybe more than—ordinary memory. What is produced may be largely true but nonetheless is still only partly true, and verification by other persons may be impossible.

Clearly, many clinical circumstances seem to require that early traumas be confronted and mastered. Such efforts are typical in the treatment of DID and may be especially needed with these and other patients when symptoms such as flashbacks are persistent or when problems such as depression and sexual inhibition have no discernable cause and do not yield to conventional treatment. But we as therapists also need to be cognizant of instances in which such confrontation leads to additional difficulties. For instance, if a memory of abuse within the family is recalled, how is the person to feel about the perpetrator or toward others who may have known but done nothing? When all is said and done, the patient is left with the dilemma of what to do with the new information. Therefore, part of working through such traumas is to come to grips with *current* psychosocial sequelae of working through past traumas.

INCORPORATING HYPNOSIS INTO PSYCHOTHERAPY

Psychotherapeutic treatment of persons with DID frequently includes judicious use of hypnosis. In this section, I outline widely accepted essential features of this form of treatment: developing self-soothing techniques, mapping the system of alternate personalities, facilitating communication between alters and with the therapist, managing abreaction, and—when possible and appropriate—aiding the process of fusion. I also discuss how dissociative processes that originally were used for sheer psychic survival can be drawn on to improve psychological health.

Treatment of individuals with DID may contain several dimensions, including periods of hospitalization, medication for symptom amelioration, group therapy, family therapy, and expressive therapies, such as art, movement, and writing. But there is little disagreement about the central role of individual psychotherapy. In the healing therapeutic crucible of a consistent, caring, nonexploitative interpersonal relationship, the person who has resorted to dissociative defenses in the face of repeated overwhelming traumas can recover the hope, trust, and dignity that were damaged by the experience. Therapy can also restore the continuity of self-experience that the reliance on dissociation had disrupted.

The growing literature on both diagnosis and treatment of DID has muted, though not silenced, those clinicians who believe that DID is largely an iatrogenic disorder created in highly hypnotizable individuals by gullible therapists who unwittingly encourage the fragmentation of personality elements in their patients by acting as if the different elements were actually different persons. The use of hypnosis was singled out as a prime offender because hypnosis can, in fact, "create" most of the phenomena characteristic of paralysis, distortion of memory, alteration of body experience, disturbance in time sense, and the experience of actions as involuntary. Indeed, there is a good deal of similarity between hypnosis and the defensive strategies used by traumatized persons, whether such strategies are consciously employed or whether, without such conscious intention, experiences become walled off from the usual flow of memory and become attached to other unintegrated aspects of identity.

Hypnosis and dissociation, however, are not identical phenomena. Their historical definitions and contemporary measurements are not the same, but hypnosis is increasingly thought of as a "controlled dissociation" and dissociation a form of "self-hypnosis." Thus, the similarity between hypnosis and dissociation has closely connected the two, and hypnosis is a valuable tool in the treatment of dissociative disorders. What was originally evoked in the individual by traumatic experiences can be beneficially influenced in treatment by controlled hypnotic interventions. Although it is true that hypnosis can simulate the phenomena of DID, there is no evidence that the profound disturbances in identity, consciousness, and memory found in DID, and the frequently accompanying symptoms of insomnia, headache, eating disorders, substance abuse, sexual dysfunction, and pervasive relationship difficulties, can be caused by hypnosis.

In the first modern treatment plan for DID, hypnosis played a key role. Subsequently, almost every prominent author outlining treatment strategies for DID advocates the judicious use of hypnosis. What follows here is a summary and outline of what is widely accepted as appropriate incorporation of hypnotic techniques into the psychotherapy of DID. It presumes a general knowledge of the clinical manifestations of DID, a grasp of how psychotherapy is conducted without hypnosis, and familiarity with the basics of hypnosis. Training in hypnosis is now easily available through both the nationally recognized professional hypnosis societies: the American Society for Clinical Hypnosis and the Society for Clinical and Experimental Hypnosis. Both organizations offer introductory, intermediate, and advanced workshops, some exclusively devoted to DID, as well as to related areas such as sexual trauma, self-hypnosis training, and abreactive techniques. Other teaching centers, such as the Menninger Clinic and numerous medical schools, also provide training in hypnosis for almost all licensed mental health professionals. Using hypnosis in the treatment of DID requires an advanced level of skill; its use in less complicated treatment situations (for example, phobias, pain control) should precede its use with DID.

Persons with DID tend to be highly hypnotizable, presumably because of their extensive use of hypnosislike dissociative strategies in coping with early life traumas. Indeed, many theorists assert that one of the necessary ingredients for the formation of DID is the capacity to dissociate. Dissociating in the face of repetitive traumas seems to strengthen that ability and may set the stage for dissociating in response to even minor stress because the "skill" may have been overlearned.

The clinician must bear in mind that these patients may not consider what they do to be self-hypnosis. Indeed, what is experienced may not seem volitional at all, but sudden and alarming lapses in self-control. "Spacing out" or "tuning out" is a commonly reported experience, with the person's mind seeming to go blank. These individuals may abruptly "wake up" in unfamiliar or even dangerous situations with no awareness of why or how they got there. Or they may feel like a passenger or observer in their own body, with the behavior or feelings not seeming like their own.

The suggestion that hypnosis may play a useful role in treatment may be taken—as it is by many nondissociative patients—as an opportunity for the therapist to exert malignant control over them. Maintaining control over themselves in the face of bewildering alterations in consciousness, behavior, and body experience has often become a major cause of concern for such patients. The idea of surrendering self-control, much less allowing another person to gain such control over them in the light of their history, may be a terrifying prospect. Obviously, a good deal of education and reassurance is needed before hypnotic interventions are begun, and education and reassurance are best provided after a therapeutic relationship is formed and some amount of trust is achieved. Eventually, the patient is advised that hypnosis will be used to put him or her in greater control, not less. The therapist will be teaching some techniques that can be used between sessions, and others that will be used in sessions by plan and with the patient's consent. The patient will learn to regulate dissociative processes that were originally used for self-protection but that have taken on a divisive and maladaptive life of their own.

And what if the patient refuses? Many successful treatments have been conducted without the formal use of hypnosis, so there is no basis for considering it indispensable. For many patients, however, it has clearly been an important aid through providing relief from anxiety and other painful and disruptive emotions; assisting communication between unintegrated parts of the total personality by whatever label they may be known (for example, alters, selves, states); relieving amnesias and abreacting traumatic experiences; achieving a sense of self-control; revising shameful and guilty self-perceptions; and fostering the assimilation of all aspects of the self and that person's life experiences.

How to Begin

Assuming a willing patient and a trained therapist, what are the first steps in the incorporation of hypnotic techniques? Simple induction techniques are usually preferable, such as eye fixation, relaxation, pleasant guided imagery, and counting. Induction techniques that involve the inability to open one's eyes (eyelid catalepsy) or to move freely (arm rigidity) should be avoided because of their compromising effect on the patient's need to retain the sense of self-control. Especially anxious patients may initially require lengthy induction procedures (twenty to forty minutes) to achieve the degree of calm and the experience of safety that eventually they will be able to produce in a matter of moments. A rapid induction technique, such as that advocated by Herbert Spiegel, may subsequently be used during the treatment session and in self-hypnosis.

The patient is shown how to evoke a sense of comfort by recalling a pleasant memory or by devising a pleasant fantasy. Here, the patient is instructed to practice producing this state of calm and pleasure periodically during the day. In time the pleasant experience can be evoked by replacing the formal induction procedure with a signal or cue word (for example, thumb and forefinger touching as a sign that "I'm O.K."). Thus, these persons learn that distressing emotions can be calmed and even replaced with pleasant ones and that they have more control over their experience than they had come to believe. Further, the therapist is providing tangible help in putting the patients more, not less, in control. Small successes build hopefulness, self-esteem, and a sense of mastery, all of which contribute to the development of the therapeutic alliance. It is important to remember that these patients have not truly felt in control for a very long time. Neither do they have any good reason to trust the therapist. Developing trust in one's capacity for self-control and in the nonexploitative, unselfish interest of another person is precious and will grow only slowly.

Along with the pleasant memory or fantasy that is used to calm hyperarousal, the patient is helped to create the image and experience of a "safe place," something like a secluded beach, secure room, or mountain fortress where no one can approach without the patient's permission. When it is agreeable to the patient, the therapist may be pictured as a presence there as well. Reliving traumatic experiences for the purpose of abreaction and mastery should not begin in the safe place, so as not to contaminate it with distress. Rather, the safe place can be a place of respite following such memory work as part of regaining calm and a sense of security (see Figure 7.1). The intrusion of bad memories or fantasies during these preparatory exercises signals a need for proceeding slowly and with caution.

Once equipped with self-hypnotic skills of self-soothing and regulation of emotion, the patient may begin to recall relatively

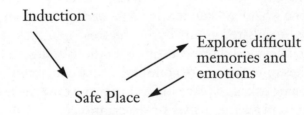

Induction

Explore difficult
memories and
emotions

Safe Place

Figure 7.1
Establishing a Comfortable and Safe Foundation
Facilitates Working Through Abreaction
Note: Figure added by editor, J. Spira.

minor traumas as the first step in eventual mastery of more serious traumas. Minor traumas would be experiences like being verbally berated or other stressful events that provoked discomfort but not significant dissociation. The practice of going into and out of trance can also be an important step in gaining control over what previously was experienced as uncontrolled "switching" between various states.

Mapping the System

As the alliance is forged and the treatment frame established, the process of *mapping the system* can begin. In the most general sense, this mapping entails eliciting the various alters and determining the circumstances of their creation, their age, gender, name, and role in the overall system. It is common to find protectors, persecutors, children, and opposite genders, as well as some alters that serve as single-minded expressions of hate, sexuality, or fear. A typical pattern is for three to five sides to emerge fairly quickly, and then four or five more to make their presence known. Less common are instances of larger numbers, sometimes over one hundred, but such manifestations are typically variations on a few themes, rather than significantly differentiated personality states. Richard Kluft has suggested the label of *complex DID* for the existence of twenty-six or more alters.

It may be possible to identify one alter that knows all of the others, making initial history gathering easier. This side may or may not be what has been termed an *inner self helper*, an element that may be enlisted as an ally in the treatment, just as it may serve a stabilizing and protective role in the overall system. Some approaches to mapping are conducted very concretely, with the patient being asked to place his or her name on a sheet of paper and then to place the names or descriptions of the other sides wherever on the sheet they belong. The various interrelationships among the different sides can thus be represented by their locations on the page. Even more concrete, but less common, is using the outline of the patient's actual body silhouette on a large piece of drawing paper, with alters being identified with respect to how they may be experienced somatically. Some alters may be experienced on the left or right side of the head or body, some in the arms and legs, and others in or near various organs.

These efforts at mapping carry the risk of retraumatizing the patient because focusing on the creation of the dissociated personality elements of necessity draws the patient toward traumatic memories. When possible, abreactions of trauma for the purpose of mastery should come about by plan, not as an inadvertent reaction to history gathering. Establishing ideomotor signaling as part of the early hypnotic training may be a valuable aid to initial mapping. The patient is told that other sides can communicate by lifting various fingers in response to questioning. One of the hands is identified, and certain fingers are designated to lift, such as the index finger for yes, the little finger for no, and another when the questioning should stop. Some therapists also identify a finger for "I don't know," but others consider this unnecessary or unproductive.

Early in the mapping process, any angry or uncooperative alters must be contacted. Some basic ground rules must be agreed to, such as ensuring safety for the patient's body, curtailing antisocial behavior, agreeing to develop no more personalities, and establishing the therapist's interest in the well-being of all the different sides. Although eventual integration of the overall personality is an understandable goal of the therapist, making this explicit at the outset may antagonize or frighten alters that may understandably regret fusion as death for them. It may mobilize resistances needlessly and, in fact, may never become the patient's goal. After the therapist makes an accurate diagnosis and educates the patient about the disorder, the treatment alliance can be based instead on the desirability of increased communication and cooperation among the various parts of the overall system; thus self-destructiveness is decreased and adaptive functioning is maximized.

Facilitating Communication

After inducing trance, the host personality can be asked to "just wait and see what happens" or even to "take a nap" so that the alters can communicate. In time, though, the host will be urged to listen in on every tolerable communication. Switching between alters can also be facilitated, with the host allowing the other sides to emerge fully for a talk with the therapist or by the host reporting what the others are saying to the therapist.

At times the host will be resistant to hearing any communications to the therapist, remaining amnestic for what transpires during part or all of the session. And it is typical for amnesias between various alters to persist, with alter B knowing about alter C, but not about alter D, and so on. The host, if need be, could be asked to communicate through ideomotor responses so as not to disrupt communication with the alter presently "out." We as therapists must remember that dissociative barriers were created for good reasons and that only a considerable degree of safety within the therapeutic relationship will allow them to relax. An internal bulletin board can be created on which messages can be left for the therapist or for the host personality. For example, one alter might warn of the imminent dangerous behavior of another, or a heretofore silent alter might announce its willingness to be known. This is a fantasy experience comparable in some respects to the independent journaling the patient may be invited to do each day—writing done in a self-induced state of reverie or receptivity to whatever may be written; this task allows the alters to express feelings and needs.

Fraser's dissociative table technique may be quite valuable in promoting internal communication. The patient is asked to picture him- or herself at a table large enough for "everyone" to be seated around in a conference-type room. From a door on the other side of the room, all of the patient's alters that are willing to be known can enter the room and sit where they please around the table. A special switch shines a spotlight on them one at a time, determining who talks. Or a microphone may be passed around the table. For alters that are initially unable to speak directly to the host or the therapist, an intermediary may be designated. Each alter may have a memory screen nearby, allowing for the recall and sharing of traumatic memories through visualizing them on the screen. The needs and fears of the various alters can be expressed, and compromise or resolution can occur, much like a group or family therapy process.

The goal of all such techniques is to promote communication and cooperation among the different components of the personality system. In the early stages, the therapist may temporarily be a repository of information not fully shared among the alters, but this practice has many pitfalls and should be held to a minimum. Preserving secrets and having "special deals" with some parts not known by others contradict the treatment goal of openness and undermine the therapist's stance of even-handedness. "Locating" information in the therapist outside the patient is but another form of dissociation.

Abreaction and Mastery

To reduce the necessity for dissociative defenses, traumatic memories held by different alters must be expressed, mastered, and assimilated into the wiser personality system. One of the most valuable uses of hypnosis is facilitating a modulated recall within the context of interpersonal safety that leads to a sense of mastery.

Numerous articles have been published about the management of abreaction with hypnotic techniques. The rudiments can be outlined as follows: after securing agreement from all of the parts that it's all right to proceed, the therapist can use age-regression techniques that allow the memory to begin just before the traumatic aspect. Such age regression may include turning back pages on a calendar of the person's life, looking through old photograph albums, browsing in a library of old books about the person's life, or selecting from a videotape collection of all special life occasions. Watkins's affect bridge technique is often effective; it enables the patient to reexperience some recent instance of the particular emotion and to follow it back to earlier instances. Here, a patient is asked to recall an earlier time when he or she had a similar feeling. Once the patient is poised at that fateful moment, the memory is allowed to proceed slowly. The goal is for the person to reexperience the event at a level of emotional arousal sufficient to be meaningful but not retraumatizing.

Pacing the recall is of crucial importance. Various distancing or "fractionating" techniques may be applied, such as first having the patient view the event as if it happened to someone else or to someone similar to the patient. The recall may be done in slow motion or watched as a film on a television screen, with the remote control switch firmly in the patient's hand to slow down or stop the action. What had been an overwhelming feeling can now be experienced for only a few moments or in highly muted form. Different alters can take turns seeing or experiencing the event, slowly absorbing its reality into the life of the entire system.

Stronger and more mature alters can be expected to master traumas before the younger and less stable ones. The patient will have been trained to communicate if any alter becomes overwhelmed. In addition to the monitoring by the therapist of the patient's breathing, pulse, color, facial expression, and posture, some form of signal or of spontaneous awakening should be available in the event that an overwhelming degree of distress is not apparent to the therapist. The patient should always be advised to remember only as much as can be tolerated (permissive amnesia). Provisions may be necessary for the patient's physical safety during abreaction because flailing of arms and legs is not uncommon. The presence of a co-therapist or trusted companion is sometimes helpful. If significant violence or psychotic disorganization is a likelihood, proceeding in a hospital setting is obviously indicated.

During the abreaction, the therapist may comment about the experience, helping the patient find words to express what at the time may have been a terrifying or sickening jumble of events. Care should be taken, however, not to guide or influence the recall in a way that might embellish or distort it. A useful strategy is to have the person take the opportunity now to tell his or her tormenter what could not have been said at the time, to express the dissociated or stifled feelings of shame, fear, or anger. The patient may even wish to punish the perpetrator in fantasy, but such a cathartic exercise is not an effort to revise the memory. Rather, it may help mobilize and integrate the entire range of feelings involved and assist in countering the earlier sense of helpless passivity. The therapist can help the patient correct distorted ideas about what happened or why so that the patient can achieve a coherent, first-person account with a tolerable degree of emotion. Mastery is achieved, in part, by the patient's becoming the narrator of the experience, acquiring the control that putting things into words can bring, and sharing the experience with a trusted other.

A standard fifty-minute hour may not be sufficient for some abreactive sessions, but some sort of time frame should be established. Whatever the plan, Kluft's rule of thirds apples: the first third of the session should be spent identifying the material to be worked with, the second third processing the material, and the final third reestablishing the patient. Some of the processing may take place while the patient is still in trance, especially in dealing with alters. Enough time should be spent with the host personality out of trance for the therapist to determine that it is fully alert and capable of departing safely. The integrative work following abreactions alone is insufficient for lasting therapeutic effect. Abreaction of every significant trauma may not be possible in those patients who have experienced prolonged cruelty over many years. The most serious traumatic events require individual attention, but others may form clusters by their similarity and be abreacted simultaneously.

Hypnosis can also be used throughout the course of treatment for symptom control and management of crisis. The patient's capacity for hypnotic responsiveness allows for what may seem like magical intervention, such as paralyzing a belligerent alter, having a frightened child alter take a prolonged nap, or temporarily creating amnesia for recent unsettling events. Such intervention, however, should be rare.

Communications among the various alters to determine the source of the crisis and to enable coping by locating and mobilizing strengths and cooperation is far preferable in the long run to coercive or manipulative control by the therapist. The ability to evoke the patient's hypnotic talents can, unfortunately, stir the therapist's countertransference fantasies of omnipotent control, just as it may fuel the patient's wish to submit passively to a healing caretaker. In any case, these patients are typically crisis-prone, especially with respect to self-mutilation and suicidal urges, and they sometimes require medication and periods of hospitalization despite their hypnotic abilities and other strengths.

Fusion and Beyond

Integration is a gradual process occurring throughout treatment that results from the progressive reduction of dissociative boundaries so that the individual's thoughts, feelings, and behaviors fit together coherently and thus provide a continuous sense of identity and ownership of experience. *Fusion* refers to the occasion when selves previously experienced as separate begin to merge. They may begin to share memories, and then all of conscious awareness (sometimes termed *co-consciousness*) before becoming increasingly similar and ceasing to be separate. Some fusions occur spontaneously as treatment proceeds, a naturally occurring outgrowth of reduced reliance on dissociation. Others need facilitation by the therapist in the form of hypnotically orchestrated images, such as of joining hands and flowing together.

Fusion may be attempted on a trial basis, and patients may spontaneously revert to separateness if done prematurely. As a rule, the therapist should not insist on promoting the fusions because the patient's readiness is more important than that of the therapist. The alters must come to realize that they indeed will continue to exist, but as part of a functional whole, rather than alone with their fear or anger.

During postfusion therapy (recommended to be two years or so), the now-integrated alters can be elicited, either directly for face-to-face interviews or through the ideomotor signals, to determine their current degree of satisfaction and to learn of any nascent difficulties within the personality system that need attention. During the postfusion period, hypnotic techniques continue to be useful not only in affect regulation but also in general ego strengthening, problem solving, and identity consolidation. The patient can rehearse new solutions to problems in fantasy, experiment with age progression to sample a desired new path of personal growth, and continue to draw self-esteem from the experience of mastery associated with the exercise of hypnotic abilities. The dissociative processes originally employed for sheer psychological survival have now become genuinely adaptive tools for the patient's developing psychological success.

∽

When properly trained, a therapist using hypnosis can greatly facilitate the therapeutic progress of the patient with DID. It may at first strike one as odd that a dissociative disorder can be treated through employing a dissociative strategy. Yet, experience shows that teaching a patient to control his or her entry into a dissociative state for comfort and psychological exploration can result in illumination of the disorder, as well as less frequent severe or uncontrolled dissociative reactions to distress.

NOTES

P. 220, *the underlying dissociative pathology may not be easily apparent:* Kluft, R. P. (1991). Clinical presentations of multiple personality disorder. *Psychiatric Clinics of North America, 14,* 605–629.

P. 220, *defensive strategies that can be thought of as similar to self-hypnosis:* Bliss, E. L. (1983). Multiple personalities, related disorders, and hypnosis. *American Journal of Clinical Hypnosis, 26,* 114–123.

P. 220, *inducing a trance state:* (see Introduction, this volume.)

P. 220, *the mind, part, person, or force that exists in the body:* Braun, B. G. (1980). Hypnosis for multiple personalities. In H. J. Wain (Ed.), *Clinical hypnosis in medicine* (pp. 209–217). Chicago: Year Book Medical.

P. 221, *Watkins's ego-state therapy:* Watkins, J. G. (1978). *The therapeutic self: Developing resonance—Key to effective relationships.* New York: Human Sciences Press.

P. 221, *can actually create the complex dissociative pathology seen in DID:* Kluft, R. P. (1982). Varieties of hypnotic interventions in the treatment of multiple personality. *American Journal of Clinical Hypnosis, 24,* 230–240.

P. 223, *expressive therapies, such as art, movement, and writing:* (see Chapter Eight, this volume.)

P. 223, *the central role of individual psychotherapy:* Turkus, J. A. (1991). Psychotherapy and case management for multiple personality disorder: Synthesis for the continuity of care. *Psychiatric Clinics of North America, 14,* 649–660.

P. 224, *and pervasive relationship difficulties, can be caused by hypnosis:* Kluft, R. P. (1982). Varieties of hypnotic interventions in the treatment of multiple personality. *American Journal of Clinical Hypnosis, 24,* 230–240; Putnam, F. W. (1989). The therapeutic role of hypnosis and abreaction. In *Diagnosis and treatment of multiple personality disorder* (pp. 218–252). New York: Guilford Press.

P. 224, *In the first modern treatment plan for DID:* Allison, R. B. (1974). A new treatment approach for multiple personalities. *American Journal of Clinical Hypnosis, 17,* 15–32.

P. 224, *DID is the capacity to dissociate:* Braun, B. G., & Sachs, R. G. (1985). The development of multiple personality disorders: Predisposing, precipitating, and perpetuating factors. In R. P. Kluft (Ed.), *Childhood antecedents of multiple personality* (pp. 37–74). Washington, DC: American Psychiatric Press; Putnam, F. W. (1985). Dissociation as a response to extreme trauma. In R. P. Kluft (Ed.), *Childhood antecedents of multiple personality* (pp. 65–97). Washington, DC: American Psychiatric Press.

P. 226, *rapid induction technique, such as that advocated by Herbert Spiegel:* Spiegel, H., & Spiegel, D. (1978). *Trance and treatment: Clinical uses of hypnosis.* New York: Basic Books.

P. 228, *Richard Kluft has suggested:* Kluft, R. P. (1988). The phenomenology and treatment of extremely complex multiple personality disorder. *Dissociation, 1*(4), 47–58.

P. 228, *inner self helper:* Comstock, C. M. (1991). The inner self helper and concepts of inner guidance: Historical antecedents, its role within dissociation, and clinical utilization. *Dissociation, 4,* 165–177.

P. 229, *signaling as part of the early hypnotic training:* Cheek, D. B., & Lecron, L. M. (1968). *Clinical hypnotherapy.* New York: Grune & Stratton.

P. 230, *Fraser's dissociative table technique:* Fraser, G. A. (1991). The dissociative table technique: A new strategy for working with ego states in dissociative disorders and ego-state therapy. *Dissociation, 4,* 205–213.

P. 231, *the management of abreaction with hypnotic techniques:* Horevitz, R. (in press). Hypnosis in the treatment of multiple personality. In J. W. Rhue, S. J. Lynn, & J. Kirsh (Eds.), *Handbook of clinical hypnosis.* Washington, DC: American Psychological Association; Putnam, F. W. (1989). The therapeutic role of hypnosis and abreaction. In *Diagnosis and treatment of multiple personality disorder* (pp. 218–252). New York: Guilford Press.

P. 231, *Watkins's affect bridge technique:* Watkins, J. G. (1971). The affect bridge. *International Journal of Clinical and Experimental Hypnosis, 19,* 21–27.

P. 233, *management of crisis:* Kluft, R. P. (1983). Hypnotherapeutic crisis intervention in multiple personality. *American Journal of Clinical Hypnosis, 26,* 73–83.

FOR FURTHER READING

Allison, R. B. (1974). A new treatment approach for multiple personalities. *American Journal of Clinical Hypnosis, 17,* 15–32.

Bliss, E. L. (1983). Multiple personalities, related disorders, and hypnosis. *American Journal of Clinical Hypnosis, 26,* 114–123.

Braun, B. G. (1980). Hypnosis for multiple personalities. In H. J. Wain (Ed.), *Clinical hypnosis in medicine* (pp. 209–217). Chicago: Year Book Medical.

Braun, B. G., & Sachs, R. G. (1985). The development of multiple personality disorders: Predisposing, precipitating, and perpetuating factors. In R. P. Kluft (Ed.), *Childhood antecedents of multiple personality* (pp. 37–74). Washington, DC: American Psychiatric Press.

Cheek, D. B., & Lecron, L. M. (1968). *Clinical hypnotherapy.* New York: Grune & Stratton.

Comstock, C. M. (1991). The inner self helper and concepts of inner guidance: Historical antecedents, its role within dissociation, and clinical utilization. *Dissociation, 4,* 165–177.

Fraser, G. A. (1991). The dissociative table technique: A new strategy for working with ego states in dissociative disorders and ego-state therapy. *Dissociation, 4,* 205–213.

Horevitz, R. (in press). Hypnosis in the treatment of multiple personality. In J. W. Rhue, S. J. Lynn, & J. Kirsh (Eds.), *Handbook of clinical hypnosis.* Washington, DC: American Psychological Association.

Kluft, R. P. (1982). Varieties of hypnotic interventions in the treatment of multiple personality. *American Journal of Clinical Hypnosis, 24,* 230–240.

Kluft, R. P. (1983). Hypnotherapeutic crisis intervention in multiple personality. *American Journal of Clinical Hypnosis, 26,* 73–83.

Kluft, R. P. (1988). The phenomenology and treatment of extremely complex multiple personality disorder. *Dissociation, 1*(4), 47–58.

Kluft, R. P. (1991). Clinical presentations of multiple personality disorder. *Psychiatric Clinics of North America, 14,* 605–629.

Putnam, F. W. (1985). Dissociation as a response to extreme trauma. In R. P. Kluft (Ed.), *Childhood antecedents of multiple personality* (pp. 65–97). Washington, DC: American Psychiatric Press.

Putnam, F. W. (1989). The therapeutic role of hypnosis and abreaction. In *Diagnosis and treatment of multiple personality disorder* (pp. 218–252). New York: Guilford Press.

Spiegel, H., & Spiegel, D. (1978). *Trance and treatment: Clinical uses of hypnosis.* New York: Basic Books.

Turkus, J. A. (1991). Psychotherapy and case management for multiple personality disorder: Synthesis for the continuity of care. *Psychiatric Clinics of North America, 14,* 649–660.

Watkins, J. G. (1971). The affect bridge. *International Journal of Clinical and Experimental Hypnosis, 19,* 21–27.

Watkins, J. G. (1978). *The therapeutic self: Developing resonance—Key to effective relationships.* New York: Human Sciences Press.

CHAPTER

8

EXPRESSIVE THERAPY

Peggy L. Dawson and John F. Higdon

Recent years have seen not only a marked increase in the diagnosing of patients with Dissociative Identity Disorder (DID), but also an apparent increase in the complexity of such patients. Challenges to the therapist are obviously raised by having a patient with alters of many ages, orientations, ways of communicating, interests, likes, dislikes, and agendas.

In our experience, patients with the DID diagnosis, characterized by alters having disparate states of mind, benefit from a range of therapeutic modalities and activities in addition to traditional verbal psychotherapy. A clinician treating such patients can be of an even greater assistance when considering augmentive modalities, such as those used by expressive and functional therapists to treat these now not-so-rare DID patients.

Such therapies as art, music, movement, and occupational therapy use arts and crafts, daily living tasks, work, social skills groups, stress management, exercise, altruistic volunteering, writing, and movement and can provide helpful choices of therapy modalities. In fact, as early as a decade ago, when the current trend in multiple personality diagnosis was on the rise, a pioneer clinician, David Caul, initially recognized and supported the use of adjunctive therapies with the (now) DID patient.

THEORETICAL PERSPECTIVE

It is well established that dissociation of identity in one person can result in the person having up to hundreds of alter personalities or fragments of personalities. As a constellation, the alters have differing ages, genders, orientations, affiliations, interests, capabilities, pursuits, memories, coping styles, emotionality, and so forth. These alternate personalities, though truly part of a whole, each meet and interact with the world in very different ways.

Furthermore, therapists have noted a tendency toward mutual polarization among various alters—that is, to varying degrees, dissociating and becoming unaware or unsympathetic toward the separate parts. Thus, this "walling off" of each aspect may allow the patient to escape awareness of differing incidents or types of abuse as they occur. DID patients who are presently in treatment and emancipated from daily abuse, however, still tend to be handicapped in everyday life activities by this splitting. These patients are bereft of the common practice of goal or priority setting that most people do by comparing and considering their wishes and responsibilities set one against the other. Consequently, uninformed by a central processing unit, the alters adopt widely diverging interests, styles, expressive behaviors, and preferences in any number of areas.

Because some or most of the alters can be aware of each other yet be driven in different directions, it is understandable that they develop animosities or competitive feelings toward each other. For instance, they may call each other names, disparage one another's contributions, and perhaps even feel angry and homicidal toward one another. Ironically, these attitudes occur even though all of the ego parts were unconsciously created to protect the same child abuse victim. This ill will and lack of cooperation can keep the DID patient in a state of frequent conflict and tension, with alters coming to act at cross-purposes with each other or with the host.

How Expressive Therapies Work

Expressive therapies, which are versatile and adaptable, have constructive ways to approach the resultant mutual hostility and lack of recognition between alters and host. Although the ultimate goal of therapy is to empower the host and to encourage the alters to work together for the good of the whole, it is ironic that the most effective way to do this is to let the alters expand. They need to gain an understanding of the diagnosis and of each other in order for this work to be done. In fact, one use of expressive therapy initially in treatment is to introduce alters to each other through a variety of means. These activities can also help the constellation explore the differing competitive egos and concomitant coping strategies that comprise the patient's system.

Later, the therapist may use expressive, cooperative, shared activities among alters. These shared creative or everyday activities can weaken barriers among the formerly unknown or disregarded alters. Opportunities for individual expression prove useful with alters because although they are truly part of a whole, each meets and interacts with his or her human and nonhuman environment on different terms.

Activities therapies have several advantages while serving the integration or internal cooperation process. For example, they are sometimes perceived by the patient as less intrusive than psychotherapy—perhaps because the patient generally chooses what to do, selects the medium by which to express him- or herself, and determines how to complete the activity. This therapy also allows for a variety of forms of expression among the constellation of alters, who usually have dissimilar skills in expression and communication.

Structured activity encourages the alters to apply their seemingly different personal histories, resources, knowledge, and interests into goal-related projects involving various artistic or inanimate objects. Different alters can even be encouraged to work as a cooperative group on projects in activities therapy.

Alters who clearly work together for the first time to accomplish a task and to attain a concrete product they can be proud of may experience feelings of competence (rather than competition). They are thus introduced to an enhanced sense of self-expression and peaceful coexistence—a situation in which alters are not, at least for the moment, at odds with each other. As teamwork is continued through activities therapy and applied to "real life" community or outpatient assignments, the patient may progress to an increased quality of life through cooperation and perhaps will even begin to consider eventual personality fusion.

Overcoming Secrecy

One of the central problems in diagnosis and treatment of DID is secrecy. Western culture's taboo against abuse of children, especially sexual abuse, has not rendered it as rare as one would like to think, for severe, repeated child abuse is a major cause of the dissociative splitting seen in DID. Violation of the abuse taboo carries an inherent secrecy and emotional loading that seems to contribute to the extreme degree of identity dissociation and activity disruption found in DID.

Here, again, activities therapy can be relevant. Non-objective art can serve the process of gaining the host's and personalities' views of the world and expressions of feelings. For example:

M R .   R

Mr. R., a former patient at the Veterans Hospital, checked into the psychiatric unit, having recently been discharged from the military because of a series of unauthorized absences. Through the consultation of a Navy psychiatrist before discharge, Mr. R. came to suspect that he had DID.

Mr. R. explained to us that he had apparently been gone from his military duties for days at a time, yet he had no recollection of where he had been or what he had done. He even received letters addressed

Figure 8.1
Mr. R.'s Illustration of Living with DID

to a person with a name similar to his own at his address. Much to his surprise, the letters were from people he didn't know. The correspondents alluded to the fine times they had shared with Mr. R. during the dates he was AWOL. Sadly, he said that other people always seemed to know more about his life than he did.

We asked Mr. R. whether he could make some kind of expressive rendering of the way this felt. He agreed, chose terra-cotta clay, and formed a bust of himself that showed his head plus a wide, elongated structure emanating from the back of it (see Figure 8.1). He described the bust by saying that, throughout his daily life, he feels that he is trailing some huge and embarrassing outgrowth. And although the outgrowth—which he says represents his problem—is obvious to others, it is literally a secret kept from himself.

Because of the mantle of secrecy that is attendant to the diagnosis, many patients are never diagnosed correctly. Treatment is even hampered by the patient's conscious or unconscious long-standing commitment to nondisclosure. Abusers in the child victim's life usually extracted promises of secrecy from their victim. They were often very convincing and seductive or, more frequently, quite overt and graphic in threatening their child victim with death or other dire consequences if he or she spoke about the abuse. The abusers may have extracted promises of secrecy through pain or offered threats to hurt the child's loved ones or to kill special pets or animals if the child disclosed. These believable threats from long ago generally result in current repression of the acts across some or most of the patient's system. It may also engender complete muteness or lack of articulation in one or several alters of a single patient.

It may be that the admonitions not to talk may enhance the abused child's natural tendency to blame him- or herself for the acts that transpired. This personal blame, shame, or guilt occurs, accompanies, and is enhanced by the abuser's threats and tends to culminate in an assurance that the abuse will not be revealed or discussed. Other factors leading to nondisclosure include the abuse's occurring long ago or when the child was preverbal, resulting in the older child or adult patient's literally having "no words" to describe the memory of the acts. Hence, in therapy some of the alters' memories of the abuse seem to take the form of nonverbal or inarticulate recollections that aren't well expressed through verbal give-and-take.

Putnam et al. concluded in their research that, among reporting MPD therapists, the most commonly reported type of alter among patients was the child alter. And some of the alters who carry the most knowledge and directly painful effects of the abuse may be children. Depending on their age and skill, children (even when they are alternate personalities) obviously cannot participate as do adults in verbal psychotherapy. Activities therapy offers them several avenues for nonverbal exploration of the memories. By encouraging artistic productions, writing, or other means of non-oral communication, the activities therapies can allow a child alter to maintain his or her verbal silence and yet to disclose how he or she feels or to describe what has happened in a nonverbal and apparently safe way. Even when the abuse occurred early in the child's life, when he or she lacked the necessary words to depict events, activities of expressive therapy allow a form of communication of memories and feelings through play, movement, and various other means. Thus, the patient is helped to work through disturbing material by using limited or no conversation while sidestepping the fear of literally *telling* about the event.

Cooperation Among Alters

Cooperation through activities is one of the foci that naturally arise after the initial introductions and roles of the alters have been established. Cooperation can be facilitated through allowing or requiring the various alters to join forces, to pool resources, and to think and work together on some project. Various activities may elicit a heretofore difficult-to-achieve spirit of comaraderie among the alters, possibly leading to eventual fusion. Just as dissimilar political units may be able to pull together and achieve a mutual respect and rapport when confronted by another entity seen as external, two or more alters may be helped toward a powerful alliance by teaming up to accomplish a mutually agreed-on goal. This alliance happens by the alters' beginning to communicate and by their teaching as well as listening to what each other knows, rather than by insisting on their own perspective. The different alters may then learn to appreciate that sharing knowledge or a talent enables one to contribute without competing, to give without giving up, and that a team spirit and mutual respect make everyday life more effective and less tumultuous.

Reframing

Positive reframing within the context of activities therapy can be another effective way of breaking down hostilities between a host and alters or among alters. To illustrate this attitude, often one or more alter personalities of a DID patient may take a disturbingly hostile attitude toward other alters or the host personality.

The therapist can address the angry alter initially by saying, "Tell me some good skills you have." If the alter feels angry and "tough," he or she may typically say, "There's nothing good about me."

The therapist can counter with, "How about if I list some things about you and you could tell me if I'm right; be honest with me now." The therapist continues with phrases like the following: "Do you know what you want? Can you figure things out? Do you express yourself through what you do?" (or other attributes a tough alter may admit to in the context of a positive reframing). If the hostile alter responds to several of these characteristics—often with the begrudging posture of a hint of a new perspective—the therapist can proceed with an attempt to "link up" two personalities: "Have you met (perhaps the passive host personality)? Do you think (the host) should be more like you?" If the tough alter responds, "Yes, he (she) ought to be more like me!" it may be the first glimmer or fostering of some form of teaching or sharing among previously incompatible alters.

This form of positive reframing and mutual cooperation can take actual experiential form in the activity clinic where a variety of modalities—for example, art, crafts, cooking, composing—lend themselves to such cooperation. We have had patients work together with their alters on many activities: for example, baking, painting pictures, exercising, gardening.

Some aspects of the creative products attained through expressive therapy seem reminiscent of Pennebaker's important work, in which he elaborates that the mere translation of one's thoughts or speech into art or writing tends to decrease the negative emotional impact of the material. Certainly, this finding is germane to the DID patient who has great stores of repressed, highly charged memories. It seems as though writing, as opposed to speaking, requires a different type of skill that uses more thought, greater articulation, and enhanced tying together of loosely organized cognitions. The act of writing itself may lead to enhanced recollection and insight into memories. A similar advantage applies to art therapy, another type of expression, perhaps in the direction of less intellectual processing and more affect.

Expressive therapies that combine at least three modalities of expression—speech, writing, and art (with a broad inclusion)—may enhance treatment, strengthen the performance of the patient in his or her environment, and empower the contributions of alter personalities who possess differing and previously incompatible modes of expression. Teamwork, an obviously important component both to cooperation among alters and as a prerequisite for integration, is encouraged in order to create products of creative expression or everyday activities. The final product represents a combination of the differing personalities' styles, skills, and perspectives of the patient.

APPLICATION OF EXPRESSIVE THERAPY

Applications of expressive therapy for patients with DID can occur in a variety of ways, depending on the patient and the stage of treatment.

Introduction to Other Alters: Use of Nonprovocative and Ego-Enhancing Activities

The person with DID may have suspected the diagnosis but not really known for sure prior to the time of treatment. In fact, the patient may even have been presented with evidence of DID, such as unacknowledged written prose, unknown clothes in the closet, completed projects, and "missed time," but repeatedly resisted acknowledging the reality of the disorder and thus firmly set a system of denial. Although this denial generally becomes a difficult symptom to broach in therapy, the task can be assisted by the expressive therapist.

Nonthreatening expressive tasks can be an effective entry into the life of the patient and show that the therapist has both interest and confidence in the patient's ability to define and express his or her situation. Once patient-therapist rapport has been established, the therapist can encourage creative work to be produced by alters and then introduced to the host or other alters. This technique is a way of helping the formerly unintroduced parts become familiar with that aspect of the system and to accept the diagnosis.

Overcoming Denial

On the one hand, drawings, journals, or other prose produced by the alters and then shown to the host while in the structured and supportive setting of therapy can be an effective and relatively gentle way to convince the host personality that alters exist. On the other hand, it seems that if evidence is presented too abruptly, without a sensible introduction or means for the host to assimilate the introduction, the patient or his or her alters may find the therapeutic process fearful and, in effect, "run away," as they are used to doing.

If initial creative evidence of the alters can be produced to the host in an insightful, pleasant, or enriching form such as a painting, baked treat, prose, or poetry, the host's current affiliations with his or her alters may eventually become less stormy than when they happened uncontrolled, unbidden, misunderstood, and often with unfortunate results in the patient's everyday life.

UNDERSTANDING STELLA

Stella, a married woman who had always been faithful to her husband as far as she knew, awoke naked one morning in a hotel room bed with a man she did not recognize. Further, her hair was dyed red, and she was wearing bright red fingernail polish, a color she claimed she'd never have chosen for herself. In addition, she had a crashing headache, and several wine bottles littered her side of the room. She got up quickly, dressed, took flight, and with great haste, resumed her everyday appearances.

While telling us this story more than a year later, Stella admitted that, at the time, she had found this to be a very upsetting and emotionally charged situation. But she had relegated the unfortunate incident to the back of her mind as she had done with so many other mysterious situations, not mentioning it to anyone and not seeking help or crediting her behavior to any kind of mental disorder. Only later, she actually sought help. And then she sought aid, not for bouts of dissociation, but for alcoholism, as one of her alters was a heavy drinker.

Stella had just completed a substance abuse program, but she mentioned that she had undertaken the treatment in a halfhearted manner. For despite the evidence of her binges—frequent empty wine bottles, hangovers, cash spent, and reports of acquaintances who claimed to have seen her tipsy in local bars—she was still not convinced. Even though she acknowledged unavoidable signs that she was drinking, she had no personal recollection of the incidents or any conscious desire to drink alcohol. At this point, the patient was evaluated for DID.

In the initial meeting, Stella had little to say and appeared withdrawn, perhaps depressed, and had, as seems typical of the hosts of many DID patients, a paucity of interests, activities, or outlets for creative expression. When we talked about typical ways in which people sometimes act and accomplish activities during dissociation, Stella showed increased interest by becoming more posturally attentive and alert and by asking brief questions. When we asked whether she had ever felt any dissociative symptoms herself, Stella made guarded comments with no definite corroboration of the diagnosis. Following the patient's lead, we pressed her no further, trying not to force insight or nonvolunteered information; rather, we set out to establish an initial rapport. Rapport, even the earliest DID (MPD) therapists agree, can "make or break" the therapeutic aims.

The patient did mention, however, that she sometimes found in her possession drawings or paintings she had no knowledge of even though these works were executed on her own paper or stationery. We wanted to capitalize on her propensity for artwork, realizing that alters often are activity specific; that is, they emerge when the chance to engage in a potential activity that interests them is offered.

Therefore, we presented several sheets of drawing paper and a box of colored pencils, with the suggestion that she might like to make some kind of composition—of course, hoping that an alter (should one exist) would accept the invitation and provide the patient and her therapists some useful artistic evidence of his or her identity or personality. And in fact, that is just what happened.

The next time we met, Stella offered a drawing. She said offhandedly that she found it on her nightstand with a note indicating that she should give the work to me. She didn't seem to be the least perplexed or surprised to acknowledge this work that appeared from "nowhere." The drawing itself was highly abstracted but clearly represented the side view of a human face with, among other designs, a wine glass upside down, inside the top of the head. It became clear later, as the alter personalities were more fully elucidated, that this picture was drawn by Stella's substance-abusing alter, Sue Anne. At the bottom of the drawing was a kind of invitation or opening to therapy, a phrase completed with handwriting unlike the patient Stella's, which said, "Come See Our World" (see Figure 8.2).

My earlier conversation with Stella and the rapport that had been established then combined this day with the new drawing and the subsequent conversation concerning the artwork. We discussed her history and the possible implications for the source of the drawing. Our conversation dovetailed with the information that Stella had been assimilating in her psychotherapy sessions. Surprisingly, she felt somewhat heartened when, in a new light, she considered her puzzling personal history relative to the recent psychotherapy information about DID, along with the creative evidence she had produced. As she discussed the possibility of this diagnosis, she claimed that she was rather relieved, having long pondered whether she her-

Figure 8.2
Stella's
Alter Sue Anne Revealing a Hidden Side

self was a person unaware of her own actions and also an alcoholic or whether she was simply going crazy. These interactions brought about Stella's first emotionally unencumbered experience with an understanding of the reality of the existence of her alters. The current evidence of dissociation received and presented by therapists who, of course, placed no blame felt very different to Stella from the earlier condemning descriptions by family and townspeople concerning the disremembered acts of her alters.

Gaining the Alters' Histories and Points of View

An alter, whether a fully formed personality or a fragment, will generally have some distinct characteristics involving the ways by which he or she relates to the environment or to others. Part of the integration or mutual cooperation process involves gaining the alter's individual history: the particular set of circumstances that has helped form his or her perspectives and influenced his or her behaviors.

Activity therapists use many media and techniques to assist this goal. These interventions can include practical as well as expressive and creative tasks. Expressive tasks may include specific applications such as music, movement, artwork, poetry and writing, play, and sand tray arranging. These various media, when presented in a gentle manner, provide opportunities not only to introduce alter personalities to one another and to the host but also to gain a sense of the alters' histories and points of view as they exist within the constellation. The therapist comes to know the alters and is able to share information about them with the host more fully by describing their preferred media or activities, as well as the methods they choose to carry out projects.

It is also important to understand the meanings that the specific activities have for the alters.

JOYCE

In Stella's case, for example, one of her alters, Joyce, worked very hard in the clinic for a few days, first carefully drawing a composition with artists' pastels and then making an abstract representation in the form of a clay collage. The collage was a flat form supporting ten outlined circles of various sizes. Some of the circles were plain, but others had a partition down the middle, and one circle contained a smaller circle. All of these forms were connected.

After she had constructed and fired the collage once, Joyce carefully glazed the completed form with a selection of colors before the final firing. She spoke little while she worked and would never relate anything about the significance of the piece. So it was amazing to us when, as soon as the piece was glazed, fired, and completed, an angry alter, Judy, emerged and smashed the whole work by throwing it to the ground.

Several days later, while engaged in a conversation with a helpful alter, Dina, I realized the significance of Judy's action. Dina was describing all of the alters, and I asked whether she could make some kind of paper-and-pencil representation of the system. Representing the system in this way is also known as *mapping* and can be used to acquaint the therapist with the system, as well as to show changes as therapy progresses. Dina sketched roughly as she named the alters and referred to them by using individual circles to augment her words and to describe each one. She went on to describe how one specific alter could almost be called a "multiple personality herself; a circle within a circle."

I asked Dina to draw a schema of the whole internal system. She responded by representing nine circles, all designed, placed, and connected in ways almost identical, though not nearly as artistic, as the work of Joyce.

Promoting Cooperation and Respect through Goal-Oriented Activities

On the one hand, the life of a patient with DID may be fractured by the various personalities that seem to vie for time to control the body with little or no regard for the work in progress or to the long-term pursuits of host or other alters. Consequently, tasks and goals are poorly organized, not prioritized, and ill-defined—often to be started but never brought to a satisfying completion in the tumultuous life of the person with DID. On the other hand, the procedures for discrete tasks of creative expression, as well as functional goals, can be well defined, having obvious outcomes and specific steps needed in order to reach the goals.

These goals, in the form of short-term doable procedures, are useful to the patient and seem to work well in the activity clinic. Here, the therapist can remind a specific host or alter to stay on task and can also discourage, by way of a contract or bargain, unbidden interruptions by other alters, as happens so often in the patient's life. After the patient has elucidated his or her goals for activity, be it creative or everyday tasks, the therapist introduces and enforces the structure for a model for time management. The well-defined activity structure with built-in agreement among the interested parties tends to encourage the alters to cooperate in proceeding with or completing a project.

When a person is initially diagnosed with DID, it is typical for each alter to perceive that he or she is perhaps the only one who really cares about a certain activity and that this activity territory must be protected against the plans or whims of other disparate engines that run the system. Activities therapy can be a means by which the alters learn to appreciate the resources of one another. For instance:

LANCE

After the initial stages of meeting the alters of Lance, a twenty-four-year-old recently diagnosed with DID, and of talking with his alters about what activities each provided to the system, one of the dominant alters, T. Porter, said that if I wanted a good look at the various entities in his system, I could ask the "artist," Kate (who he claimed was good for little else) to draw portraits of them. When I later asked Kate to do this, she was pleased—especially so since T. Porter had suggested it. Once the drawings were done (see Figures 8.3 and 8.4), I asked Kate to describe the strengths and personal resources of each personality. During this time, I also invited the other personalities to listen in. Kate's presentation, including illus-

Figure 8.3
Lance's Artistic Alter Kate

trations, had been accomplished within just over a week. The alters seemed to be impressed by her efficient completion of the task, as well as complimented by her lucid descriptions of them all.

Adding to the confusion about interests at cross-purposes is the consideration that the alters of one patient tend to process their world differently from one another, and they even hold varied

Figure 8.4
Drawing by Another Feminine Alter of Lance

perceptions of themselves. Artwork may be used for alters who are willing to participate in this way as a compatible and quick means to elucidate or describe some of the points of view of various alters. For instance:

When Lance was recently diagnosed with DID, he was instructed to relax, clear his mind, close his eyes, and do some deep breathing before he completed the drawing task at hand. The goal was to select artists' pastel chalks that he thought were most appropriately colored and then, using only the chalk color and varieties of line, to represent a symbol for a commonly felt emotion. The emotion under consideration here was anger.

Lance appeared to relax deeply for about thirty seconds, his eyes closing and his head dropping. Then he opened his eyes abruptly while suddenly sitting up erect and looked straight at me. He smiled and in a coquettish female voice said, "And who are you?"

I responded by asking the same question of him, and he introduced himself as Rachel. I inquired whether this personality had heard me describe the task at hand to Lance. She giggled and assured me that she had heard the instructions but went on to say that she did not feel angry—now or ever. She had, though, apparently observed others who did feel anger and said that judging from what she saw, she would give the representation a try.

This alter chose a bright blue pastel and, as she drew, moved her hand jauntily across the paper as if drawing a pattern of flouncy lace. As she completed her drawing, I asked whether any others were around whom, like her, I hadn't met and who might want to do a drawing for me. She suggested that, for a drawing of anger, Trina might oblige.

After bidding me a coy good-bye, Rachel closed her eyes for a moment and then opened them a few seconds later. Rachel's cheery smile had gone from the patient's face and was replaced with a glare. The formerly upbeat character of Rachel was transformed. This hostile presence had solidly crossed arms and legs, locked tightly, one across the other. This alter seemed much more reluctant to speak, so I inquired about identity. She icily informed me that her name was Trina, with the assurance that, having heard the previous requests for a symbolic anger drawing, she could tell me more than I wanted to know about that topic.

Trina then grabbed a red pastel and made a quick, large diagonal sawtooth pattern on the paper, pressing so hard that she broke the pastel stick twice as she worked. Once Trina's pattern was established in red, she immediately followed over the top of this pattern with a black pastel, again stabbing at the paper and breaking this color as well.

After Trina's contribution and her brief explanation of the work, I asked whether I could see Lance again. When he came back to control of the body, he sensed that no time had intervened since he last saw me. He was quite taken aback to note that his hands had gotten soiled with chalk. I explained to him how that had happened. After he got over his surprise about the appearance of the two previous artistic interlopers, he was interested to know the points of view of these two female alters and to see their work.

On looking at their products, Lance commented that these drawings gave him a new understanding. He said he had always been
quite ashamed to find among his belongings evidence of what he had
considered to be his own repressed feminine proclivities. This evidence apparently took various forms and could be anything from a
nicely arranged vase of flowers sitting on a delicate doily to some
blatantly suggestive female lingerie under his pillow. Having before
had no sense of where these things came from, he had considered
them bizarre manifestations. Now, he said, their meaning took on a
broader perspective.

Improving Function

The everyday activities of a person with DID are often made difficult by the lack of coordination between the competing drives
and motives of the patient and by the patient's lack of acceptance
of the alters. One goal of therapy is to help the alters get along
with, accept, and encourage one another and allow goals to be
met. This objective can be facilitated through creative activities
that can have carryover to the patient's daily life.

BETTY

One of Betty's alters, Susie, had performed all of the cooking duties
throughout Betty's adult life. Betty indicated in occupational therapy that one of her priorities for the near future was to assume the
responsibility for this chore. Susie, however, was reluctant to give
up her task. This situation obviously called for some negotiation.
Susie, the current cook, was also interested in ceramics, and so in a
bargain negotiated by the activity therapist, Betty proposed that
Susie would come out at scheduled times to work on her personal
ceramic project while Betty would learn to cook and bake. Susie
agreed not to take control of the body while Betty was cooking, but

rather to offer her advice on the procedures—in essence, to *be there* as her coach.

Perhaps Susie accepted this bargain because she liked the idea of consulting with Betty, seeing herself as an activity expert in the area of cooking. She was also very keen about the chance to complete a ceramics project—a medium with a processing time that takes days and has many discrete steps, steps that would have been impossible to achieve in the old system of chaotic planning with no external guidance.

Expressive activities can help the host and alters develop much-needed broader perspectives in their everyday life. If you had asked Betty about her interests when she first entered therapy, she would have told you she held only one role—that of a university student. Generally, a single interest was typical of Betty's life and also of the lives of her nearly twenty alters. Even though she was now a veteran (the military having been a rather adventurous undertaking to embark on), Betty claimed that she was not even the one who had enlisted in the Army; it had been one of her alters.

Having a paucity of activities and a dearth of means by which to be constructive and to express herself, Betty chose to make a small redwood box in the activity clinic. She was uninitiated about even the most basic of tools but generally was eager to try. It soon became apparent that power tools were terribly frightening to her. Whether a sander or a band saw, the host's body literally trembled and cowered as the machine motor began to work. As if on this cue, the "tough" alter, Bobbi, would emerge to complete the power tool task. Bobbi, when she appeared, always had a mad look on her face, was apt to swear at others, and tended to bluster for no apparent cause. Even though she was helping Betty, Bobbi often cursed at the host at times like these. Thus, Bobbi's actions and words combined in a kind of contradiction. While her actions apparently rescued Betty from a tremendous anxiety, at the same time Bobbi's words cursed Betty as pitiful and weak for not being able to carry out the needed task herself. Some further differences between the two existed. For example, Bobbi was much more abrupt in her movements than

Betty, and Bobbi sometimes stuttered. When Bobbi was questioned about her personal history, she maintained that she was raised in Betty's house and perceived that she accepted much of the abuse meant for the young Betty. She felt that she had endured, was now rather rugged, and was proud of it.

Although Bobbi did indeed have a intimidating demeanor, she consistently appeared to stand up for the rights of Betty or of any other alters who she judged had been treated unfairly. At first Bobbi's contributions in the clinic were generally limited to those mentioned above. As therapy progressed, however, and she saw that concrete goals could be attained, she seemed to change and even began completing bona fide altruistic chores. These chores included helping make adaptive equipment out of wood for disabled veterans and keeping certain areas of the clinic in order. Along with her positive expansion of behaviors and duties came a welcome broadening of her demeanor.

WORKING TOWARD INTEGRATION

Expressive therapies are effective in the later stages of therapy. A proper foundation must be laid, however, before integration is attempted. Work following integration is also valuable in helping the patient continue to cope.

Preintegration Considerations

Imagine how difficult it would be to join forces with another to complete a self-descriptive painting that someone else has begun or to share in a subjective artistic impression of an event with someone else. Completed creative tasks that describe or symbolize oneself are obviously personal. The difficulty of this task sharing is made even more challenging when animosity or unclear communication exists between the partners. Consequently, after treatment has proceeded to a point where the alters acknowledge each other and communicate, we have used shared expressive tasks among them to facilitate the process of mutual cooperation or integration. The patient and his or her alters' cooperative participation in tasks of creative personal meaning have served both as a barometer for integration or cooperation and as a means to foster it. These concrete tasks allow for the strong opinions of each personality to be voiced, be considered by another, be acted on quickly, and result in a concrete product. In Lance's case, one of his now-communicating alters decided to share with Lance a memory of an abusive incident that had occurred when two men took him out to an isolated wooded area, molested him, and then abandoned him there. The alter drew the more specific information: how the men appeared, what colors they were wearing, and the form of the car that had transported them. As the drawing progressed, Lance was asked to come out frequently to absorb, empathize, and perhaps sense the familiarity of the scene *he* had been subjected to. After the initial illustrations were done, Lance continued the drawing by completing the background. When the cooperative composition was finished, Lance seemed to gain an increased empathy for the alter and a greater understanding of the incidents to which he had been subjected.

The joint construction of a magazine picture collage also constitutes a helpful shared give-and-take task for the host and alters. Because (in our experience) it generally seems easier for the alters to see things through the eyes of the host than it does for the host to see things through the eyes of the alters, the collage assignment is phrased thus: "You, Lance, are to work together today with J. Porter to choose pictures from a magazine and to paste them down, making a composition of the things that you like or dislike and so forth. J. Porter will look through your eyes and will let you know when, according to him, a picture that he views as appropriate should be included. You, Lance, are in charge of the task but are expected to include pictures he chooses, as well as pictures of your own. Work together to paste and complete the composition."

This is a fascinating task to watch because initially the host may tend to deny the inclusion of those alter's pictures that the host finds incompatible or offensive to his or her own way of thinking. The host may even flip quickly through pages that the alter shows or might show an interest in. In fact, it is not unusual for the frustrated alter to actually come out and select and cut his or her own pictures, complaining that the host would not consider these choices for inclusion in the collage.

It is also revealing to ask the alters to communicate their opinions of the collage once it is completed. They may see things that are quite cogent in each other's contributions—things that the other personality didn't recognize at first. The personalities always tend to mention the greatest differences that exist between them that are symbolized in specific symbols through the activity and composition of the collage. When this discussion can proceed as a reasonable give-and-take, it may set a precedent for continued discussion on varied points of view.

Postintegration Work

Once an alter or alters have agreed to cooperate or integrate, much work still remains to be done. The personality agreement or fusion is strengthened when the therapist maintains involvement, allowing for a smoother transition to the host's inclusion of these parts of him- or herself. In our experience, when alters are integrated, the host is not only inundated by a flood of retrieved memories but also is jostled by new psychological perspectives. Perhaps the host will even see colors as more vibrant or claim to have other enhanced sensory experiences. With a sense of increased vitality, the host may exhibit more enthusiasm, insight, and initiative for creative tasks.

While incorporating this newly found part of him- or herself, the host may experience difficulty in making sense of these new perceptions and consequently may find artistic endeavors comforting to compose. Also, a perceived loss certainly exists in the system after an integration. The remaining unintegrated alters may miss the integrated personalities, who to them have lost their former voices and perceived presence in order to become part of the host's life.

When Mr. R. was integrated with two of his alters, not only the remaining alters but also he himself began to miss the gregarious company and sound social advice he had been receiving in the past weeks from Mike, now a part of himself. Yet in a visit with Mr. R. some months later, after he had moved away, he seemed to have adjusted to the integration, confiding, "I was never funny at all before, but now when I say something really clever that makes other people laugh, I know that is the Mike part of me talking."

CADENCE OF THERAPY

It takes time and consistent interaction to establish rapport with the patient and his or her alters, to gain their trust and to learn their histories. Most therapists of DID agree that treatment is labor intensive and tends to be counterproductive when hurried. By the nature of the diagnosis, the patient is inherently unstable and holds the potential for self-damaging acts. Although expressive therapies augment what is being accomplished in psychotherapy and supports those goals, it can also unexpectedly bring forth material that causes an abreaction. For instance:

Unfortunate results occurred after the patient Betty, who had acknowledged her DID diagnosis, consented to and was subsequently videotaped in occupational therapy for the purpose of meeting her alters later through viewing the tape. We wanted Betty to become aware of the activities, resources, and talents that alter embodied. When the viewing occasion occurred a day after the filming, however, the patient ran out of the viewing room in shock as she actually realized how the dissociation manifested. This patient, though she seemed to cognitively accept and deal with the implications of her condition, was apparently not emotionally ready. A setback to therapy then occurred because one of the patient's alters—a young woman named Janelle, who considered herself to be a beauty queen—was appalled to see herself on video speaking and moving as she knew she did but now occupying an older, heavy-set woman's body. This dismay caused a problem when Janelle, a main personality until now, seemed to disappear from the patient's constellation of alters for several weeks. Her absence finally broken by a telephone call, Janelle whispered (in order, she said, that the other alters wouldn't hear her conversation) when she asked to come back to the activity clinic to finish a ceramic project she had been working on. She sounded sad, whimpered, and said she was quite ashamed to find that she looked like the host. Janelle even suggested that perhaps she should wear a cover over her head when she returned so that she wouldn't be so ashamed to have others see her.

The above patient's emotional response may not be so different from that of most adult DID patients who have long-standing, hard-held denial, fear, and resistance to knowing their true diagnosis. Consequently, tact, consistency, and a sensitivity to the patient's readiness for different stages of therapy are imperative—both to reduce the shock of the reality of the diagnosis, as well as to decrease the dread of the host for the alters.

∽

Obviously, in these days of managed care, there may be less opportunity for long inpatient stays and protracted daily creative therapies for the patient. Most therapy for DID patients, however, is currently completed on an outpatient basis. Many, if not all, of the expressive techniques and activities described in this chapter that augment and serve the integration process can be profitably used by a treating therapist. Specific expressive therapies, when allowed for, certainly can be integrated into an outpatient program. In fact, most of these outpatient "homework" activities take on added significance when completed in the real-life environments of home, community, and personal relationships.

As outlined, expressive tasks offer the alters and host means other than verbal psychotherapy by which to develop a fuller appreciation of each other and of the need to work cooperatively. The tasks can be fun as well as practical. Responsibility for making appropriate choices is left up to the patient but is monitored by the therapist. This arrangement can be facilitated by agreements between host and alters or even by written contracts between alters or host and alters. Often, this is the first time in his or her life that someone has helped the patient with the many personalities to actually address his or her personal life in a way that is honest and useful. Furthermore, creative products can serve as an outgrowth and independent symbol of each personality's perspective. We have found that this encouragement of the individual alters acts as a catalyst for acceptance and change throughout the total system. So, the therapist here finally becomes a kind of arbitrator—considering the priorities of the various alters and then, with the host, deciding which plans and wishes must be modified and selecting those that uphold the overall goals and desires of the patient. It seems ironic, but is generally the case, that the chance to make personal statements and exert their will encourages the various alters to later participate more fully in integration and cooperation and to appreciate that the opportunity for individual choice and expression, so often compromised in the daily life of the person with DID, has at last been honored.

NOTES

P. 239, *complexity of such patients:* Bliss, E. L. (1980). Multiple personalities: A report of 14 cases with implications for schizophrenia and hysteria. *Archives of General Psychiatry, 37,* 1383–1385; Greaves, G. B. (1980).

Multiple personality: 165 years after Mary Reynolds. *Journal of Nervous and Mental Disorders, 168,* 577–596; Kluft, R. P. (1984b). Treatment of multiple personality disorder: A study of 33 cases. *Psychiatric Clinics of North America, 7,* 9–29; Putnam, F. W., Guroff, J. J., Silberman, E. K., Barban, L., & Post, R. M. (1986). The clinical phenomenology of multiple personality disorder: Review of 100 recent cases. *Journal of Clinical Psychiatry, 47,* 285–293.

P. 239, *David Caul:* Caul, D. (1984). Group and videotape techniques for multiple personality disorder. *Psychiatric Annals, 14*(1), 43–50.

P. 240, *or unsympathetic toward the separate parts:* Kohut, H. (1971). *The analysis of the self.* New York: International Universities Press.

P. 240, *types of abuse as they occur:* Beahrs, J. O. (1982). *Unity and multiplicity: Multilevel consciousness of self in hypnosis, psychiatric disorder, and mental health.* New York: Brunner/Mazel.

P. 241, *lack of recognition between alters and host:* Kluft, E. S. (Ed.) (1993). *Expressive and functional therapies in the treatment of multiple personality disorder.* Springfield, IL: Thomas.

P. 242, *eventual personality fusion:* Dawson, P. L. (1990). Understanding and cooperation among alter and host personalities. *American Journal of Occupational Therapy, 44,* 994–997.

P. 244, *abused child's natural tendency to blame him- or herself for the acts:* Lister, E. D. (1982). Forced silence: A neglected dimension of trauma. *American Journal of Psychiatry, 138,* 872–876; Summit, R. C. (1983). The child sexual abuse accommodation syndrome. *Child Abuse and Neglect, 7,* 177–193.

P. 244, *Putnam et al. concluded in their research:* Putnam, F. W., Guroff, J. J., Silberman, E. K., Barban, L., & Post, R. M. (1986). The clinical phenomenology of multiple personality disorder: Review of 100 recent cases. *Journal of Clinical Psychiatry, 47,* 285–293.

P. 246, *previously incompatible alters:* David Caul, 1982, personal communication.

P. 246, *Pennebaker's important work:* Pennebaker, J. W. (1993). Putting stress into words: Health linguistic and therapeutic implications. *Behavior Research and Therapy, 31,* 539–548.

P. 249, *can "make or break" the therapeutic aims:* Allison, R. A. (1980). *Minds in many pieces: The making of a very special doctor.* New York: Rawson, Wade; Braun, B. G., & Sachs, R. G. (1986). Mapping techniques for multiple personality disorder. In B. G. Braun (Ed.), *Dissociative disorders: Proceedings of the Third International Conference on Multiple Personality/Dissociative States* (p. 64). Chicago: Rush University; Wilbur, C. B. (1984). Treatment of multiple personality. *Psychiatric Annals, 14,* 27–31.

P.252, *has helped form his or her perspectives and influenced his or her behaviors:* Kluft, R. P. (1984a). Aspects of the treatment of multiple personality disorder. *Psychiatric Annals, 14,* 51–55.

P. 252, *Expressive tasks may include specific applications such as music:* Pickett, E., & Sonnen, C. (1993). Guided imagery and music: A music therapy approach to multiple personality disorder. In E. S. Kluft (Ed.), *Expressive and functional therapies in the treatment of multiple personality disorder* (pp. 143–167). Springfield, IL: Thomas.

P. 252, *movement:* Baum, E. Z. (1991). Movement therapy with multiple personality disorder patients. *Dissociation, 4,* 99–104.

P. 252, *artwork:* Cohen, B. M., & Cox, C. T. (1989). Breaking the code: Identification of multiplicity in artistic productions. *Dissociation, 2,* 132–137; Fuhrman, N. L. (1988). Art interpretation and multiple personality. *Dissociation, 1*(4), 33–49; Jacobson, M. L. (1985). Manifestations of abuse in the art work of an inpatient diagnosed with multiple personality disorder [Summary]. In B. G. Braun (Ed.), *Dissociative disorders: Proceedings of the Third International Conference on Multiple Personality/Dissociative States* (p. 32). Chicago: Rush University; Mills, A., & Cohen, B. M. (1993). Facilitating the identification through art: The diagnostic drawing series. In E. S. Kluft (Ed.), *Expressive and functional therapies in the treatment of multiple personality disorder* (pp. 39–66). Springfield, IL: Thomas.

P. 252, *poetry and writing:* Cohen, B. M., Giller, E., & Giller, W. L. (1991). *Multiple personality from the inside out.* Lutherville, MD: Sidran Press.

P. 252, *play:* Fagan, J., & McMahon, P. P. (1984). Incipient multiple personality in children: Four cases. *Journal of Nervous and Mental Disease, 172,* 26–36; Olson, J. A. (1986). The use of play in the treatment of patients with MPD. In B. G. Braun (Ed.), *Dissociative disorders: Proceedings of the Third International Conference on Multiple Personality/Dissociative States* (p. 33). Chicago: Rush University; Olsen, J. A. (1993). The therapeutic use of play in the treatment of patients with multiple personality disorder. In E. S. Kluft (Ed.), *Expressive and functional therapies in the treatment of multiple personality disorder* (pp. 201–217). Springfield, IL: Thomas; Ross, C. A. (1989). *Multiple personality disorder: Diagnosis, clinical features, and treatment.* New York: Wiley.

P. 252, *sand tray arranging:* Sachs, R. G. (1990). The sand tray technique in the treatment of patients with dissociative disorders: Recommendations for occupational therapists. *American Journal of Occupational Therapy, 44,* 1045–1047; Sweig, T., & Sachs, R. (1993). Applications of sandplay to the treatment of multiple personality and dissociative disorders. In E. S. Kluft (Ed.), *Expressive and functional therapies in the treatment of multiple personality disorder* (pp. 189–220). Springfield, IL: Thomas.

P. 253, *Representing the system in this way is also known as mapping:* Braun, B. G., & Sachs, R. G. (1986). Mapping techniques for multiple personality disorder. In B. G. Braun (Ed.), *Dissociative disorders: Proceedings of the Third International Conference on Multiple Personality/Dissociative States* (p. 64). Chicago: Rush University.

P. 254, *encourage the alters to cooperate in proceeding with or completing a project:* Dawson, P. L. (1990). Understanding and co-operation among alter and host personalities. *American Journal of Occupational Therapy, 44,* 994–997.

P. 255, *they even hold varied perceptions of themselves:* Fine, C. G. (1988). Thoughts on the cognitive perceptual substrates of multiple personality disorder. *Dissociation, 1*(4), 5–10; Fine, C. G. (1991). Treatment stabilization and crisis prevention: Pacing the therapy of the multiple personality disorder patient. *Psychiatric Clinics of North America, 14,* 661–675.

P. 263, *treatment is labor intensive and tends to be counterproductive when hurried:* Fine, C. G. (1991). Treatment stabilization and crisis prevention: Pacing the therapy of the multiple personality disorder patient. *Psychiatric Clinics of North America, 14,* 661–675.

P. 264, *the potential for self-damaging acts:* Kluft, R. P. (1991). Hospital treatment of multiple personality disorder: An overview. *Psychiatric Clinics of North America, 14,* 695–719.

P. 264, *bring forth material that causes an abreaction:* Kluft, R. P. (1987). An update on multiple personality disorder. *Hospital and Community Psychiatry, 38,* 363–373.

P. 265, *can be integrated into an outpatient program:* Dawson, P. L. (1993). Occupational therapy for inpatients and outpatients with multiple personality disorder. In E. S. Kluft (Ed.), *Expressive and functional therapies in the treatment of multiple personality disorder* (pp. 245–257). Springfield, IL: Thomas.

FOR FURTHER READING

Allison, R. A. (1980). *Minds in many pieces: The making of a very special doctor.* New York: Rawson, Wade.

Baum, E. Z. (1991). Movement therapy with multiple personality disorder patients. *Dissociation, 4,* 99–104.

Beahrs, J. O. (1982). *Unity and multiplicity: Multilevel consciousness of self in hypnosis, psychiatric disorder, and mental health.* New York: Brunner/Mazel.

Bliss, E. L. (1980). Multiple personalities: A report of 14 cases with implications for schizophrenia and hysteria. *Archives of General Psychiatry, 37,* 1383–1385.

Braun, B. G. (1986). Issues in the psychotherapy of multiple personality disorder. In B. G. Braun (Ed.), *Treatment of multiple personality disorder* (pp. 1–28). Washington, DC: American Psychiatric Press.

Braun, B. G., & Sachs, R. G. (1986). Mapping techniques for multiple personality disorder. In B. G. Braun (Ed.), *Dissociative disorders: Proceedings of the Third International Conference on Multiple Personality/Dissociative States* (p. 64). Chicago: Rush University.

Caul, D. (1984). Group and videotape techniques for multiple personality disorder. *Psychiatric Annals, 14*(1), 43–50.

Cohen, B. M., & Cox, C. T. (1989). Breaking the code: Identification of multiplicity in artistic productions. *Dissociation, 2,* 132–137.

Cohen, B. M., Giller, E., & Giller, W. L. (1991). *Multiple personality from the inside out.* Lutherville, MD: Sidran Press.

Dawson, P. L. (1990). Understanding and co-operation among alter and host personalities. *American Journal of Occupational Therapy, 44,* 994–997.

Dawson, P. L. (1993). Occupational therapy for inpatients and outpatients with multiple personality disorder. In E. S. Kluft (Ed.), *Expressive and functional therapies in the treatment of multiple personality disorder* (pp. 245–257). Springfield, IL: Thomas.

Fagan, J., & McMahon, P. P. (1984). Incipient multiple personality in children: Four cases. *Journal of Nervous and Mental Disease, 172,* 26–36.

Fine, C. G. (1988). Thoughts on the cognitive perceptual substrates of multiple personality disorder. *Dissociation, 1*(4), 5–10.

Fine, C. G. (1991). Treatment stabilization and crisis prevention: Pacing the therapy of the multiple personality disorder patient. *Psychiatric Clinics of North America, 14,* 661–675.

Fuhrman, N. L. (1988). Art interpretation and multiple personality. *Dissociation, 1*(4), 33–40.

Greaves, G. B. (1980). Multiple personality: 165 years after Mary Reynolds. *Journal of Nervous and Mental Disorders, 168,* 577–596.

Jacobson, M. L. (1985). Manifestations of abuse in the art work of an inpatient diagnosed with multiple personality disorder [Summary]. In B. G. Braun (Ed.), *Dissociative disorders: Proceedings of the Third International Conference on Multiple Personality/Dissociative States* (p. 32). Chicago: Rush University.

Kluft, E. S. (Ed.). (1993). *Expressive and functional therapies in the treatment of multiple personality disorder.* Springfield, IL: Thomas.

Kluft, R. P. (1984a). Aspects of the treatment of multiple personality disorder. *Psychiatric Annals, 14,* 51–55.

Kluft, R. P. (1984b). Treatment of multiple personality disorder: A study of 33 cases. *Psychiatric Clinics of North America, 7,* 9–29.

Kluft, R. P. (1987). An update on multiple personality disorder. *Hospital and Community Psychiatry, 38,* 363–373.

Kluft, R. P. (1991). Hospital treatment of multiple personality disorder: An overview. *Psychiatric Clinics of North America, 14,* 695–719.

Kohut, H. (1971). *The analysis of the self.* New York: International Universities Press.

Lister, E. D. (1982). Forced silence: A neglected dimension of trauma. *American Journal of Psychiatry, 138,* 872–876.

Mills, A., & Cohen, B. M. (1993). Facilitating the identification through art: The diagnostic drawing series. In E. S. Kluft (Ed.), *Expressive and functional therapies in the treatment of multiple personality disorder* (pp. 39–66). Springfield, IL: Thomas.

Olson, J. A. (1986). The use of play in the treatment of patients with MPD. In B. G. Braun (Ed.), *Dissociative disorders: Proceedings of the Third International Conference on Multiple Personality/Dissociative States* (p. 33). Chicago: Rush University.

Olson, J. A. (1993). The therapeutic use of play in the treatment of patients with multiple personality disorder. In E. S. Kluft (Ed.), *Expressive and functional therapies in the treatment of multiple personality disorder* (pp. 201–217). Springfield, IL: Thomas.

Pickett, E., & Sonnen, C. (1993). Guided imagery and music: A music therapy approach to multiple personality disorder. In E. S. Kluft (Ed.), *Expressive and functional therapies in the treatment of multiple personality disorder* (pp. 143–167). Springfield, IL: Thomas.

Pennebaker, J. W. (1993). Putting stress into words: Health linguistic and therapeutic implications. *Behavior Research and Therapy, 31,* 539–548.

Putnam, F. W., Guroff, J. J., Silberman, E. K., Barban, L., & Post, R. M. (1986). The clinical phenomenology of multiple personality disorder: Review of 100 recent cases. *Journal of Clinical Psychiatry, 47,* 285–293.

Ross, C. A. (1989). *Multiple personality disorder: Diagnosis, clinical features, and treatment.* New York: Wiley.

Sachs, R. G. (1990). The sandtray technique in the treatment of patients with dissociative disorders: Recommendations for occupational therapists. *American Journal of Occupational Therapy, 44,* 1045–1047.

Summit, R. C. (1983). The child sexual abuse accommodation syndrome. *Child Abuse and Neglect, 7,* 177–193.

Sweig, T., & Sachs, R. (1993). Applications of sandplay to the treatment of multiple personality and dissociative disorders. In E. S. Kluft (Ed.), *Expressive and functional therapies in the treatment of multiple personality disorder* (pp. 189–220). Springfield, IL: Thomas.

Wilbur, C. B. (1984). Treatment of multiple personality. *Psychiatric Annals, 14,* 27–31.

PART THREE

INPATIENT
INTERVENTIONS

9

HOSPITAL TREATMENT

Richard P. Kluft

In this chapter, I will note some concerns about the hospital treatment of Dissociative Identity Disorder (DID) and discuss a pragmatic approach to the use of inpatient care as a therapeutic modality. I will indicate the considerations that underlie my management of DID in a hospital setting and discuss the principles and practices that follow from them.

Numerous advances in the understanding and psychotherapeutic treatment of DID patients have initiated a new era in which specialized care is increasingly available and accessible. Many DID patients will achieve stable remission in treatment with expert clinicians experienced in the treatment of DID. But neophytes providing specific treatment can achieve more favorable results than experienced therapists who decline to address DID directly. The development of dedicated Dissociative Disorders Units (DDUs) has demonstrated the feasibility of treating DID patients with an intensity and expertise hitherto unanticipated. Techniques developed in such settings have been adapted to the unique needs of particular general psychiatric programs.

Traditionally, DID has been regarded as a rarity. Notwithstanding Stengel's 1943 pronouncement that DID was extinct, contemporary studies using reliable and valid screening instruments and structured interviews demonstrate that DID is a clinical commonplace. Ross, Norton, and Wozney found that 3.3

percent of sequentially admitted patients in a Canadian general psychiatric population suffered previously undiagnosed DID. Saxe, van der Kolk, Berkowitz, et al. found that 4 percent of patients in a Harvard hospital had previously unrecognized DID. Boon and Draijer reported that 5 percent of the psychiatric patients at a Dutch psychiatric hospital had previously undiagnosed DID. DID will be diagnosed by most mental health practitioners who are alert to its gross and subtle manifestations and prepared to initiate a systematic assessment of dissociative phenomena.

Managed care must contend with large numbers of DID patients whose conditions respond only to the intense psychotherapeutic treatments that are often discouraged because of their expense. The mental health professions must address with alacrity the possibility that at the very moment in time DID patients are being identified with greater frequency and referred for a type of care that has been demonstrated to be effective, economic and social forces may threaten to render such treatment unavailable to all but the affluent few. This would be a dire blow indeed to a group of patients whose disorder often stems from the failure of responsible individuals to offer them adequate nurture, protection, and consolation.

A New Model of Hospital Care for DID

Modern conceptualizations of the appropriate role of hospital care are driven largely by the psychopharmacological paradigms and economic concerns. It is considered ideal to mobilize the patient in short order and expend the minimal amount of time, effort, and funding in doing so. Efforts to mobilize the full armamentarium of the mental health sciences on behalf of a suffering patient in a compassionate and supportive environment may be considered undesirable because it is costly and time-consuming.

Such an orientation may be useful in stemming the regression of a medication-responsive psychotic or overwhelmed patient, tiding the characterologically vulnerable individual through a period of distress or decompensation and supporting the situationally upset as they reequilibrate. However, it is a questionable model for the delivery of care to a population of patients whose condition is not primarily medication responsive.

DID patients' episodes of dysfunction and dysphoria often involve such pervasive problems that relatively brief admissions are likely to fail to bring them to a level of function at which they can move forward in outpatient therapy alone. That is, for many DID patients, the brief hospital stay suppresses, rather than resolves, the issues that led to the hospitalization. This suppression may set the stage for either another hospitalization or a therapeutic stalemate if the patient settles down but has not achieved what he or she needs to achieve in order to proceed safely in an outpatient setting. In such instances, efforts to move forward outside the hospital are likely to result in recurrent distress and dysfunction, with the need for rehospitalization. Each subsequent rehospitalization may once again prove too brief and the treatment too cursory and superficial to be of genuine benefit to the patient.

Plainly stated, the function of inpatient treatment is to build a better outpatient. The treatment of DID is primarily an outpatient enterprise, highly dependent on continuity of treatment by the primary therapist to maximize its chances of success. Inpatient treatment is almost always ancillary to outpatient treatment. I work on the premise that, except in the rarest of instances, hospital care is a precious commodity in short supply, not to be squandered in a profligate or thoughtless manner, but to be used to address emergencies and/or to achieve goals that are essential to the progress of the overall therapeutic process.

To be effective in achieving this mission, the hospital stay must not only provide containment, structure, and support through a period of crisis but also must address effectively whatever emotional burdens, deficits in coping, and vulnerabilities precluded the outpatient management of the concerns that led to the hospital admission. It must also facilitate the patient's readiness to continue with his or her outpatient treatment.

An admission is especially beneficial when some therapeutic intervention sets in motion a process of change that acquires its own momentum or when the patient seizes on the hospital stay as an opportunity for self-initiated and self-directed growth. Although on many occasions very brief hospital stays suffice to meet the needs of the DID patient, all too often they do not, and the patient is discharged in a very unsatisfactory state.

Adjusting the Treatment to the Patient

Effective hospital care for DID must address the clinical realities of the condition, rather than attempt to force the proverbial square peg into a round hole. If an inpatient setting that disparaged the use of medication and other biological therapies failed to treat a patient with major depression or a bipolar disorder with the appropriate medication and other modalities, we would be outraged. The situation of the DID patient who receives suboptimal treatment, however, is not likely to be responded to with similar forcefulness.

The treatment of choice for DID is intensive psychotherapy, facilitated when necessary by hypnosis. When an inpatient program proposes to treat DID without an emphasis on the established treatment of choice, few voices (besides those of the patients) are raised in protest. Even though the first-line treatment is intensive psychotherapy and to withhold it might expose the patient to the risk of unnecessary morbidity and even death by a preventable suicide, unit chiefs and administrators often protest the use of their hospitals to support such endeavors. They may protest that providing the DID patient with appropriate psychotherapy is disruptive to the milieu and causes other patients (and staff members) to complain that the DID patient is receiving different and "special" treatment.

Consequently, it is often easier for hospital staff to turn a blind eye to the needs of the DID patient. Worse still, they are comforted in their withholding this "treatment of choice" by the knowledge that DID is sufficiently controversial that, should they be sued, eminent and prestigious authorities can be found to aver that DID does not exist, is an iatrogenic artifact, or is an erroneous diagnosis based on the misinterpretation of the phenomena of another disorder. Furthermore, they may maintain that the DID manifestations will vanish when misguided treatment efforts are discontinued.

DID Patient at Risk

Let me try to provide a context for appreciating the fact that many DID patients will require a period of hospital care sometime during the treatment of their illness. DID patients are particularly crisis-prone and vulnerable. It is often difficult to realize that these often bright, talented, and gifted individuals who appear so strong in so many ways are simultaneously highly at risk for the deterioration of their adaptive capacities. To my mind, what is most impressive (and counterexpectational to predictions of those who maintain that DID is iatrogenic and that recommended treatments encourage regressive dependency) is that although 74 percent of Ross, Norton, and Wozney's 236 DID patients reported having been hospitalized, most had been hospitalized prior to the diagnosis of DID. Thus, hospitalization is less common following the diagnosis and the institution of treatment for DID. This finding suggests that despite the difficulties associated with the treatment of DID, the patient will decompensate less frequently in specific treatment than in treatment that fails to address their condition.

In my own practice, 85 percent of patients referred to me in a decompensated state will require hospital care within six months. However, of patients I can begin in treatment with my own protocol for strengthening the patient before approaching traumatic material, I hospitalize only 15 percent to 20 percent over the remainder of their treatment. Thus, I find that the best way to reduce the costs of the hospital care of DID patients is to be extremely generous with the use of the hospital for decompensated cases but to promote the use of treatment approaches that minimize the likelihood that future hospital care will be required once the patient is able to resume outpatient treatment.

As mentioned above, DID patients are often quite vulnerable and crisis-prone. Most of them fight bravely to remain in control of themselves and collapse only when they are exhausted by their efforts. Consequently, an incident of disequilibrium may be more a "preview of coming attractions" than an isolated event that can be resolved with alacrity. The likelihood of future destabilization makes it helpful for the health- and cost-conscious professional to ask whether both patient and pocketbook will be better served by regarding each hospitalization as an opportunity to promote the long-term goals of the therapy, in addition to addressing the immediate crisis, by taking what I call a "stabilization-plus" perspective.

To place this point of view in perspective, let me introduce the reader to what I call "the mathematics of misery" and then note some of the clinical features of trauma victims in general and DID patients in particular that render the traumatized DID patient especially vulnerable to destabilization. First consider the impact of trauma by using sexual assault as a model. A single unwelcome sexual experience, for example, can have a devastating impact on a victim's mental health. We can all agree that the plight of the rape or incest victim is particularly unfortunate.

Suppose that a given individual with DID has been sexually exploited for ten years. This is the average number of years of abuse that has been alleged by a cohort of 355 DID patients. If the average abuser imposes himself or herself on the victim twice a week and has access to that victim for fifty weeks per year, "the mathematics of misery" dictates that the future adult DID patient may have had one thousand unwanted sexual experiences. If the abuser can exploit the victim no more than once a week, the victim may have had five hundred unwanted sexual experiences. If the victim can be approached only once a week for one month per year, he or she still may have had forty unwanted sexual experiences, which is quite a lot to deal with.

A person who has suffered such extensive exploitation is likely to suffer many sequelae. The sense of self is damaged, and there are many disruptive affective and behavioral consequences. The patient's cognition may be disrupted as well, and relatedness will be impaired. Pathological secrecy is not uncommon. Revictimization is highly likely. It is also likely that such a person will have much instability in his or her life and frequently will be unable to turn to others for assistance without behaving in ways that may create similar instability in the relationship with the helper(s) or establishing relationships in which past patterns of exploitation may be recapitulated. It is difficult to engage such a damaged person rapidly and to move aggressively in treatment. Even in optimal hospital settings, it is not unusual for the DID patient to need days, if not more than a week, to begin to work constructively with a hospital staff with which he or she has had no prior connection.

As we turn to the aspects of vulnerability that are more particular to DID patients than to trauma victims in general, additional concerns arise. Table 9.1 presents a summary of factors that make DID patients inherently unstable and vulnerable, factors that one must be prepared to consider and perhaps address in the effort to achieve stabilization-plus and to "build a better outpatient." If such factors are not borne in mind, it will be difficult to appreciate why at times an intelligent, talented, and personable DID patient may be hospitalized more frequently and for longer periods than a severely psychotic individual. Unfortunately, great strengths do not invariably compensate for great weaknesses. The DID patient is often a patchwork quilt of the most diverse combinations of assets and liabilities.

The more of these factors that play a role in the DID patient's life, the more he or she is virtually "an accident looking for a place to happen" and the more challenging the mission of the hospital treatment in undertaking the stabilization-plus necessary to build a better outpatient. The patient for whom several or most of the factors in Table 9.1 are operative is likely to prove more difficult to treat rapidly than the patient for whom only a few are problematic.

Table 9.1
Factors Contributing to the Vulnerability and
Instability of DID Patients

1. An ongoing and available observing ego is absent.

2. Usually autonomous ego functions are disrupted.

3. Information necessary for coping is unavailable because of amnesia.

4. Absence of co-consciousness means efforts with one alter may not help the others.

5. Pseudodelusional (often with both belief and disbelief in different alters) convictions of separateness may cause one alter to fail to relate to another's plight, to see another alter's difficulties as to its own advantage, and even to attack another alter.

6. Switching after activity makes it difficult to learn from experience.

7. Inconsistent, dysfunctional, and demanding behavior may drive away supports.

8. Inner battles and switching may lead to ego-disruptive quasi-psychotic symptoms.

9. Alters' narcissistic investment in separateness and beliefs that therapy might "kill them" may lead to alters opposing treatment.

10. Severe moral masochism (as in self-punitive self-censure) is evident.

11. Repetition by reenactment of self-endangering patterns is evident.

12. Concomitant "sitting duck syndrome" (as in proneness to revictimization) is evident.

13. Cognitive impairments diminish coping capacity and accurate assessment of circumstances.

14. Intrusive flashback phenomena are apparent.

Table 9.1 *(continued)*

15. Fantasy-proneness (patient may be unable to distinguish between what has been thought and what has occurred) is evident.

16. High hypnotizability to heterohypnosis (the induction of trance by another), self-hypnosis, and spontaneous trance, which, because of high absorption and suggestibility, leads to the intensification of the emotional potency of stimuli.

17. There is frequent comorbidity with other mental disorders that also enhance vulnerability/instability.

18. Exquisite sensitivity to issues of actual or feared separation and loss is apparent.

19. Current societal preoccupation with both child abuse and the denial of the reality of child abuse allegations creates a "trigger dense" environment in which the DID patient experiences frequent and often disquieting overstimulation.

20. Because intrafamilial abuse is often alleged, it is rare for a DID patient to have a supportive family of origin.

The perspective offered above has not been documented by any systematic research. It is consistent with the frequently made clinical observation, however, that a subgroup of DID patients is repeatedly rehospitalized for a series of admissions that fail to bring them to a level of function and resilience that permits them to move beyond their unfortunate cycle of decompensations and rehospitalizations. To be effective, the hospital setting must be prepared to identify the relevant stressors (situational and intrapsychic), explore the characteristic manner in which the DID patient responds to those stressors (behaviorally and subjectively), help the DID patient process the stressors and their impact on him or her, and equip the patient with tools adequate to the task of making him or her more resilient in the face of those stressors. Anything less simply sends the accident looking for a place to happen back out to happen again.

PRINCIPLES OF ADEQUATE HOSPITAL TREATMENT

To achieve such objectives, the hospital must be prepared to bring to bear the necessary expertise to effect them. Let's examine what expertises and qualities are necessary to support the inpatient treatment of DID patients, acknowledging that, with some exceptions (those related to providing dignified care for the patient), a given DID patient may or may not require them during any given admission. Table 9.2 indicates these prerequisites.

Most of the items in Table 9.2 are self-explanatory; others may require clarification. For example, without support for the idea of treating this patient population (item one), it will be tempting to redefine their pathology (often by mandate of the unit chief) as something that can be addressed within existing patterns of care or to decide that a patient should be transferred out if problematic. If it is possible for a disgruntled individual to interdict the delivery of appropriate care by appealing up the chain of command, it is likely that serious treatment will prove impossible.

Communication (item six) must be more than the exchange of information, professional "howdy-dos," lectures by the treating professional or referral source as to how the nurses should conduct themselves with the patient, and protests by nursing staff about the perceived burden imposed by the admission of the patient and the support of the treatment program. Communication must address candidly the problems to be solved and solve them in a constructive manner. Abstract principles and shoulds are not preeminently effective. The participants in the communication are adult rather than child-adolescent learners. They will question the relevance of, if not resent, interactions that do not address the resolution of daily problems. It is more

Table 9.2
Prerequisites for the Competent
Hospital Treatment of DID Patients

1. Administrative support for the mission of treating DID patients

2. Adequate supervision and support for frontline staff who actually are with the patients and must contend with their switching and traumatic material

3. The presence of (or consultative access to) expertise in both the individual treatment and the nursing management of DID patients

4. A willingness on the part of unit staff to support a psychotherapy-centered admission

5. Easy access to educational materials, consultation, and supervision so that staff can move from a position of uncertainty to one of mastery

6. Excellent problem-solving-oriented communication between the referral source and the treating professional and between the treating professional and the treatment team

7. Treatment goals that both address the stabilization-plus objective and acknowledge the (actual rather than "business as usual") limitations on resources that may exist, both in terms of the unit's capacities and the financial aspects of supporting the admission

8. A treatment regimen that will avoid (1) "mission creep" (the expansion of goals beyond resources), (2) regression that is not an inevitable part of attaining certain therapeutic goals, and (3) disrupting unit function more than is absolutely necessary to achieve stabilization-plus

9. Staff and treating professionals' possessing understanding and skills relevant to intervention with regard to unique DID behaviors and phenomena, such as switching; hypnotic, autohypnotic, and spontaneous trance; and the alter states

(continued)

Table 9.2 *(continued)*

10. General expertise in the management of a wide range of psychiatric disorders so that comorbid psychopathologies can be addressed promptly and competently

11. Primary nursing care provided by someone who will not go on vacation or leave during the likely duration of the patient's stay

12. Sufficient staff professionalism that (1) disagreements over the DID diagnosis and its treatment will not be leaked to or otherwise imposed on the patient; (2) staff will not attempt to impress on the patient their own judgments and opinions that differ from those of the treating professional; (3) mechanisms exist to address splitting phenomena, both those generated by the patient and those generated by the staff's different perceptions of the patient and/or his or her condition

13. A mechanism that will both allow necessary procedures to take place (noisy abreactions, restraint sessions, hypnosis, and drug-facilitated interviews) and buffer the rest of the unit from their potentially disruptive impact

14. A treating professional readily available to both the treatment team and the referral source

15. Roles and prerogatives of all involved caregiving professionals made clear and reclarified whenever necessary

16. A procedure to manage any complaints made by the DID patient about his or her care, lest the immediate world become involved in a chaotic melange

17. Discussions on matters of confidentiality with the patient and all concerned, who must appreciate that the staff cannot be effective on the patient's behalf if they are not informed about the progress of the treatment and its major concerns

important for an evening-shift nurse to know what to do when a child alter cowers beneath a piece of furniture and will not emerge than it is for him or her to receive a lecture about the origin of child alters and their need for reassurance and nurture.

It is not uncommon for the treatment of a DID patient to be troubled by persistent objections that it requires more of the staff than does work with other patient groups. Because something is not the norm, it is protested (item seven). Intensive care, surgical, delivery room, premature nursery, or emergency ward staffs would be unlikely to raise such an issue. Most medical and surgical professionals appreciate that some cases are simply more demanding than others and call on more of their skills and energy.

This type of protest is more frequently encountered in the freestanding psychiatric hospital than in the psychiatric unit of a general hospital, where the "nursing culture" and milieu remain more under the influence of the psychiatric nurses' ongoing interaction with colleagues who deal with wide varieties of patients. Unfortunately, nursing services in psychiatric hospitals can become removed from the considerations discussed in Table 9.2 and lose sight of the wide range of needs that patients may have, through no fault of their own.

Setting Realistic Expectations

It is also extremely important to avoid admitting a patient for a treatment that has insufficient funding. As cruel as it is to withhold hospital care from a suffering patient, it is more heartless still to begin very extensive projects that have no chance of being completed before the patient will have to be discharged or transferred to a state facility at which it is unlikely that the treatment can be completed.

A typical scenario: an outpatient therapist will perceive that a patient is having difficulty with painful material and is starting to decompensate. The therapist will request hospital care to do this work in a structured and safe environment. If the patient is admitted and is completely cooperative (a circumstance that one cannot count on), he or she is likely to take a week or so to open up to the new therapist and may require a similar amount of time to shut down and restabilize in order to be safe on an outpatient basis. If the patient has thirty days of insurance, that means only approximately two weeks will be available for work on the powerful material; that is likely to be insufficient.

The patient will be better served by a brief admission of a week or so dedicated to containment and to developing a relationship with the inpatient therapist, followed by a focus in the outpatient treatment on strengthening the patient before approaching difficult material again. Should such work destabilize the patient again, ideally the patient can return to a known environment and familiar therapist and deal briefly with the upsetting material while shutting down other material and alters. Suppose the patient requires a week to connect and restabilize and two brief admissions of four days each to weather brief crises. The patient and the therapy will have profited more from less hospital care than had he or she become involved in an unrealistically ambitious admission that depleted funding and left him or her shell-shocked rather than restabilized.

At the Dissociative Disorders Unit of the Institute of Pennsylvania Hospital (DDU), we try to prevent admissions with global goals and meager resources with which to attain them. Instead, we attempt to educate the referring therapist about what is reasonable to expect. Unfortunately, we often learn later that the patient has been admitted elsewhere to attempt the heroic endeavor and has wound up in a state hospital, often unable to function for a protracted period.

Mission Creep

Under item eight, I have listed the probably unfamiliar term *mission creep*. This is a contemporary military expression that refers implicitly to the dangers and problems that develop when a force sent to accomplish a particular mission and equipped to do so finds its mission enlarged and changed (the "creep") so that sight is lost of the original objective and increasing time and resources become committed to attaining the expanded or altered goals. The original purpose of the mission is abandoned and never achieved, and the force may become mired in an increasingly complicated task that is increasingly unlikely to be accomplished expeditiously or successfully.

Mission creep is menacing to the patient, the referring and treating therapists, the hospital staff, and the funder of the admission; it is particularly likely to occur when an admission is open-ended or its goals are global or vaguely formulated. It can exhaust and demoralize the patient, who becomes overwhelmed by the opening up of so much painful material without any sign of its resolution, with the exacerbation of dissociative symptoms, and by the sense of being out of control. He or she may end the admission unable to return to the premorbid level of function and knowing that the hospital has failed to help and that it is no longer possible to go to the hospital at a time of distress because coverage has been exhausted.

The therapists may feel impotent or incompetent and become overwhelmed by what has escaped from the Pandora's box that has been opened. They may feel a sense of failure and guilt, which the patient will perceive as their sensing that he or she cannot be helped. Not infrequently, they begin to withdraw from the patient. Conflict and mutual recrimination between the outpatient and hospital-based therapist may take place. The hospital staff feel powerless. They have exhausted themselves on the patient's behalf without seeing their efforts bear fruit. Their sense of mastery and competence with regard to work with DID will suffer, and they may approach the next DID admission with dread. The source of the funding will be less than delighted. Monies will have been expended without proof of tangible benefit to the patient and with some indications that the patient has been harmed rather than helped by the hospitalization. It will be very easy for the funding source to conclude that the professionals involved are incompetent, that DID cannot be treated, and that efforts should be made to minimize expenditure on behalf of other patients with a similar diagnosis.

Unfortunately, at times, mission creep may occur despite the best and most focused efforts of all concerned in the treatment of a newly diagnosed patient, an acutely traumatized patient, or a previously mismanaged or incompletely understood patient. All of these cases have too many unknown factors and unpredictable elements for accurate treatment planning. When several of these factors co-occur, chaos may be inevitable. For example, a patient being sexually exploited by her previous therapist was hospitalized after a brutal rape by a stranger. In the course of the admission, DID was diagnosed. The trauma of the rape had reactivated virtually the full range of her earlier misfortunes, superimposing the features of both an acute stress reaction and Posttraumatic Stress Disorder (Delayed Type) on the DID. Therapeutic engagement was complicated by the erotizing of her ongoing treatment.

More common forms of mission creep exist. In some instances, the therapist and the patient either never establish or wander away from the essential goals of the admission. In the first case, often either the therapist is relatively unfamiliar with the treatment of DID or the mandate from the referral source is impossibly broad. For example, a psychiatrist who had never treated DID was assigned such a patient. He allowed the patient to express herself freely on a wide variety of topics that were of concern to her, and she became quite agitated as she did so. Because the material produced was new and strange and because work with alters was a novel experience, he set about simply getting to know the patient, her alters, and her history. Soon, she was "wide open," and her insurance was on the verge of exhaustion. Although the patient felt very positive about the psychiatrist, she was discharged in a disorganized state, unable to return to her job or to function well at home.

A closely related form of mission creep occurs when an inpatient therapist agrees to follow a plan that is unrealistic. A psychologist assigned to treat a DID patient learned that the referring therapist hoped the admission could be used to "abreact and work through the satanic ritual abuse" felt to be unsafe to handle in an outpatient setting. She began and found that one lurid account led to another, with the patient deteriorating all the while, flooded with progressively more and more unsettling material. At the end of the patient's insured days, she was suicidal and decompensated. She was transferred to a state hospital.

The most common form of mission creep occurs, however, when the therapist allows distraction, curiosity, or the patient's or referring therapist's unrealistic hopes and demands or fantasy-proneness to hamstring common sense. For example:

A patient who had always retained conscious awareness of paternal incest had become overwhelmed and suicidal when she began to have flashbacks of these events and to hear the inner voice of an alter identified with her father menacing and urging her to kill herself. Within two days of admission, she found herself at odds with her primary nurse, whom she found cold and uncaring. Exploring this, her therapist found that the nurse reminded her of her mother. As this was further explored, it appeared that the mother knew about the incest, and the patient began to report fantasies that her mother might have abused her as well.

A week was spent in exploring her relationship with the nurse and in pursuing the issue of the mother. In group the patient was upset by talk of abortions. Soon, she became convinced that she had suffered one or more incestuous pregnancies and abortions, and this became the focus of discussion. One evening, another patient confided in her that she had suffered satanic ritual abuse, and the patient herself had a nightmare that night about such matters. This, too, was explored.

By now three weeks had passed, during which only two days had been directed to the exploration and treatment of her chief complaint (incest memories, related flashbacks, and problematic alters). The referring therapist was upset but accepted the inpatient therapist's reasoning that the emergence of the above material would speed and shorten the overall therapy. The patient was pleased because she thought that real progress had been made and that she was now "really getting to the bottom of things." The stress of this all, however, destabilized her alter system.

Discharged, the patient remained unable to cope and had to go on disability. She now had flashbacks of incest, incest pregnancies, abortions, maternal neglect and abuse, and satanic ritual abuse. She was switching frequently and unable to handle even the more mundane aspects of her life without great difficulty. Although this approach may be useful in a slower, more consistent outpatient setting, it is clearly inappropriate for intensive brief inpatient treatment.

The fact that certain treatments useful in work with DID patients may be strange, noisy, and labor-intensive and thereby unsettling to the milieu (item thirteen) cannot be allowed to preclude their use. Conversely, the skilled practitioner will realize that, more often than not, such procedures should not be an everyday aspect of the DID patient's treatment. Traditional prolonged abreactive sessions may be replaced with fractionated abreactions, which are more tolerable for both the patient and the milieu. Daily abreactive work exhausts and destabilizes more patients than it helps and should be discouraged in most cases. Abreaction without processing and enhancing the understanding of what has occurred and its impact on the patient can degenerate into retraumatization mistaken for skilled treatment. The same considerations apply to restraint sessions and drug-facilitated interviews.

Importance of Communication

Complaints against staff and therapists by DID patients are frequent and often vociferous (item sixteen). Their anticipation and dread of harm, as well as their fears of being disliked and rejected, beget a host of problematic attitudes, utterances, and behaviors, often designed to master or control such eventualities. Their negative and traumatic transferences are difficult to abide, and their use of projective identification and splitting-like defenses can attach odious connotations to those involved in their care. At times it is difficult to bear in mind that such processes are unconscious in the main, especially in DID patients about whom one often entertains the notion that some alter consciously knows about and controls everything with spiteful malice or in whom alters will take the grandiose stance that they, in fact, have brought about all that occurs. Countertransference management with such patients can be a fine art.

I have found it useful to establish a chain of communication for such complaints that does not place the referring therapist or concerned others in any role of responsibility but that does recognize and respect their concerns. Such persons are easily seen by the patients as "courts of appeal" against the unreasonable demands and pressures imposed by staff and the inpatient therapist. I have found it useful to acknowledge and address the reality components of complaints while still insisting on holding firm to the "mission of the admission" and to decline to invest much time in the exploration of such grievances.

In another era, when hospital stays were quite long and milieu programs more psychodynamic and more intense, these protests would have been approachable as valuable derivatives of core conflicts that could be explored with great benefit. For better or worse, however, with shorter stays, less psychodynamic focus, and less powerful milieux, a session spent with the patient ventilating about the slowness and personal shortcomings of the medication nurse, for example, may constitute 5 percent of the psychotherapy time for a one-month admission (four weeks at five sessions per week), a scandalous waste of scarce resources.

Our DDU team has found it useful to assign the role of the hearer of the grievances to a social worker or an administrative nurse and to discuss the grievance in rounds. I have found it useful to tell my patients of my concern that although their complaints need to be addressed, such a focus in our sessions is counterproductive and detrimental to our achieving what we need to achieve and that we will use no more than five minutes to review such considerations.

SPECIAL ASPECTS OF TREATMENT IN A DEDICATED DISSOCIATIVE DISORDERS UNIT (DDU)

Although I have no objective data that support the superiority of specialized dissociative disorders units or programs (DDUs), I can compare my own experience of treating DID patients for over a dozen years in a general hospital psychiatric unit and on unspecialized floors of a private psychiatric hospital with the experience of treating them on a DDU. I also have learned a great deal from having visited many general and DDU units, consulting to many hospitals that were considering establishing a DDU, and discussing with visitors to my DDU their impressions of its advantages and disadvantages. Interestingly, although most patients have praised the DDU for what it has to offer, a small but vocal minority find them to be too overwhelming, aggressive, or intense, and they loathe them.

It is my experience that if a general hospital psychiatric unit or general psychiatric unit approximates the conditions noted in Table 9.2, it is very possible to do excellent work with DID. In the absence of those conditions, however, DID treatments in such settings may proceed under so many disadvantages and burdens as to make an optimal level of care unlikely. I have seen so many wonderful therapeutic breakthroughs on specialized DDUs with dedicated staffs and wonderful milieux that have established warm, supportive, and healing cultures that I have become convinced that such units can be profoundly powerful agencies of healing. Some of their potential benefits are listed in Table 9.3.

Anything that powerful, however, has the potential to subserve less appropriate ends. Table 9.4 presents an outline of some

Table 9.3
Benefits of a Dedicated DDU

1. There is universal staff expertise with DID.

2. The DID patient is not special or different.

3. Treatment of the DID patient is not special or different and is supported and familiar.

4. Milieu culture disparages acting up and makes patients feel more normal and human.

5. Special group therapies make the benefits of group treatment available without the usual disruptions.

6. Staff routinely can apply interventions commonly only done by experts.

7. As a consequence, there is more rapid interdiction of crises and regressions and quicker remobilizations.

8. Peer pressures from other skilled therapists and administrators discourage misadventures.

9. There is no staff-induced staff splitting over matters of belief or disbelief regarding DID; general patient-induced splitting is more readily addressed.

10. Staff competence and confidence quiet many DID patients' fears.

11. There is much peer support to do the difficult work of therapy and integration.

12. Expert consultation is readily available without significant delay.

13. The unit director acts as ombudsman for patient care issues.

Table 9.4
Relative Cautions about Treatment in Dedicated DDUs

1. Dedicated DDUs can prove overwhelming to the newly diagnosed DID patient still fearful of the diagnosis.

2. It is virtually inevitable that one patient's upset will trigger upset in some others, so such settings can be highly stimulating.

3. Patients' accounts may more readily be contaminated by what the patients hear from others.

4. Patients may model on peers in their attempts to understand and control themselves.

5. Patients who feel unready to deal with their own issues may find themselves triggered nonetheless by what they hear from others in groups.

6. Vicarious traumatization by others' accounts is not uncommon.

7. Unmotivated patients may find that such programs do not (and cannot) support their stances (and thus cause anxiety) and confront the causes too forcefully for them to tolerate.

8. Some such programs have been dominated by unwise and oversimplified approaches to treatment.

9. Patients with severe narcissistic issues of entitlement or who need to feel special and unique are invariably upset to find they are considered to be "like everyone else."

10. For some patients, admission to a DDU is perceived as a public revelation of their abuse backgrounds, and issues of mortification and perceived stigmatization preclude their making good use of such programs.

11. The attorneys of DID litigants may be concerned that, in such a program, interventions and contaminations might occur that could damage the DID litigants' credibility in court.

12. If the goals of the admission are not kept in mind or if mission creep occurs, the same powerful forces for recovery may be turned toward fomenting a massive regression and decompensation.

13. Patients may immerse themselves in their peers' issues as a defense against addressing their own.

potential drawbacks associated with treatment in dedicated DDUs. In my experience of directing a DDU for six years, concerns one and twelve have been the most consistently problematic, although they have not been very frequent.

It is typical for a newly diagnosed DID patient admitted to a DDU to think that he or she has gone "through the looking glass" into a very strange world indeed. The first two or three days are very alarming, with the patient wanting to deny the disorder and fearing being turned into the sort of "freak" that he or she imagines inhabits the DDU. Most, however, rapidly settle down because they appreciate that they are being understood and because the peers they meet seem to be very much like themselves, hurt people who very much wish they could escape both their hurt and the disorder that is its consequence. A small minority insist on leaving abruptly; another small minority remain but stay entrenched in intense resistance and/or denial so profound that their admission achieves less than one would hope for.

The failure to arrive at reasonable goals or the onset of mission creep has occurred at times despite my team's best efforts. These protracted situations are unsettling and discouraging. They have occurred in under 3 percent of our admissions. Unfortunately, in our unit they have tended to occur and have been most likely to elude all efforts to prevent them under the circumstances noted above. I illustrate this with a vignette from my own practice.

A DID patient was admitted after an episode of self-injury. An alter associated with this incident was identified, and the goals decided on were (1) to deal with the repercussions of this on the alter system, (2) to achieve a safety contract with the alter that had done the self-harm, (3) to teach that alter to manage the pressures that had preceded the self-injury, and (4) to abreact the trauma that had made the alter vulnerable to the pressures to which it had succumbed.

After achieving goals one and two, the patient went on a pass with her husband. She alleges that, on arriving home, he went to a store to make a purchase and a prior abuser came to the door and persuaded a child alter to let him into their home, whereupon he raped her. Unfortunately, she did not report this incident until a week after it was alleged to have occurred, because it was apparently dissociated at once. In the meanwhile, I had pursued abreactive work with the patient, who began to decompensate instead of demonstrating relief (as she had when prior traumas had been abreacted). By the time I was apprised of the recent rape, the admission had consumed over half of her remaining coverage, and she was "wide open" with respect to the material we were working on, the breakthrough of the rape experience, and the experiences of several other alters I had not planned to work with but that had been triggered by the reverberations of the rape within the alter system.

We exhausted her benefits before she was very stable, and her posthospital course was rocky in the extreme. In this case, I can hardly fault myself or the patient for the mission creep, but its pernicious impact occurred nonetheless. Fortunately, this is the exception rather than the rule on a smoothly functioning DDU.

LENGTH OF ADMISSIONS

Given the objective of stabilization-plus, it stands to reason that the length of the hospital stay is usually correlated with the interaction of several factors: how ambitious the goals are that the admission aspires to achieve; the overall ego strength, motivation, and resilience that the patient can bring to bear; the resilience of the alters that bear the burden of carrying on day-to-day life; the impact of comorbidity on Axes I through III; the intensity of the stress in the patient's life; and the presence or absence of external supports. Refer to my earlier work for additional discussion of the subjects in this section.

Brief Admissions (Days to Two Weeks)

Brief admissions address very discrete problems, either on an emergency or preplanned basis. Among these problems are the working through of distressing material containing flashbacks or reenactments and working with one or a small number of alters that are out of control or threatening to harm the patient or others. Intervening may or may not require the use of special procedures, such as restraint sessions and drug-facilitated interviews.

Other goals may be (1) the assessment of a puzzling episode of dysfunctional behavior that cannot be explained on the basis of what is known but that suggests the possibility of dire consequences if unexplored and (2) the provision of an external prosthesis for a temporarily overwhelmed individual with basically good strengths. Often, such individuals are transiently overwhelmed by traumatic material, passive influence experiences, or real or imagined rejection.

Short Admissions (Two to Eight Weeks)

Short admissions are typical when material has overwhelmed or seems about to overwhelm a patient and it appears that it will have to be worked through definitively to guarantee the patient's safety and stability. Other goals that may require this length of stay are resolution of conflicts among alters that threaten the patient's well-being; containment of alters' dangerous impulses toward other persons; lessening of any overwhelming crises in the patient's life; aiding of any alters that cope with daily life that have become disabled; dealing with autohypnotic pseudopsychotic symptoms that have become disruptive; dealing with several alters to restabilize the patient; dealing with switching when it is rapid, chaotic, and disruptive; and treating of alters to the point of integration in order to bring about stability. Further goals may be diagnostic evaluation of a puzzling case; adjustment of a medication regimen; support and safety during an essentially medical or surgical hospitalization; and treatment of a co-existing or intercurrent mental disorder.

Intermediate-Length Admissions (Six Weeks to Three Months)

Intermediate is a controversial length of hospitalization for DID patients. Braun believes that admissions of this length can lead to regressions that themselves will necessitate further hospital treatment. In contrast, I have found this length of stay necessary for those DID patients with sufficient character pathology or ego weakness that it must be dealt with in addition to the DID psychopathology. Such patients either require more time to achieve the goals attained in short admissions by more stable patients or are so fragile that one must approach the attainment of these goals in a far more gradual and gentler manner to avoid precipitating a regression.

Additional indications for admissions of this length are patients with rapid and chaotic switching that does not respond to standard measures; entrenched self-destructiveness; stabilization that cannot be effected without treating many alters; and the nature of the personality system being such that every issue must be dealt with across many alters. Still further moderate-length stays are characteristic of patients who have severe intercurrent eating disorders and those who allege ritualistic abuse. The latter have their own form of severe instability and escalating chaos.

Long Admissions (Three to Six Months)

Patients likely to require long stays or a series of admissions in rapid sequence (particularly if the patient's coverage so necessitates) are those with chronic but severe and active suicidality or homicidality, severe concomitant psychopathology, profound resistance, massive decompensation, the disruption of reality testing by autohypnotic "psychotic" features, or the absence of a single strong host or a group able to collaborate effectively to address daily living. Also, some patients of great complexity can become decompensated across so many alters that a tremendous amount of work must be done to remobilize the patient.

There also are two small groups of DID patients. The first includes those whose switching is so rapid and dysfunctional that the therapist is confronted with virtual "personality salad." Such patients may hardly be able to complete a sentence without switching. The second includes patients who are so badly injured and whose alter systems are so dysfunctional that major reconstruction will be necessary to help the patient and considerable regression must be tolerated to get to the patient at a level at which he or she could be reached.

Extended Admissions (More Than Six Months)

Extended admissions are necessary for the most severely decompensated of patients. In my experience, such patients invariably either have been the victims of therapist-patient sexual exploitation (or its equivalent by other caretaking staff) or have been severely mistreated in prior psychotherapies. Trying to treat patients who are severely decompensated and who have had experiences that cause the very treatment process to be severely contaminated is like swimming upstream against a brisk current. Nonetheless, it is worth the effort and is often successful in the long run.

Success with This Treatment Philosophy

The principles described previously are born of clinical experience. I developed them in the course of learning about DID during the last quarter century. They are largely consistent with what other experienced clinicians of recognized expertise in the field would endorse. As with all of my clinical thinking, they bear the influence of my close collaboration with Bennett G. Braun, M.D., for fifteen years; my directing a DDU for six years with David L.

Fink, M.D., and Catherine G. Fine, Ph.D.; and more recently my collaboration with Ira Brenner, M.D. My discussions with George Ganaway, M.D., have also influenced me. His still-unpublished thoughts on running a DDU milieu are most instructive.

The most substantial documentation of the efficacy of these principles has been the feedback I have received from those who have sought to implement them in their own facilities and practices. It appears that these principles have been more effective in governing the delivery of good care than the ideas that were previously in place. In my own practice, during the last three years, I have managed to achieve stabilization-plus in all but three of the patients I have hospitalized, all of whom had not been my patients as outpatients. As a unit director and consultant who can recommend but not enforce his recommendations, I have been impressed not only by the productivity of this model but also by the chaotic and unproductive admissions of patients with whom this model is not applied and with whom mission creep not infrequently occurs.

This model implicitly, and at times explicitly, subscribes to the tactical integrationalist model of treatment, a term I have used to describe approaches to therapy that use a series of adroit interventions to achieve a series of small therapeutic goals that build on one another toward integration. For a more elaborate description, see Fine. In essence, this model carries out a series of short-term therapies under the rubric of a long-term treatment; one does a piece of work, stabilizes, solidifies gains, prepares for the next piece of work, and so forth. The tactical integrationalist model attempts to stabilize and prevent crises.

THERAPEUTIC PRACTICES AND GUIDELINES

In previous sections, I have stressed approaches that support and create the appropriate therapeutic environment for practice guided by the treatment philosophy elaborated above. Here, I discuss and outline more concrete aspects of the hospital management of the DID patient.

Preempting Chaotic Admissions
(Through Preparing Good First Steps)

Clarification of expectations and an understanding of roles is very important. Without it the DID patient (and perhaps all other parties as well) may have an uncomfortable, frustrating, and discouraging experience. Unrealistic fantasies and expectations are by no means uncommon. They are of three main varieties: (1) powerful wishes, (2) transference-based fantasies, and (3) misunderstandings about what is possible.

1. *Powerful wishes.* Putnam's expression of the DID patient's wishes is excellent. He points out that, from the preadmission perspective of the patient, the hospital may appear a welcome asylum in which

> the wearying internal vigilance required to keep dangerous alters from causing harm can be relaxed and replaced by the hospital staff's eternal watchfulness. Patients may believe that the hospital is a place where they can get "rest" or be "put to sleep" for a while. They may see it as a place of refuge from intrusive family members or other external threats. They may be seeking a place to let out the most dangerous of alters, who dare not emerge in the therapist's office.

The DID patient's encounter with staff demands for self-control and self-containment may be a rude awakening, in deep conflict with the wishes to be nurtured, cared for, accepted as he or she is and to be allowed to "get it all out." The assurances of others that "the hospital will be able to handle you" are rapidly reinterpreted to mean that the hospital is a place of sanctioned retraumatization. Although many DID patients rapidly identify with the mission of the hospital, many hold fast to their sense of grievance and not only fight the hospital staff but also vow never to return to such a place and, on discharge, are reluctant to share materials with their therapist that might suggest the need for inpatient care.

2. *Transference-based fantasies.* This type of negative reaction is related to the transference-based notion that the hospital is a

house of horrors in the first place; this reaction goes beyond the patient's merely projecting past abusive relationships and scenarios on the staff and the situation. It certainly is true that many DID patients have had and continue to have hospital stays in which their diagnoses are missed and that they received inappropriate and sometimes detrimental treatment. It is also the case that many DID patients continue to encounter hospital staff members who treat their disorder as a joke and try to talk them out of it or ridicule them and the person who made the diagnosis. These reality concerns set aside, however, it is not uncommon for DID patients to interpret the hospital setting in terms of their actual or feared mistreatment elsewhere.

The normal routines and constraints essential to running a hospital unit with appropriate safety and containment may be perceived as coercive, uncaring, and sadistic. Compromises to personal privacy inherent in institutional life are perceived as humiliating intrusions, and restriction to a limited area is understood as a cruel punishment, often misunderstood as a reenactment of childhood confinements. Staff members charged with enforcing the regulations and norms of the unit are often misperceived as abusive.

When the DID patient perceives himself or herself as threatened, alters specialized to react to threats may be mobilized. It is not uncommon for such alters to be oppositional and/or disruptive; in recent years, many have followed the litigious tenor of the times and have proven assiduous "jailhouse lawyers." Other frequently encountered responses are overtly aggressive alters; the presentation of child alters that, if not indulged and/or treated, will be "protected" by alters believing they are justified in behaving in an angry manner in the "child's" defense; alters that deny difficulties and feign wellness to press for discharge; and alters that behave provocatively in order to motivate those involved in their care to discharge them. The latter response may involve assaultive or destructive behavior designed to force administrative discharge.

3. *Misunderstandings.* Misunderstandings invariably overlap with fantasies and transferences but are based on failures to

appreciate what is possible and what is not possible in a given setting and within a given time frame. At times the referring therapist may be the source of the misunderstanding. Let me illustrate a common scenario:

MELISSA

Melissa's alters thought they needed to express their feelings without inhibitions and constraints, yet they feared hurting their diminutive and motherly outpatient therapist, Dr. B, and driving her away with their intense negative feelings, from which they protected her. Dr. B concurred that it was unlikely these emotions could be expressed safely in her office. When self-destructive pressures mounted, Dr. B arranged to hospitalize Melissa. Both she and Melissa hoped it would be possible to deal not only with her self-destructiveness but also with the emotions they felt unable to contain on an outpatient basis. Therefore, in the minds of Melissa and Dr. B, the admission had an implicit agenda that Melissa would discharge in the hospital setting what could not be handled with Dr. B in her office.

When Melissa entered the DDU, her behavior toward staff was rude and aggressive. Efforts to contain and redirect her led to Melissa's protesting that this was what she needed to do. She disrupted art and movement therapy groups with behaviors she thought were in her therapeutic interest. When she was verbally assaultive to a nurse and threatened to punch the woman, Melissa was placed in restraints. When I interviewed her as unit director, I elicited from her her beliefs that she had to vent all unacceptable feelings in the DDU and integrate all "bad" alters in order to continue in treatment with Dr. B. I learned that Dr. B, who was actually terrified of Melissa, was supporting this behavior.

Consequently, I took steps to disabuse Dr. B of her misunderstandings and insisted that she and the inpatient psychiatrist meet with Melissa together to determine reasonable goals for the hospital stay. Once all three concurred that a reasonable goal would be to bring the aggressive and angry alters into the treatment with a contract against acting on their anger, Melissa became manageable. Dr. B sought ongoing consultation for her further work with Melissa, and the long-term resolution of matters proved satisfactory.

First Steps

It is crucial to determine the stabilization-plus discharge criteria and to ascertain what must be achieved to bring them about. Often, this is a less complicated matter than the clinician might imagine. If the patient is involved in a systematic psychotherapy of DID that more or less follows one of the currently popular models or series of stages, the general rule of thumb (summarized as Table 9.5) is to achieve safety and stability and move the patient forward by

1. Bringing problematical alters under the governance of a safety contract

2. Processing and/or containing whatever material is proving difficult to manage and is either destabilizing or threatening to destabilize the patient

3. Helping the patient deal with whatever interpersonal uproar or rejection is distressing him or her

4. Enhancing the patient's coping capacities with respect to the class of destabilizing events that has necessitated hospital care

5. Attending to comorbidity concerns

6. Neutralizing trigger phenomena that may have destabilized the patient

7. Anticipating and addressing matters of damage control and fallout prevention

8. Moving the patient back on course toward the appropriate concerns of the phase of therapy that he or she is in (see Table 9.6).

Let me illustrate the above with a case vignette in which the stabilization-plus model is contrasted with the more passive

Table 9.5
Summary of Tasks Needing to Be Achieved
During the Hospital Stay

1. Provide a safety contract (or equivalent assurances).
2. Detoxify emergent material.
3. Manage uproar/rejection.
4. Enhance coping regarding destabilizing factors.
5. Attend to comorbidity concerns.
6. Neutralize triggers.
7. Attempt to minimize damage and fallout from admission and its precipitants.
8. Move the patient toward phase-specific therapy concerns.

Table 9.6
Phases of Treatment for DID

1. Establishment of the therapy
2. Preliminary interventions
3. History gathering and mapping
4. Metabolism of the trauma
5. Move toward integration-resolution
6. Integration/resolution
7. Learning of new coping skills
8. Solidifying of gains and working through
9. Follow-up

approach of merely containing the patient as he or she restabilizes. Leslie had two identical episodes that prompted hospital care. On the first occasion, she was treated by another doctor; on the second, by myself.

LESLIE

Leslie was a thirty-two-year-old woman whose DID had been diagnosed three months previously. Her therapist had moved to explore traumatic material, and she had begun to have more frequent amnestic spells and flashbacks. She had begun to feel compelled to kill herself. One night, she took an overdose of prescription medication. She did not recall consciously willing to do it; she watched herself as she took the pills, unable to stop. It felt so unreal that she thought perhaps it was just a dream. Only when she felt back in control of herself and noticed that indeed her bottles of prescribed medication lay empty and that she was groggy and hardly able to walk did she appreciate the deep trouble was genuinely in and call for an ambulance. When medically cleared, she was transferred to a psychiatric facility.

At that hospital, she gave a history consistent with DID but showed no clear evidence of active dissociation. She had no apparent active suicidal ideation. She was discharged after three days to her outpatient therapist. Three weeks later, an identical incident occurred. For reasons irrelevant here, the patient was transferred to me when medically cleared. Again, she gave a history consistent with DID but showed no clear evidence of active dissociation. She had no active suicidal ideation.

My approach differed from my predecessor's. With evidence suggesting that a relatively autonomous alter was involved in the ingestion, I did not accept the patient's statement that she was without suicidal ideation as a representation of the entire human being. I asked to talk with the alter or alters involved in the ingestion. After some initial reluctance, the alter that had ingested the medication agreed to talk, and I learned from that alter the treatment was beginning to discuss abuse by an uncle. Several alters identified with the uncle and were determined to kill the patient or to intimidate her so that she would make no further revelations. I learned that not only was the patient discussing abuse in treatment, but she also had become engrossed in watching highly provocative talk shows on abuse and abuse-related topics. After watching one such show, the patient had begun to get more vivid and explicit flashbacks. It seemed that everything would pour out momentarily. That night, there had been an ingestion.

I asked the alters promoting suicide about any other ways in which they could have conveyed their misgivings about making revelations to the alters that participated eagerly in treatment, and to the therapist, so that such extreme communications would not be necessary. I made it clear that all alters were welcome in the treatment, even those with suicidal or hostile feelings, but insisted that such communication be in words, rather than in actions. When I learned that there was no co-consciousness, that the uncle-identified alters were aware of the usually prevailing alters and their thoughts and activities but not vice versa, I considered creating co-consciousness hypnotically. I did not know the patient well enough, however, to be sure that such an avenue of communication would not be co-opted into the inner struggles among the alters. Consequently, I persuaded the patient to have written dialogues in a journal. Although the process was not smooth, within a few days I had persuaded the usual alters to attend to the concerns of the uncle-identified alters and vice versa. At this point, I could get a safety contract from all alters.

During this time, I determined there was no significant comorbidity or interpersonal rejections or uproars to address and pursued several courses of action with regard to the traumatic material. First, I determined from the patient and her therapist that therapy was really just beginning and that most of the tasks of the initial phases of therapy had not been accomplished. Consequently, the patient had been asked to do painful abreactive work appropriate for Stage Four (Metabolism of trauma) before accomplishing the tasks of Stages One through Three (Establishing the therapy; Preliminary interventions; History gathering and mapping). The patient had not yet developed the skills to contain the traumatic recollections, images, and flashbacks.

As I requested access to alters and was granted it, it was possible to discuss with the patient's alters which materials could be put out of awareness and which alters associated with traumas were prepared to "go to sleep," reclaiming their materials and participation in life at a later date, when the patient would be prepared to deal with them. This task was accomplished by means of hypnotic temporizing techniques. These involve efforts to contain overwhelming affects, disconcerting issues, and both unsettled and unsettling alters when they are not being worked with in a treatment session or an assigned therapeutic task.

I further instructed the patient how to rid herself of excessive uncomfortable affect by autohypnotic and other methods. I also persuaded the patient's therapist of the need to backtrack and strengthen the patient before approaching the traumatic material yet again. Finally, a certain amount of traumatic material remained intrusive. By isolating the alter involved with the experiences in question from the other alters, I abreacted enough to take pressure off this alter without upsetting the others in the process. I made it a point to discuss the possibility of further episodes of flashbacks and dysphoria being triggered by provocative talk shows and educated her about the tendencies of soap operas to pick up whatever is "hot" on talk shows to spice up their plots. We agreed that she would be best served by modifying her viewing habits.

I helped her understand that material that emerges in therapy is best understood as the beginning of understanding, rather than as unquestionable truth. She confessed that she had become very upset, feeling she had to act on what was emerging, and was relieved to be "granted a reprieve." I helped her reframe her admission as "boot camp for the rest of the therapy," rather than proof of her fragility.

I left unstated that my predecessor had been less than helpful and that her therapist had pushed her too rapidly. The former was a nonfactor, and the latter, whose relationship with the patient was rather solid, was able to appreciate the need to redirect the focus of treatment and seemed prepared to do so. I saw nothing to be gained and much to be lost by taking a critical stance. The therapist did a good deal of relevant reading while the patient was in the hospital.

If the reader refers back to Table 9.5, it will be apparent that the essential bases had been touched. After fifteen days, the patient was discharged back to the referring therapist. On two-year follow-up, the patient is progressing well, and the therapist has become very knowledgeable about the treatment of DID. There have been some rough moments requiring brief increases in the frequency of sessions, but no readmissions.

My treatment of the patient might be perceived as very aggressive by a therapist who prefers to take a permissive stance and await developments, and as extravagant by those whose primary motivation is to limit inpatient costs. However, it might be regarded as compassionate and caring by a therapist eager to save this woman from becoming a "revolving door patient" whose life and career might be destroyed by a disruptive series of admissions. It might be understood to be a bargain by an economy-oriented person able to appreciate the long-term savings accrued thereby.

Clear Communication

Clearly, the first steps are of crucial importance. Ideally, (1) the outpatient therapist and the patient have come to an agreement and have defined the objectives the admission should attain, and (2) these goals can be communicated successfully to the professional in charge of the inpatient treatment.

As indicated throughout this chapter, however, this is not often the case. When the inpatient-treating professional must develop the goals with the patient, it often is important to explore the fantasies, misunderstandings, and unrealistic hopes very promptly; to assess what must be done to achieve the "generic" admission tasks listed in Table 9.5; and to appreciate whether more elaborate goals must be achieved to bring about the stabilization-plus admission. For example, it may be necessary to do abreactive work to reduce the inner chaos in the alter system or lessen the destabilizing pressures on the alter system, or to work extensively with an alter or alters that cannot or will not agree to making the patient safe.

Once such goals become relatively clear, it must be explained to the patient and to the referring therapist; the support of the latter is very important, especially if the therapist had a different understanding. Furthermore, it becomes important to help both therapist and patient appreciate where the work proposed for the hospital stay fits in the context of the overall treatment process.

I find it useful to talk about the phases of therapy, to explain where the patient fits in that scheme, and to indicate how the proposed work will facilitate the next work in the outpatient treatment. For example, on the second hospital day, I said to Leslie words to this effect:

> Leslie, I appreciate that the last few weeks have been very difficult and demoralizing for you. Right now, you have all sorts of painful images flashing into your awareness; it's almost as if some mental dam has broken and you are being flooded. It's coming so fast and furiously that even though you are a very strong woman, you are being overwhelmed. As if that were not enough, parts of your mind about which you have little or no awareness are also being threatened by what has happened, and the ways that they try to cope with it all are endangering your life.
>
> Although you and your therapist would like us to just get all this trauma out and handled and done with, that task will have to be approached very gently and carefully over a period

of months or even years. It's more important to keep you safe and functioning than it is to rush to deal with this material, and again I want to emphasize that trying to deal with it all rapidly is doing therapy just as if it were traumatization, piling more on you than you or anyone could handle.

We are going to try to get to know all the parts of your mind involved in this upset and the suicide attempts, and we are going to try to make them comfortable as partners in the treatment. That means we will be working on strengthening all of you as a total human being and preparing you to handle the traumatic stuff gradually and bit by bit. We are going to try to shut down all of the painful material we can, and what we can't, we will try to process as gently as we can in a step-by-step manner. We also are going to teach you how to break up and contain flashbacks and to contain or even rid yourself of these storms of powerful feelings.

To do this, we will have to help the various parts communicate more effectively, and in words rather than actions. Another way of saying this is that you seem to have jumped into the deep end of the pool before you have become a strong swimmer. We are going to try to bring you back to dry land and help you become strong enough to begin your treatment on a firmer footing. There's all the time in the world to get to the deep water, and there is no rush to do that before you are good and ready.

Foundations for a Good Experience

Although it may be impossible to avoid some turmoil in the hospital care of a DID patient, the cumulative experience of those familiar with their hospital care offers some guidelines that are especially useful to bear in mind in the general psychiatric setting. In DDU environments, the milieu and the specialized nursing and overall care plans act specifically to enforce many of these recommendations.

Braun; Ross; Sackheim, Hess, and Chivas; and I concur that it is useful to discuss the concerns a DID patient is likely to have both before and throughout an actual admission. Communication is essential and may require strenuous efforts to avoid misunderstandings and splitting. Although the DID patient may prove a potent stimulus to splitting and may make active efforts to bring this about, it has been my experience that most of the splitting attributed to DID patients is generated by or is a response to the staff's own "splitness" with regard to the DID diagnosis and the issues raised by DID patients.

If the staff of the unit to which the DID patient is admitted have not been successful with previous DID patients or are not familiar with DID, it is important for the person in charge of the treatment to discuss his or her objectives with the staff and to have reasonable expectations based on a realistic appraisal of what the unit is able to offer. This procedure is not meant to alleviate the responsibility of units that have not addressed the needs of DID patients. It is more an acknowledgment that such units cannot be expected to "get up to speed" in the course of the admission in question and that efforts to do so will lead to unproductive turmoil and mutual recrimination.

It has been my experience that trying to lecture such a staff about DID or to change their attitudes toward DID are universally unproductive. Instead, matter-of-fact problem solving backed with ready access to the professional in charge of the treatment is more likely to be productive. This stance openly acknowledges that (1) the staff are likely adult learners who tend to learn in terms of how to solve work-related problems, rather than to absorb abstractions or acquire information; (2) it is easier to put the emphasis on achieving professional mastery and competence than on trying to change attitudes (many of which may be hostile to DID); and (3) many staff will experience the novelty of treating a DID patient as an unwelcome burden, rather than as an opportunity for professional growth, and will be delighted to learn skills that make their jobs easier. It is likely that most units will include staff members who believe and will continue to believe that DID is not real and that DID patients are being misdiagnosed and perhaps mismanaged. Cooperation is a reasonable goal; conversion is not.

Several general recommendations developed and published before specialized DDUs became available have proven useful in helping units deal with DID patients.

1. *Negotiate a contract.* When possible, it is useful to negotiate a contract with the patient to acknowledge the reasons for the admission, to cooperate with the unit's regulations, and to establish the criteria for discharge. This task should be on a behavioral level whenever practical.

2. *Anticipate impact on staff.* The treating professional should openly anticipate the probable impact of the DID diagnosis and patient on the staff and the milieu. Encourage a cooperative effort even in the face of strong disagreement. I reluctantly admit that an often effective ploy is to assure balky staffs or staff members that if they back the treatment play effectively, they are likely to be rid of the patient much sooner than if the patient feels unaccepted and acts out or regresses. Expect problems to raise their heads repeatedly. The staff and the milieu will have to work through the DID issue gradually. Rapid resolutions are infrequent. The dedicated caregiver is likely to become demoralized if he or she expects an enthusiastic reception for DID or a prompt resolution to staff's misgivings.

3. *Support the staff.* The treating professional should predict the possibility of staff splitting as noted above and encourage staff to contact him or her about crises before instituting significant responses whenever possible. It is useful to check in by telephone with those nursing shifts with which the professional has little or no contact on a regular basis. It is imperative that the staff not feel abandoned and unsupported.

4. *Provide structured groups.* It is useful to anticipate the DID patient's likely response to the various therapeutic modalities and to indicate which ones the DID patient may have difficulty tolerating. In general, DID patients will do best in structured groups and often tolerate nonverbal more easily than purely verbal

groups. Therefore, unstructured general verbal groups may prove disruptive to and become disrupted by DID patients. Conversely, art, movement, music, cognitive-behavioral, psychoeducational, and occupational therapy groups may prove very helpful. Unit meetings often are tolerated poorly, with the DID patient either "trancing out" or quivering in fear in a terrified alter. The price of excusing the DID patient from such a meeting, however, may be a degree of isolation or specialness that is more problematic than the behavior noted above. In general, if the patient cannot contract to attend a group in an alter or group of alters capable of abiding within the norms of the group, it may be preferable to excuse him or her.

The frequently heard injunction that the DID patient must promise not to switch in group is completely unrealistic and therefore unreasonable. My personal approach on a general unit is to ask the DID patient across all alters to restrict switching to those alters that can pass for the patient's usual presentation fairly well and to request them to listen in throughout the group so that, should they emerge, they can continue participation without unduly distressing other patients. Usually, this request will have to be made a few times before the patient can conform his or her behavior within these boundaries, but the results are worth the effort.

5.   *Provide single rooms.* I believe that the DID patient does best in a single room. This arrangement spares another patient a potential burden and offers the DID patient a place of refuge. The unit may be saved many crises. It is unfair to another patient to have a roommate who is often abreacting, awakening from nightmares in a disoriented state, has disruptive and child alters needing to express themselves, and so forth. For example, it is normative for child alters to color, seek nurture, and play with stuffed animals, but the average milieu cannot tolerate such behavior in its common areas. On our DDU, child alters are told to go to their rooms, and protective alters are instructed to provide nurture, which is not a staff function in any more than a general sense.

6. *Clarify rules.* The treating professional should personally explain unit rules to the patient after having requested all alters to listen and should insist on reasonable compliance. Apart from the DDU setting, I try to do this with a member of the nursing staff present to discourage splitting and attempts to argue over "what the nurse said" and "what the doctor said." When an alter that is represented as not knowing and/or not comprehending and/or unable to follow the unit rules is confronted with the fact of a rule's having been broken, it is most effective to take a firm but kindly and nonpunitive stance but to make no exceptions. I do not want my DID patient to suffer the dubious honor of being special; nor do I want to be seen as either corruptible or vulnerable to seduction into the multiple reality disorder and inner world of DID.

7. *Address the patient.* Much time and effort has been wasted fretting over how to respond to the alters' self-perceived differences, especially whether to address them by their separate names. To save much unnecessary strife and conflict, I strongly recommend that the patient be told that he or she must respond to the legal name in all personalities and under all circumstances and in all group and unit settings. Without this convention, an unrealistic burden is imposed on the unit.

In one-to-one interactions, however, I suggest with equal emphasis that the patient be called whatever he or she wants to be called. In this manner, social convention is retained in deference to unit function, but the patient's subjective reality is acknowledged when to do so will not be disruptive. To force the patient to maintain a uniformity of names or the presence of a particular alter usually reinforces the alters' perceived need to demonstrate their reality and invites unproductive disputes.

Psychiatrists with a track record of success in treating DID concur that meeting the DID patient as he or she experiences him- or herself ultimately erodes, rather than reinforces, the separateness. My clinical axiom is "DID is that mental disorder that dissolves in empathy." It has served me well in the integration of more than 150 DID patients. Here, empathy is reinforced by using each alter's name. To summarize: in a group or in a unit situation, a single name should be acceptable to the patient, whereas in one-on-one interactions, the alters' preferred names should be used if the patient so requests.

8. *Remain in alters appropriate to the situation.* It must be made clear to the DID patient and staff that the patient is expected to attend activities in alters that are able to conform their behavior within reasonable limits. See number three.

9. *Explain the patient's responsibility.* It must be explained to the DID patient and the staff that it is not the staff's obligation to either recognize the different alters or to change their behaviors when different alters are encountered. If the patient wants staff to be aware that a particular alter is out, it is the patient's duty to clarify this.

10. *Define staff roles.* It is crucial to define the roles of the various staff members and to make it clear which, if any, will relate to issues surrounding the alters and traumatic materials, in addition to the professional doing the psychotherapy. Clearly, at times any staff member may have to respond to a crisis and do an intervention, so such role distinctions cannot be rigid and absolute. Before the establishment of our DDU, on our general units the nurses and psychiatric technicians would talk with whatever personality was out and were comfortable requesting the return of a more appropriate personality if the patient was unable to manage him- or herself. They would remain in a supportive role, facilitating adaptive coping, to help the patient deal with the impact of what had been recovered in therapy. They were instructed to avoid exploratory work and to direct any effort to introduce new material (except in the context of a crisis) back to the individual therapy. On our DDU, the nurses have been instructed in the use of many techniques to help patients shut down abreactions and flashbacks and to elicit and deal directly with alters in connection with issues of coping and safety. They do not, however, initiate exploration of new material; nor do they continue the exploration of traumas.

11. *Maintain focus.* Because the DID patient often is extremely sensitive, he or she may become preoccupied with minor incidents, disagreements, and misunderstandings. It is necessary to encourage and even insist that the DID patient remain focused on the goals of the admission and to emphasize that the unit will do its imperfect best on behalf of the patient and will encourage the patient to do his or her imperfect best to attend to the purpose of the admission despite any distractions.

12. *Define the role of the outpatient therapist.* It is imperative to define the role and prerogatives of the referring therapist with regard to the hospital treatment. It is also essential to define the degree of contact that will be allowed during the inpatient stay. Some authorities advocate arranging temporary privileges for the outpatient therapist in some instances. Others see it as desirable for the outpatient therapist to play an important role in developing the goals of the admission but to play a minimal role in the treatment.

Such a variety of arrangements are practiced in different settings that I can offer no more definitive advice than that whatever is decided on must be clear and adhered to. I have borne witness to numerous debacles (and even played an unwitting role in several) in which an intrusive outpatient therapist called the patient daily and sat in judgment of the inpatient treatment, even telling the patient not to follow certain advice. I also have seen inpatient therapists keep themselves so remote from the referring therapists that the goals of the admission were never shared and agreed on and led to a less than satisfactory outcome. Also, I have seen inpatient therapists undermine the stature of the outpatient therapist, with devastating impacts on the ongoing therapy.

Unfortunately, one encounters instances in which the outpatient therapist is clearly lacking in skill or for some other reason is not well suited to address the patient's therapeutic needs. In some such situations, it becomes necessary to help the therapist and the patient come to a parting of the ways. I have built a process into our DDU program that attempts to identify such problems rapidly and to address them if they are amenable to correction. Often, we can help a therapist to a better under-standing of how to conduct the treatment and how to manage boundary issues. When this understanding does not appear pos-sible, we try to arrange the best possible outcome for all con-cerned.

ISSUES ARISING IN THE TREATMENT OF DID

A number of concerns typically arise in connection with the treatment of DID patients. The difficulties they pose are inversely proportionate to the unit's experience with DID and other traumatized populations.

Thus, for a psychobiologically oriented unit, the use of hyp-nosis, powerful abreactions, and drug-facilitated interviews and the spending of considerable amounts of time in individual psy-chotherapy sessions may pose a considerable challenge. A unit accustomed to managing trauma victims, however, will already be quite familiar with most of the phenomena that DID patients and their treatment will present. Suffice it to say that it is always useful to explain the procedures that one plans to use and to anticipate the patient's likely response to them.

It is a major error to limit one's efforts and discussions exclu-sively to the primary nurse assigned the patient's care. Nursing is a hierarchical profession, and nurses with administrative responsibility often are uncomfortable when new procedures without established protocols or precedents are introduced, and it is their job to oversee the nursing aspects thereof. It is no secret that often nurses think they must "pick up the pieces" after whatever transpires during therapy sessions. Therefore, it is important to discuss the proposed treatment with the nurses and psychiatrists charged with administering the unit. It is important to have their support.

For example, a psychiatrist began the inpatient treatment of a DID patient. After each session, the patient was severely dis-organized and required nursing care at such a level that the unit's chief nurse thought efforts on behalf of this patient detracted from the care the nurses could give to the unit as a whole. She complained vociferously to the unit's administrative psychiatrist, who insisted the patient be seen by a consultant known to be hostile to DID. Subsequently, it became impossible to continue the work planned for the admission.

Use of Hypnosis

Although hypnosis has a long history in psychiatry and can play a number of useful roles with DID patients, it remains mysterious and strange to many mental health professionals. Because DID patients are highly hypnotizable when cooperative with hypnotic procedures, it is helpful to demystify and explain it and indicate the role it will play in treatment. It is also important to help staff appreciate that the DID patient has autohypnotic and spontaneous trance experiences. I have helped my own DDU staff apply interventions to curtail crises and interdict spontaneous abreactions that do not involve the induction of hypnosis but that draw on the patient's own autohypnotic capacities.

Drug-Facilitated Interviews

On occasion, drug-facilitated interviews are useful. It is important to schedule such interviews when nursing staff will not be unduly inconvenienced if their assistance is advisable. I recommend tape-recording all such sessions because the patient may not register in memory what is retrieved under such circumstances. De Vito has described a treatment in which amobarbital-facilitated interviews were a major aspect of the therapy and included appropriate orders and protocols in that communication. Under some circumstances, it may be preferable to use a benzodiazepine, rather than a barbiturate.

I prefer lorazepam to diazepam because the latter is quite irritating to the vein and may cause a phlebitis. I also have found it useful to consider, instead of intravenous medication, a sublingual dose of proprietary lorazepam given seventy-five to ninety minutes before the interview. The generics do not appear to be designed for sublingual usage; patients uniformly declare that their taste is foul.

Restraint Sessions

At times a patient will claim to be unable to control certain violent alters that must be accessed for the treatment to proceed. The patient may warn that these alters will inevitably attack someone else or attack their own body or do some other unacceptable act. At times it is the therapist's perception that he or she might have difficulty containing the patient during certain work. At such times, a restraint session may be considered. Patients undergoing such procedures should sign informed consents in advance.

In some jurisdictions, laws regulating the use of restraints may virtually preclude holding such sessions. The therapist who plans to attempt restraint sessions should discuss the proposed course of treatment with those administratively in charge of the unit. I have heard many anecdotal accounts of head nurses refusing to allow such procedures or of administrative psychiatrists forbidding them. For a detailed discussion of restraint sessions, see Young.

On my DDU, we try to avoid restraint sessions whenever possible. They cannot be continued on an outpatient basis, so making them a mainstay of treatment virtually guarantees additional admissions. I frequently will use "hypnotic restraints" by suggesting that the body will remain immobile from the neck down, apart from respiration, until the suggestion is removed. Nonetheless, they are often employed when the therapist has reason to believe that the session may become physical.

Explosive Material

It is not uncommon for the DID patient to be concerned with experiences whose veracity is unknown but whose potential explosiveness is beyond question. The DID patient may wish to discuss this material in various groups on the unit and to share it with other patients. This material may be so distressing to other patients, however, that a decision must be made whether or not such open expression can be tolerated.

I hold strong opinions on this matter and share them, acknowledging that they are no more than opinions. I think that if a patient comes to the hospital to work on his or her difficulties, he or she should not suffer the superimposition of additional unnecessary burdens. It is acceptable for trauma victims to share no more than the general nature of their experiences in appropriate therapeutic settings, but not in conversation with peers. The appropriate setting for the detailed discussion of traumas is individual psychotherapy. It is not consistent with compassionate treatment, however, to prohibit the patient from discussing any "overflow" in his or her contact time or with the nurse assigned to him or her.

Aspects of the Management of Abreactions

It is not uncommon for a patient with DID to be overwhelmed by intrusive flashbacks of traumas at the time of admission and to require work with this material to achieve stabilization. Nor is it unusual for work with a problematic alter to require accessing and dealing with traumatic material that may require abreaction. The noise of abreactive work may be disruptive to the unit, and working with patients processing traumatic material may prove unsettling to staff, especially to those who may have suffered their own misfortunes. Furthermore, abreactive work holds the potential to destabilize the patient should it not be circumspect and contained. Abreaction in and of itself is of uncertain value. It is clear that, out of the context of a planful therapy designed to help patients move toward mastery, abreaction may prove to be no more than retraumatization.

Many more issues surround abreaction than can be addressed in this chapter. The interested reader may wish to consult additional sources. The ideas expressed here draw mostly on Kluft. Here, I note only a few considerations.

Abreactive sessions (other than sessions in which fractionated abreactions occupy a small portion of the session time) should not be held one after another, day after day. The most important aspect of abreactions is the processing and working through of what has been abreacted. That is what leads to mastery and release from the grip of the past. Consequently, although patients may require a hospital setting in order to do abreactive work safely, they cannot do vigorous abreactive work on a daily basis. Two or three abreactive sessions per week should be regarded as a maximum. Although in the past many therapists have used very long sessions in order to do abreactive work, such long sessions are difficult to do in many hospital settings, and it is not helpful to plan to do them without the advice and consent of nursing and psychiatric administrators.

Perhaps the best way for the treatment of DID to wear out its welcome is for the inpatient therapist to leave the patient distraught and out of control as he or she leaves the unit and for nursing staff and others to be confronted with a very chaotic situation indeed for the next several hours. Two useful approaches to bear in mind mitigate such problems: the rule of thirds and fractionated abreactions. I developed both of these in order to do abreactive work without decompensating or otherwise endangering DID patients.

The rule of thirds holds that, to do planned abreactive work with DID (or trauma victims in general), one should try to get into the material one is trying to address within the first third of the session so that the remainder of the first third and the entire second third of the session can be used to do the abreactive work; retain the last third to process the material of the abreaction and to restabilize the patient. For inpatients who already have demonstrated their ability to do abreactive work without decompensating, one may occasionally press a little beyond the two-thirds point unless the material is especially difficult.

Fractionated abreactions involve using a series of techniques to do abreactive work in small bits. By their very nature, they teach the patient that traumas can be mastered in a planful series of small steps. Consequently, the patient can be taught to do abre-active work on an ongoing basis and thereby is prepared to continue doing this safely and without decompensation on an outpatient basis. Use of such techniques in the impatient setting can make it possible to do abreactive work without destabilizing either the patient or the milieu. These techniques are rather recently developed and as yet are not widely known or practiced. They are much easier to use in conjunction with hypnosis.

Who's on First?

At times it may be necessary or useful to allow alters that are not usually involved in day-to-day affairs to remain in control of the body for periods of time. When this is done, staff must be informed of the situation and its rationale, lest they be concerned or feel compelled to take steps to bring back the alters with which the staff are more familiar.

For example, in one patient the host became aware of some memories it was previously unaware of and became so overwhelmed that it could not function. The host was put to sleep hypnotically until more work could be done in the next session. Another alter that had not been out in several years and was markedly different from the host in voice and demeanor was asked to take over in the interim. Apprised of the situation, nursing staff, although uncomfortable, were supportive of the intervention.

Safety Concerns

At times a DID patient will be placed on restrictions because of safety concerns related to one or more alters. Then, when these alters are no longer in evidence, other alters will protest the restrictions and insist that they are not at risk. In such situations, it is most practical to get safety contracts across all alters, rather than take at face value the fluctuating surface manifestations of the alter system. Nursing staff must be empowered to insist on assurances of safety and control from the patient. A patient who cannot give a good faith contract on behalf of all alters should not be regarded as safe, despite some alters' protests. It is rarely if ever appropriate to override nursing staff's expressions of concern in these matters. The patient who tries to contract with only the therapist or some other individual but will not contract with others is creating circumstances that cannot be accepted because splitting of the staff is a virtually inevitable consequence of leaving this type of arrangement in place.

Medication Concerns

Staff must be made aware that medication cannot be relied on to contain or control dissociative symptoms. Partial and confusing responses to psychopharmacological interventions are not uncommon, and the patient's response to medication may be different or inconsistent across alters. It is not unusual for the psychiatrist attempting to palliate the DID patient's distress to develop an elaborate polypharmacy regimen that appears disconcerting to the purist but that represents the most effective approach at that moment. Such efforts should not be judged by abstract criteria, but rather by whether they succeed in helping the patient. The interested reader is referred to a helpful review article by Loewenstein.

Concerned Others

It is very difficult to make generalizations about dealing with the concerned others of DID patients. At times the DID patient will not grant permission for them to be interviewed. It is not infrequent for the concerned others to be somewhat pathological and cause the therapist to doubt whether they will be useful supports or more likely to exploit the DID patient with whatever information they are given. Constructive, concerned others may need assistance coming to grips with the DID patient's situation. It is most important that the DID patient's concerned others be assessed rapidly but thoroughly so that treatment planning and discharge planning, which should proceed hand in hand, can be informed and knowledgeable as soon as possible.

Cautions and Limitations of the Stabilization-Plus Approach

The stabilization-plus approach to the hospital treatment of DID is a compassionate and efficient model. It is based on the tactical integrationalist stance. The main cautions and limitations that must be kept in mind relate to the heterogeneity of the DID patient population. Not all can be treated, and not all who can be treated will respond in a uniform manner. Some DID patients simply refuse to cooperate with the interventions that are necessary to support this approach. Some DID patients have additional comorbidity that impairs their capacity to use this model of treatment. For such patients, the hospital stay must focus on containment and address the co-occurring psychopathology; the "plus" of stabilization-plus cannot be addressed. Some patients' benefits are managed in such a way that the logic of this approach will not be accepted.

This model is ideal for use in the context of a managed care plan that is considering the lifetime prognosis of those whose care it supervises. Such a plan will appreciate the logic of an approach that, by its very nature, attempts to strengthen the patient and ultimately remove the patient from that group of DID patients who are major users of costly inpatient services. However, this model may appear less than desirable to those plans administered with the objective of minimizing costs on a year-by-year basis (and trying to demonstrate that their contract with the payer should be renewed); administrators of such plans may find it preferable to defer expenses whenever possible. This type of stance would lead reviewers to insist that patients be discharged the moment there is no active indication for hospital stay on the basis of suicidality or homicidality. Such a plan would be shortsighted and in the best interests of neither the patient nor the managed care company.

I conclude as I began. As therapists we now have at our disposal the means to treat a large percentage of DID patients with increasing efficacy and are capable of creating hospital programs that not only will stabilize most DID patients but also hold the potential to catalyze their outpatient psychotherapy. Whether we seize this opportunity or let it elude our grasp depends in the main on forces and pressures far beyond the purview of the mental health sciences.

NOTES

P. 275, *expert clinicians experienced in the treatment of DID:* Kluft, R. P. (1982). Varieties of hypnotic interventions in the treatment of multiple personality. *American Journal of Clinical Hypnosis, 24,* 230–240; Kluft, R. P. (1984a). Aspects of the treatment of multiple personality disorder. *Psychiatric Annals, 14,* 51–55; Kluft, R. P. (1984b). Multiple personality in childhood. *Psychiatric Clinics of North America, 7,* 121–134; Kluft, R. P. (1985). The natural history of multiple personality disorder. In R. P. Kluft (Ed.), *Childhood antecedents of multiple personality* (pp. 197–238). Washington, DC: American Psychiatric Press; Kluft, R. P. (1986). Personality unification in multiple personality disorder (MPD): A follow-up study. In B. G. Braun (Ed.), *Treatment of multiple personality disorder* (pp. 29–60). Washington, DC: American Psychiatric Press; Kluft, R. P. (1993c). The treatment of dissociative disorder patients: An overview of discoveries, successes, and failures. *Dissociation, 6,* 87–101.

P. 275, *to address DID directly:* Coons, P. M. (1986). Treatment progress in 20 patients with multiple personality disorder. *Journal of Nervous and Mental Disease, 174,* 715–721; Kluft, R. P. (1985). The natural history of multiple personality disorder. In R. P. Kluft (Ed.), *Childhood antecedents of multiple personality* (pp. 197–238). Washington, DC: American Psychiatric Press; Kluft, R. P. (1993c). The treatment of dissociative disorder patients: An overview of discoveries, successes, and failures. *Dissociation, 6,* 87–101.

P. 275, *Techniques developed in such settings:* Kluft, R. P. (1992a). Enhancing the hospital treatment of dissociative disorder patients by developing nursing expertise in the application of hypnotic techniques without formal trance induction. *American Journal of Clinical Hypnosis, 34,* 158–167; Young, W. C. (1986). Restraints in the treatment of a patient with multiple personality. *American Journal of Psychotherapy, 50,* 601–606; Young, W. C., Young, L. J., & Lehl, K. (1991). Restraints in the treatment of dissociative disorders: A follow-up of twenty patients. *Dissociation, 4,* 74–78.

P. 275, *Ross, Norton, and Wozney:* Ross, C. A., Norton, G. R., & Wozney, K. (1989). Multiple personality disorder: An analysis of 236 cases. *Canadian Journal of Psychiatry, 34,* 413–418.

P. 276, *Saxe, van der Kolk, Berkowitz, et al.:* Saxe, G. N., van der Kolk, B. A., Berkowitz, R., Chinman, G., Hall, K., Lieberg, G., & Schwartz, J. (1993). Dissociative disorders in psychiatric inpatients. *American Journal of Psychiatry, 150,* 1037–1042.

P. 276, *Boon and Draijer:* Boon, S., & Draijer, N. (1993). *Multiple personality disorder in the Netherlands: A study on reliability and validity of the diagnosis.* Amsterdam: Swets & Zeitlinger.

P. 276, *to offer them adequate nurture, protection, and consolation:* Kluft, R. P. (1984c). Treatment of multiple personality disorder. *Psychiatric Clinics of North America, 7,* 9–29; Kluft, R. P. (1993a). Basic principles in conducting the psychotherapy of multiple personality disorder. In R. P. Kluft & C. F. Fine (Eds.), *Clinical perspectives on multiple personality disorder* (pp. 19–50). Washington, DC: American Psychiatric Press.

P. 278, *The treatment of choice for DID:* Kluft, R. P. (in press-a). Dissociative identity disorder. In G. O. Gabbard (Ed.), *Treatments of mental disorders: The DSM-IV edition.* Washington, DC: American Psychiatric Press; Putnam, F. W., & Loewenstein, R. J. (1993). Treatment of multiple personality disorder: A survey of current practices. *American Journal of Psychiatry, 150,* 1048–1052; Smith, W. (1996). Chapter Seven, this volume.

P. 279, *encourage regressive dependency:* Ross, C. A., Norton, G. R., & Wozney, K. (1989). Multiple personality disorder: An analysis of 236 cases. *Canadian Journal of Psychiatry, 34,* 413–418.

P. 279, *I hospitalize only 15 percent to 20 percent:* Kluft, R. P. (1991a). The hospital treatment of multiple personality disorder. *Psychiatric Clinics of North America, 14,* 695–719; Kluft, R. P. (1993b). The initial stages of psychotherapy in the treatment of multiple personality disorder patients. *Dissociation, 6,* 145–161; Kluft, R. P. (1993c). The treatment of dissociative disorder patients: An overview of discoveries, successes, and failures. *Dissociation, 6,* 87–101.

P. 280, *DID patients are often quite vulnerable and crisis-prone:* Kluft, R. P. (1984a). Aspects of the treatment of multiple personality disorder. *Psychi-*

atric Annals, *14*, 51–55; Kluft, R. P. (1991a). The hospital treatment of multiple personality disorder. *Psychiatric Clinics of North America*, *14*, 695–719.

P. 280, *cohort of 355 DID patients:* Schultz, R., Braun, B. G., & Kluft, R. P. (1989). Multiple personality disorder: Phenomenology of selected variables in comparison to major depression. *Dissociation*, *2*, 45–51.

P. 281, *The sense of self is damaged:* Putnam, F. W. (1990). Disturbances of "self" in victims of childhood sexual abuse. In R. P. Kluft (Ed.), *Incest-related syndromes of adult psychopathology* (pp. 113–132). Washington, DC: American Psychiatric Press.

P. 281, *The patient's cognition may be disrupted:* Fine, C. G. (1990). The cognitive sequelae of incest. In R. P. Kluft (Ed.), *Incest-related syndromes of adult psychopathology* (pp. 161–182). Washington, DC: American Psychiatric Press; Fish-Murray, E., Koby, E. V., & van der Kolk, B. A. (1987). Evolving ideas: The effect of abuse on children's thought. In B. A. van der Kolk (Ed.), *Psychological trauma* (pp. 89–110). Washington, DC: American Psychiatric Press.

P. 281, *relatedness will be impaired:* Kluft, R. P. (1990a). Dissociation and subsequent vulnerability: A preliminary study. *Dissociation*, *3*, 167–173; Kluft, R. P. (1990c). Incest and subsequent revictimization: The case of therapist-patient sexual exploitation, with a description of the sitting duck syndrome. In R. P. Kluft (Ed.), *Incest-related syndromes of adult psychopathology* (pp. 263–287). Washington, DC: American Psychiatric Press.

P. 281, *Pathological secrecy is not uncommon:* Schultz, R. (1990). Secrets of adolescence: Incest and developmental fixations. In R. P. Kluft (Ed.), *Incest-related syndromes of adult psychopathology* (pp. 133–160). Washington, DC: American Psychiatric Press.

P. 281, *Revictimization is highly likely:* Kluft, R. P. (1990a). Dissociation and subsequent vulnerability: A preliminary study. *Dissociation*, *3*, 167–173.

P. 281, *has had no prior connection:* Braun, B. G. (1993). Aids to the treatment of multiple personality disorder on a general psychiatric inpatient unit. In R. P. Kluft & C. G. Fine (Eds.), *Clinical perspectives on multiple personality disorder* (pp. 155–175); Kluft, R. P. (1993a). Basic principles in conducting the psychotherapy of multiple personality disorder. In R. P. Kluft & C. F. Fine (Eds.), *Clinical perspectives on multiple personality disorder* (pp. 19–50). Washington, DC: American Psychiatric Press.

P. 282, *proneness to revictimization* [in Table 9.1]: Kluft, R. P. (1990c). Incest and subsequent revictimization: The case of therapist-patient sexual exploitation, with a description of the sitting duck syndrome. In R. P. Kluft (Ed.), *Incest-related syndromes of adult psychopathology* (pp. 263–287). Washington, DC: American Psychiatric Press.

P. 287, *their need for reassurance and nurture:* Kluft, R. P. (1990b). Educational domains and andragogical approaches in teaching psychotherapists about multiple personality disorder. *Dissociation, 3,* 188–194.

P. 288, *to be safe on an outpatient basis:* Braun, B. G. (1993). Aids to the treatment of multiple personality disorder on a general psychiatric inpatient unit. In R. P. Kluft & C. G. Fine (Eds.), *Clinical perspectives on multiple personality disorder* (pp. 155–175). Washington, DC: American Psychiatric Press; Kluft, R. P. (1991a). The hospital treatment of multiple personality disorder. *Psychiatric Clinics of North America, 14,* 695–719.

P. 292, *fractionated abreactions:* Fine, C. G. (1991). Treatment stabilization and crisis prevention: Pacing the therapy of the multiple personality disorder patient. *Psychiatric Clinics of North America, 14,* 661–675; Kluft, R. P. (1988). On treating the older patient with multiple personality disorder: "Race against time or make haste slowly?" *American Journal of Clinical Hypnosis, 30,* 257–266; Kluft, R. P. (in press-b). The management of abreactions. In B. Cohen & J. Turkus (Eds.), *Multiple personality disorder: Continuum of care.* New York: Jason Aronson.

P. 293, *traumatic transferences:* Loewenstein, R. J. (1993). Posttraumatic and dissociative aspects of transference and countertransference in the treatment of multiple personality disorder. In R. P. Kluft & C. G. Fine (Eds.), *Clinical perspectives on multiple personality disorder* (pp. 511–585). Washington, DC: American Psychiatric Press.

P. 293, *can be a fine art:* Kluft, R. P. (1991a). The hospital treatment of multiple personality disorder. *Psychiatric Clinics of North America, 14,* 695–719; Kluft, R. P. (1994). Countertransference in the treatment of multiple personality disorder. In J. P. Wilson & J. D. Lindy (Eds.), *Countertransference in the treatment of PTSD* (pp. 122–150). New York: Guilford Press; Loewenstein, R. J. (1993). Posttraumatic and dissociative aspects of transference and countertransference in the treatment of multiple personality disorder. In R. P. Kluft & C. G. Fine (Eds.), *Clinical perspectives on multiple personality disorder* (pp. 511–585). Washington, DC: American Psychiatric Press.

P. 298, *Refer to my earlier work:* Kluft, R. P. (1991a). The hospital treatment of multiple personality disorder. *Psychiatric Clinics of North America, 14,* 695–719.

P. 300, *Braun:* Braun, B. G. (1986). Issues in the psychotherapy of multiple personality disorder. In B. G. Braun (Ed.), *Treatment of multiple personality disorder* (pp. 1–28). Washington, DC: American Psychiatric Press; Braun, B. G. (1993). Aids to the treatment of multiple personality disorder on a general psychiatric inpatient unit. In R. P. Kluft & C. G. Fine (Eds.), *Clinical perspectives on multiple personality disorder* (pp. 155–175). Washington, DC: American Psychiatric Press.

P. 302, *tactical integrationalist model of treatment:* Kluft, R. P. (1988). On treating the older patient with multiple personality disorder: "Race against time or make haste slowly?" *American Journal of Clinical Hypnosis, 30,* 257–266; Kluft, R. P. (1993c). The treatment of dissociative disorder patients: An overview of discoveries, successes, and failures. *Dissociation, 6,* 87–101.

P. 302, *see Fine:* Fine, C. G. (1991). Treatment stabilization and crisis prevention: Pacing the therapy of the multiple personality disorder patient. *Psychiatric Clinics of North America, 14,* 661–675.

P. 303, *Putnam's expression:* Putnam, F. W. (1989). *Diagnosis and treatment of multiple personality disorder.* New York: Guilford Press.

P. 306, *popular models or series of stages:* Braun, B. G. (1986). Issues in the psychotherapy of multiple personality disorder. In B. G. Braun (Ed.), *Treatment of multiple personality disorder* (pp. 1–28). Washington, DC: American Psychiatric Press; Kluft, R. P. (1991a). The hospital treatment of multiple personality disorder. *Psychiatric Clinics of North America, 14,* 695–719; Kluft, R. P. (1991b). Multiple personality disorder. In A. Tasman & S. M. Goldfinger (Eds.), *American Psychiatric Press annual review of psychiatry* (Vol. 10, pp. 161–188). Washington, DC: American Psychiatric Press; Putnam, F. W. (1989). *Diagnosis and treatment of multiple personality disorder.* New York: Guilford Press; Ross, C. A. (1989). *Multiple personality disorder: Clinical phenomenology, diagnosis, and treatment.* New York: Wiley.

P. 307, *Table 9.6:* Kluft, R. P. (1991). The hospital treatment of multiple personality disorder. *Psychiatric Clinics of North America, 14,* 695–719.

P. 309, *tasks of the initial phases of therapy:* Kluft, R. P. (1991b). Multiple personality disorder. In A. Tasman & S. M. Goldfinger (Eds.), *American Psychiatric Press annual review of psychiatry* (Vol. 10, pp. 161–188). Washington, DC: American Psychiatric Press; Kluft, R. P. (1993b). The initial stages of psychotherapy in the treatment of multiple personality disorder patients. *Dissociation, 6,* 145–161.

p. 310, *hypnotic temporizing techniques:* Kluft, R. P. (1989). Playing for time: Temporizing techniques in the treatment of multiple personality disorder. *American Journal of Clinical Hypnosis, 32,* 90–98.

P. 314, *Braun:* Braun, B. G. (1993). Aids to the treatment of multiple personality disorder on a general psychiatric inpatient unit. In R. P. Kluft & C. G. Fine (Eds.), *Clinical perspectives on multiple personality disorder* (pp. 155–175). Washington, DC: American Psychiatric Press.

P. 314, *Ross:* Ross, C. A., Norton, G. R., & Wozney, K. (1989). Multiple personality disorder: An analysis of 236 cases. *Canadian Journal of Psychiatry,* *34,* 413–418.

P. 314, *Sackheim, Hess, and Chivas:* Sackheim, D. K., Hess, E. P., & Chivas, A. (1986). General principles for short-term inpatient work with multiple personality disorder. *Psychotherapy, 25,* 117–124.

P. 314, *and I concur:* Kluft, R. P. (1991a). The hospital treatment of multiple personality disorder. *Psychiatric Clinics of North America, 14,* 695–719.

P. 314, *issues raised by DID patients:* Kluft, R. P. (1984a). Aspects of the treatment of multiple personality disorder. *Psychiatric Annals, 14,* 51–55.

P. 315, *DDUs became available:* Kluft, R. P. (1984a). Aspects of the treatment of multiple personality disorder. *Psychiatric Annals, 14,* 51–55; Kluft, R. P. (1991a). The hospital treatment of multiple personality disorder. *Psychiatric Clinics of North America, 14,* 695–719.

P. 317, *inner world of DID:* Kluft, R. P. (1984a). Aspects of the treatment of multiple personality disorder. *Psychiatric Annals, 14,* 51–55; Kluft, R. P. (1991a). The hospital treatment of multiple personality disorder. *Psychiatric Clinics of North America, 14,* 695–719; Kluft, R. P. (1993a). Basic principles in conducting the psychotherapy of multiple personality disorder. In R. P. Kluft & C. F. Fine (Eds.), *Clinical perspectives on multiple personality disorder* (pp. 19–50). Washington, DC: American Psychiatric Press.

P. 318, *issues of coping and safety:* Kluft, R. P. (1992a). Enhancing the hospital treatment of dissociative disorder patients by developing nursing expertise in the application of hypnotic techniques without formal trance induction. *American Journal of Clinical Hypnosis, 34,* 158–167.

P. 319, *some authorities:* Braun, B. G. (1993). Aids to the treatment of multiple personality disorder on a general psychiatric inpatient unit. In R. P. Kluft & C. G. Fine (Eds.), *Clinical perspectives on multiple personality disorder* (pp. 155–175). Washington, DC: American Psychiatric Press.

P. 321, *play a number of useful roles with DID patients:* Kluft, R. P. (1992b). Hypnosis with multiple personality disorder. *American Journal of Preventive Psychiatry and Neurology, 3,* 19–27; Kluft, R. P. (1992c). The use of hypnosis with dissociative disorders. *Psychiatric Medicine, 10,* 31–46.

P. 321, *the patient's own autohypnotic capacities:* Kluft, R. P. (1992a). Enhancing the hospital treatment of dissociative disorder patients by developing nursing expertise in the application of hypnotic techniques without formal trance induction. *American Journal of Clinical Hypnosis, 34,* 158–167.

P. 321, *de Vito:* de Vito, R. A. (1993). The use of Amytal interviews in the treatment of an exceptionally complex case of multiple personality disorder. In R. P. Kluft & C. G. Fine (Eds.), *Clinical perspectives on multiple personality disorder* (pp. 227–240). Washington, DC: American Psychiatric Press.

P. 322, *discussion of restraint sessions, see Young:* Young, W. C. (1986). Restraints in the treatment of a patient with multiple personality. *American Journal of Psychotherapy, 50,* 601–606; Young, W. C., Young, L. J., & Lehl, K. (1991). Restraints in the treatment of dissociative disorders: A follow-up of twenty patients. *Dissociation, 4,* 74–78.

P. 323, *consult additional sources:* Fine, C. G. (1991). Treatment stabilization and crisis prevention: Pacing the therapy of the multiple personality disorder patient. *Psychiatric Clinics of North America, 14,* 661–675; Hammond, D. C. (Ed.). (1992). *Handbook of hypnotic suggestions and metaphors.* New York: W. W. Norton; Kluft, R. P. (1989). Playing for time: Temporizing techniques in the treatment of multiple personality disorder. *American Journal of Clinical Hypnosis, 32,* 90–98; Kluft, R. P. (in press-b). The management of abreactions. In B. Cohen & J. Turkus (Eds.), *Multiple personality disorder: Continuum of care.* New York: Jason Aronson; Steele, K., & Colrain, J. (1990). Abreactive work with sexual abuse survivors: Concepts and techniques. In M. Hunter (Ed.), *The sexually abused male: Vol. 2. Application of treatment strategies* (pp. 1–55). Lexington, MA: Lexington Books; Watkins, J. (1992). *Hypnoanalytic techniques: Vol. 2. The practice of clinical hypnosis.* New York: Irvington.

P. 323, *The ideas expressed here draw mostly on Kluft:* Fine, C. G. (1991). Treatment stabilization and crisis prevention: Pacing the therapy of the multiple personality disorder patient. *Psychiatric Clinics of North America, 14,* 661–675; Kluft, R. P. (1989). Playing for time: Temporizing techniques in the treatment of multiple personality disorder. *American Journal of Clinical Hypnosis, 32,* 90–98; Kluft, R. P. (in press-b). The management of abreactions. In B. Cohen & J. Turkus (Eds.), *Multiple personality disorder: Continuum of care.* New York: Jason Aronson.

P. 324, *endangering DID patients:* Kluft, R. P. (1989). Playing for time: Temporizing techniques in the treatment of multiple personality disorder. *American Journal of Clinical Hypnosis, 32,* 90–98; Kluft, R. P. (1991b). Multiple personality disorder. In A. Tasman & S. M. Goldfinger (Eds.), *American Psychiatric Press annual review of psychiatry* (Vol. 10, pp. 161–188). Washington, DC: American Psychiatric Press; Kluft, R. P. (1993a). Basic principles in conducting the psychotherapy of multiple personality disorder. In R. P. Kluft & C. G. Fine (Eds.), *Clinical perspectives on multiple personality disorder* (pp. 19–50). Washington, DC: American Psychiatric Press.

P. 324, *to do abreactive work in small bits:* Fine, C. G. (1991). Treatment stabilization and crisis prevention: Pacing the therapy of the multiple personality disorder patient. *Psychiatric Clinics of North America, 14,* 661–675; Kluft, R. P. (1989). Playing for time: Temporizing techniques in the treatment of multiple personality disorder. *American Journal of Clinical Hypnosis, 32,* 90–98; Kluft, R. P. (in press-b). The management of abreactions. In B. Cohen & J. Turkus (Eds.), *Multiple personality disorder: Continuum of care.* New York: Jason Aronson.

10

SHORT-TERM,
PROBLEM-ORIENTED
INPATIENT TREATMENT

Colin A. Ross

I have been treating Dissociative Identity Disorder/Multiple Personality Disorder (DID) on an inpatient basis since 1985 and have been Director of a Dissociative Disorders Unit (DDU) at Charter Behavioral Health System of Dallas since 1991. Charter is a freestanding, private, for-profit institution and part of a chain of hospitals owned by Charter Medical Corporation.

During the past two years, our inpatient census has averaged fifteen to twenty patients, with an average length of stay in the range of eighteen to twenty-one days. We also average about five patients in partial hospitalization, who participate in the same program as the inpatients.

I function as attending physician on an average of three to five patients, conduct a cognitive therapy group three times a week, consult to other physicians admitting to the unit, and review cases at staff meetings on a weekly basis, as well as deliver a limited amount of individual psychotherapy. About one-third of our patients are from out of state, so we have a caseload biased toward difficult and refractory cases and deal with a full range of types of insurance.

When I moved from Canada to Texas in 1991, I had only worked in the Canadian health care system and only as a full-time salaried academic. I learned quickly that, to survive in the volatile and unstable psychiatric health care marketplace, one must adapt continuously to rapidly changing conditions. For instance, insurance reimbursement for psychological testing of inpatients has almost vanished in the past two years. I have therefore developed an acute care, problem-oriented treatment approach that is operationalized and couched in language palatable to managed care and that results in substantial clinical improvement in most cases. The approach is a refinement of the methods described in texts by myself and Frank Putnam.

One of the physicians admitting to our unit was the former director of a long-term inpatient psychotherapy unit in another state, on which the first patient case conference was held six weeks after admission. Another did his residency in a hospital that had an average inpatient length of stay of one year. Timberlawn, the most famous freestanding psychiatric hospital in Dallas, had an average length of stay of eighty-two days just five years ago, which has been reduced to fourteen days. Many insurers now consider inpatient care to be regressive if the patient has been in the hospital for thirty days. In this regulatory and insurance environment, behavioral management and containment must be effective quickly.

OVERALL PHILOSOPHY OF
OUR TREATMENT APPROACH

In devising the DDU Master Treatment Plan (see Table 10.1), a number of considerations went through my mind. My goal was not to treat DID as such because a psychiatric diagnosis is not in and of itself an indication for inpatient admission. I devised a set of clinical problems warranting inpatient treatment that were generic and similar to those in general adult psychiatry. I wanted the treatment to be operationalized because this would provide good clinical care, be palatable to managed care reviewers, and lay a foundation for scientific treatment outcome studies. I use the first person plural much of the time in this chapter because I refer to the DDU treatment team as a whole.

On our DDU, we treat problems, not alter personalities, memories, or DID. The most common presenting problems by far are suicidal and homicidal ideation, often accompanied by cutting, burning, suicide attempts, threatened assault, and possession of handguns.

The unit follows the usual ethical and procedural rules of inpatient psychiatry, and we make an effort not to treat the patients as special in any way. We have a system of levels of care, pass privileges, behavioral expectations, and consequences that are similar to those one would find on any general adult inpatient unit. Patients are held responsible for the behavior of all alter personalities, and the usual and natural consequences of destructive or regressive behavior are in place.

The goal of treatment is to return the person to a functional outpatient status as quickly as possible while teaching the person coping and recovery skills that can be applied on an outpatient basis in ongoing living and therapy. The emphasis of the treatment is not on memory recovery or abreaction, and we have instituted many measures to contain, limit, and discourage spontaneous countertherapeutic abreactions. Most of the treatment is conducted in an adult problem-solving psychoeducational mode. This does not mean that there is not a great deal of intense emotion expressed and processed on the unit or that there is no acting out. The tone of the therapeutic milieu, however, involves clear expectations for hard work, healthy behavior, and focused recovery.

We regularly discuss in both individual and group therapy the problem of historical accuracy of childhood trauma memories. The position of the doctors and therapists working on the unit is that patients are responsible for their own feelings, thoughts, memories, and behaviors. Professionals can neither prove nor disprove the reality of the memories, and that is not their job. The content of the memories is regarded as a minor element in the treatment, which takes place at a structural and process level.

(Text continues on page 346)

Table 10.1
Charter Behavioral Health System of Dallas Dissociative Disorders Unit Master Treatment Plan

1. Diagnosis
   i. Dissociative amnesia _____
   ii. Dissociative fugue _____
   iii. Depersonalization disorder _____
   iv. Dissociative identity disorder _____
   v. Dissociative disorder—not otherwise specified _____
   vi. Major depressive disorder _____
   vii. Borderline personality disorder _____
   viii. Substance abuse _____

2. Problems
   i. Suicidal ideation or attempt _____
   ii. Homicidal ideation or attempt _____
   iii. Severe anxiety _____
   iv. Severe depression _____
   v. Severe posttraumatic symptoms _____
   vi. Nonsuicidal self-harm _____
   vii. Chaotic, disorganized, or regressed behavior _____
   viii. Inability to function at work or home _____
   ix. Dangerous behavior, victim of ongoing abuse _____
   x. Abusive behavior toward others _____
   xi. Other specific problems _____

3. Interventions
   I. Suicidal Ideation or Attempt
   i. Ensure safety _____
   ii. Map personality system _____
   iii. Identify involved persecutor personality
       and its motivation _____
   iv. Reframe persecutor's behavior in system as positive _____
   v. Contract with persecutor for no self-harm for a
       specified period of time _____
   vi. Devise alternative behaviors to meet
       the persecutor's objectives _____
   vii. Determine whether persecutor is carrying out
       behavior by itself or is controlled or motivated
       by another personality _____

Table 10.1 *(continued)*

viii. Contract with persecutor to be called out in
future sessions   _____

ix. Reframe persecutor alter(s) as positive for
frightened child alters and host   _____

x. Empathize with persecutor's own pain,
fear, and dysphoria   _____

xi. Encourage dialogue between persecutor and host _____

II. Homicidal Ideation or Attempt

i. Ensure safety   _____

ii. Map personality system   _____

iii. Identify homicidal personality and its motivation _____

iv. Reframe alter's behavior as positive in intention
(for example, to protect other alters and
the body) if possible   _____

v. Contract with homicidal personality for no violence
for a specified period of time   _____

vi. Devise alternative behaviors to meet the
homicidal personality's objectives   _____

vii. Determine whether homicidal personality is carrying
out behavior by itself or is motivated or controlled
by another personality   _____

viii. Contract with homicidal personality to be
called out in future sessions   _____

ix. Reframe homicidal alter's behavior as positive for
other relevant alters and host   _____

x. Empathize with the homicidal alter's own pain,
fear, and dysphoria   _____

xi. Encourage dialogue between homicidal alter and host _____

III. Severe Anxiety
(Strategies may apply to both generalized anxiety and panic attacks)

i. Anxiolytic medication   _____

ii. Relaxation audiotape   _____

iii. Relaxation/meditation/grounding techniques   _____

iv. Modify caffeine intake and other physiological
contributors   _____

Table 10.1 *(continued)*

    v. Modify identifiable environmental stressors on
unit contributing to anxiety or work on desensitizing
patient to them

    vi. Map personality system   _____

    vii. Identify alter(s) in system who are most anxious
and from whom the anxiety is originating   _____

    viii. Identify specific memories/fears/personality system
conflicts contributing to anxiety   _____

    ix. Identify protector/soothing alters who can reduce
anxiety from inside and contract with them, taking
vii and viii into account   _____

    x. Put extremely anxious alters to sleep inside
temporarily   _____

    xi. If anxiety is caused by potentially violent alters
threatening to come out, review strategies for
suicidal and homicidal ideation   _____

    xii. If anxiety is caused by an emerging memory,
refer to strategies for posttraumatic symptoms   _____

IV. Severe Depression

    i. Review and/or readminister Beck Depression
Inventory   _____

    ii. Assess suicidal ideation and ensure safety   _____

    iii. Map personality system   _____

    iv. Identify whether depression is affecting most of
the personality system or only a few alters   _____

    v. Antidepressant medication   _____

    vi. Modify environmental stressors contributing
to depression   _____

    vii. Set limits on lethargic, withdrawn behavior;
reinforce nondepressed behavior   _____

IF ONLY THE HOST PERSONALITY IS DEPRESSED:

    viii. Establish communication, co-consciousness
between host and nondepressed alters   _____

    ix. Help nondepressed alters and host share executive
control in a way that improves overall function   _____

    x. Determine whether any alters are deliberately
making the host depressed; if so, refer to strategies
for suicidal ideation   _____

Table 10.1 *(continued)*

___

xi. Modify cognitive errors contributing to depression;
always remember that wherever you find depression,
anger is not far away   _____

V. Severe Posttraumatic Symptoms
    i. Ensure safety during any abreactions   _____
    ii. Map personality system   _____
    iii. Medication   _____
    iv. Relaxation audiotape   _____
    v. Relaxation/meditation/grounding techniques   _____
    vi. Modify identifiable environmental triggers on unit
        contributing to PTSD symptoms if feasible   _____
    vii. Identify specific alters from whom memories
        are emerging   _____
    viii. Determine the general nature of the memories
        involved in the current symptom   _____
    ix. Identify protector/soothing alters inside who can
        reduce the flashbacks, rate of memory recovery,
        and level of arousal from the inside   _____
    x. Stage recovery of memories through dreams,
        journals, art therapy, internal visualization without
        full abreaction   _____
    xi. Contract with any persecutors amplifying the
        PTSD symptoms to reduce the rate of flashbacks   _____

These interventions are focused on the hyperarousal component of
PTSD; the psychic numbing component is much less likely to be a
focus of inpatient treatment.

VI. Nonsuicidal Self-Harm

The difference between suicide attempts and deliberate self-harm
is often unclear, and both can occur together in the same behavior.
Deliberate self-harm involves burning, scratching, head banging,
picking, minor cutting, and other behaviors clearly not intended to
cause death. The persecutor's motivation is usually to punish the
host, let out the bad feelings, relieve tension or depersonalization,
appease angry alters temporarily, experience a euphoric rush, show
outside people that the pain is real, or simply to see blood. The
interventions are the same as for suicidal ideation in principle, but
the content is not focused on a desire to die.

___

Table 10.1 *(continued)*

i. Ensure safety _____

ii. Map personality system _____

iii. Identify involved persecutor personality and its motivation _____

iv. Reframe persecutor's behavior in system as positive _____

v. Contract with persecutor for no self-harm for a specified period of time _____

vi. Devise alternative behaviors to meet the persecutor's objectives _____

vii. Determine whether persecutor is carrying out behavior by itself or is motivated or controlled by another personality _____

viii. Contract with persecutor to be called out in future sessions _____

ix. Reframe persecutor alter(s) as positive for frightened child alters and host _____

x. Empathize with persecutor's own pain, fear, and dysphoria _____

xi. Encourage dialogue between persecutor and host _____

VII. Chaotic, Disorganized, or Regressed Behavior

i. Ensure safety _____

ii. Map system _____

iii. Identify involved personality and the reason for its behavior (fear, abreaction, infantile alter, hallucinating alter) _____

iv. Call out a behaviorally controlled alter _____

v. Talk through to other alters; ask for a switch or soothing from inside _____

vi. If iii–v are unsuccessful after a few minutes, escort to patient's room or quiet room _____

vii. Do not allow patient out of room until behavior is controlled; iii–v may be repeated in patient's room or quiet room _____

viii. Medication _____

IF BEHAVIOR IS CAUSED BY UNCONTROLLED RAPID SWITCHING:

ix. Medication _____

x. Talk to system as a whole and explain the need for reduced switching _____

Table 10.1 *(continued)*

---

    xi. If ix–x ineffective, escort to patient's room or
quiet room   _____

    xii. Do not allow patient out of room until
behavior is controlled   _____

VIII. Inability to Function at Work or Home
    i. Map system   _____
    ii. Identify alters who have carried out these functions
in the past or could perform them in the future   _____
    iii. Contract with these alters to work toward being in
control at necessary times   _____
    iv. Identify other problems from problem list that are
contributing to this problem and choose relevant
interventions   _____

IX. Dangerous Behavior, Victim of Ongoing Abuse
    i. Map system   _____
    ii. Identify alters involved in behavior and
their motivation   _____
    iii. Reframe alter's behavior in system as positive   _____
    i v. Identify how behavior is a reenactment of
childhood trauma   _____
    v. Devise alternative behavior to meet the alter
personality's objectives   _____
    vi. Modify social factors contributing to entrapment in
abuse or make appropriate referrals   _____
    vii. Interview others involved in abusive behavior
if feasible   _____

X. Abusive Behavior Toward Others
    i. Ensure safety   _____
    ii. Inform child protection, police, or other agencies
as required   _____
    iii. Medication   _____
    iv. Map system   _____
    v. Identify alters involved in behavior and
their motivation   _____
    vi. Reframe abusive alters' behavior as a reenactment
of childhood trauma if feasible   _____

Table 10.1 *(continued)*

---

vii. Reframe abusive alters' behavior as positive in
   intention if feasible (for example, protecting
   child alters)   _____
viii. Contract for no assaultive behavior   _____
  ix. Devise alternative strategies to meet alters' objectives _____
   x. Set behavioral limits and consequences   _____
  xi. Encourage dialogue between assaultive alters and host _____
 xii. Instruct all alters that responsibility and
   consequences for behavior belong to the
   person as a whole   _____

XI. Other Specific Problems
   i. Identify problem   _____
  ii. Map system   _____
 iii. Specify necessary interventions   _____

Source: Dallas Dissociative Disorders Unit. Reprinted with permission.

A majority of patients admitted to the unit have childhood memories of cult ritual abuse; an increasing minority have memories of military mind control experimentation. Most of the time, it is clinically impossible to differentiate historically real from confabulated memories.

We do not change our staffing, procedures, or coverage on cult holidays and have not observed an increase in acting out on these dates. We do not take down artwork or make other changes in the physical environment when patients say they contain cult triggers, and we do not keep people in the hospital any longer than we otherwise would because of claims about ongoing cult accessing or involvement. Our explanations for these policies involve straightforward statements about the world being full of potential triggers and it not being the function of health care insurance companies to protect citizens from criminal assault or violations of their rights. The focus of treatment is on internal ambivalence about the trauma and attachment to the perpetrator, not on modifying the environment.

The treatment model is a trauma-dissociation model, so a general assumption is made that most, if not all, individuals admitted to the unit experienced severe traumas of some type during childhood. In perhaps 10 percent of cases, there is a strong suspicion or actual consensus in the treatment team that the DID is a false-positive diagnosis and that the person actually has a mixture of Axis II pathology, Axis I nondissociative pathology, and dissociative disorder not otherwise specified. The treatment plan for these patients is not fundamentally different from that for full DID cases, however, because resolution of conflict between dissociated elements of the psyche is still required. The problem of the differential diagnosis of DID is usually discussed in a psychoeducational manner with such patients.

We rarely refuse consent to have patients read their charts on request, and we maintain an open treatment system. This means we prefer the referring therapist to provide the inpatient therapy whenever possible, and we try to involve outside resources and support persons in the treatment and discharge planning.

The atmosphere of the unit is that of a teaching hospital. Several psychiatry residents have done rotations on the unit, a number of people have completed two thousand hours of master's level licensure clinical contact, and we regularly have mental health professionals of all kinds visiting the unit and sitting in on groups. Patients do not have the option of refusing to allow visitors to sit in on groups, although they have this option for individual therapy sessions.

Our goal is to have the atmosphere of the unit be calm, adult, and healing. It's countertherapeutic to have spontaneous abreactions occurring in the hallway, the day room, in front of the nursing station, or in other public areas of the hospital. During the last three years, we have reduced the amount of acting out, physical restraint, intramuscular medications, spontaneous abreaction, self-mutilation, head banging, and other self-abusive behavior to a small fraction of the baseline in late 1991. By early 1994, the number of nursing incident reports per patient on the DDU did not differ statistically from the rate in the rest of the hospital. This reduction was achieved by slow and difficult learning, including reversing the assumption that such behavior was an inevitable concomitant of productive trauma therapy. It is not.

BEHAVIORAL MANAGEMENT TECHNIQUES

Our program at Charter has a number of components designed to reduce self-destructive behavior and to focus the patients on recovery. These include containing abreaction, transferring out, levels of care, staff expectations, medications, anger management, structure, and dedicated staff. Seventy per cent of the people admitted to the unit meet criteria for borderline personality disorder, so borderline behavioral management is an everyday part of the work. I consider it a remarkable achievement to have a dozen or more severely self-destructive borderline patients housed on the same unit with no more acting out than elsewhere in the hospital.

Containing Abreaction

In an effort to contain the amplification of ritual abuse memories by mutual contagion and the triggering of other patients with graphic ritual abuse stories, we established an optional ritual abuse group in which descriptions of details of the trauma were allowed. Patients not wishing to attend this group had the option of attending an alternative concurrent group. Eventually, we canceled the ritual abuse group altogether because graphic discussion of such memories triggered too much acting out and did not appear to be therapeutic for the individuals or the milieu. Canceling the ritual abuse group and stipulating that details of childhood trauma cannot be described in most or all of the other groups has markedly stabilized the unit.

Likewise, we shifted the emphasis in our child alter group from play therapy with child alters to the personality system as a whole acquiring socialization skills, and we renamed the group socialization group. This apparently minor change in name and emphasis appeared to further stabilize the unit. We shifted the content and expectations of the groups away from abreaction and memories and toward acquisition of skills, problem solving, and psychoeducation. Patients are often referred to the unit, having received a year or more of therapy for DID but not yet having acquired basic interpersonality communication or problem resolution skills despite much "memory work" having been done.

Transferring Out

A major intervention with immediate and dramatic impact on the amount of acting out on the unit was to institute a policy of transferring acting-out patients to the general adult unit for behavioral containment and stabilization. Although this policy was initially perceived as a form of punishment, discussion during community meetings and group therapy has resulted in general agreement among patients that this policy helps preserve a safe, working atmosphere on the unit. A number of patients have returned to the unit after such temporary transfers, expressing positive feelings about the helpfulness of the intervention.

The ultimate banishment is the threat of transfer to a state hospital. It is well understood in the milieu that the DDU is a tertiary-care intensive psychotherapy unit and that chronically self-destructive patients who require long-term inpatient care are likely to be transferred to a state facility. Such transfers, which occasionally occur, require group processing before and after the event. We try to frame transfer to the state hospital in a positive light, but this is difficult. In the regulatory environment of the next five years, such transfers may become more common because regulators will lower the level of suicidal ideation they consider to be tolerable for safe discharge and because insurers will increase the level required for reimbursement. How providers will survive financially and legally when the gate to the state facility is closed remains to be seen.

Levels of Care

The management of levels of care on the DDU is complicated, as is the behavioral analysis required. For instance, self-mutilation need not always be responded to with a drop in privilege levels. If the balance of forces inside the patient is tipped toward regression and hospital dependency, then reducing levels in response to self-mutilation actually rewards and reinforces the behavior. In such cases, a steady increase in levels toward a fixed discharge date is most therapeutic.

Another patient, however, will perceive a reduction in privilege levels as a powerful, noxious stimulus and will work diligently on system communication and cooperation to avoid such consequences. The general principle is that the behavioral reinforcers must be constructed in a case-by-case fashion to optimize function and to speed recovery. Simpleminded or cookbook behavioral interventions do not work on a DDU. We usually discuss our behavioral management strategies with patients in a direct manner.

For instance, in a cognitive therapy group, I explained to the patients how the relationship between self-mutilation and inpatient status works for patients with managed insurance policies. The host personality of a particular patient who was the focus of discussion, I said, should be thankful to the "bad" alters who cut and burned enough to ensure that she met inpatient criteria, which she would not have without their planned and deliberate efforts. In general, for all DDU patients, it is necessary to become nonsuicidal gradually in order to get sufficient work done to truly be stabilized by discharge.

Interestingly, the insurance company rewards the patient for being initially suicidal and self-mutilative. If the patient miscalculates and remains suicidal too long, however, the insurance reviewer then defines her as a bad borderline and so the treatment gets defined as regressive and benefits are cut off. Then, if the level of suicidal ideation is too high, transfer to state hospital becomes necessary. A narrow window exists—which varies, depending on the particular insurance policy—during which it is strategically advantageous to be actively suicidal. Also, I pointed out, too many admissions result in a bad borderline diagnosis, so overuse of the strategy in terms of repeat admissions also backfires. The effect of this discussion is to reward the "bad" alters for their helpful behavior, thereby forming a treatment alliance with them while setting firm limits and consequences for excessive self-mutilation or suicidal ideation.

Staff Expectations

Another element of our behavioral management is the expectations set by staff. We expect patients to work hard psychotherapeutically and not to act out (we define acting out as a failure of commitment to recovery). In group I regularly define behaviors as disruptive, avoidant, self-destructive, and unhealthy in a direct, confrontational, yet supportive manner. I define these behaviors as symptoms of childhood trauma and the goal of treatment as the substitution of flexible, adaptive behaviors. One major theme of treatment is to analyze current behaviors, roles, feelings, and cognitions as reenactments of childhood trauma: the best behavioral management technique is good therapy.

Skeptics about DID often say that the suggestibility of individuals with DID puts them at high risk for regression, dependency on the therapist and the hospital, entrenchment in the sick role, confabulation, and increasing disability. Although this is true, the inverse is also true: properly managed, DID patients can be "suggested" into health. In a well-balanced treatment program, the suggestibility of DID patients can be a great asset. When the demand characteristics of the milieu are for higher function, stable behavior, and recovery, this can have a powerful effect. Proper management of the suggestibility of DID patients does not involve simple extinction techniques because recovery from the degree of impairment seen in patients on our unit requires years of hard work.

Medications

As mentioned, the amount of intramuscular medications used on the unit has dropped dramatically as other methods of containment have been improved. We now use physical restraint about once a quarter and do not use planned voluntary physical restraints at all.

I formerly used ultra high-dosage benzodiazepines, which I define as twenty milligrams or more per day of lorazepam, fairly often, but this has been unnecessary for over a year. It's uncommon for me to prescribe ten milligrams per day of lorazepam or clonazepam for more than the first week of hospitalization. This reduction in usage of benzodiazepines has not been accompanied by an increase in the use of any other classes of medications. Most often, patients under my care are discharged on simplified medication regimens, compared with their preadmission polypharmacy.

We have also abandoned barbiturate-facilitated interviews because they were usually regressive and followed by dramatic acting out within the first twenty-four hours postinterview. We discovered the obvious—namely, that rapid penetration of the defenses with a barbiturate angered the alters who had been protected by those barriers. Over time, we learned that demands for Amytal interviews were usually symptomatic of a lack of commitment to the sustained, painful, laborious work of therapy. Also, as the memories in and of themselves have become less and less the target of therapy, the need for barbiturate interviews has declined. We use phenothiazines as an alternative to benzodiazepines on a limited basis, largely to avoid the problems with abuse, tolerance, and dependence that make the benzodiazepines so problematic.

Anger Management

Another element of our behavioral management is anger management therapies, which we continue to refine. We have a number of groups specifically dedicated to anger processing and management and make the healthy expression and modulation of traumatic rage a major theme of treatment. Future modifications of the program will involve building in more structured methods of discharging and expressing anger for patients to use in group and individual therapy and privately. Above all, we define the anger as a legitimate and biologically normal reaction to chronic childhood trauma.

I regularly provide a desensitization model of therapy in general and anger work in particular during cognitive therapy group. I define *anger* as the phobic stimulus and explain the rationale for systematic desensitization. Patients have to learn to tolerate their anger in manageable increments. This, coupled with the learning of new anger management skills and the correction of cognitive errors about anger, provides a treatment approach grounded in a large literature concerning cognitive-behavioral treatment of phobias. In the view of most DID patients in the early and mid phases of treatment, one can be either murderously enraged or completely shut down, with no other options available. A psychoeducational element of the anger therapy involves teaching about the pathological modeling that DID patients received from their parents during their childhoods.

Structure

Structure is a major component of behavioral management, irrespective of the content of the structured time. The more unstructured, unscheduled time there is, the more acting out there will be. We therefore have a full complement of groups and try to build in as much structure as possible on the weekends while allowing for rest time. All must be managed within the shrinking financial resources of the health care system.

From a cost management point of view, there is a trade-off between reducing the amount of staff to save money in a climate of steadily declining reimbursement while not thinning the resources so much that the resulting extra patient acting out requires additional staff to manage.

Dedicated Staff

Finally, we have trained staff and a physically separate self-contained unit with a lockable door. The fact that the door must be locked when individuals are at risk of acting out creates peer pressure not to act out. Having staff who choose to work on the DDU, rather than who are resentful of that assignment, is immensely helpful. The less extraneous professional, patient, cleaning staff, and other traffic on the unit, the more settled it will be. Behavioral management of the patients is infinitely easier if they are not being goaded by hostile, projecting, disbelieving, or blaming mental health professionals and doctors. Many problems vanish as soon as the patients can be housed on a separate DDU and are no longer housed on a general adult unit.

BASIC STRUCTURE AND CORE PRINCIPLES

The core of our program—because this extremely difficult patient population requires subtle, complex management—is the patient's relationships with the individual therapist, the physician, and the group therapy. It's a constant struggle to maintain a quality program with shrinking resources. The core therapy groups receive cognitive therapy, DID education, DID process group, anger management, psychodrama, art therapy, and recreational therapy. These occupy about forty hours a week.

Each patient receives at least three hours a week of individual psychotherapy, in addition to medical rounds by the attending physician. Other staff in the health system who interact with the patients are also knowledgeable about DID, including utilization review, intake, and administrative staff. A DDU cannot function without supportive, committed administration. I would not try to establish a dissociative disorders program in an administratively neutral or hostile environment.

In my charts, I write a physician's progress note on the first day I see the patient; it begins with a brief summary of the essentials of the case, including demographics, diagnosis, and presenting problem. I then write an itemized treatment plan that is updated continuously and charted in daily notes throughout the rest of the admission. A typical initial treatment plan reads as follows:

1. Increase interpersonality communication and cooperation.
2. Form a treatment alliance with key persecutor alters, reframe their behavior as positive in intention, and devise alternative behavioral strategies to meet the system's needs.
3. Foster the development of nondissociative coping strategies.
4. Correct key trauma-driven cognitive errors.
5. Limited trauma memory processing related to presenting suicidal ideation.
6. Two to three weeks in the hospital, possibly one to two weeks in day hospital.

This itemization provides an operationalized treatment plan that can be followed easily by the utilization review personnel and the individual therapist. Notice that the plan includes the key words *cognitive* and *behavioral* because managed care reviewers are unlikely to pay for the analysis of transference or resolution of intrapsychic conflicts defined in the vocabulary of object relations theory. The same work, stated in cognitive-behavioral terms, is much more likely to receive coverage. Certain types of charting are more likely to be perceived as evidence of *regressive therapy*. This is why the word *limited* is used in reference to memory work and the word *abreaction* is never used except to describe spontaneous abreactions, which are defined as symptoms and targets of therapy. One should not be wedded to the vocabulary of any one school of psychotherapy and should be prepared to shift terminology as required.

The treatment, in my hands, is a technically eclectic blend of cognitive, systems, and dynamic approaches, with the main emphasis on cognitive therapy. At the core is the formation of treatment alliances with persecutor alter personalities and increasing interpersonality communication and cooperation. The goal is to shift the system from a state of civil war to one of negotiation and mutual problem solving.

In the psychoeducational component of therapy, I teach the alters repeatedly that they are all parts of one person and live in the same body. When child alters are cutting or burning, it is almost always the case that they think the current date is 1962 or some equivalent year from childhood. They rarely understand that they are cutting their own body. Getting them to understand that the body has grown up and that the abuse has stopped is a key element in getting the cutting to stop. Many cognitive errors need to be addressed in this work.

Rather than discuss the principles of therapy at length in the abstract, I illustrate them here in action through case examples. The cases are composites of many individuals.

A PRESENTING PROBLEM OF SUICIDAL IDEATION

A thirty-year-old woman with six prior admissions to other facilities had been in DID therapy for two years. She reported a history of domestic incest and satanic ritual abuse. She said she needed to be in the hospital to be protected from her cult alters, who wanted to take her to a ceremony on an upcoming cult holiday. Recent self-inflicted lacerations and cigarette burns were evident on her forearms and thighs. She was clinically depressed but had failed to respond to adequate trials of several classes of antidepressants. Trazodone was started and increased to a dosage of four hundred milligrams every hour, which helped her insomnia, posttraumatic nightmares, and depressive symptoms.

There was no collateral verification of the reality of any of her trauma history, she declined consent to contact first-degree relatives, and prior medical records were not illuminating. Her referring therapist believed literally in the reality of the ongoing satanic cult involvement.

THE INITIAL INTERVENTION

The host personality was firmly entrenched in the victim role and tried to place the treatment team in the rescuer role, with the cult-aligned alter personalities functioning as the perpetrators. The initial intervention was to reframe the cult alters as helpful, rather than as enemies. I pointed out to the host personality, using Socratic questioning methods, that the reason she met inpatient criteria was the deliberate, focused efforts of her cult alters, who had been cutting, burning, and creating command hallucinations for suicide. Without their efforts, she would not have been able to get into the hospital and would not have been safe from the cult on the cult holiday. Here, I was using the host personality's belief in the reality of the ongoing ritual abuse as leverage to correct her cognitive errors about the cult alters being her enemies.

Once the host personality accepted this logic, I proceeded to analyze for her the logical possibilities that flowed from the fact that the cult alters got her into the hospital. Whatever their intentions, I said, the outcome of their behavior was protective; therefore, they were actually functioning as protectors. From this it followed that only one of two options was possible: (1) the cult alters were not really all powerful and controlling, as the host thought, and she was able to get herself admitted despite their wishes; and (2) the cult alters really were controlling the situation, and therefore they actually wanted to be in the hospital and to get away from the cult—they just couldn't admit it yet. This logic locked the host personality into either being empowered herself or regarding her persecutory alters as protectors; both are essential preliminary steps toward resolving the presenting problem of suicidal ideation and self-mutilation.

I pointed out how the cutting and burning conveniently escalated as the cult holiday approached, and I tightened the therapeutic double-bind by saying that either the cult alters must be so dumb that they don't realize their behavior will result in hospitalization, or they actually wanted to be admitted. The host couldn't opt for the conclusion that her alters were dumb, because I had defined them as part of herself; more important, the cult alters were placed in a bind of having to admit their desire to get free of the cult in order not to be classified as dumb. At this point, I had indirectly engaged the cult alters in therapy without even talking with them, knowing they would be listening to my conversation with the host.

Next, I asked the host personality what would have happened if she had not had the cult alters and had had to endure the trauma of the rituals directly herself. This line of questioning led quickly to the conclusion that the cult alters were a great asset to the host, were created by her to protect her from the trauma of the cult, and were only carrying out the role she had assigned them. It was hardly fair for the host to be faulting them for doing their job. This line of questioning created guilt in the host about viewing the cult alters as bad, which further softened her stance toward them. I then pointed out that the cult alters had to be highly skilled at their roles in the rituals in order for the host to survive because failure to perform adequately would have resulted in the body suffering more extreme abuse. In fact, the ideological commitment of the cult alters to the cult was actually a necessary survival strategy, rather than evidence of the need for spiritual warfare against them.

The psychoeducational component of the work was to teach the host and the alters about anger: the host had considered the anger of the cult alters to be evidence of their allegiance to Satan. In fact, the anger is normal and unavoidable. It is a legitimate and healthy reaction to chronic childhood trauma. The question is what to do with it and how to channel it in a healthy direction. To fault and reject the cult alters for being angry is highly unfair when they have done the difficult job of holding and containing that intolerable affect for so many years. In fact, faulting them for being angry makes them more hurt, angry, and resentful and even more likely to cut and burn.

COLLABORATING WITH THE ALTERS

By this point, the presenting problem has been redefined as the solution to the real problem: this is the classical family therapy intervention, in which the behavior of the identified patient is redefined as a system strategy for maintaining homeostasis. The so-called bad alters have been cutting and burning to protect the body from the cult, their error being that this strategy is actually damaging the body. The goal of treatment, then, becomes the creation of an alternative strategy that is less self-destructive. Devising such a strategy requires discussion and cooperation between the host and the cult alters.

One can intervene paradoxically with the cult alters early in the admission, even before they have taken executive control during individual therapy sessions and anger management groups. I discuss the workings of the health care system directly with satanic alter personalities and point out to them that the average length of stay on our unit is just under three weeks. I explain that therefore my goal is the same as theirs: to get the body out of the hospital as soon as possible. I point out that we only differ on what to do postdischarge, with the alters advocating return to the cult or completed suicide. I point out that the way to get out of the hospital on schedule, without a transfer to the state hospital, is for the self-abusive behavior to stop. It therefore becomes in the best interests of the cult-aligned alter personalities to maintain stable behavior. I also sidestep power struggles with these alters by saying that working with me instead of against me will prevent a great deal of unnecessary conflict between them and the staff, which I define as "hassle," implying that it is street smart for the alters to avoid conflict.

I hire the cult alters as consultants to the therapy by asking them to keep a close eye on me and the rest of the treatment team and to report to me on any unsatisfactory behavior they observe. I define myself as the expert on DID and say that they are the experts on the system, not me, because I have only just met them. Because they have years of experience at managing and protecting the system, their advising me will prevent me from stumbling around in the dark, making errors, and stirring up secrets that need to be protected. In saying this, I have defined the alters as protectors while focusing on other matters, and the cult alters are placed in the position of implicitly agreeing that they are protectors.

I point out to the host, with the persecutor alters listening, that it is smart not to trust me too much. This tactic builds trust by paradoxically defining a lack of trust as a skill, rather than as a deficit. I point out that the host personality and the child alters have been repeatedly victimized because they have been too trusting and unassertive. Since the cult alters hold all the anger and aggression, the host personality could benefit from a sharing of anger by the cult alters; it would make her stronger and more assertive. It is not fair for the cult alters to define the host as a wimp; they have been holding all of her non-wimp attributes. She is bound to be weak because they have all the strength. I know they have all the strength because they are the ones who understood what it took to keep the body safe and to get it into the hospital prior to the cult holiday.

I always take advantage of my knowledge that satanic ritual abuse personality systems are usually organized in layers, with the cutting and burning alters receiving direction from higher-ranking alters who often are identified as demons. I ask the cutting alters whether they are afraid they would get in trouble if they stopped cutting, and they almost always answer in the affirmative. I then talk through to the alters at the top of the system and say that I would like to work directly with them. I point out that it is a nuisance for the system for me to be interacting with low-ranking alters, who then have to worry about retaliation from higher up while the high-ranking alters have to go to all the effort of monitoring and controlling the cutters. It would be much less hassle for everyone if I could just work directly with the bosses.

At this point, it is important to contract with the high-ranking alters for protection of the secrets. Often, the referring therapist has been working far too much on memory recovery and abreaction, which has reinforced the resistance and acting out of the cult alters, which in turn reinforces the host's cognitive errors about them being bad and demonic. I invert this to a stance in which it is essential to keep the secrets protected and to pace the therapy at a tolerable rate.

The host personality now needs to be reeducated about the nature of therapy because she usually sees trauma memory recovery as the core of treatment and sees active posttraumatic symptoms as evidence of hard work. Again in a Socratic mode, I ask the host personality what she thinks is the reason for the cult alters being so far away in the background. She always thinks that this is evidence of their evil nature and power over her. In fact, they are farthest away because they hold the worst feelings and secrets and need the most protection. I tell the host that the cult alters almost always turn out to be children and the most traumatized parts of the system. This is why they have trouble understanding about being in the same body, use magical thinking almost exclusively, and are unwilling to take executive control. This perception of the cult alters markedly increases the host's empathy for them because they now have victim status, and she must be a perpetrator if she is mean or rejecting toward them. Just like the child alters she already sees as victims, they need safety and internal soothing.

The host personality receives education about *identification with the aggressor*, which is the psychodynamic principle inherent in the creation of cult alter personalities. This is defined as a clever survival strategy in which the power of the perpetrator is internalized to create a developmentally protective illusion of safety and control in the traumatized child's mind. Although it is an illusion, the identification actually works to buffer and modulate the overwhelming sense of powerlessness and helplessness.

DEALING WITH THE UNDERLYING ISSUES

By this point in the therapy, the emphasis shifts from the satanic ritual abuse to the underlying cognitive errors and psychodynamic conflicts. It is not necessary or helpful to take a position that the ritual abuse is confabulated; that merely entrenches system resistance and shows a lack of respect for the person's defenses. The same dynamic conflicts exist and are the target of therapy, whether the memories are accurate or incorrect. The underlying problem is attachment to the perpetrator. This statement is equally true whether the trauma is domestic incest or cult ritual abuse, and I point out repeatedly in cognitive therapy group that the same basic problems exist for all trauma survivors, ritual and nonritual. This stance eliminates the need to discuss the ritual abuse at a content level: only a minute fraction of good therapy is devoted to ritual abuse content.

The attachment to the perpetrator, who is usually the father, has several elements. One function of the defenses is to protect the host personality from grief: the host's task in recovery is to mourn the loss of the father she never had. She has to let go of the false images of the father. These images include the immensely powerful and seductive satanic high priest, who valued his special daughter as future high priestess of the cult; the good father who was always there and never hurt his daughter in any way; the inhuman criminal who has no good features; and the man who is *her father* but not *my father*, in the view of some alters. It seems unlikely that these defenses and false images would be required if the father really had been non-abusive, healthy, and emotionally available.

Separation from the father and relinquishing of the identification with the aggressor are also frightening because they uncover the overwhelming terror, helplessness, and powerlessness of the traumatized child. To not be bad, responsible for the abuse, and deserving of the abuse means that one was, in truth, a helpless victim. For many years, it has been better to be bad and self-punitive in order to perpetuate the attachment to the perpetrator despite the cost in ongoing abusive relationships and failure to separate and individuate. This statement is true because, for the time-locked alters in the back of the system, the emergency state of childhood continues timelessly.

At a more mundane level, the overreliance on dissociative defenses and the impairment caused by Axis I and II psychopathology has made the everyday world a lonely and overwhelming place. Rather than being unskilled and alone, it is better to have expertise and power in a confabulated world of satanic ritual abuse, or in a real one, if the memories are accurate. Separation from the perpetrator can be resisted because it may result in having to live alone and be self-supporting, with no father-protector to fall back on.

Attention to these underlying conflicts and dynamics shifts the focus of therapy onto everyday problems of current living. It is remarkable how many patients enter the hospital to be protected from the cult, when the underlying issue is a need to be disentangled from an unsatisfying or abusive relationship or simply to get time out from the demands of the world. While satanic cults certainly may exist, the focus of therapy is on *psychological* matters, on the domain of expertise of mental health care providers.

By going through these steps, the composite patient attained all the goals of the initial treatment plan. The cult alters were working cooperatively with the host and other protectors, and a solid contract protected the secrets and paced the therapy at a tolerable level. The hospital therapist had spoken with the out-of-state referring therapist several times, and the ongoing outpatient treatment plan had been modified to emphasize current functioning and conflict resolution. Various practical changes in the patient's social supports and outside resources had been made, and she had attended a number of groups in our sexual compulsivity program to deal with problems of this nature.

After three weeks as an inpatient, she was no longer clinically depressed or actively suicidal and was discharged. At discharge, the satanic alter personalities acknowledged that they were parts of the same person, were glad to have missed the rituals on the cult holiday, and were committed to working with the host personality to build a better life. Future admissions to deal with cult-aligned alters on other system levels that had not yet been engaged in treatment were anticipated. Long-term prognosis for stable integration of the DID was considered good.

COGNITIVE THERAPY GROUP

Before closing, I briefly describe the cognitive therapy group I run on the unit three times a week. The group lasts for an hour. Each Monday, or whenever there are new patients, I begin by explaining who I am, what group this is, and how it works. The group is a general process group in which patients can talk about anything that is troubling them. The only rule is that we do not discuss details of the childhood trauma. I take care of the cognitive part, and it involves my focusing on how their thought patterns are affecting their feelings and behavior. They do not need to worry about how to do cognitive therapy because I take care of that. Sometimes one person will use the whole hour, sometimes it will be more of a group discussion, but usually two or three people will do some work, with the others giving feedback. We rotate around so that the same person does not dominate the group and most people have a chance to do some work during an admission.

The group consists of rotating individual therapy and group psychoeducation, with feedback from group members. We do not deal with group process as such, except to comment on disruptive behavior or projections onto other group members. Also, we do not talk about complaints, dissatisfactions, or other milieu and hospital issues. Group members vary from those who have just been diagnosed to day hospital patients in the late preintegration phase of therapy. Most patients sit on chairs, but sitting on the floor and bringing stuffed animals into group are allowed. Patients leaving the group for brief time-outs is allowed, but if this becomes excessive, it is addressed and limits are set.

I deal with the issues and problems described in the case example. I specifically and repeatedly remind patients that the alters are all parts of one person and part of a survival strategy based on the cognitive and dissociative functions of the normal child's mind. The problem is that the survival strategy of childhood is not working well in the changed conditions of adulthood.

I find the cognitive therapy group to be productive and the quality of work done by the patients to be very high. I am constantly impressed by the commitment to recovery, intellectual acuity, problem-solving skills, humor, and resiliency of these courageous survivors. They grasp convoluted cognitive loops, internal paradoxes, and other subtleties quickly, despite frequent trancing out, switching, and other mobilizations of autohypnotic defenses during group. The group is not "intellectual" and involves a great deal of display and processing of affect in a contained fashion. DID patients are capable of sustained, intensive, profitable group therapy and respond to the work ethic of the milieu in the majority of cases. As is true of all major mental illnesses, a subset of patients are so entrenched in Axis II psychopathology that they cannot use the program productively, but we are learning more and more about how to engage even the most chronic and difficult cases in meaningful therapy.

DID is one of the few mental disorders, by the way, for which managed care companies will certify inpatient treatment with psychotherapy as the primary treatment modality.

∾

DID can be treated on a subspecialty inpatient unit with good short-term outcomes that satisfy the demands of a managed health care system. The treatment is practical, grounded, and effective, although this has not been documented in systematic treatment outcome studies. The emphasis on our Dissociative Disorders Unit at Charter Behavioral Health System of Dallas is on rapid stabilization, return to outpatient care, cognitive-behavioral therapy, psychoeducation, anger management, and the development of a flexible repertoire of nondissociative coping strategies. Medications, primarily benzodiazepines and the newer serotonergic antidepressants, are used regularly, and the number of nursing incident reports on the unit has been reduced to a level that does not differ significantly from the overall rate in the institution.

Running a DDU is an unending exercise in innovation, adaptation, and making do with resources that are less than ideal. We are currently conducting six-year prospective outcome follow-ups on a sample of 103 inpatients by using a battery of self-report measures and structured interviews. The efficacy of the treatment of DID can be studied by using existing measures and the usual methods of monitoring treatment response.

NOTE

P. 338, *described in texts by myself and Frank Putnam:* Putnam, F. W. (1989). *Diagnosis and treatment of multiple personality disorder.* New York: Guilford Press; Ross, C. A. (1989). *Multiple personality disorder: Diagnosis, clinical features, and treatment.* New York: Wiley.

ABOUT THE AUTHORS

Judith Armstrong, Ph.D., is a clinical associate at the University of Southern California. She is in private practice in Los Angeles, specializing in clinical and forensic work with dissociative disordered and traumatized patients. She developed and directed the Dissociative Disorders Assessment Research Program at the Sheppard and Enoch Pratt Hospital and has published and presented extensively on the assessment of dissociative disorders. She is a fellow of the International Society for the Study of Dissociation and the Society for Personality Assessment.

Peggy L. Dawson, M.Ed, OTR, currently teaches occupational therapy at the University of Missouri–Columbia. She began working with DID patients twelve years ago while employed as an occupational therapist at a veterans hospital and has worked with both hospitalized and outpatient Dissociative Identity Disordered populations. She has described various treatment applications and pertinent activity at numerous state, national, and international workshops, as well as through her professional writings. Most recently (1993), she described various occupational therapy (OT) treatment approaches in a chapter entitled "Occupational Therapy for Inpatients and Outpatients with Multiple Personality Disorder" in E. S. Kluft (Ed.) *Expressive and Functional Therapies in the Treatment of Multiple Personality Disorder.*

Catherine G. Fine, Ph.D., is clinical assistant professor in psychiatry at Temple University School of Medicine, program coordinator of the Dissociative Disorders Unit at the Institute of Pennsylvania Hospital, associate editor of the journal *Dissociation*, and past president of the International Society for the Study of Dissociation, and has a private practice as clinical psychologist. She is coeditor (with Richard Kluft) of *Clinical Perspectives on Multiple Personality Disorder.*

John F. Higdon, Ph.D., is a clinical psychologist at the Truman Memorial Veterans Hospital in Columbia, Missouri, and associate professor of psychiatry in the School of Medicine, University of Missouri–Columbia. He treats a wide range of psychiatric disorders and has published in the areas of Dissociative Identity Disorder, Paranoid Disorder, and aggression.

Richard P. Kluft, M.D., is a psychiatrist and psychoanalyst in Philadelphia, where he is senior attending psychiatrist and director of the Dissociative Disorders Program at the Institute of Pennsylvania Hospital, is clinical professor of psychiatry at Temple University School of Medicine, serves on the faculty of the Philadelphia Psychoanalytic Institute, and is a lecturer of psychiatry at the Harvard Medical School. He is the author of more than two hundred publications and the editor of *Childhood Antecedents of Multiple Personality*, *Treatment of Victims of Sexual Abuse*, *Incest-Related Syndromes of Adult Psychopathology*, and (with Catherine G. Fine) *Clinical Perspectives on Multiple Personality Disorder*. He is editor-in-chief of *Dissociation* and has served as president of both the International Society for the Study of Dissociation and the American Society of Clinical Hypnosis and has been treating dissociative disorders for twenty-five years.

Stephen S. Marmer, M.D., Ph.D., is on the clinical faculty in the Department of Psychiatry and Biobehavioral Medicine at UCLA School of Medicine and the senior faculty at Southern California Psychoanalytic Institute. He also has a private psychiatric practice in Los Angeles.

Gary Peterson, M.D., is an experienced therapist, speaker, and author in the area of psychological trauma and dissociative disorders. He has been an advisor to the Child and Adolescent and the Psychiatric Systems Interface (Dissociative) Disorders Work Groups of the American Psychiatric Association Task Force on *DSM-IV*. He chairs the Diagnostic Taxonomy Committee of the

International Society for the Study of Dissociation. He is president and co-founder of the North Carolina Triangle Society for the Study of Dissociation; is board certified in psychiatry and child psychiatry; is clinical associate professor of psychiatry and research associate professor of psychology at the University of North Carolina at Chapel Hill; and is a psychiatrist in practice in Chapel Hill, North Carolina.

Colin A. Ross, M.D., is the director of the dissociative disorders program at Charter Behavioral Health System of Dallas and an associate clinical professor of psychiatry at Southwestern Medical Center. He is the past president of the International Society for the Study of Dissociation and author of more than one hundred publications, including *Multiple Personality Disorder: Diagnosis, Clinical Features, and Treatment* (1989); *The Osiris Complex: Case Studies in Multiple Personality Disorder* (1994); *Pseudoscience in Biological Psychiatry* (1995); and *Satanic Ritual Abuse: Principles of Treatment.*

Daniel J. Siegel, M.D., received his medical degree from Harvard University and did his postgraduate training in pediatrics, general psychiatry, and child and adolescent psychiatry at UCLA. He studied child development, attachment theory, memory, and narrative as a National Institute of Mental Health–UCLA research fellow following his clinical training and presently serves as acting director of training in child and adolescent psychiatry at UCLA. He is the founder and coordinator of the Cognitive Sciences Study Group and a member of the Cognitive Sciences Research faculty at UCLA. He teaches and writes on subjects including child development, psychotherapy, cognition, memory, trauma, and dissociation.

William Smith, Ph.D., is dean of the Karl Menninger School of Psychiatry and Mental Health Sciences. He is a diplomate of the American Board of Clinical Psychology and of the American Board of Psychological Hypnosis.

James L. Spira, Ph.D., M.P.H., is on the faculty of the Department of Psychiatry and the Department of Medicine at Duke University School of Medicine and director of the program in health psychology at Duke's medical rehabilitation facility, the Center for Living. A licensed psychologist, he completed his graduate training at the University of California at Berkeley and a postdoctoral fellowship in psychiatry at Stanford University School of Medicine. His research focuses on modifying acute stress reactions due to medical crises. A member of the American Red Cross Mental Health Disaster Relief Services, he also teaches psychotherapeutic methods for persons suffering from acute stress reactions following environmental catastrophes, and offers professional training courses in hypnotherapy and the therapeutic uses of meditation.

Moshe S. Torem, M.D., serves as chairman of the Department of Psychiatry and Behavioral Sciences at Akron General Medical Center and professor and chairman of the Department of Psychiatry, Northeastern Ohio University's College of Medicine. He is recent past president of the International Society for the Study of Dissociative Disorders.

INDEX

A

Abreaction: defined, *li;* destabilization caused by, 263–265, 290–292; through expressive therapies, 263–265; fractionated versus intensive, 292, 324–325; management of, in hospital setting, 323–325; readiness for, 85; to resolve traumatic memories, 67–69, 145, 231–234; versus retraumatization, 229; spontaneous, containment/discouragement of, 310, 313, 321, 323, 339, 347, 348–349; in tactical integration perspective, 94

Absorption: measures of, 20; tendency toward high, *xxvii*

Abstraction, *xxvii, xxviii, xxxi*

Abuse: defined, *li;* and differential diagnosis, *xxv, xxxii;* disclosure of, premature, 151, 167–168, 221–222; and dissociation, in history, 136–137; duration/frequency of, and sequelae, 280–281; and etiology, *xxvi–xxvii,* 137; nondisclosure of, factors in, 242–245; nondisclosure of, and suicidal ideation, 308–309; ongoing, of children with Dissociative Identity Disorder, 144–145, 149, 167; ongoing, inpatient interventions for, 345; preverbal, 244–245; in psychotherapy experiences, 301; repressed memories of, *xlix–xlx;* sadistic, and hypnosis, 152; towards others, inpatient interventions for, 345–345. *See also* Cult abuse; Ritual abuse; Trauma, childhood

Abuser alters. *See* Persecutory alters

Academic alters, 147

Acting out. *See* Aggressive behavior; Behavioral management; Self-harm; Suicidal ideation/behavior

Adler, A., *xxxiv, xxxviii*

Adolescent alters, 96

Adolescent Dissociative Experiences Scale (A-DES), 23–24

Adolescents: assessment of, 23–24; treatment of, 150. *See also* Children with Dissociative Identity Disorder

"Aetiology of Hysteria," 136

Affect bridge technique, 231–232

Affect regulation/tolerance: and behavioral control, 84–85, 352–353; and self, 57–59

Affectivity, 55–57

Age regression techniques, 231

Agency, 55–57

Aggressive alters, 27, 31, 58–59; and hospitalization, 153, 305–306; restraint sessions for, 322. *See also* Angry alters; Persecutory alters

Aggressive behavior, 208; in children, 23; inpatient interventions for, 345–345

Aggressor, identification with, 361–362. *See also* Perpetrators

Alcohol, and medication interactions, 109, 110

Alcohol dependence: alter-specific, 248–251; medication for, 114, 125; and medication prescribing, 156. *See also* Substance abuse

Alcoholics Anonymous, 90

Alexander, F., 207–208

Alprazolam (Xanax), 106, 107, 108, 109, 111, 124

Alters: active versus inactive modes of, 139–140; addressing of, by name, 317–318; adolescent, 96; affects of, 58–59; aggressive, 27, 31, 58–59, 153, 305–306, 322; angry, 96, 159–161, 229, 257–258, 245–247, 304; asleep, 139–140; awake, 138–139; behavior of, in hospital setting, 325; child, 96, 159–161, 244–245, 304, 348–349, 356; in children, 147, 150–151; co-conscious, 138–139, 234; cognitive development of, 159–161; cognitive therapy with, in case example, 356–363; communication among, 138, 165–166, 202, 230–231, 262, 355–356; communication with, *xxxvi–xxxvii*, 230–231; and con-comitant diagnoses, *xxiii*; confidentiality issues with, *xxxvii, xlv*, 62, 157–159, 231; conflict among, 240, 245–247, 355–356; and conflict, 188; conscious awareness of, 62–63, 138–141, 147; contracting with, 161, 309, 325–326; cooperation among, through cognitive therapy, 355–356, 358–361; cooperation among, through goal-related projects, 241–242, 245, 246–247, 254–260, 261–262; and core identity, 56–57; cult, 356–363; dead, 140–141; defensive benefits of, 34, 190–191, 212; defined, *li;* and differential diagnosis, *xxv;* emergence of, through expressive therapies, 247–251, 252–254, 264–265; emergence of, through hypnosis, 220–222; equal attention to, versus playing favorites, *xxxvi,* 16, 72, 196–197, 206; hierarchy among, 360; infant, 164–165; and medication, *xxxiv,* 103, 105; models of responsibility held by, 85, 95–97; mute, 165–166; narrative charting for, 65–66; and narrative construction, 46, 65, 209–210; nature of, *xx–xxi;* and nocturnal enuresis, 164–165; number of, *xx,* 228; over-worked, 92–93, 96; past versus future orientation in, 92, 96; persecutory, 96, 159–161, 355, 357–361; and posttraumatic memory processes, 52, 53; protector, 95, 260, 304, 357–361; and psychologi-cal testing, 12–14, 15–16; reframing of, 245–247, 357–358; self-helper, 197, 206, 228; as self-objects, 189–190, 200; sexual, 188; and sleep problems, 163–164; and somatic symptoms, 161–162; and suicidal/self-harm ideation, 159–161, 356–363; and therapeutic responsibility, 84; and transference, 204–206; treatment alliance with, 355, 358–361; unconscious, *xlv. See also* Host personality; Integration; Mapping; Splitting; Switching

American Society for Clinical Hypnosis, 224

Amitriptyline (Elavil), 118, 119, 121, 161

Amnesia, among alters, 138, 230. *See also* Dissociative Amnesia

Amobarbital, 321

Amoxapine (Asendin), 118, 121

Amytal, *xxv, xxxiv, li,* 352

Anger, *xl;* management of, 352–353

Angry alters: adolescent, 96; in case example, 257–258; in hospital treatment, 304; reframing of, 245–247; and self-harm prevention, 159–161, 229. *See also* Aggressive alters; Persecutory alters

Anticonvulsants, 155

Antidepressant medication, 116–120; age and, 120; for children, 153, 155; cost and, 120; dose ranges for, 121; drug interactions with, 115; efficacy of, *xxiii;* generic and trade names for, 121, 124; newly released, 124–127; patient choice and, 120; previous use of, 119; safety in, 117; side effects of, 118–119; symptom profile for, 117–118; timing for, 120

Antihistamines, sedative, 114

Anxiety: in assessment process, 15–16; inpatient interventions for, 341–342; medications for, 106–116, 156

Anxiolytic medications, 106–116, 156
Armstrong, J., 3–37, 204
Art therapy, 247, 255–258, 261–262.
   See also Expressive therapies
Asleep alters, 139–140
Assessment, 3–4; of adolescents,
   23–24; and alters, 12–14, 30–31;
   anxiety in, 15–16; behavioral observation in, 7–8; of children, 22–23;
   cognitive, 25–27; discrepancy in
   results of, 12–14, 34; and Dissociative Identity Disorder literature,
   8–9; of dissociative symptoms,
   19–25; establishing safety in, 14–17;
   framework of, for dissociative disorders, 6–8; goals of, 4–6; personality, 27–34; and PTSD test
   literature, 9–10; strategies for,
   6–11; structure versus flexibility in,
   18–19; symptom fabrication/con-
   cealment in, 10–11, 24, 28–29; test
   battery for, 19–34; testing alliance
   in, 11–19; testing by patient in,
   18–19; of whole personality, 12–14
Astemizole (Hismanal), 124
Attachment, childhood: disorganized,
   60; idealized figure of, 62; and
   identification with the aggressor,
   361–362; and narrative construction, 45–46; in psychotherapy,
   60–62; and state transitions, 42
Authority figures, 89, 91
Autobiographical memory. *See*
   Explicit memory
Avoidant behavior, and posttraumatic
   memory, 51, 68–69
Awake alters, 138–139

B

Balint, M., 189
Behavioral management, 84–85; indi-
   vidualized, 350–351; medication
   for, 120–122; techniques of, in
   inpatient setting, 348–354
Behavioral observation, in assessment,
   7–8

Benzodiazepines, 106–113; for children, 156; dose ranges for, 109;
   drug interactions with, 110–111;
   generic and trade names of, listed,
   109; for interviewing patients, 321;
   for restraint, 352; withdrawal from,
   107–108
Berkowitz, R., 276
Berne, E., 148–149
Bertrand, A.-J.-F., 136
Beta-blockers, 116, 122, 124, 155
Beta endorphins, 125
Beyond the Pleasure Principle (Freud),
   208
BI-PAP treatment, 123
Blame: and models of responsibility,
   84, 86, 88, 89–90, 91; and secrecy
   about abuse, 244; the victim, 86.
   See also Responsibility
Bleeding, interalter, 139, 164
Body-mind disconnection, 69–70
Bonding, *xxxviii–xxxix*. *See also*
   Attachment
Boon, S., 276
Borderline Personality Disorder
   (BPD): and deficiency, 189; and dif-
   ferential diagnosis, 22, 212; and
   Dissociative Identity Disorder,
   xxxvi, 212–213; and insurance cov-
   erage, 350–351; as secondary diag-
   nosis, *xxiii*, 212–213, 348; splitting
   in, 192; and therapeutic relation-
   ship, *xxxv*
Bowlby, J., 189
Brand-Bartlett, A., 206
Braun, B. G., 82, 100, 105, 116, 122,
   125, 300, 301, 314
Brenner, I., 206, 302
Breuer, J., 185
Brickman, P., 83, 84–86, 90
Buchele, B., 206
Buddhist meditation technique,
   xliii–xliv
Bupropion (Wellbutrin), 117, 118,
   119, 121
Buspirone (BuSpar), 114–115

C

C-PAP treatment, 123
Carbamazepine (Tegretol), 108, 122
Caretaker alters, 96
Carlson, E., 21, 23
Caul, D., 239
Change, and models of responsibility, 85–93
Characteristics, rapid shifts in, 23. *See also* Switching
Charcot, J.-M., 190
Charter Behavioral Health System, Dissociative Disorders Unit, 337–365; behavioral management in, 348–354; Master Treatment Plan of, 338, 340–346; philosophy of, 338–339, 346–348; structure of, 354–356; therapeutic principles of, 354–365
Charting. *See* Mapping
Child alters, 96, 244–245, 304; group therapy for, 348–349; self-harm behavior of, 159–161, 356
Child development: and affect regulation, 57–59; and development of core self, 55–57; and nurturing, 188–190; of personality, stages of, *xxxviii–xxxvl, xlvi, liii*; splitting in, 192. *See also* Attachment
Child Dissociation Checklist (CDC-Version 3.0), 22–23
Childhood memories, inability to recall, in general population, 53–54. *See also* Memory; Trauma, childhood
Children with Dissociative Identity Disorder: alter relationships in, 147, 157–159, 165–166; assessment/diagnosis of, 22–24; expressive therapies for, 151; family-environmental issues in, 141, 142–143; family interventions for, 149–150; group therapy for, 150–151; hallucinatory/dissociative symptoms in, 146; hospitalization of, 152–154; hypnotherapy for,

151–152; individual psychotherapy for, 146–149; interalter confidentiality in, 157–159; medication for, 153, 154–157; mute alters in, 165–166; nocturnal enuresis in, 164–165; ongoing abuse of, 142–143, 149, 167; pain control for, 161–162; safety issues in treatment of, 167–168; sleep problems of, 162–164; theoretical perspectives on, 135–141; therapeutic principles for, 141–143, 144–145; treatment of, versus adults, 144–145; treatment of, length of, 143, 146; treatment of, stages of, 144–145, 147
Chivas, A., 314
Chlordiazepoxide (Librium), 106, 107, 109, 111–112
Chlorprothixene (Taractan), 116, 121, 122
Choice: in medication, 120; in therapeutic goals, 73–74
Chu, J., 126
Clomipramine (Anafranil), 118
Clonazepam (Klonopin), 105, 106, 107, 108, 109, 112, 122, 123, 352
Clonidine, 105
Clorazepate (Tranxene), 106, 109
Co-consciousness, 138–139, 234
Cognition: hot versus cold, 40–43, 72; and memory, 44–49
Cognitive assessment tests, *xxiv*, 25–27
Cognitive-behavior therapy (CBT), *xli–xlii*
Cognitive patterns, 41–42
Cognitive science approach, 39–74; to defining Dissociative Identity Disorder, 49–52; goals of, 73–74; memory processes in, 43–49; narrative in, 43–45, 49, 57, 65–66; to psychotherapy, 54–75, 147; to therapeutic relationship, 40–43
Cognitive therapy, 355–356; compensatory model in, 93; in inpatient case example, 356–363; tactical

integration perspective in, 94
Cognitive therapy group, 353, 363–364
Coherency, 55–57
Cold cognition, 40–43
Collage project, 262
Comfort, within self, *xxxviii–xxxix*, 189; in Dissociative Identity Disorder versus Borderline Personality Disorder, 212; and transitional object relatedness, 200–202
Communication: among alters, 138, 165–166, 202, 230–231, 262, 355–356; here-and-now, *xl–xli*; through hypnosis, 230–231; therapist with alters, *xxxvi–xxxvii*, 230–231, 355, 358–361
Comorbidity, *xxiii–xxiv*; with Borderline Personality Disorder, *xxiii*, 212–213, 348; and managed care, 168–169; and medication, 99–100, 103–104, 116–117, 124–125, 127–128. *See also* Alcohol dependency; Borderline Personality Disorder; Depression; Posttraumatic Stress Disorder; Substance abuse
Compensatory model, 91–93, 94, 95, 97
Confidentiality, interalter, *xxxvii*, *xlv*, 62, 157–159, 231
Conflict, 187–188; interalter, 240, 245–247, 355–356
"Confusion of Tongues Between Adults and Children," 136–137
Consciousness: of alters, levels of, 138–141; cognitive processes in, 40; in dissociative versus non-dissociative states of mind, 53; division of, and dissociation, 51, 53, 62–63; versus memory, 45
Containment: in hospital setting, 303, 304; of spontaneous abreaction, 310, 313, 321, 323, 339, 347, 348–349
Contamination, symptom, 90–91, 199, 296, 348

Continuity of self, 55–57, 74
Contracting: among alters, for safety, 161, 309, 325–326; with patient, regarding hospitalization, 315
Control: over behavior, 84–85; and hypnosis, 225, 226–227, 234; and models of responsibility, 84. *See also* Behavioral management; Responsibility
Coons, P., 100
Coping skills: among alters, 15–16, 32; developing new, *xli–xlii*, *xlvii*. *See also* Behavioral management; Functioning, daily
Core self, 55–57, 74
Countertransference: in assessment process, 17; and attachment, 61; based on "fixing the problem," 93; in hospital setting, 293; and parallel dissociation, 205–206; in psychoanalytic approach, 203–207; in psychotherapy, 71–73
Crisis, vulnerability to, 279–284
Crisis management: hospitalization for, 299–300; hypnosis for, 233–234
Cult abuse, *xxvi–xxvii*, 216–217; in cognitive therapy case example, 356–363; focus on underlying issues in, versus content, 361–362; triggers of, and patient responsibility, 346. *See also* Ritual abuse
Cult alters, 356–363
Cult holidays, 346, 356

D

Dawson, P. L., 239–271
Day residue, 213
Dead alters, 134–140
Declarative memory. *See* Explicit memory
Dedicated dissociative disorders units (DDUs), 275, 294–298; benefits of, 294, 295; cautions about, 294, 296–298; for short-term, problem-oriented treatment, 337–365. *See also* Charter Behavioral Health

System, Dissociative Disorders Unit

Defense theory, 190–191, 208

Deficiency, 188–190

Denial, overcoming, 145, 247–251

Dependency, in medical model of responsibility, 87–89

Depersonalization: defined, *li–lii;* measures of, 20, 25

Depression: in children, 153; in host personality, 342–343; inpatient interventions for, 342–343; as secondary diagnosis, *xxiii,* 117

Derealization: defined, *lii;* measures of, 20

Desensitization, 353

Desipramine (Norpramin), 117, 118

Despine, A., 81–82

Destabilization: due to inadequate hospital treatment, 288, 290–292, 297–298; patient vulnerability to, 297–281

de Vito, R. A., 321

Diagnosis, *xix–xxv,* 144; cognitive science approach to, 53–54; concomitant, *xxiii,* 103–104; diagnostic questions for, *xxiv–xxv;* differential, *xxii,* 10, 22, 33, 347; *DSM-IV* criteria for, *xx;* hypnosis for, 220–222; inaccuracy in, *xxiii–xxiv, xxxii,* 20–21, 24; labels of, 4–5; patient acceptance/rejection of, 145, 247–251, 264–265; of patient prior to Dissociative Identity Disorder, *xxxii, xlvi;* in problem-oriented inpatient treatment, 340; psychological tests for, *xxiv–xxv,* 19–34; using dreams for, 214. *See also* Assessment; Comorbidity

Diagnostic and Statistical Manual of Mental Disorders (DSM-I), 183

Diagnostic and Statistical Manual of Mental Disorders (DSM-II), 183

Diagnostic and Statistical Manual of Mental Disorders (DSM-III), 183

Diagnostic and Statistical Manual of Mental Disorders (DSM-III-R), xx, *lii,* 183

Diagnostic and Statistical Manual of Mental Disorders (DSM-IV), xix–xx, lii, 183

Diazepam (Valium), 106, 107, 108, 109, 112–113, 115

Diphenhydramine (Benadryl), 114

Disorganized behavior, inpatient interventions for, 344–345

Dissociated relatedness, 24

Dissociation: body-mind, 69–70; controlled versus uncontrolled, *xxix–xxxi, lii,* 223; defined, *lii;* development of, 49–52, 136–137; in Dissociative Identity Disorder versus Borderline Personality Disorder, 212; familial/intergenerational, 149; history of theories on, 136–137; versus hypnosis, 223–224; between implicit and explicit memory, 48–49, 67–69; measures of, for adults, 19–22; measures of, for children, 22–24; narrative and, 43–46, 65–66, 208; psychoanalytical view of, 193–195; structured interviews for, 24–25

Dissociative ability: and etiology, *xxviii–xxx,* 224–225; and hypnotizability, 224–225

Dissociative Amnesia: cognitive development of, 51, 69; defined, *lii;* and differential diagnosis, *xxii, xxiv, xxv;* measures of, 23

Dissociative Disorder-Not Otherwise Specified (DD-NOS): in children, 147–149; defined, *lii;* ego-state-oriented therapies for, 148–149; in inpatient treatment, 347; as interim diagnosis, *xxiv*

Dissociative disorders: in children, 147–148; history of theories of, 81–82, 136–137. *See also* Depersonalization; Derealization; Dissocia-

tive Amnesia; Dissociative Fugue; Dissociative Identity Disorder
Dissociative Disorders Interview Schedule (DDIS), 24
Dissociative Experiences Scale (DES), *xxiv*, 19–22
Dissociative Fugue, and differential diagnosis, *xxii, xxv*
Dissociative Identity Disorder (DID): assessment for, 7–34; benefits of studying, *xvii–xix*; versus Borderline Personality Disorder, 212–213; in children, 135–169; cognitive science approach to, 39–74; complex, 228; as defensive disorder, 190–191; deficiency and, 190; defined, 49–52, 219–220; developmental course of, *xlvi*; diagnosis of, *xix–xxv*, 53–54, 220–222; etiology of, *xxvi–xxxii*, 137; and false versus repressed memory debate, *xlix–l*, 215–217; history of, 81–82, 136–137, 183–186, 207–208; identity issues in, 195; instability in, 279–284; long-term versus brief psychotherapy for, *xvii–xix, xxiii–xxiv, l,* 168–169; models of helping for, 85–97; naming of, 183, 195; patient denial about, 247–251, 264–265; prevalence of, *xvii*, 275–276; prognosis for, 190; psychotropic medication for, 99–128; readings on, 131–132, 176–181, 237–238, 269–271; resurgence of interest in, 81–82, 185; as spectrum disorder, 212–213; trauma models of, 137, 186–187; treatment of, in adults versus children, 144–145; treatment of, tasks/stages in, 144–145, 307. *See also* Alters; Children with Dissociative Identity Disorder; Diagnosis; Etiology; Treatment
Dissociative table technique, 230–231
Doxepin (Sinequan), 118, 119, 121
Draijer, N., 276

Dreams: nightmare, 51; therapeutic use of, 213–215; waking, 214
Droperidol (Inapsine), 116, 121, 122
Drug interactions: with benzodiazepines, 110–111; with buspirone, 115
Dual diagnosis. *See* Comorbidity

E

Early memory. *See* Implicit memory
Eating disorders, 300
Ego and the Id, The (Freud), 185–186
Ego states, defined, 148. *See also* Alters
Ego-state-oriented therapies, 148–149, 221
Ego-state therapy, 148, 221
Ellis, A., 87
Empathy, 189, 190, 208; limitations of, 317–318
Enlightenment model, 89–91, 96
Enuresis, nocturnal, 164–165
Episodic memory. *See* Explicit memory
Erickson, E., *liii*
Erickson, M., *liii*, 32
Etiology, *xxvi–xxxii*; abuse in, severity of, *xxx–xxxii*; and cognitive development, 49–52; and deficiency, 188–190; dissociative ability in, *xxviii–xxx*, 224–225; gender in, *xxviii, xxxii*; and lack of family support/protection, *xxvii–xxviii*; parental modeling in, 149; trauma in, *xxvi–xxvii*, 136–137, 184, 186–187, 190–191, 207–208, 242
Evans, F., 101
Eve, 141, 184
Existential approach, *xxxviii, xl–xli*; and moral model of responsibility, 87
Exner Comprehensive System, 32
Explicit memory, 46–49; and dissociative development, 49–50, 51; and resolving traumatic memories,

67–69, 147, 208–211; and secondary process, 194–195. *See also* Memory; Narrative

Exploration developmental stage, *xxxix*

Expressive therapies: abreaction in, 263–265; advantages of, 241–242, 246–247, 265–266; applications of, 247–263; combined with psychotherapy, 197–198, 223, 239–266; for children, 146, 151; for determining alter characteristics, 252–254; for improving daily functioning, 258–260; for integration, 261–262; for interalter cooperation, 241–242, 245, 246–247, 254–260, 261–262; media of, 252; modalities of, 247; for overcoming denial of diagnosis, 247–251; for overcoming secrecy, 242–245; postintegration, 263; theoretical perspective on, 240

Externalization, *xxvii*, 216

F

Fairbairn, W. R. D., *xxvii–xxviii, li, liii*, 189

False memory syndrome, *xlix–xlx*, 215–217

Family interventions, for treating DID-children, 149–150

Family support/nonsupport: and deficiency, 189, 200; and etiology, *xxvii–xxviii*, 92; and narrative construction, 43–44, 45, 46

Family therapy, with alters, *xxxvi–xxxvii*, 358

Fantasy: and early childhood abuse memories, *xlix*; extension of, versus existential focus, *xl–xli*; measures of, 20; as safe haven, 60; tendency toward, *xxviii, xxxi*

Father, attachment to, 361–362

Fees, 198–199

Ferenczi, S., 136–137

Fine, C. G., 302

Fink, D., 212, 302

Flashbacks: medication for, 120–122; and posttraumatic memory processing, 51, 68–69; during psychological testing, 9–10, 16–17

Fluoxetine (Prozac), 117, 118, 119, 121, 124, 155

Flurazepam (Dalmane), 109

Fluvoxamine (Luvox), 123, 124–125

Follow-up therapy (postintegration), *xlvi, xlviii*; and conflict, 188; expressive therapies in, 263; hypnosis in, 235; tasks of, 145

Food and Drug Administration, 116, 155

Frankl, V., 87

Fraser, G. A., 230

Freud, S., *liii*, 81, 136, 185–186, 189, 190, 191–192, 207, 208, 210

Functioning, daily, *xxi–xxii*; cognitive-behavior therapy for improving, *xli–xlii*; expressive therapies for improving, 258–260; inpatient interventions for, 345

Fusion, *xlvi, xlvii–xlviii*; versus alter death, 140; defined, *lii–liii*, 234; readiness for, 234. *See also* Integration

Future orientation, 92, 96

G

Gainer, M., 128

Ganaway, G., 302

Gender, and etiology, *xxviii, xxxii*

Gestalt therapy, 149

Glossary of terms, *li–liv*

Gmelin, 183

Group, defined, *liii*

Group therapy: for child alters, 348–349; for children, 150–151; cognitive, 353, 363–364; for hospitalized patients, 315–316, 348–349, 354; for ritual abuse patients, 348

Guntrip, H., 189

H

Halazepam (Paxipam), 109
Haloperidol (Haldol), 115, 121, 122
Headaches, in children, 161–162
Hess, E. P., 314
Higdon, J. F., 239–271
Homicidal ideation, 339; inpatient interventions for, 341
Hospital treatment, *xxxii, xxxiii;* abreaction management in, 323–325; administrative support in, 284, 285, 354; admission to, 287–288, 298–302; brief, 277, 278, 299; for children, 152–154; and concerned others, 326–327; containment in, 303, 304; conventional models of, 276–278; in dedicated dissociative disorders units (DDUs), 275, 294–298, 337–365; disruptive nature of, to milieu, 286, 292; and Dissociative Identity Disorder instability, 279–284; drug-facilitated interviews in, 321–322, 352; expectations of, unrealistic, 287–288, 303–306, 311–313; explosive material in, appropriate sharing of, 322–323; extended, 301–302; failure of, 278–279; first steps in, 306–311; in freestanding psychiatric hospital versus psychiatric unit, 287; goals of, 306, 307, 311–313; guidelines for, 313–320; hypnosis in, 321; inadequate resources in, 285, 287–288, 297–298; intermediate-length, 300; lengths of, 298–302; long-term, 300–301; medication in, 326; "mission creep" in, 285, 288–292, 297–298; misunderstandings in, 304–306, 308–311; and "model-patient" alters, 153; objectives of, 277–278, 283–284; outpatient therapist involvement in, 153–154, 289, 319–320; patient complaints in, 286, 292–294; phases of, 307; pre-requisites for adequate, 284–294; prevalence of Dissociative Identity Disorder patients in, 275–276, 279–280; restraint sessions in, 322; roles in, 318, 319–320; room arrangements in, 316; rule clarification in, 317; safety in, 325–326; short-term, 299–300; short-term, problem-oriented, 337–365; specialized, for children, 154; "stabilization-plus" approach to, 280, 281, 301–302, 306–313, 320–328; staff communication in, 284, 285, 286, 287, 292–294, 314–315, 320–321; staff skepticism in, 314–315; staff splitting in, 315, 317, 326; symptom contamination in, 296; symptom suppression in, 153, 277; therapeutic practices in, 302–313, 320–327; transference-based fantasies about, 303–304; use of alters' versus patient's names in, 317–318. *See also* Dedicated dissociative disorders units; Problem-oriented inpatient treatment
Host personality: alters' hostility against, 159–161, 359–360; in children, 147; defined, 138; depression in, 342–343; grief work of, 361–362; overworked, 92–93, 96; and pain control, 162; postintegration, 263; providing information to, 159, 166–167; role of, in hypnosis, 230, 233; role of, in interalter communication, 262
Hot cognition, 40–43
Hydroxyzine (Atarax, Vistaril), 114
Hyperamnesia, 51
Hyperarousal, 51
Hypervigilance, *xxxi*, 51
Hypnosis: abreaction in, 231–234; benefits of, 222–226; cautions with, 221–222; for children, 151–152; combined with psychotherapy, 222–235; components of, *xlv*; for

containment of traumatic material, 310; control in, 225, 226–227, 234; for crisis management, 233–234; for diagnosis, 220–222; versus dissociation, 223–224; in ego-state therapy, 148; first steps in, 226–228; goals of, 222; in hospital treatment, 321; ideomotor signaling in, 229, 230; for imposing restraint, 322; induction of, *xliv*, 226–228; integration phase in, *xliv*; interalter communication through, 230–231; and legal testimony, 152; mapping the system in, 220–221, 228–229; for mastering traumatic memories, 231–234; by perpetrators, 152; for recovering traumatic memories, 221–222; safe place in, 227; self-soothing in, 226–228; susceptibility to, 220, 224–225; symptom creation/simulation due to, 221, 223, 224; time frame for, 233; training for, 152, 224; uses of, *xlii–xlv*, 219; utilization phase of, *xliv*. *See also* Self-hypnosis

Hysteria, 207

I

Identity, 195
Identity diffusion, 195
Ideomotor signaling, 229, 230
Imagery, tendency toward, *xxvii*
Imipramine (Tofranil), 118, 121
Implicit memory, 46–49; and dissociative development, 49–50, 51, 66–69; and posttraumatic symptoms, 66–69; and primary process, 193–195, 208, 209
Impulse control, medication for, 120–122. *See also* Behavioral management
Incest, and dissociation, 136–137. *See also* Abuse; Trauma, childhood
Inderal. *See* Propranolol
Individuation, *xxxix*
Induction of hypnosis, *xliv*, 226–228;

rapid, 226; techniques of, 226
Infant alters, 164–165
Information: disclosure of, premature, 151, 167–168, 221–222; gathering of, *xxxv–xxxvi*, *xlv*, 62–63; therapist-provided versus patient retrieval of, 166–167. *See also* Confidentiality
Inpatient therapy. *See* Hospital treatment; Problem-oriented inpatient treatment
Insomnia, medication for, 125–126
Instability, of Dissociative Identity Disorder patients, 279–284; factors contributing to, 282–283
Instinctual drives, 189
Institute of Pennsylvania Hospital, Dissociative Disorders Unit, 288
Integration, *xlvi*, *xlvii–xlviii*; approaches to, 211; defined, *lii*; expressive therapies for, 261–263; and healing, 73–74; and hypnosis, 234; and identity issues, 195; psychoanalytic approach to, 211–212; stage of, 145; strategic, 211–212; tactical, 94, 302. *See also* Fusion; Postintegration
Intermediate treatment stages, *xlvii*
Interpersonal approach, *xxxviii–xl*; and assessment, 5–6; for children, 146
Intrusive symptoms, and posttraumatic memory, 51, 68–69. *See also* Flashbacks; Posttraumatic symptoms

J

Janet, P., 136, 190

K

Kernberg, O., *liii*
Klein, M., 192
Klonopin. *See* Clonazepam
Kluft, R. P., 16, 82, 100, 105, 142, 143, 144–145, 154, 233, 275–335
Kohut, H., *liii*, 188, 189, 201

L

Late memory. *See* Explicit memory

Legal issues: of dedicated dissociative disorders units, 296; of hypnosis, 152; and lawsuits versus treatment, 215–216; of medication for children, 155; of restraints, 322

Libido theory, 189

Lithium, 155

Loewenstein, R. J., 32, 104–105, 326

Long-term psychotherapy, *xvii–xix, xxxiii–xxxiv, l,* 168–169. *See also* Psychotherapy

Lorazepam (Ativan), 106, 107, 109, 113, 321–322, 352

M

Madness of King George, The, 208

Mahler, M., *liii,* 192

Malingering/Factitious Disorders, *xxiii*

Managed care: and expressive therapies, 265; and hospitalization, 276, 327–328, 365; language to use for, 338, 355; and long-term versus brief psychotherapy, *xvii, xviii–xix, l,* 168–169; and prevalence of Dissociative Identity Disorder, 276; and self-harm, 350–351; and structured activities versus free time, 353; and treating children, 168–169; and treating Dissociative Identity Disorder, *l,* 276; and treatment flexibility, 338

Mapping: defined, *li;* in expressive therapies, 253–254; in hypnosis, 220–221, 228–229; narrative, 65–66; in psychoanalytic therapy, 202–203

Maprotiline (Ludiomil), 118, 119, 121

Marmer, S. S., 183–218

"Mathematics of misery," 280–281

MCMI, *xxiv*

Medial temporal lobe memory system, 48

Medical model, 87–89, 96

Medication, *xxxii, xxxiv;* for alter-specific versus whole personality, 103, 105, 127; antidepressant, 116–120, 124–127; anxiety/anxiolytic, 106–116; for children, 153, 154–157; combined with psychotherapy, 100–105, 127; Dissociative Identity Disorder-specific considerations in, 102–104, 127–128; efficacy of, 104–105; for flashbacks, 120–122; ground rules for, 104–105; in hospital settings, 326, 352; for impulse control, 120–122; for interview facilitation, 321–322, 352; newly released, 123–127; for nocturnal myoclonus, 122–123; and placebo effect, 100–102, 119; for rapid switching, 116, 122; sabotage of, by alters, 103; safety in, 117, 128; for sleep apnea, 122–123, 128; stimulant, 155–156; uses of, for Dissociative Identity Disorder patients, 99–100. *See also* Antidepressant medication

Meditation, *xxix;* and self-hypnosis, *xliii–xliv*

Memory: basic principles of, 44–47; versus consciousness, 45; and dissociative development, 49–52, 53; experiential versus correspondent dimensions of, 45; implicit versus explicit, 46–49; interpersonal influences on, 46; and narrative, 43–44, 45–46, 65–66; and problem-oriented approach, 339, 349; process of, 44; psychoanalytic approach to, 215–217; psychological influences on, 50; reconstruction versus reproduction in, 44–45; recovery of, through hypnosis, 221–222, 231–234; source monitoring in, 45; trauma influences on, 46–52; traumatic, resolution of, 66–69, 145, 147, 190–191, 207–211; validity of, 339, 346. *See*

also Explicit memory; Implicit memory; Trauma, childhood
Memory talk, parent-child, 43–44, 46
Menninger Clinic, 224
Metacognition, 49, 63–64
Methadone, 124
Methylphenidate (Ritalin), 155–156
Midazolam (Versed), 106
Military mind control experimentation, 346
Mindlin, E., 184
Minnesota Multiphasic Personality Inventory-2 (MMPI-2), *xxiv*, 28–30
Mirroring, 189, 208
"Mission creep," 285, 288–292, 297–298
Monoamine oxidase inhibitors (MAOIs), 117, 125, 127
Montgomery, S., 127
Moral model, 86–87, 96
Morris, L., 101
Motivation, 189
Multimodal treatment, 100, 223, 239. *See also* Psychotherapy, individual
Multiple Personality Disorder Assessment Research Project, 32
Mute alters, 165–166

N

Naltrexone (ReVia), 123, 125
Narcissistic personality disorder, 189
Narrative, 43–45; effects of trauma on, 49; versus memory, 45–46; in psychoanalytic psychotherapy, 190–191, 208–211; in psychotherapy, 57, 65–66, 69, 72, 145, 147
Nefazodone (Serzone), 123, 125–126
Negative placebo effect, 101
Neural net, 40, 44
Neuroleptic medication, 116; for children, 156–157; for posttraumatic symptoms, 120–122, 126
Neurotic conflict, 187–188
Nightmares, 51
Nocturnal myoclonus, medical treatments for, 122–123

Nondeclarative memory. *See* Implicit memory
Norton, G. R., 275–276, 279
Nortriptyline (Pamelor), 118, 121
Nurturing, inadequate, 189–190, 200–202

O

Object constancy, 192–193
Object relations theory, *xxxviii–xxxvl*; and deficiency, 188–189; defined, *liii*; and transitional object relatedness, 200–202
Obsessive-compulsive disorder, medication for, 124–125
Oedipal conflict, 187–188, 192
Opiate addiction, 125
Orne, M., 103
Outpatient therapy, *xxxii*, *xxxiii–xxxiv*. *See also* Expressive therapies; Medication; Psychoanalytic approach; Psychotherapy, individual
Overdiagnosis, 20–21, 25, 347
Oxazepam (Serax), 109

P

Pain control, for children, 161–162
Parallel dissociation, 205
Parallel distributed processing (PDP), 40, 93
Parent-child relationship: and deficiency, 189–190, 200–202; and narrative construction, 43–44, 45, 46
Paroxetine (Paxil), 117, 118, 119, 121, 124
Passive influence, 23–24, 139, 147
Pennebaker, J. W., 246
Perls, F., 149
Perpetrators: attachment to, 361–362; fantasized punishment of, 233; identification with, 361; and nondisclosure, 244
Perphenazine (Trilafon), 116, 121, 122
Persecutory alters, 96; forming treat-

ment alliances with, 355, 358–361; positive reframing of, 357–361; voices of, 159–161. *See also* Aggressive alters; Angry alters
Personality, defined, *xx*
Personality development, *xxxviii–xxxvl, xlvi, liii. See also* Child development
Personality disorders: and differential diagnosis, *xxii, xxv;* as secondary diagnosis, *xxiii. See also* Borderline Personality Disorder; Narcissistic Personality Disorder
Personality states, defined, *xx. See also* Alters
Personality tests, *xxiv*, 17, 27–34; projective, 30–34; structured, 28–30
Peterson, G., 135–181
Phenothiazines, 352
Physicians Desk Reference (PDR), 116
Placebo effect: in children, 155; and medication efficacy, 100–102, 119, 155
Play therapy: for child alters, 348; for children, 146
Postintegration stage, *xlvi, xlviii;* and conflict, 188; expressive therapies in, 263; hypnosis in, 235; tasks of, 145
Posttraumatic Stress Disorder (PTSD): and abreaction, *li;* in children, 155; and differential diagnosis, *xxii, xxv;* and hyper-vigilance, *xxxi;* and medication, 155; and psychological testing, 9–10, 32–33; as secondary diagnosis, *xxiii*
Posttraumatic symptoms: inpatient interventions for, 343; medication for, 105, 120–123, 126, 155; memory elements of, 51; and resolution of traumatic memories, 66–69; in therapists, 93. *See also* Flashbacks
Prazapam (Centrax), 109
Primary process, 193–195, 208, 209
Problem-oriented inpatient treatment, 337–365; anger management

in, 352–353; behavioral management techniques in, 348–354; case example of, 356–363; and childhood trauma memories, 339, 349; cognitive therapy in, 356–365; diagnosis in, 340; goal of, 339; group therapy in, 348–349, 353, 354, 363–365; and high expectations, 351; interventions used in, 340–346; medications used in, 352; for non-Dissociative Identity Disorder patients, 347; patient responsibility in, 339; philosophy of, 338–339, 346–348; problems presented in, 339, 340; staff of, 351; structure of, 354–356; structured activities in, 353; therapeutic principles of, 354–356; and trauma-dissociation model, 347; treatment plan for, 355
Problem-solving ability, *xxix, xxx*, 349
Procedural memory. *See* Implicit memory
Projective tests, *xxiv*, 30–34
Propranolol (Inderal), 105, 108, 116, 122, 124, 155
Protection, failure of, *xxvii–xxviii*, 60–61, 92
Protector alters, 95; in case example, 260; in hospital treatment, 304; persecutor alters reframed as, 357–361
Protriptyline (Vivactil), 117, 119, 121
Psychoanalytic approach: to Borderline Personality Disorder versus Dissociative Identity Disorder, 212–213; classical, 189; concepts of, 186–195; conflict in, 187–188; countertransference in, 203–207; defense theory in, 190–191; deficiency in, 188–190; dissociation in, 193–195; to dreams, 213–215; and history of Dissociative Identity Disorder, 183–186; identity in, 195; to integration, 211–212; mapping in, 202–203; to memory, 215–217;

repression in, 193–195; to responsibility, 89; splitting in, 191–193; summarized, 217–218; therapeutic alliance in, 196–203; transference in, 203–207; transitional object relatedness in, 200–202; trauma in, 186–187, 190–191; to treatment, 196–217; "working through" cure in, 207–211

Psychoeducation, 339, 353, 356, 358, 360–361

Psychogenic Amnesia. *See* Dissociative Amnesia

Psychogenic Fugue. *See* Dissociative Fugue

Psychopharmacotherapy. *See* Medication

Psychosis, and differential diagnosis, *xxii*, 25–26

Psychotherapy, individual: based on cognitive sciences approach, 54–75; for children, 146–149; combined with expressive therapies, 239–266; combined with hypnosis, 222–235; combined with medication, 100–105; dissociation during, 198; ego-state-oriented, 148–149; essentials of, *xxxiv–xlviii*; financing of, 198–199; goals of, 73–74; long-term versus brief, *xvii–xix*, *xxiii–xxiv*; and models of responsibility, 81–97; narrative construction in, 190–191, 208–211; and patient choice, 73–74; physical contact in, 197; psychoanalytic approach to, 196–217; stages of, for adults and children compared, 144–145; traumatic-memory work in, 66–69. *See also* Cognitive science approach; Hospital treatment; Hypnosis; Problem-oriented inpatient treatment; Psychoanalytic approach; Therapeutic alliance

Putnam, F. W., 19, 22, 23, 100, 142, 144–145, 147, 244, 303, 338

Puysegur, 136

Q

Quazepam (Doral), 109

R

Rapaport, D., 32

Rapport development, *xxxv*, 249. *See also* Therapeutic relationship

Rational emotional therapy, 87

Readings: on Dissociative Identity Disorder, 131–132, 176–181, 237–238, 269–271; limitation on patient, 199

Recognition, *xxv*

Redecision therapy, 149

Reenactment, 102–103, 186, 202, 208; inpatient interventions for, 345; through transference, 203–204

Reframe technique, *liii*; for persecutory alters, 245–247, 357–361

Regressed behavior, inpatient interventions for, 344–345

Regressive therapy, 350, 355

Reparenting, *xxxviii*, *liii*, 208

Repressed memories, *xlix–xlx*, 215–217. *See also* Memory

Repression: versus dissociation, 50; versus division, *xlix*; psychoanalytic approach to, 193–195

Responsibility: alters' models of, 85, 95–97; cause and effect and, 84; compensatory model of, 91–93, 94, 95, 97; enlightenment model of, 89–91, 96; medical model of, 87–89, 96; models of, 85–93; and models of helping, 81–83; moral model of, 86–87, 96; nature of therapeutic, 83–85; patient's perspective of, 94–95; therapist's perspective of, 94

Restraint sessions, 322, 352

Retraumatization: through abreaction, 85; through hypnosis, 221–222, 229; through ongoing dissociation, 73; wish for, 303

Risperidone (Risperdal), 123, 126

Ritual abuse: in cognitive therapy case

example, 356–363; defined, *liii;* and etiology, *xxvi–xxvii;* group therapy for, 348; and hierarchical alter systems, 360; and hospitalization, 300; memories of, 346; psychoanalytic approach to, 216–217; and treating children, 150; underlying issues versus content of, 362. *See also* Cult abuse

Rorschach Inkblot Test, *xxiv,* 30, 32–34

Ross, C. A., 7, 24, 100, 275–276, 279, 314, 337–365

S

Sackheim, D. K., 314

Safety: during abreaction, 232; within assessment process, 14–17; and attachment, 60–62; contracting with alters for, 161, 309, 325–326; in hospital setting, 325–326; and interalter confidentiality, 157–159; patient attitudes toward, and differential diagnosis, *xxv;* in treatment, 61–62, 73, 144; in treatment of children, 167–168

Saxe, G. N., 276

Schafer, R., 191, 209

Schizophrenia/Schizophreniform Psychosis, and differential diagnosis, *xxii, xxv*

Schizotypal Personality Disorder, and differential diagnosis, *xxii, xxv*

Secondary process, 194–195, 209

Secrecy about childhood trauma: and dissociative development, 49; factors in, 242–245; and interalter confidentiality, 157–158; and narrative development, 44; overcoming, through expressive therapies, 242–245; and suicidal behavior, 308–309

Secrecy among alters, *xxxvii, xlv,* 62, 157–158, 231

Selective serotonin reuptake inhibitors (SSRIs), 117, 124

Self: affect regulation and, 57–59; core, 55–57, 74; deficiency in, 188–190; sense of, and autobiographical narrative, 65; and transitional object relatedness, 200–202

Self-harm, *li;* and child alters' cognitive development, 159–161, 356; of children, 23, 159–161; inpatient interventions for, 343–344, 350–351, 356–361; inpatient reduction of, factors in, 347–348; and insurance coverage, 350–351; medication for, 125; prevention of, through negotiating with alters, 159–161, 229

Self-helper alters: use of, in hypnosis, 228; use of, limitation on, 197, 206

Self-hypnosis, *xxix;* versus dissociation, 223, 225; meditation technique for, *xliii–xliv;* uses of, *xliii*

Self-image, negative, 90–91

Self-objects, 189–190, 200–202

Self psychology, 201, 208

Self-soothing, 212; in hypnosis, 226–228. *See also* Comfort

Semantic memory. *See* Explicit memory

Sensation, *xxix, xxxi*

Serial/linear thinking, 40, 65

Sertraline (Zoloft), 118, 119, 121, 124

Sessions: initial, *xlvii;* length of, 198; number of, per week, 198

Sexual abuse, and development of dissociation, 136–137. *See also* Abuse; Trauma, childhood

Sexual alters, 188

Sexual behavior, in children, 23

Shapiro, A., 101

Sharing, interalter, 139

Sharpley, A., 126

Sheppard Pratt Hospital, 26, 32

Side effects: of antidepressants, 118–119, 127; of antihistamines, 114; of benzodiazepines, 107; of beta-blockers, 116; of buspirone, 115; of neuroleptics, 156–157

Siegel, D. J., 39–74
Sinemet, 123
Sleep apnea, medical treatments for, 122–123, 128
Sleep problems: in children, 162–164; medical treatments for, 122–123, 125–126
Smith, W., 219–238
Smoking, and medication, 112
Social referencing, 58
Socialization group, 348–349
Society for Clinical and Experimental Hypnosis, 224
Sociopsychological model, 83
Somatic problems, in children, 161–162
Space lapse, *xxv*
Spacing out, 25, 212, 225
Spiegel, H., 226
Spira, J. L., *xvii–lv*
Splitting: as adaptive coping style, *xxx–xxxii, xlvi;* defined, *liv;* and interalter conflict, 240; severity of, and severity of trauma, *xxx–xxi;* types of, 191–193, 212–213. *See also* Alters
Stabilization: behavioral techniques for, in inpatient program, 348–354; for children, 144, 147
Stabilization-plus approach, 280, 281, 301–302, 306–313, 320–327; limitations of, 327–328. *See also* Hospital treatment
State hospitals, 249
State transitions, development of abrupt, 41–42
States of mind: and core self development, 56; dissociative versus non-dissociative, 53
Steinberg, M., 24
Stengel, 275
Stern, D., 55
Stimulant medication, 155–156
Stoller, R., 184
Stressors, 283–284
Structured Clinical Interview Device-

Dissociative version (SCID-D), *xxiv*, 24–25
Studies in Hysteria (Freud, Breuer), 185
Substance abuse: history of, and medication prescribing, 156; medication for, 114–115, 124, 125
Suggestion: avoidance of, 215, 232–233; positive use of, 351
Suicidal ideation/behavior: and alter cognitive development, 159–161; alters' communication about, *xlv;* in case example, 356–363; inpatient interventions for, 340–341, 356–363; and insurance coverage, 350–351; and nondisclosure of abuse, 308–309
Sullivan, H. S., *xxxiv, xxxviii*
Sumatriptan (Imitrex), 161
Supersensitization, *xlii*
Support: lack of, *xxvii–xxviii*, 60–61, 92; splitting for, *xxx*
Support groups, negative influences of, 90–91, 199
Suppression, 50
Switching, *xx, xxi;* defined, *liv;* as diagnostic criteria, *xxv;* during group therapy, 316; rapid, hospital interventions for, 301, 344–345; rapid, hypnotherapy for controlling, 122; rapid, medication for controlling, 116, 122
Sybil, 184
Symptom concealment, 10–11, 24
Symptom contamination, 90–91, 199, 296, 248
Symptom fabrication/exaggeration, 10–11, 24, 28–29; and hypnosis, 221, 223, 224
Symptom reinforcement, 10–11, 90–91, 199, 296, 348, 350, 355

T

Tactical integration perspective, 94, 302
Teaching hospital, 347
Tellegen Absorption Scale (TAS), *xxiv*

Temazepam (Restoril), 109
Terfenadine (Seldane), 124
Testing alliance, 11–19
Tests, *xxiv–xxv;* cognitive, 25–27; for dissociation, 19–25; personality, 27–34. *See also* Assessment
Thematic Aptitude Test (TAT), *xxiv,* 30–32
Therapeutic pluralism, 82
Therapeutic relationship: and affect regulation/tolerance, 58–59; alliance in, 196–207; and attachment theory, 60–62; boundaries in, 71–73, 198, 199; cognitive science approach to, 40–43; existential approach in, *xxxviii, xl–xli;* experiential aspect of, 70–73; facilitating compensatory model in, 96–97; and information gathering, *xxxv–xxxvi;* information retrieval in, 166–167; and interalter confidentiality, 158–159; interpersonal relationship in, *xxxviii–xl,* 70–73; and long-term psychotherapy, *xviii;* and medication, 101–102, 105, 128, 156–157; metacognitive ability and, 64; models of helping in, 82–83; psychoanalytic approach to, 196–207; rapport in, *xxxv,* 249; responsibility in, models of, 85–97; responsibility in, nature of, 83–85; safety in, 61–62, 73; and social referencing, 58; therapist availability in, 196, 197; therapist's role in, 71–73, 83, 201–202; transitional object relatedness in, 200–202. *See also* Countertransference; Psychotherapy, individual; Testing alliance; Transference
Thioridazine (Mellaril), 116, 156–157
Thirds, rule of, 154, 233, 324
Thought disorder, 25–26
Three Faces of Eve, The, 141
Timberlawn, 338
Time lapse, *xxiv*
Torem, M. S., 99–132
Training, therapist, 152, 168, 224

Trance logic, 103
Trance states, spontaneous, 23, 321
Transactional analysis (TA), 148–149
Transference, 42–43, 61; in enlightenment model, 91; in hospital setting, 303–304; interpretation of, 206–207; and placebo effect, 100–102, 119; in psychoanalytic approach, 203–207; traumatic, 102–103, 293
Transference neurosis, 203
Transferring-out intervention, 349
Transitional object relatedness, 200–202
Tranylcypromine (Parnate), 117, 119, 121
Trauma, childhood: abreaction of, in hospital setting, 323–325; and core-self development, 55–56; effects of, on cognitive pattern development, 41–42; effects of, on memory processes, 46–52; effects of, on test results, 28–29; and etiology, *xxvi–xxvii,* 137, 184, 186–187, 190–191, 207, 242; focus on, versus identity issues, 195; and forgotten childhoods, 53–54; history of theories on, 136–137; memories of, mastering of, 231–234, 323–325; memories of, and problem-oriented approach, 339, 346; memories of, resolution of, 66–69, 145, 147, 190–191, 207–211, 231–234; memories of, uncovering through expressive therapies, 261–262; memories of, uncovering through hypnosis, 221–222, 231–234; memory of, *xlix–l;* and metacognitive development, 63–64; ongoing, in children with Dissociative Identity Disorder, 142–143, 149, 167; physical/sexual versus psychological, 187; preverbal, 244–245; severity of, and severity of dissociation, *xxx–xxxi;* and sleep problems, 163–164; and splitting defense, 193;

and therapeutic alliance formation, 201–202. *See also* Abreaction; Abuse; Memory

Traumatic Content Index, 32–33

Traumatic overlay, during psychological testing, 16–17

Traumatic transference, 102–103, 293

Trazodone (Desyrel), 117, 118, 121, 125

Treatment: essentials of, *xxxiv–xlviii;* modalities of, *xxxii–xxxiv;* stages of, *xlvii–xlviii,* 144–145, 307. *See also* Expressive therapies; Hospital treatment; Hypnosis; Medication; Problem-oriented inpatient treatment; Psychoanalytic approach; Psychotherapy, individual

Tree-House-Person Test, *xxiv*

Triazolam (Halcion), 106, 109

Tricyclic antidepressants, 117

Triggers: cult, 346; in dedicated dissociative disorders units, 296; to implicit memories, 67–68; ritual abuse, 348

Trimipramine (Surmontil), 118, 121

Trust, and interpersonal approach, *xxxviii–xxxix*

Tulving, E., 48

U

Unconscious alter, *xlv*

V

van der Kolk, B. A., 276

Venlafaxine (Effexor), 123, 126–127

Video recording, of amytal interviews, *li*

Vigilance: alert/suspended, *xxi;* hyper/hypo, *xxxi,* 51

Voices: in children/adolescents, 23, 146, 150, 159–161; in Dissociative Identity Disorder versus schizophrenia, *xxii,* 26; medication for, 156–157; self-deprecatory/persecutory, 159–161

W

Watkins, J. G., 221

Wechsler Adult Intelligence Scale-Revised (WAIS-R IQ), *xxiv,* 25–26

West, L. J., 184

Wiesel, E., 210

Wilbur, 82

Winnicott, D. W., 189, 200

Winnocot, K., *liii*

Wolin, R., 126

"Working through," 190–191, 207–211

Workplace functioning, *xxi–xxii. See also* Functioning, daily

Wozney, K., 275–276, 279

Writing, 246, 309. *See also* Expressive therapies

Y

Yalom, I., *xxxv*

Young, W. C., 322